THE
MYSTERY
KNIGHT

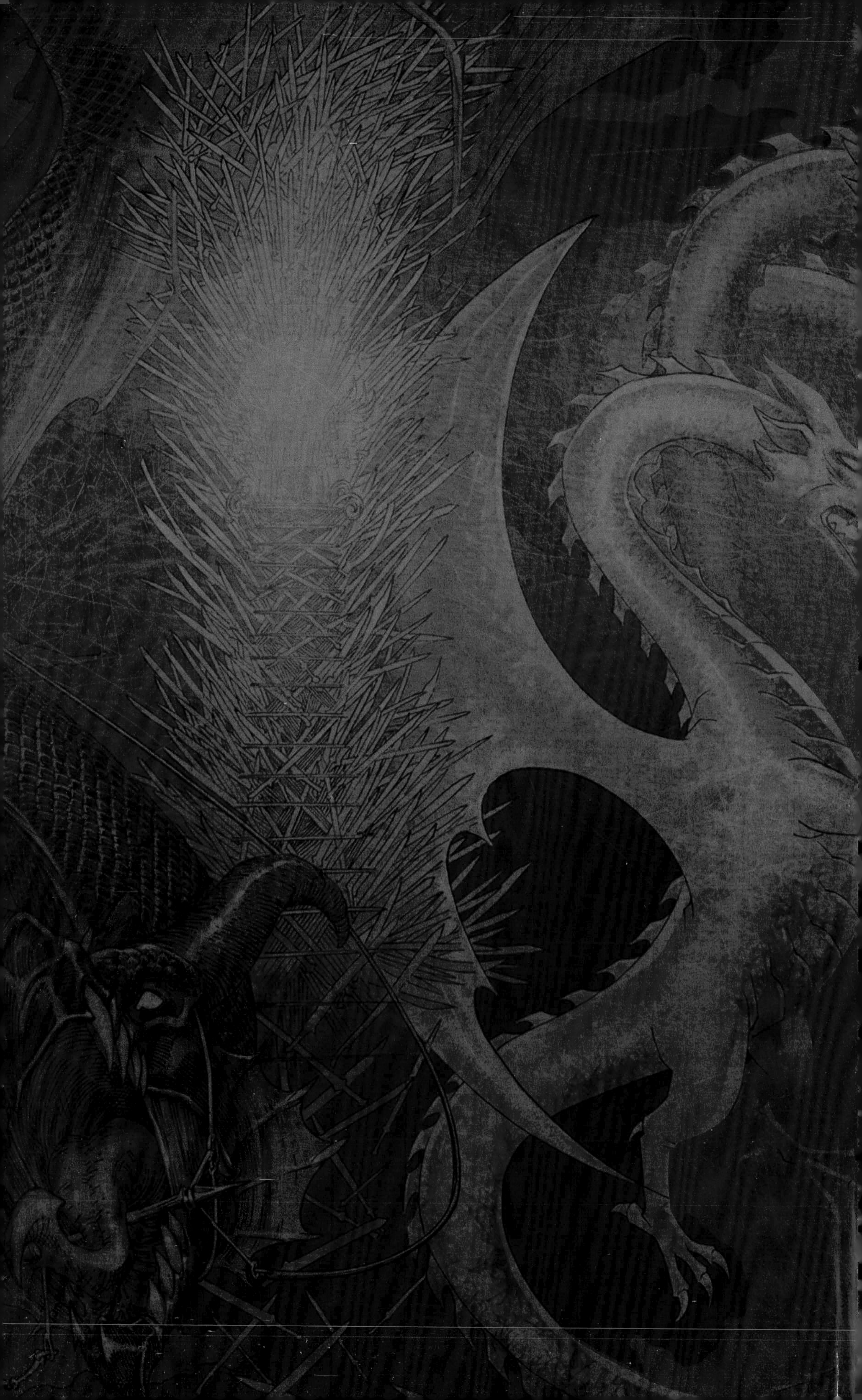

GEORGE R.R. MARTIN

THE MYSTERY KNIGHT

ADAPTED BY
BEN AVERY

ART BY
MIKE S. MILLER

COLORS BY
J. NANJAN & SIVAKAMI MOHAN

LETTERING BY
BILL TORTOLINI

HARPER
Voyager

Harper*Voyager* an imprint of
HarperCollins*Publishers* Ltd
1 London Bridge Street
London SE1 9GF

www.harpercollins.co.uk

First published by HarperCollins*Publishers* 2017
1

Copyright © George R.R. Martin 2017
Graphic novel interior design by William Tortolini

George R.R. Martin asserts the moral right to
be identified as the author of this work

A catalogue record for this book is available from the British Library

ISBN: 978-0-00-825323-3

Set in Optima

Printed and bound in Slovakia by Neografia a.s.

MIX
Paper from
responsible sources
FSC C007454

FSC™ is a non-profit international organisation established to
promote the responsible management of the world's forests. Products
carrying the FSC label are independently certified to assure consumers
that they come from forests that are managed to meet the social,
economic and ecological needs of present and future generations,
and other controlled sources.

Find out more about HarperCollins and the environment at
www.harpercollins.co.uk/green

THE MYSTERY KNIGHT

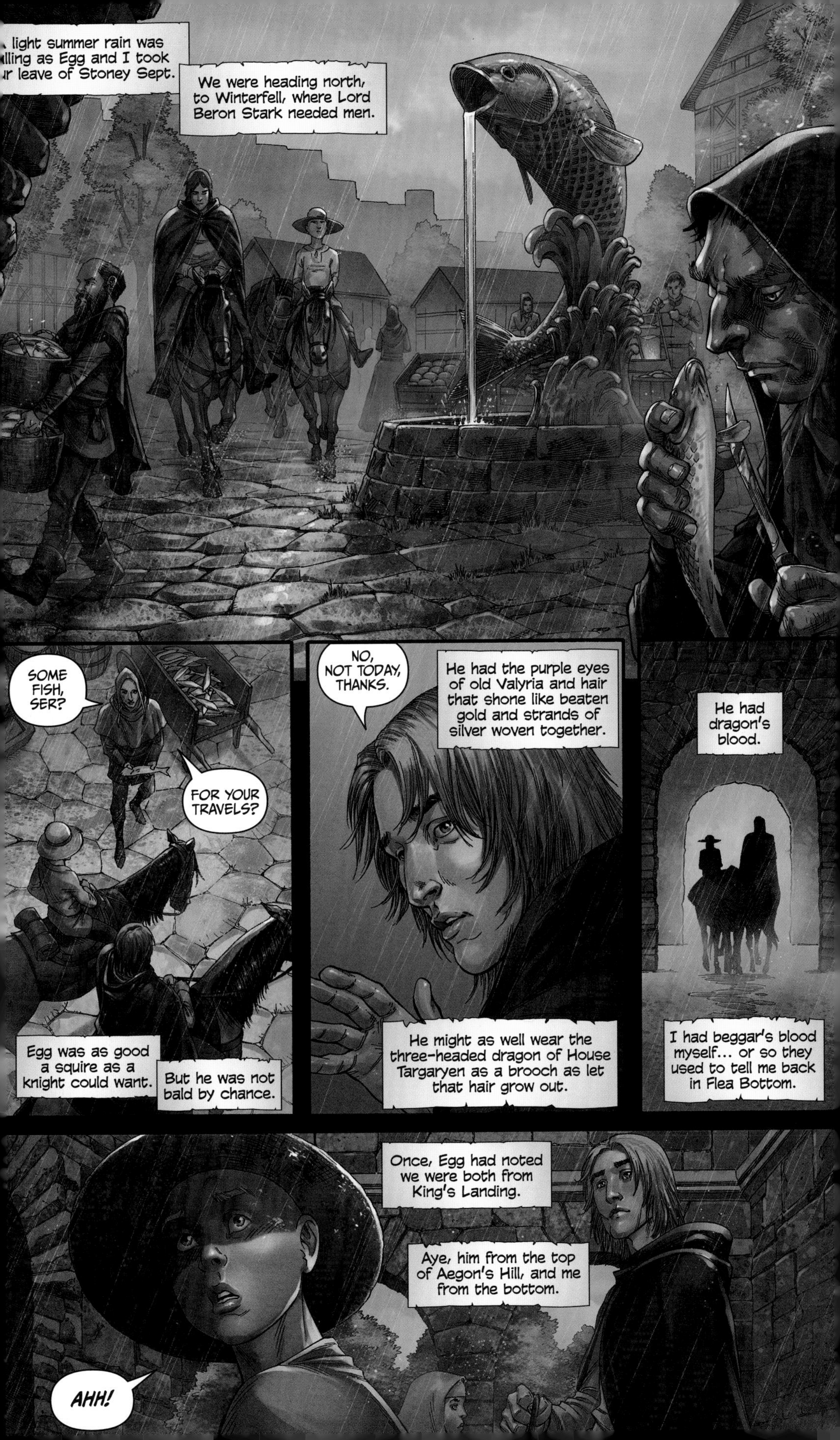
A light summer rain was falling as Egg and I took our leave of Stoney Sept.
We were heading north, to Winterfell, where Lord Beron Stark needed men.
SOME FISH, SER?
FOR YOUR TRAVELS?
Egg was as good a squire as a knight could want.
But he was not bald by chance.
NO, NOT TODAY, THANKS.
He had the purple eyes of old Valyria and hair that shone like beaten gold and strands of silver woven together.
He might as well wear the three-headed dragon of House Targaryen as a brooch as let that hair grow out.
He had dragon's blood.
I had beggar's blood myself... or so they used to tell me back in Flea Bottom.
Once, Egg had noted we were both from King's Landing.
Aye, him from the top of Aegon's Hill, and me from the bottom.
AHH!

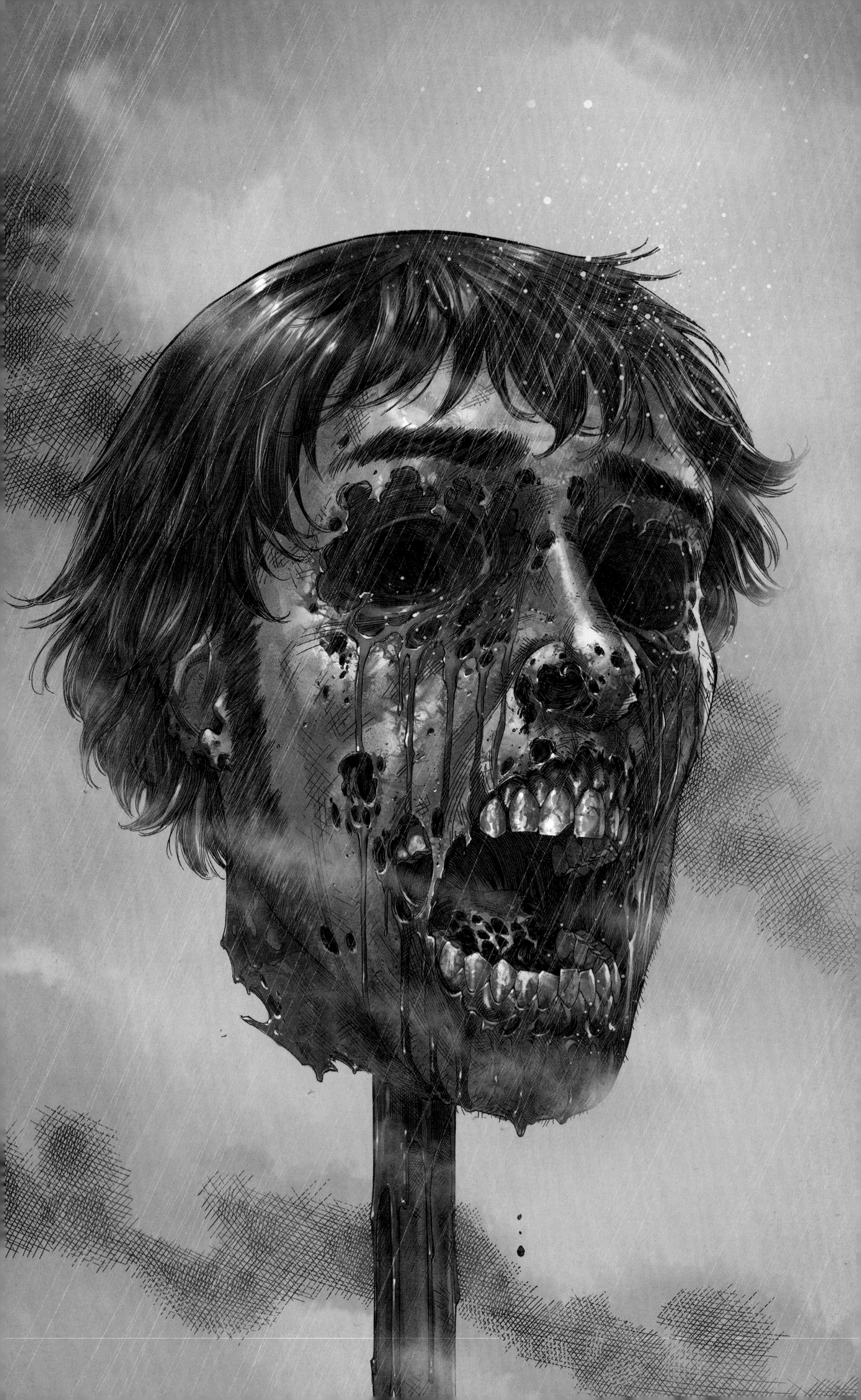

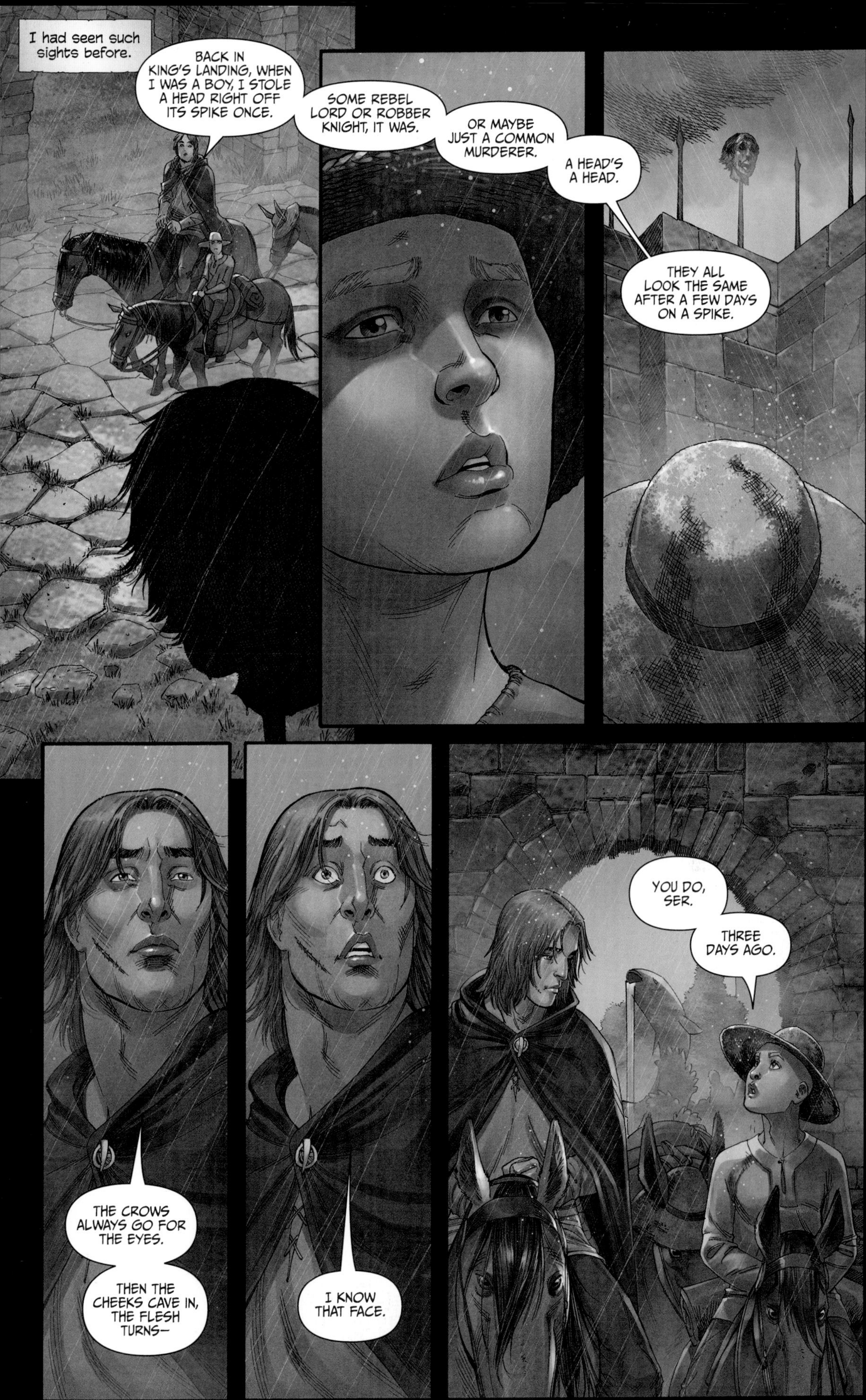

I had seen such sights before.
BACK IN KING'S LANDING, WHEN I WAS A BOY, I STOLE A HEAD RIGHT OFF ITS SPIKE ONCE.
SOME REBEL LORD OR ROBBER KNIGHT, IT WAS.
OR MAYBE JUST A COMMON MURDERER.
A HEAD'S A HEAD.
THEY ALL LOOK THE SAME AFTER A FEW DAYS ON A SPIKE.
THE CROWS ALWAYS GO FOR THE EYES.
THEN THE CHEEKS CAVE IN, THE FLESH TURNS—
I KNOW THAT FACE.
YOU DO, SER.
THREE DAYS AGO.

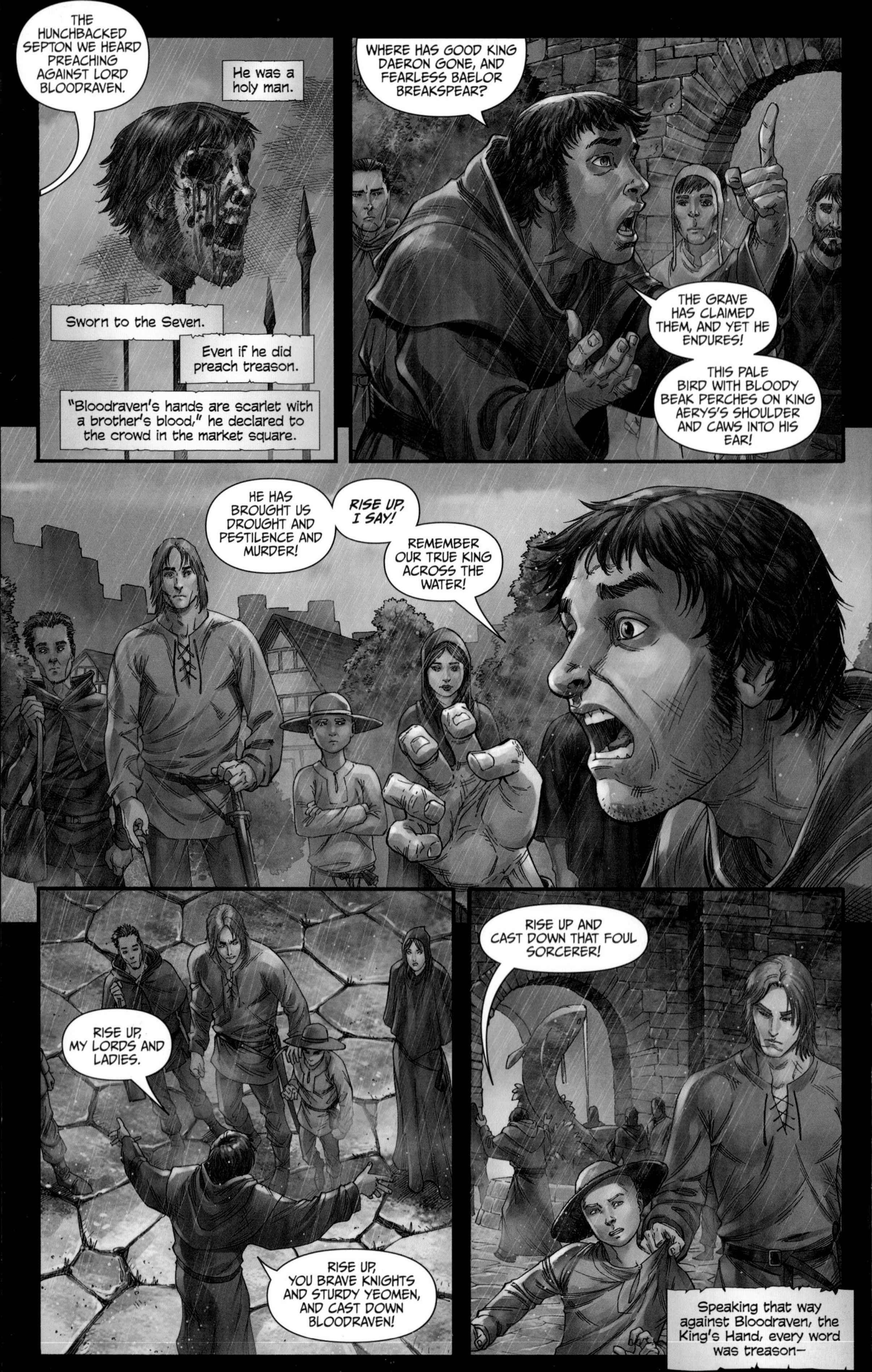
THE HUNCHBACKED SEPTON WE HEARD PREACHING AGAINST LORD BLOODRAVEN.
He was a holy man.
Sworn to the Seven.
Even if he did preach treason.
"Bloodraven's hands are scarlet with a brother's blood," he declared to the crowd in the market square.
WHERE HAS GOOD KING DAERON GONE, AND FEARLESS BAELOR BREAKSPEAR?
THE GRAVE HAS CLAIMED THEM, AND YET HE ENDURES!
THIS PALE BIRD WITH BLOODY BEAK PERCHES ON KING AERYS'S SHOULDER AND CAWS INTO HIS EAR!
HE HAS BROUGHT US DROUGHT AND PESTILENCE AND MURDER!
RISE UP, I SAY!
REMEMBER OUR TRUE KING ACROSS THE WATER!
RISE UP, MY LORDS AND LADIES.
RISE UP, YOU BRAVE KNIGHTS AND STURDY YEOMEN, AND CAST DOWN BLOODRAVEN!
RISE UP AND CAST DOWN THAT FOUL SORCERER!
Speaking that way against Bloodraven, the King's Hand, every word was treason–

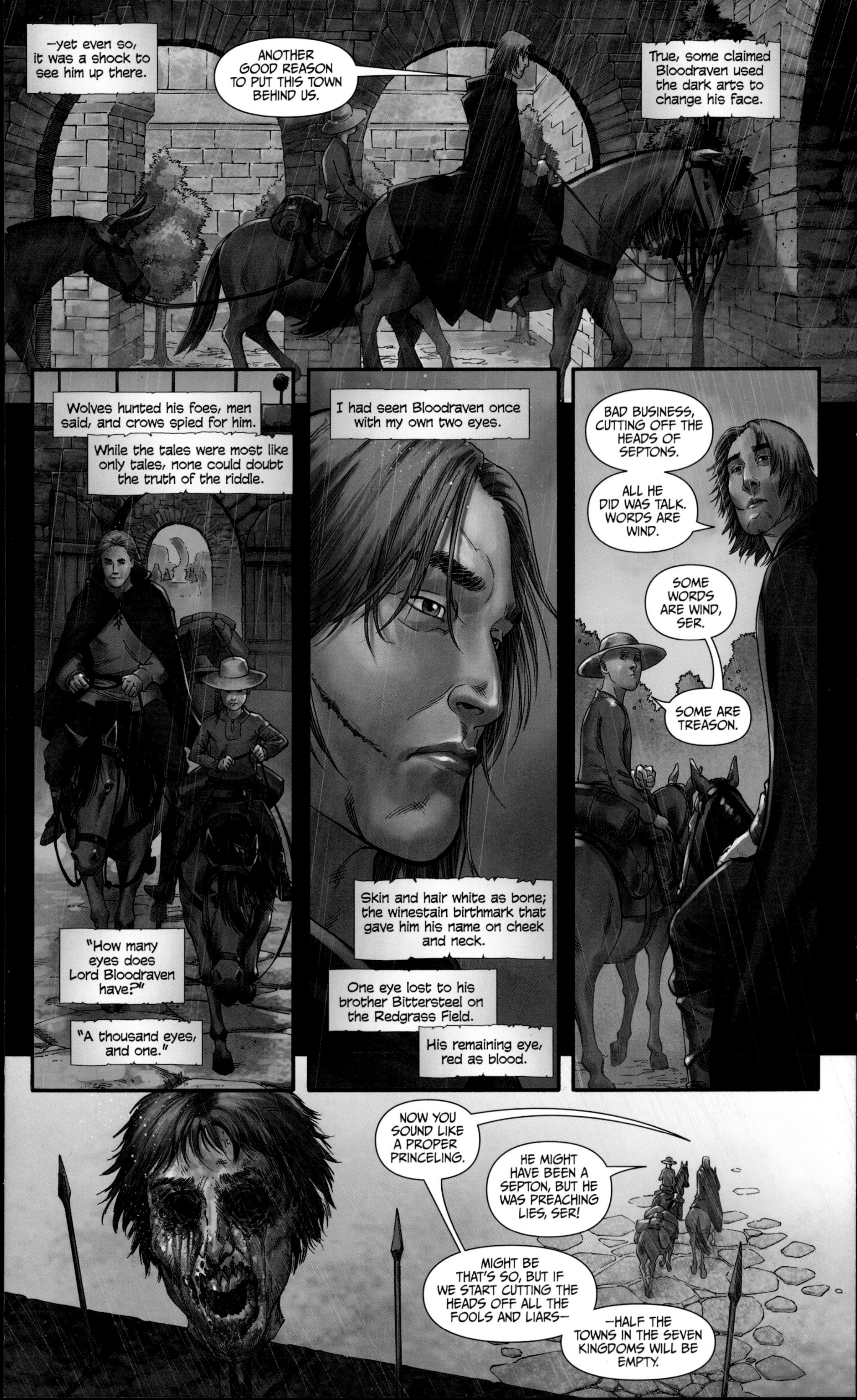
—yet even so, it was a shock to see him up there.
ANOTHER GOOD REASON TO PUT THIS TOWN BEHIND US.
True, some claimed Bloodraven used the dark arts to change his face.
Wolves hunted his foes, men said, and crows spied for him.
While the tales were most like only tales, none could doubt the truth of the riddle.
"How many eyes does Lord Bloodraven have?"
"A thousand eyes, and one."
I had seen Bloodraven once with my own two eyes.
Skin and hair white as bone; the winestain birthmark that gave him his name on cheek and neck.
One eye lost to his brother Bittersteel on the Redgrass Field.
His remaining eye, red as blood.
BAD BUSINESS, CUTTING OFF THE HEADS OF SEPTONS.
ALL HE DID WAS TALK. WORDS ARE WIND.
SOME WORDS ARE WIND, SER.
SOME ARE TREASON.
NOW YOU SOUND LIKE A PROPER PRINCELING.
HE MIGHT HAVE BEEN A SEPTON, BUT HE WAS PREACHING LIES, SER!
MIGHT BE THAT'S SO, BUT IF WE START CUTTING THE HEADS OFF ALL THE FOOLS AND LIARS—
—HALF THE TOWNS IN THE SEVEN KINGDOMS WILL BE EMPTY.

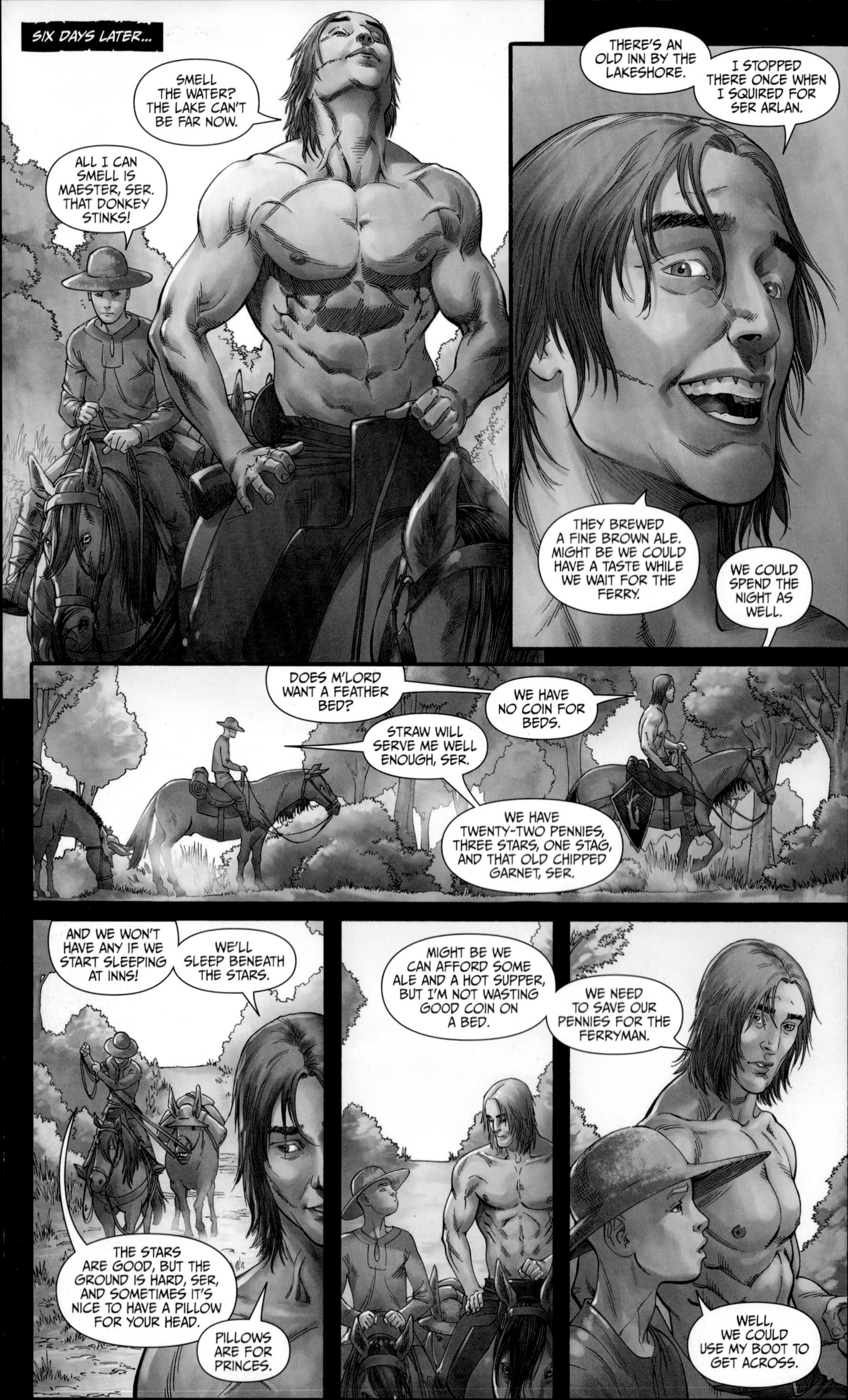
SIX DAYS LATER...
SMELL THE WATER? THE LAKE CAN'T BE FAR NOW.
ALL I CAN SMELL IS MAESTER, SER. THAT DONKEY STINKS!
THERE'S AN OLD INN BY THE LAKESHORE.
I STOPPED THERE ONCE WHEN I SQUIRED FOR SER ARLAN.
THEY BREWED A FINE BROWN ALE. MIGHT BE WE COULD HAVE A TASTE WHILE WE WAIT FOR THE FERRY.
WE COULD SPEND THE NIGHT AS WELL.
DOES M'LORD WANT A FEATHER BED?
WE HAVE NO COIN FOR BEDS.
STRAW WILL SERVE ME WELL ENOUGH, SER.
WE HAVE TWENTY-TWO PENNIES, THREE STARS, ONE STAG, AND THAT OLD CHIPPED GARNET, SER.
AND WE WON'T HAVE ANY IF WE START SLEEPING AT INNS!
WE'LL SLEEP BENEATH THE STARS.
THE STARS ARE GOOD, BUT THE GROUND IS HARD, SER, AND SOMETIMES IT'S NICE TO HAVE A PILLOW FOR YOUR HEAD.
PILLOWS ARE FOR PRINCES.
MIGHT BE WE CAN AFFORD SOME ALE AND A HOT SUPPER, BUT I'M NOT WASTING GOOD COIN ON A BED.
WE NEED TO SAVE OUR PENNIES FOR THE FERRYMAN.
WELL, WE COULD USE MY BOOT TO GET ACROSS.

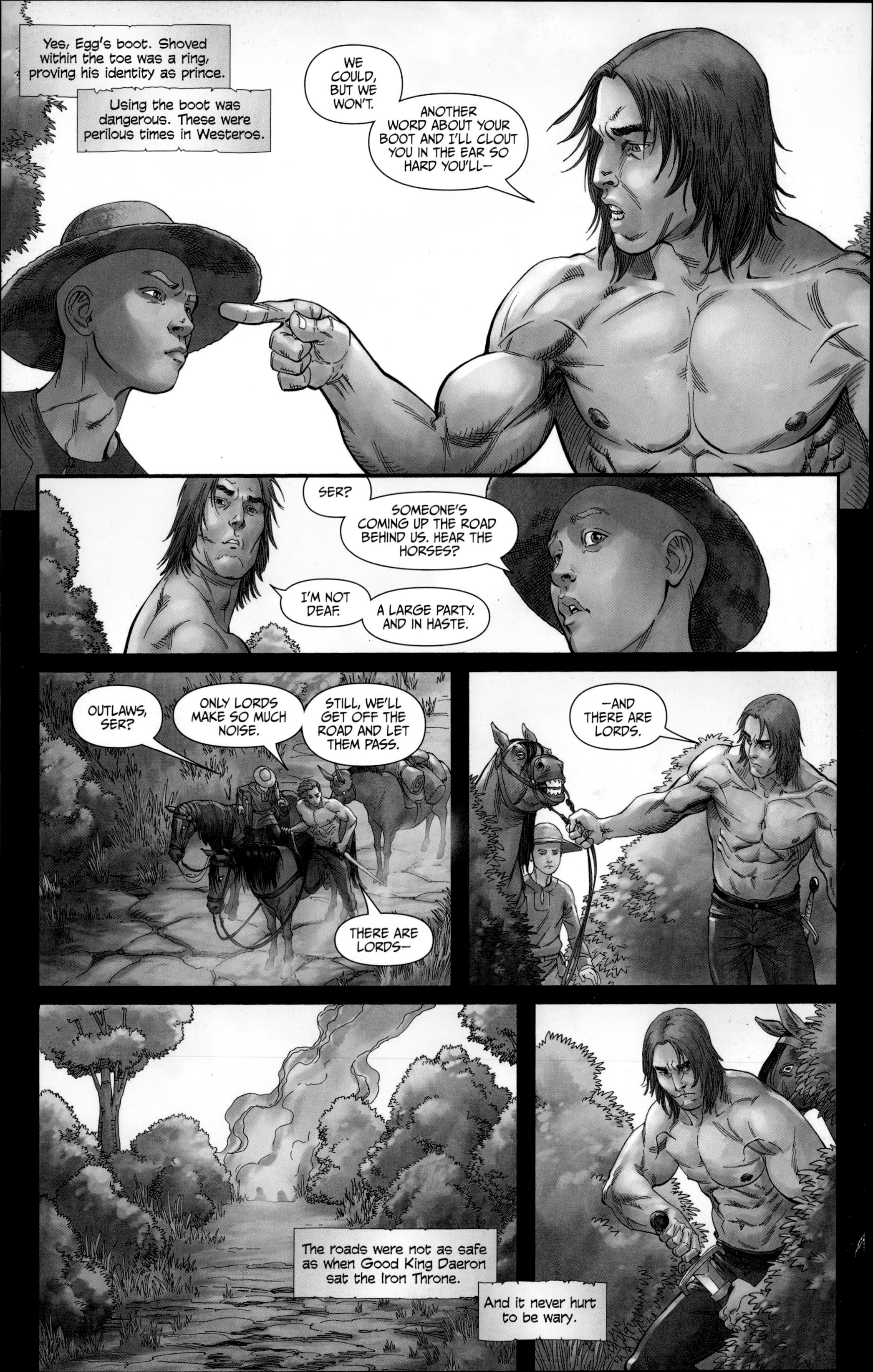

Yes, Egg's boot. Shoved within the toe was a ring, proving his identity as prince.
Using the boot was dangerous. These were perilous times in Westeros.
WE COULD, BUT WE WON'T.
ANOTHER WORD ABOUT YOUR BOOT AND I'LL CLOUT YOU IN THE EAR SO HARD YOU'LL—
SER?
SOMEONE'S COMING UP THE ROAD BEHIND US. HEAR THE HORSES?
I'M NOT DEAF.
A LARGE PARTY. AND IN HASTE.
OUTLAWS, SER?
ONLY LORDS MAKE SO MUCH NOISE.
STILL, WE'LL GET OFF THE ROAD AND LET THEM PASS.
THERE ARE LORDS—
—AND THERE ARE LORDS.
The roads were not as safe as when Good King Daeron sat the Iron Throne.
And it never hurt to be wary.

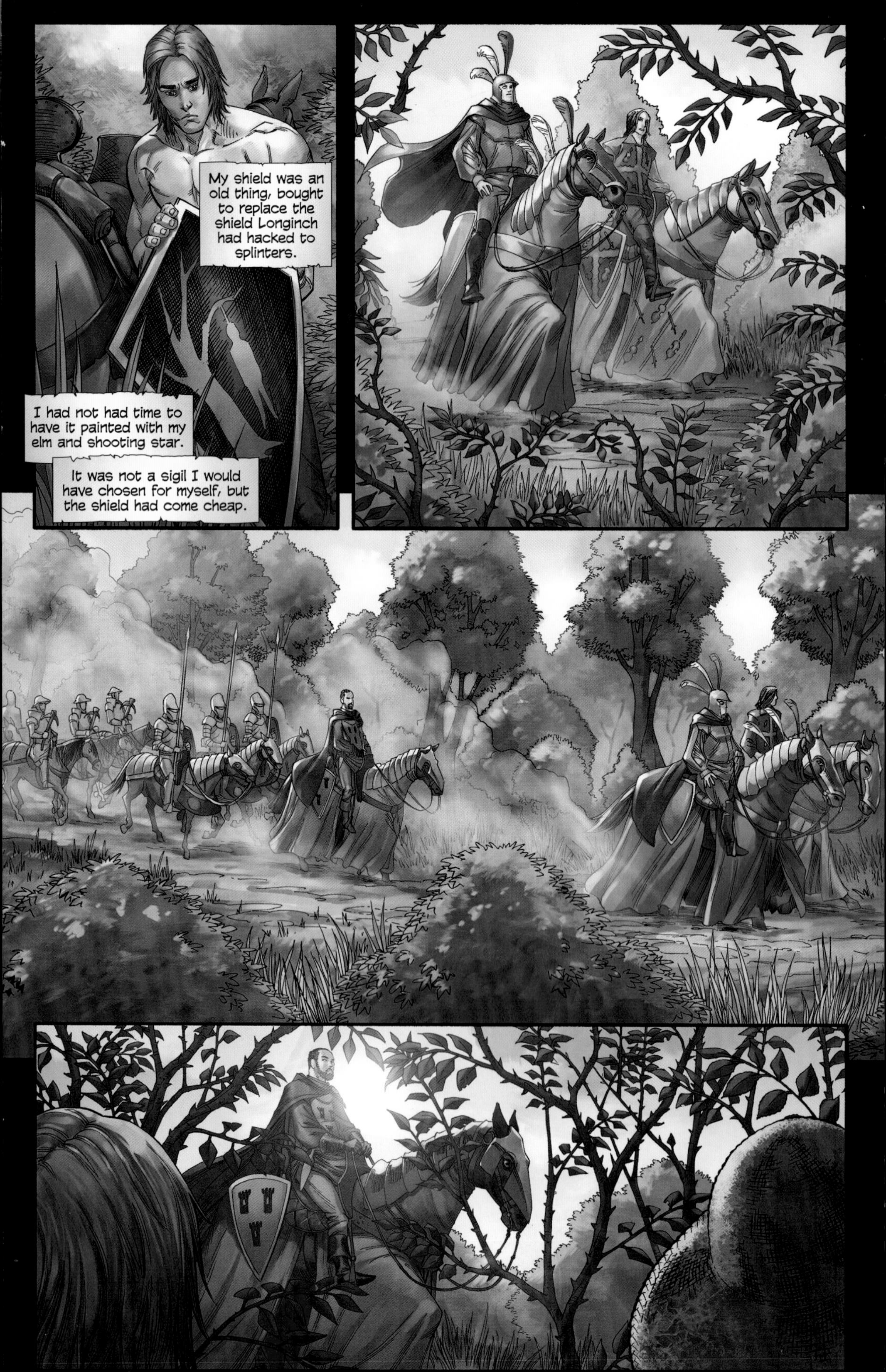
My shield was an old thing, bought to replace the shield Longinch had hacked to splinters.
I had not had time to have it painted with my elm and shooting star.
It was not a sigil I would have chosen for myself, but the shield had come cheap.

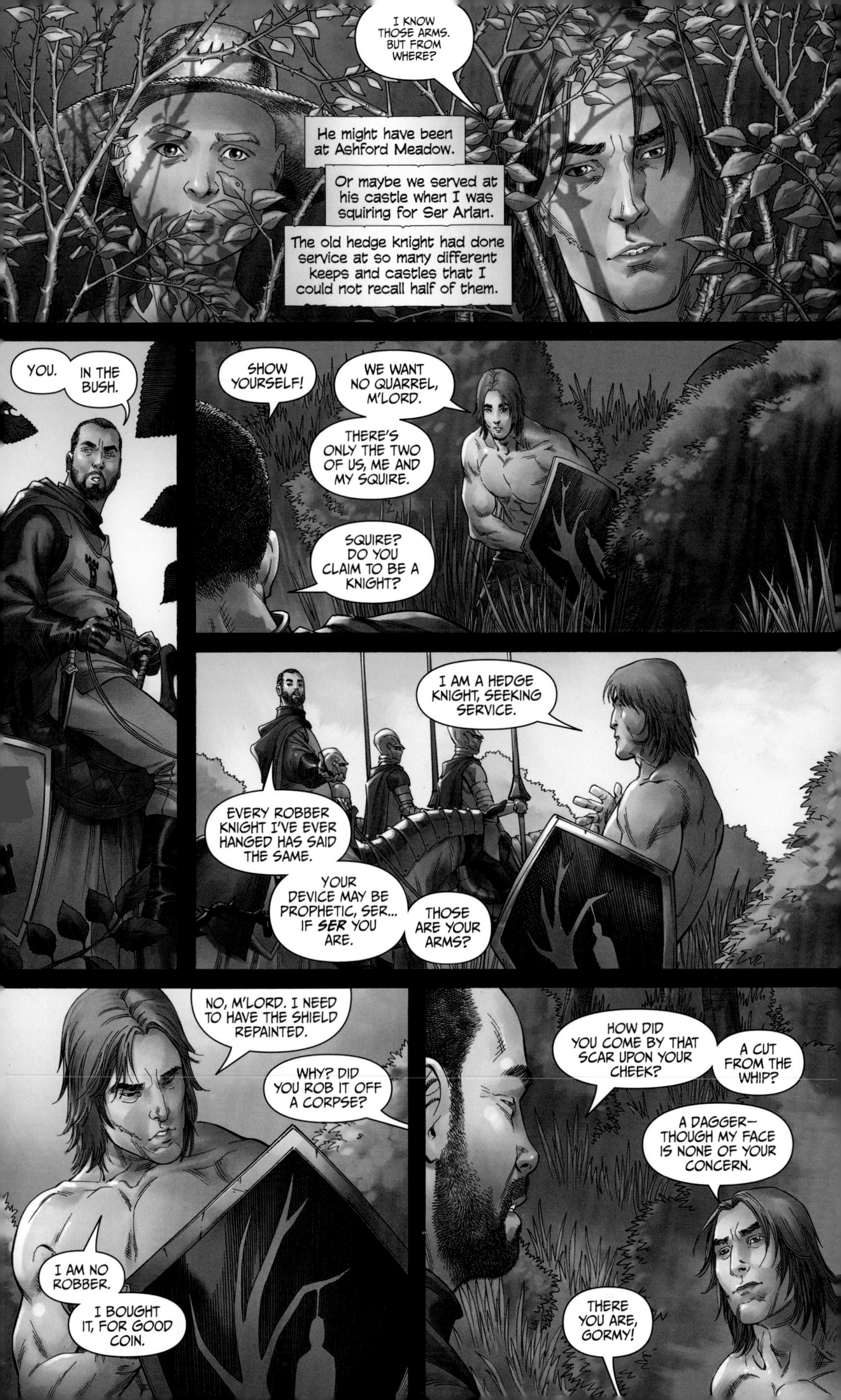
I KNOW THOSE ARMS. BUT FROM WHERE?
He might have been at Ashford Meadow.
Or maybe we served at his castle when I was squiring for Ser Arlan.
The old hedge knight had done service at so many different keeps and castles that I could not recall half of them.
YOU.
IN THE BUSH.
SHOW YOURSELF!
WE WANT NO QUARREL, M'LORD.
THERE'S ONLY THE TWO OF US, ME AND MY SQUIRE.
SQUIRE? DO YOU CLAIM TO BE A KNIGHT?
I AM A HEDGE KNIGHT, SEEKING SERVICE.
EVERY ROBBER KNIGHT I'VE EVER HANGED HAS SAID THE SAME.
YOUR DEVICE MAY BE PROPHETIC, SER... IF SER YOU ARE.
THOSE ARE YOUR ARMS?
NO, M'LORD. I NEED TO HAVE THE SHIELD REPAINTED.
WHY? DID YOU ROB IT OFF A CORPSE?
I AM NO ROBBER.
I BOUGHT IT, FOR GOOD COIN.
HOW DID YOU COME BY THAT SCAR UPON YOUR CHEEK?
A CUT FROM THE WHIP?
A DAGGER— THOUGH MY FACE IS NONE OF YOUR CONCERN.
THERE YOU ARE, GORMY!

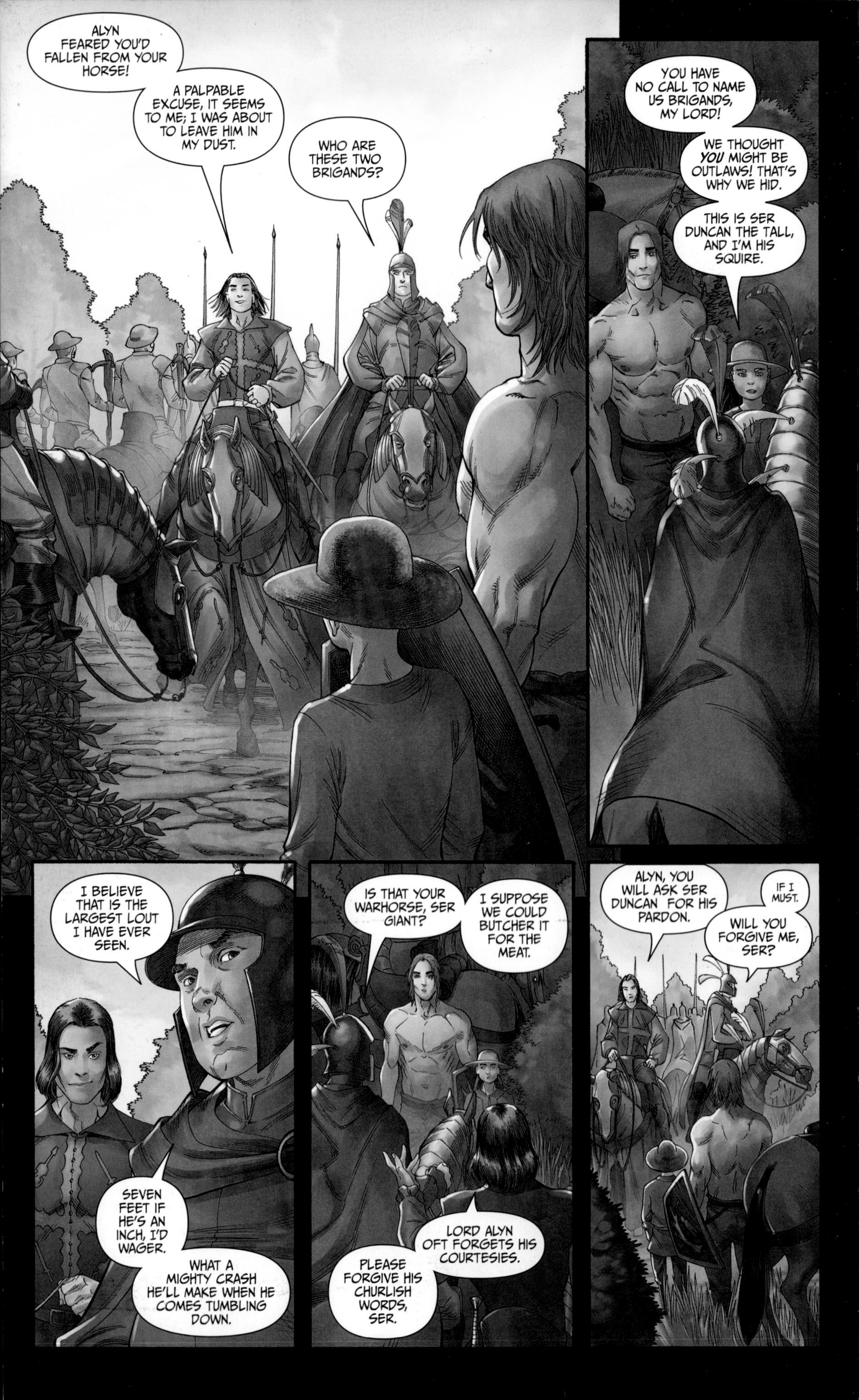
ALYN FEARED YOU'D FALLEN FROM YOUR HORSE!
A PALPABLE EXCUSE, IT SEEMS TO ME; I WAS ABOUT TO LEAVE HIM IN MY DUST.
WHO ARE THESE TWO BRIGANDS?
YOU HAVE NO CALL TO NAME US BRIGANDS, MY LORD!
WE THOUGHT *YOU* MIGHT BE OUTLAWS! THAT'S WHY WE HID.
THIS IS SER DUNCAN THE TALL, AND I'M HIS SQUIRE.
I BELIEVE THAT IS THE LARGEST LOUT I HAVE EVER SEEN.
SEVEN FEET IF HE'S AN INCH, I'D WAGER.
WHAT A MIGHTY CRASH HE'LL MAKE WHEN HE COMES TUMBLING DOWN.
IS THAT YOUR WARHORSE, SER GIANT?
I SUPPOSE WE COULD BUTCHER IT FOR THE MEAT.
LORD ALYN OFT FORGETS HIS COURTESIES.
PLEASE FORGIVE HIS CHURLISH WORDS, SER.
ALYN, YOU WILL ASK SER DUNCAN FOR HIS PARDON.
IF I MUST.
WILL YOU FORGIVE ME, SER?

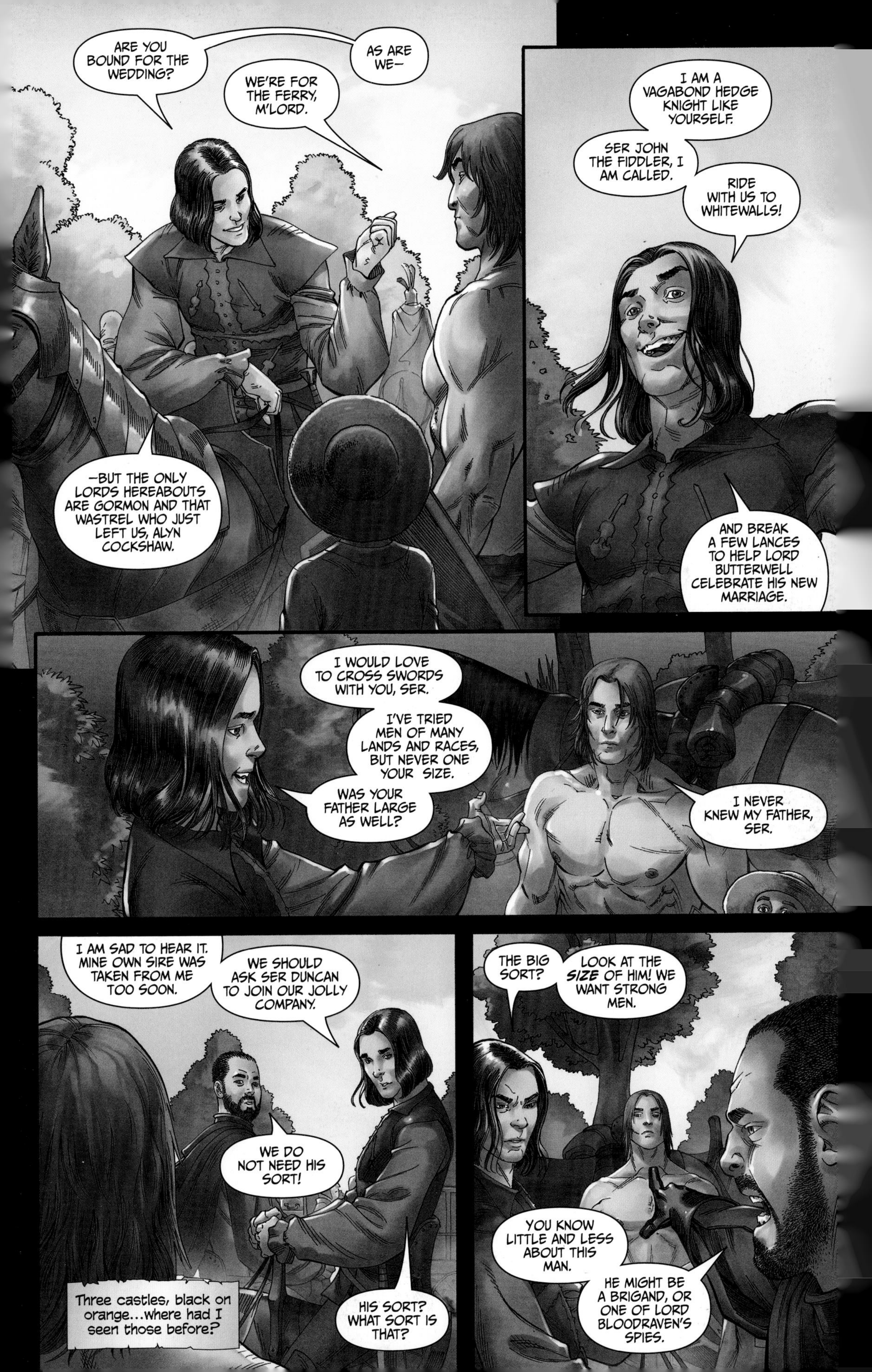
ARE YOU BOUND FOR THE WEDDING?
AS ARE WE–
WE'RE FOR THE FERRY, M'LORD.
–BUT THE ONLY LORDS HEREABOUTS ARE GORMON AND THAT WASTREL WHO JUST LEFT US, ALYN COCKSHAW.
I AM A VAGABOND HEDGE KNIGHT LIKE YOURSELF.
SER JOHN THE FIDDLER, I AM CALLED.
RIDE WITH US TO WHITEWALLS!
AND BREAK A FEW LANCES TO HELP LORD BUTTERWELL CELEBRATE HIS NEW MARRIAGE.
I WOULD LOVE TO CROSS SWORDS WITH YOU, SER.
I'VE TRIED MEN OF MANY LANDS AND RACES, BUT NEVER ONE YOUR SIZE.
WAS YOUR FATHER LARGE AS WELL?
I NEVER KNEW MY FATHER, SER.
I AM SAD TO HEAR IT. MINE OWN SIRE WAS TAKEN FROM ME TOO SOON.
WE SHOULD ASK SER DUNCAN TO JOIN OUR JOLLY COMPANY.
WE DO NOT NEED HIS SORT!
Three castles, black on orange...where had I seen those before?
HIS SORT? WHAT SORT IS THAT?
THE BIG SORT?
LOOK AT THE *SIZE* OF HIM! WE WANT STRONG MEN.
YOU KNOW LITTLE AND LESS ABOUT THIS MAN.
HE MIGHT BE A BRIGAND, OR ONE OF LORD BLOODRAVEN'S SPIES.

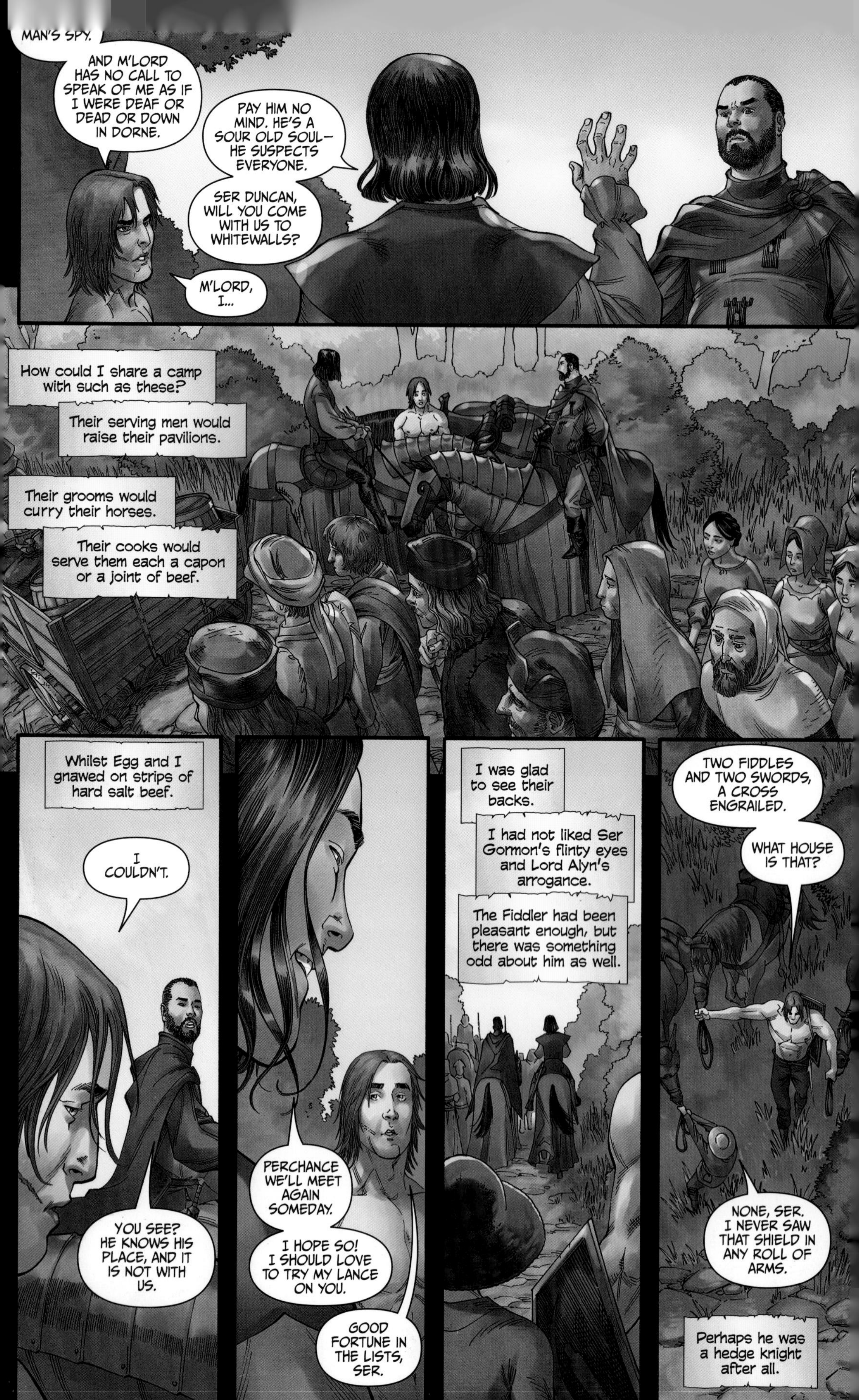
MAN'S SPY.
AND M'LORD HAS NO CALL TO SPEAK OF ME AS IF I WERE DEAF OR DEAD OR DOWN IN DORNE.
PAY HIM NO MIND. HE'S A SOUR OLD SOUL— HE SUSPECTS EVERYONE.
SER DUNCAN, WILL YOU COME WITH US TO WHITEWALLS?
M'LORD, I...
How could I share a camp with such as these?
Their serving men would raise their pavilions.
Their grooms would curry their horses.
Their cooks would serve them each a capon or a joint of beef.
Whilst Egg and I gnawed on strips of hard salt beef.
I COULDN'T.
YOU SEE? HE KNOWS HIS PLACE, AND IT IS NOT WITH US.
PERCHANCE WE'LL MEET AGAIN SOMEDAY.
I HOPE SO! I SHOULD LOVE TO TRY MY LANCE ON YOU.
GOOD FORTUNE IN THE LISTS, SER.
I was glad to see their backs.
I had not liked Ser Gormon's flinty eyes and Lord Alyn's arrogance.
The Fiddler had been pleasant enough, but there was something odd about him as well.
TWO FIDDLES AND TWO SWORDS, A CROSS ENGRAILED.
WHAT HOUSE IS THAT?
NONE, SER. I NEVER SAW THAT SHIELD IN ANY ROLL OF ARMS.
Perhaps he was a hedge knight after all.

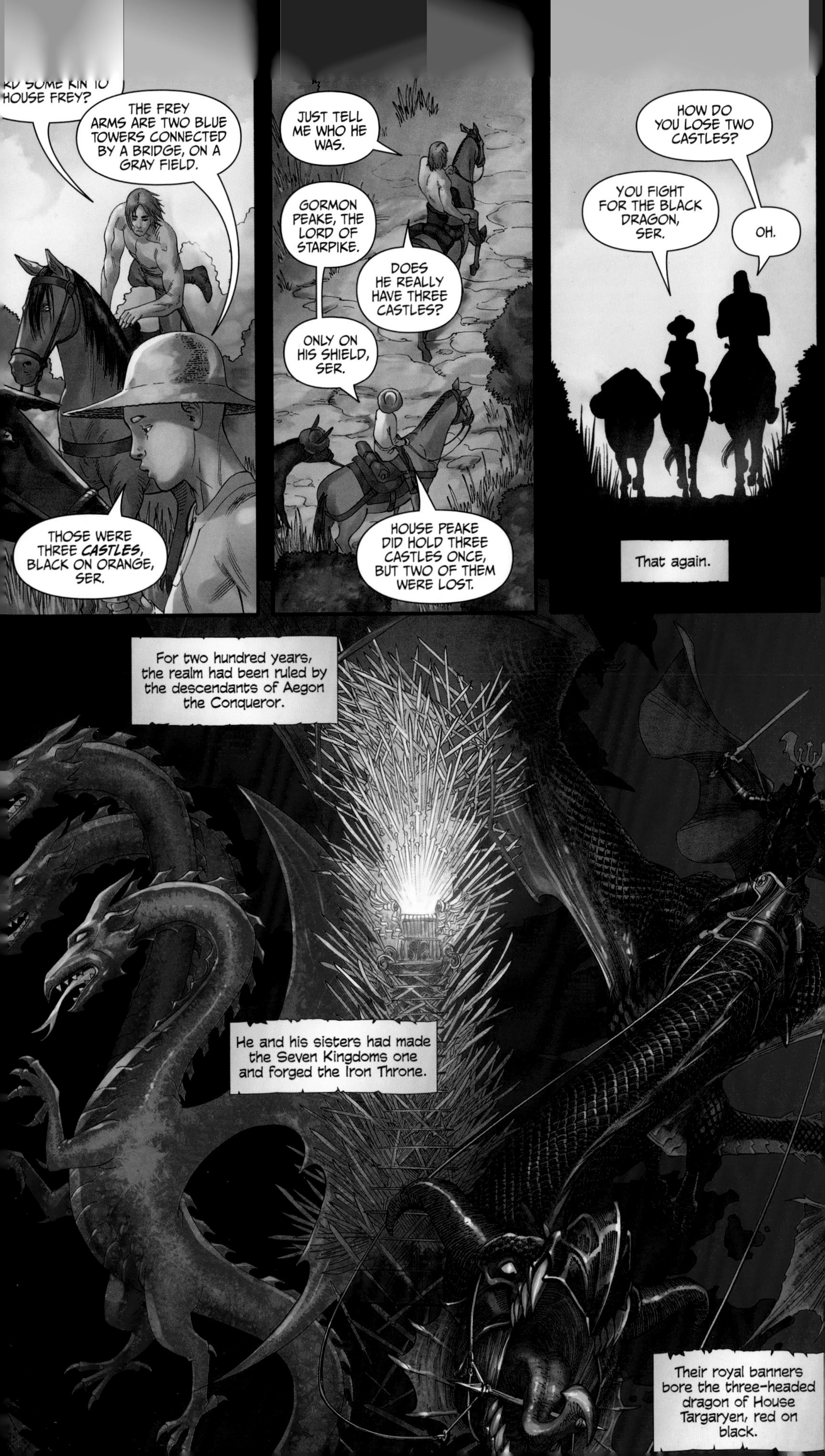

...HOUSE FREY?
THE FREY ARMS ARE TWO BLUE TOWERS CONNECTED BY A BRIDGE, ON A GRAY FIELD.
THOSE WERE THREE *CASTLES*, BLACK ON ORANGE, SER.
JUST TELL ME WHO HE WAS.
GORMON PEAKE, THE LORD OF STARPIKE.
DOES HE REALLY HAVE THREE CASTLES?
ONLY ON HIS SHIELD, SER.
HOUSE PEAKE DID HOLD THREE CASTLES ONCE, BUT TWO OF THEM WERE LOST.
HOW DO YOU LOSE TWO CASTLES?
YOU FIGHT FOR THE BLACK DRAGON, SER.
OH.
That again.
For two hundred years, the realm had been ruled by the descendants of Aegon the Conqueror.
He and his sisters had made the Seven Kingdoms one and forged the Iron Throne.
Their royal banners bore the three-headed dragon of House Targaryen, red on black.

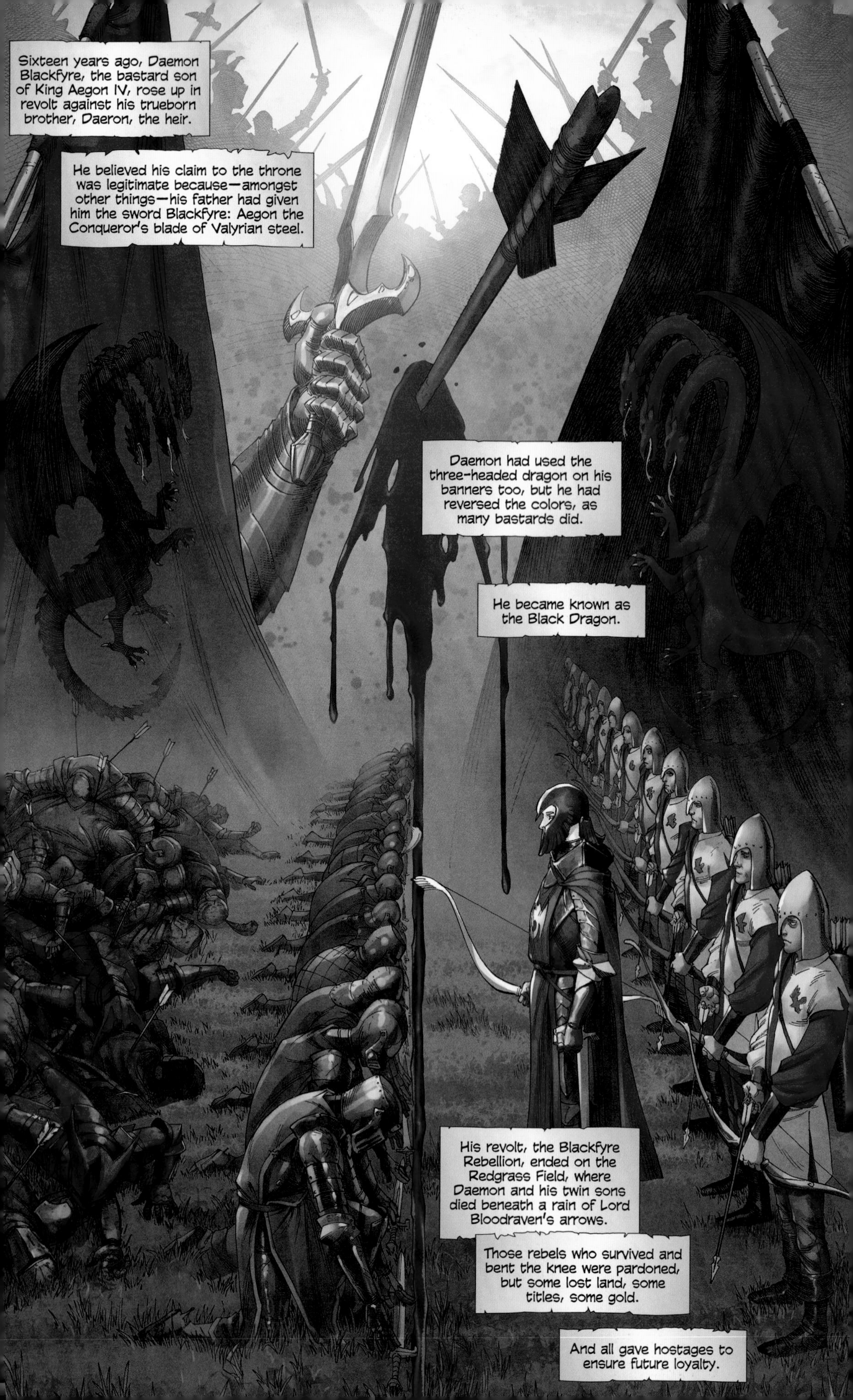
Sixteen years ago, Daemon Blackfyre, the bastard son of King Aegon IV, rose up in revolt against his trueborn brother, Daeron, the heir.
He believed his claim to the throne was legitimate because—amongst other things—his father had given him the sword Blackfyre: Aegon the Conqueror's blade of Valyrian steel.
Daemon had used the three-headed dragon on his banners too, but he had reversed the colors, as many bastards did.
He became known as the Black Dragon.
His revolt, the Blackfyre Rebellion, ended on the Redgrass Field, where Daemon and his twin sons died beneath a rain of Lord Bloodraven's arrows.
Those rebels who survived and bent the knee were pardoned, but some lost land, some titles, some gold.
And all gave hostages to ensure future loyalty.

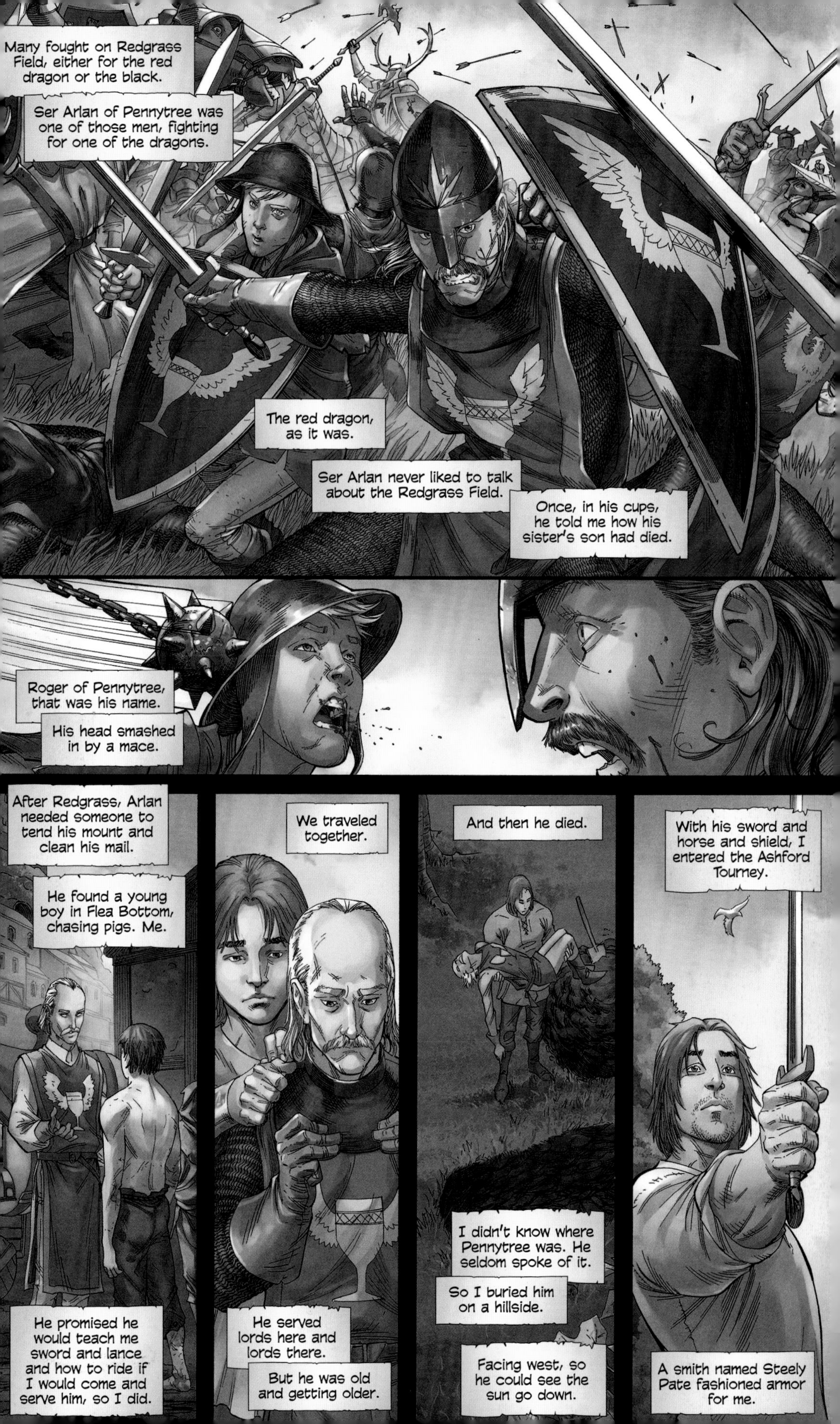
Many fought on Redgrass Field, either for the red dragon or the black.
Ser Arlan of Pennytree was one of those men, fighting for one of the dragons.
The red dragon, as it was.
Ser Arlan never liked to talk about the Redgrass Field.
Once, in his cups, he told me how his sister's son had died.
Roger of Pennytree, that was his name.
His head smashed in by a mace.
After Redgrass, Arlan needed someone to tend his mount and clean his mail.
He found a young boy in Flea Bottom, chasing pigs. Me.
He promised he would teach me sword and lance and how to ride if I would come and serve him, so I did.
We traveled together.
He served lords here and lords there.
But he was old and getting older.
And then he died.
I didn't know where Pennytree was. He seldom spoke of it.
So I buried him on a hillside.
Facing west, so he could see the sun go down.
With his sword and horse and shield, I entered the Ashford Tourney.
A smith named Steely Pate fashioned armor for me.

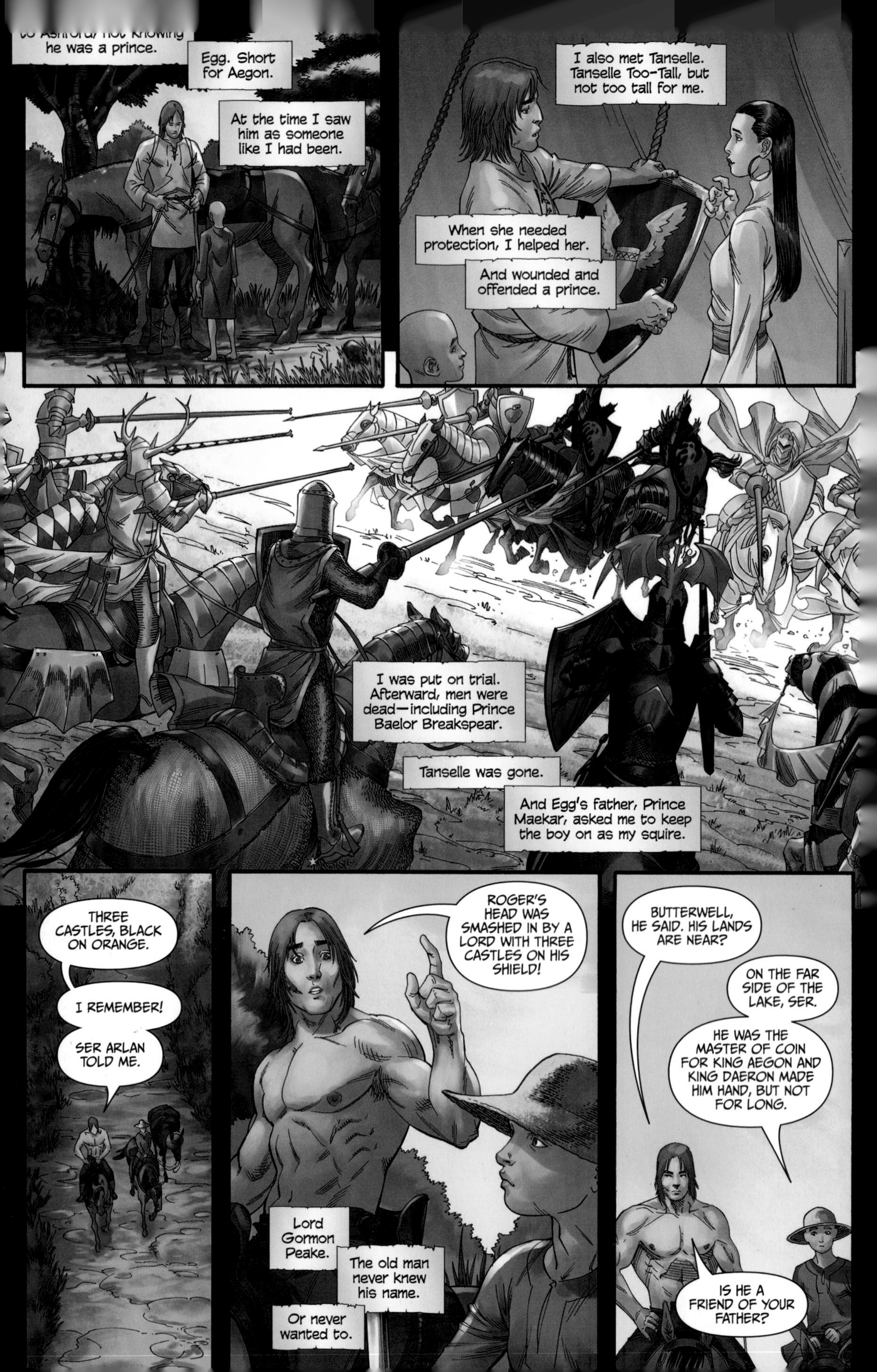

he was a prince.
Egg. Short for Aegon.
At the time I saw him as someone like I had been.
I also met Tanselle. Tanselle Too-Tall, but not too tall for me.
When she needed protection, I helped her.
And wounded and offended a prince.
I was put on trial. Afterward, men were dead—including Prince Baelor Breakspear.
Tanselle was gone.
And Egg's father, Prince Maekar, asked me to keep the boy on as my squire.
THREE CASTLES, BLACK ON ORANGE.
I REMEMBER!
SER ARLAN TOLD ME.
ROGER'S HEAD WAS SMASHED IN BY A LORD WITH THREE CASTLES ON HIS SHIELD!
Lord Gormon Peake.
The old man never knew his name.
Or never wanted to.
BUTTERWELL, HE SAID. HIS LANDS ARE NEAR?
ON THE FAR SIDE OF THE LAKE, SER.
HE WAS THE MASTER OF COIN FOR KING AEGON AND KING DAERON MADE HIM HAND, BUT NOT FOR LONG.
IS HE A FRIEND OF YOUR FATHER?

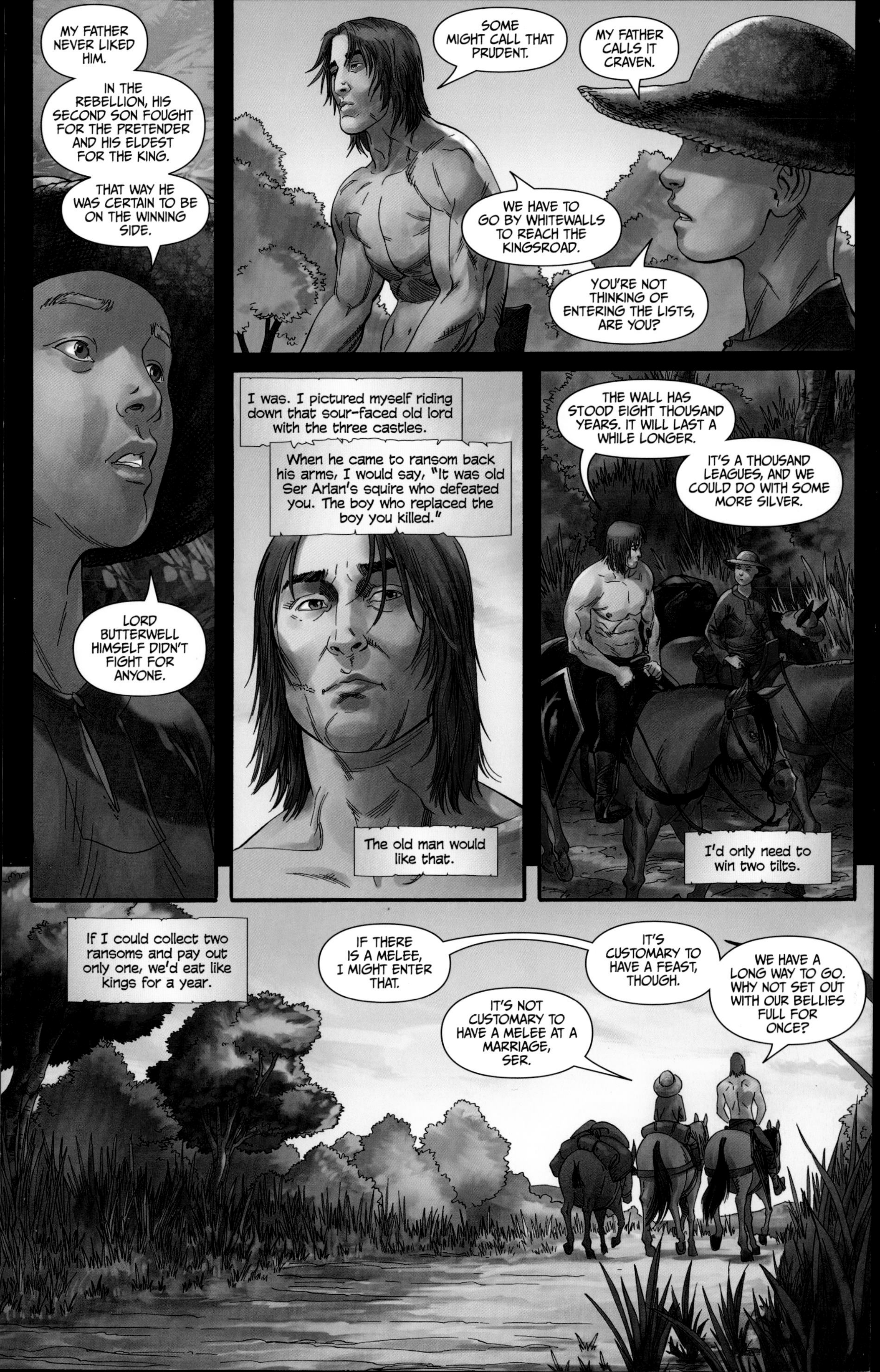
MY FATHER NEVER LIKED HIM.
IN THE REBELLION, HIS SECOND SON FOUGHT FOR THE PRETENDER AND HIS ELDEST FOR THE KING.
THAT WAY HE WAS CERTAIN TO BE ON THE WINNING SIDE.
LORD BUTTERWELL HIMSELF DIDN'T FIGHT FOR ANYONE.
SOME MIGHT CALL THAT PRUDENT.
MY FATHER CALLS IT CRAVEN.
WE HAVE TO GO BY WHITEWALLS TO REACH THE KINGSROAD.
YOU'RE NOT THINKING OF ENTERING THE LISTS, ARE YOU?
I was. I pictured myself riding down that sour-faced old lord with the three castles.
When he came to ransom back his arms, I would say, "It was old Ser Arlan's squire who defeated you. The boy who replaced the boy you killed."
The old man would like that.
THE WALL HAS STOOD EIGHT THOUSAND YEARS. IT WILL LAST A WHILE LONGER.
IT'S A THOUSAND LEAGUES, AND WE COULD DO WITH SOME MORE SILVER.
I'd only need to win two tilts.
If I could collect two ransoms and pay out only one, we'd eat like kings for a year.
IF THERE IS A MELEE, I MIGHT ENTER THAT.
IT'S NOT CUSTOMARY TO HAVE A MELEE AT A MARRIAGE, SER.
IT'S CUSTOMARY TO HAVE A FEAST, THOUGH.
WE HAVE A LONG WAY TO GO. WHY NOT SET OUT WITH OUR BELLIES FULL FOR ONCE?

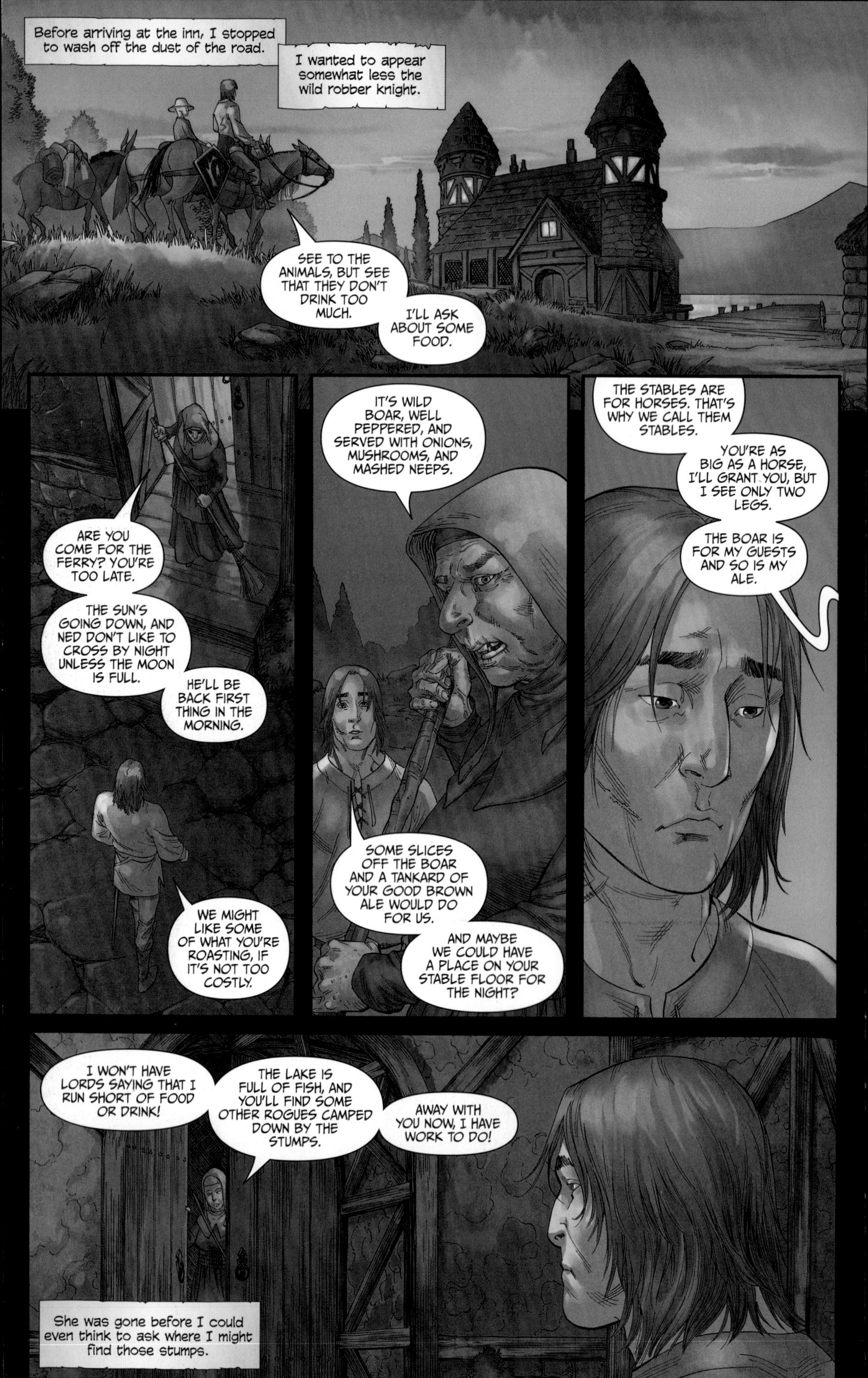

Before arriving at the inn, I stopped to wash off the dust of the road.
I wanted to appear somewhat less the wild robber knight.
SEE TO THE ANIMALS, BUT SEE THAT THEY DON'T DRINK TOO MUCH.
I'LL ASK ABOUT SOME FOOD.
ARE YOU COME FOR THE FERRY? YOU'RE TOO LATE.
THE SUN'S GOING DOWN, AND NED DON'T LIKE TO CROSS BY NIGHT UNLESS THE MOON IS FULL.
HE'LL BE BACK FIRST THING IN THE MORNING.
WE MIGHT LIKE SOME OF WHAT YOU'RE ROASTING, IF IT'S NOT TOO COSTLY.
IT'S WILD BOAR, WELL PEPPERED, AND SERVED WITH ONIONS, MUSHROOMS, AND MASHED NEEPS.
SOME SLICES OFF THE BOAR AND A TANKARD OF YOUR GOOD BROWN ALE WOULD DO FOR US.
AND MAYBE WE COULD HAVE A PLACE ON YOUR STABLE FLOOR FOR THE NIGHT?
THE STABLES ARE FOR HORSES. THAT'S WHY WE CALL THEM STABLES.
YOU'RE AS BIG AS A HORSE, I'LL GRANT YOU, BUT I SEE ONLY TWO LEGS.
THE BOAR IS FOR MY GUESTS AND SO IS MY ALE.
I WON'T HAVE LORDS SAYING THAT I RUN SHORT OF FOOD OR DRINK!
THE LAKE IS FULL OF FISH, AND YOU'LL FIND SOME OTHER ROGUES CAMPED DOWN BY THE STUMPS.
AWAY WITH YOU NOW, I HAVE WORK TO DO!
She was gone before I could even think to ask where I might find those stumps.

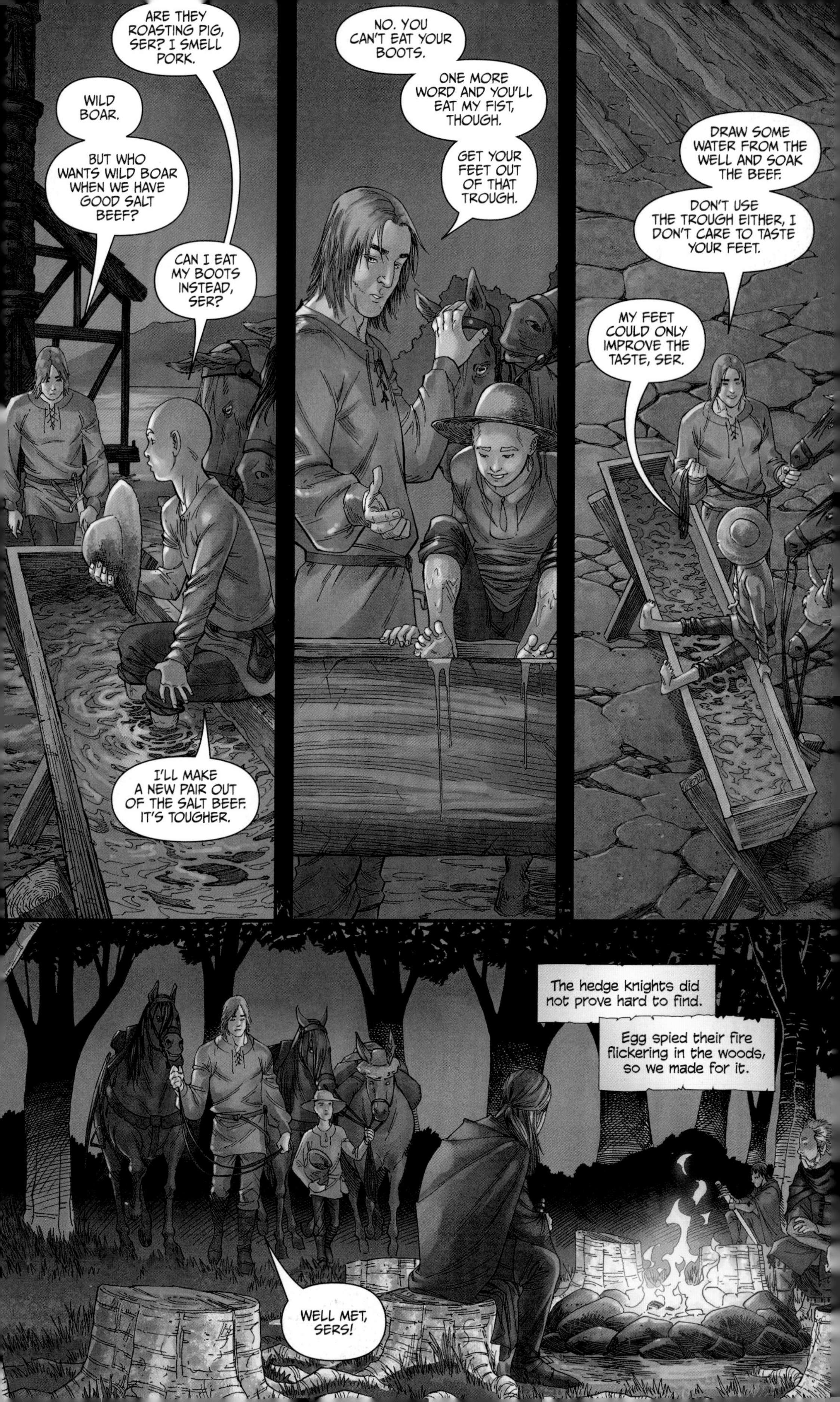
ARE THEY ROASTING PIG, SER? I SMELL PORK.
WILD BOAR.
BUT WHO WANTS WILD BOAR WHEN WE HAVE GOOD SALT BEEF?
CAN I EAT MY BOOTS INSTEAD, SER?
I'LL MAKE A NEW PAIR OUT OF THE SALT BEEF. IT'S TOUGHER.
NO. YOU CAN'T EAT YOUR BOOTS.
ONE MORE WORD AND YOU'LL EAT MY FIST, THOUGH.
GET YOUR FEET OUT OF THAT TROUGH.
DRAW SOME WATER FROM THE WELL AND SOAK THE BEEF.
DON'T USE THE TROUGH EITHER, I DON'T CARE TO TASTE YOUR FEET.
MY FEET COULD ONLY IMPROVE THE TASTE, SER.
The hedge knights did not prove hard to find.
Egg spied their fire flickering in the woods, so we made for it.
WELL MET, SERS!

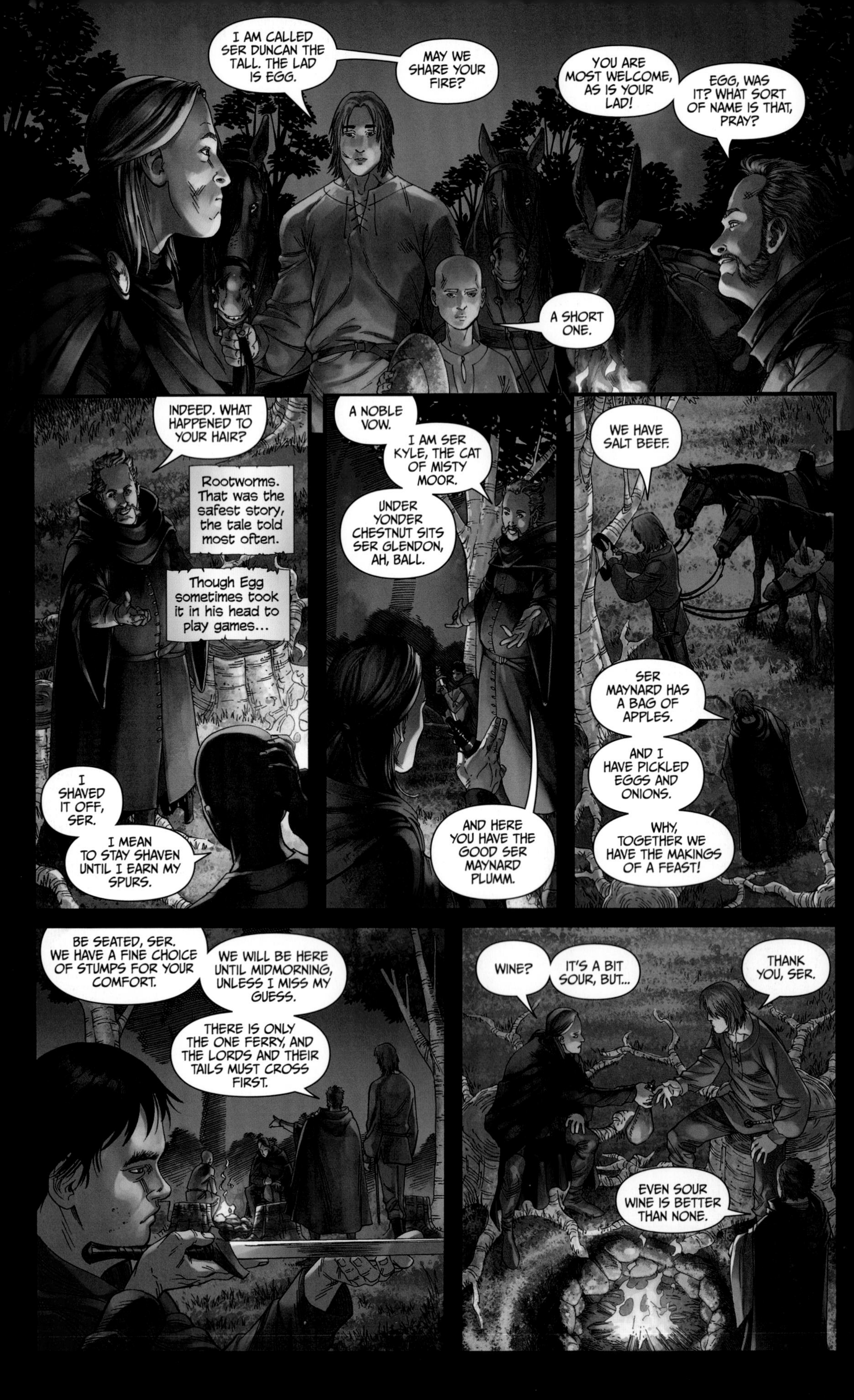
I AM CALLED SER DUNCAN THE TALL. THE LAD IS EGG.
MAY WE SHARE YOUR FIRE?
YOU ARE MOST WELCOME, AS IS YOUR LAD!
EGG, WAS IT? WHAT SORT OF NAME IS THAT, PRAY?
A SHORT ONE.
INDEED. WHAT HAPPENED TO YOUR HAIR?
Rootworms. That was the safest story, the tale told most often.
Though Egg sometimes took it in his head to play games...
I SHAVED IT OFF, SER.
I MEAN TO STAY SHAVEN UNTIL I EARN MY SPURS.
A NOBLE VOW.
I AM SER KYLE, THE CAT OF MISTY MOOR.
UNDER YONDER CHESTNUT SITS SER GLENDON, AH, BALL.
AND HERE YOU HAVE THE GOOD SER MAYNARD PLUMM.
WE HAVE SALT BEEF.
SER MAYNARD HAS A BAG OF APPLES.
AND I HAVE PICKLED EGGS AND ONIONS.
WHY, TOGETHER WE HAVE THE MAKINGS OF A FEAST!
BE SEATED, SER. WE HAVE A FINE CHOICE OF STUMPS FOR YOUR COMFORT.
WE WILL BE HERE UNTIL MIDMORNING, UNLESS I MISS MY GUESS.
THERE IS ONLY THE ONE FERRY, AND THE LORDS AND THEIR TAILS MUST CROSS FIRST.
WINE?
IT'S A BIT SOUR, BUT...
THANK YOU, SER.
EVEN SOUR WINE IS BETTER THAN NONE.

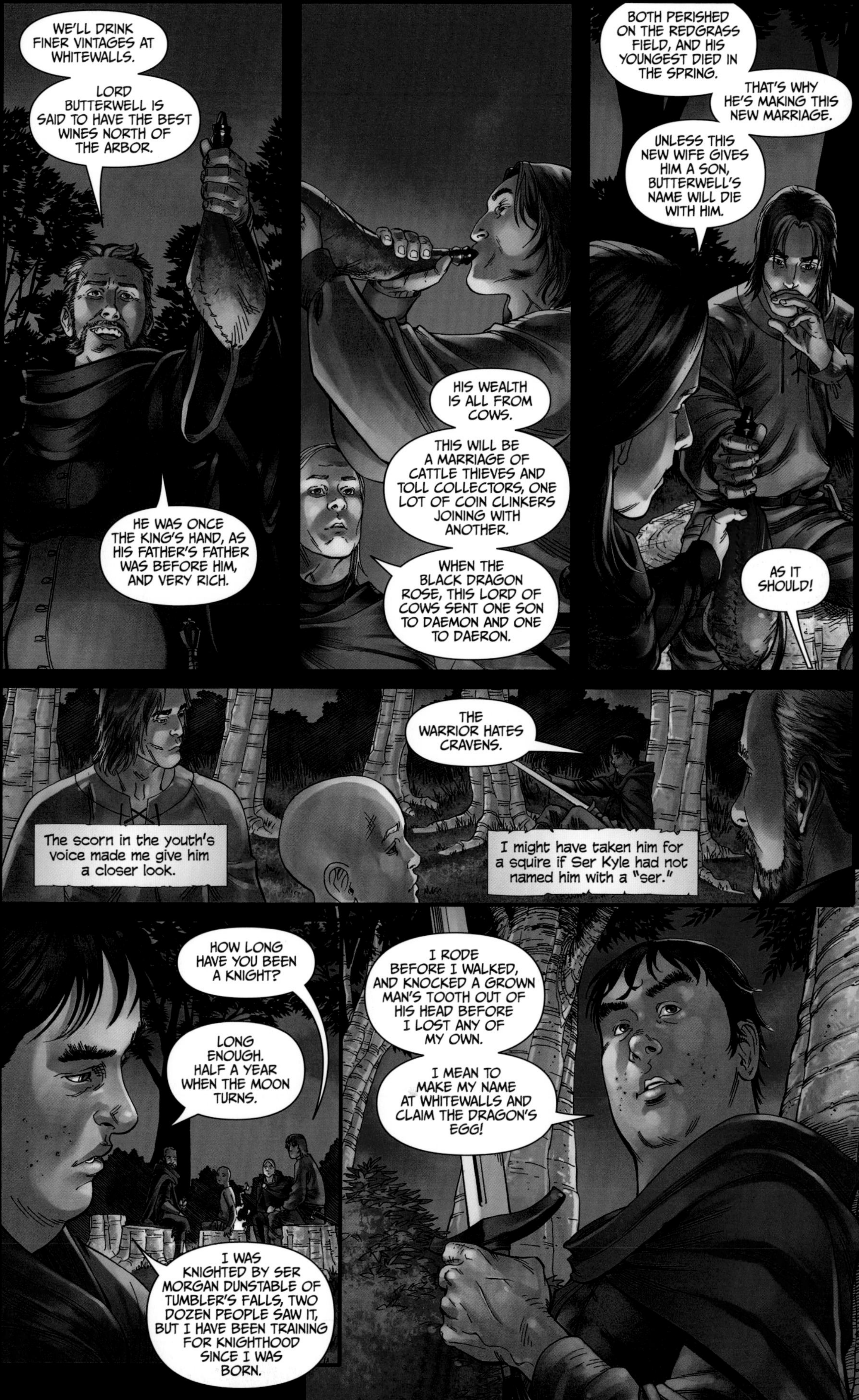
WE'LL DRINK FINER VINTAGES AT WHITEWALLS.
LORD BUTTERWELL IS SAID TO HAVE THE BEST WINES NORTH OF THE ARBOR.
HE WAS ONCE THE KING'S HAND, AS HIS FATHER'S FATHER WAS BEFORE HIM, AND VERY RICH.
HIS WEALTH IS ALL FROM COWS.
THIS WILL BE A MARRIAGE OF CATTLE THIEVES AND TOLL COLLECTORS, ONE LOT OF COIN CLINKERS JOINING WITH ANOTHER.
WHEN THE BLACK DRAGON ROSE, THIS LORD OF COWS SENT ONE SON TO DAEMON AND ONE TO DAERON.
BOTH PERISHED ON THE REDGRASS FIELD, AND HIS YOUNGEST DIED IN THE SPRING.
THAT'S WHY HE'S MAKING THIS NEW MARRIAGE.
UNLESS THIS NEW WIFE GIVES HIM A SON, BUTTERWELL'S NAME WILL DIE WITH HIM.
AS IT SHOULD!
THE WARRIOR HATES CRAVENS.
The scorn in the youth's voice made me give him a closer look.
I might have taken him for a squire if Ser Kyle had not named him with a "ser."
HOW LONG HAVE YOU BEEN A KNIGHT?
LONG ENOUGH. HALF A YEAR WHEN THE MOON TURNS.
I WAS KNIGHTED BY SER MORGAN DUNSTABLE OF TUMBLER'S FALLS, TWO DOZEN PEOPLE SAW IT, BUT I HAVE BEEN TRAINING FOR KNIGHTHOOD SINCE I WAS BORN.
I RODE BEFORE I WALKED, AND KNOCKED A GROWN MAN'S TOOTH OUT OF HIS HEAD BEFORE I LOST ANY OF MY OWN.
I MEAN TO MAKE MY NAME AT WHITEWALLS AND CLAIM THE DRAGON'S EGG!

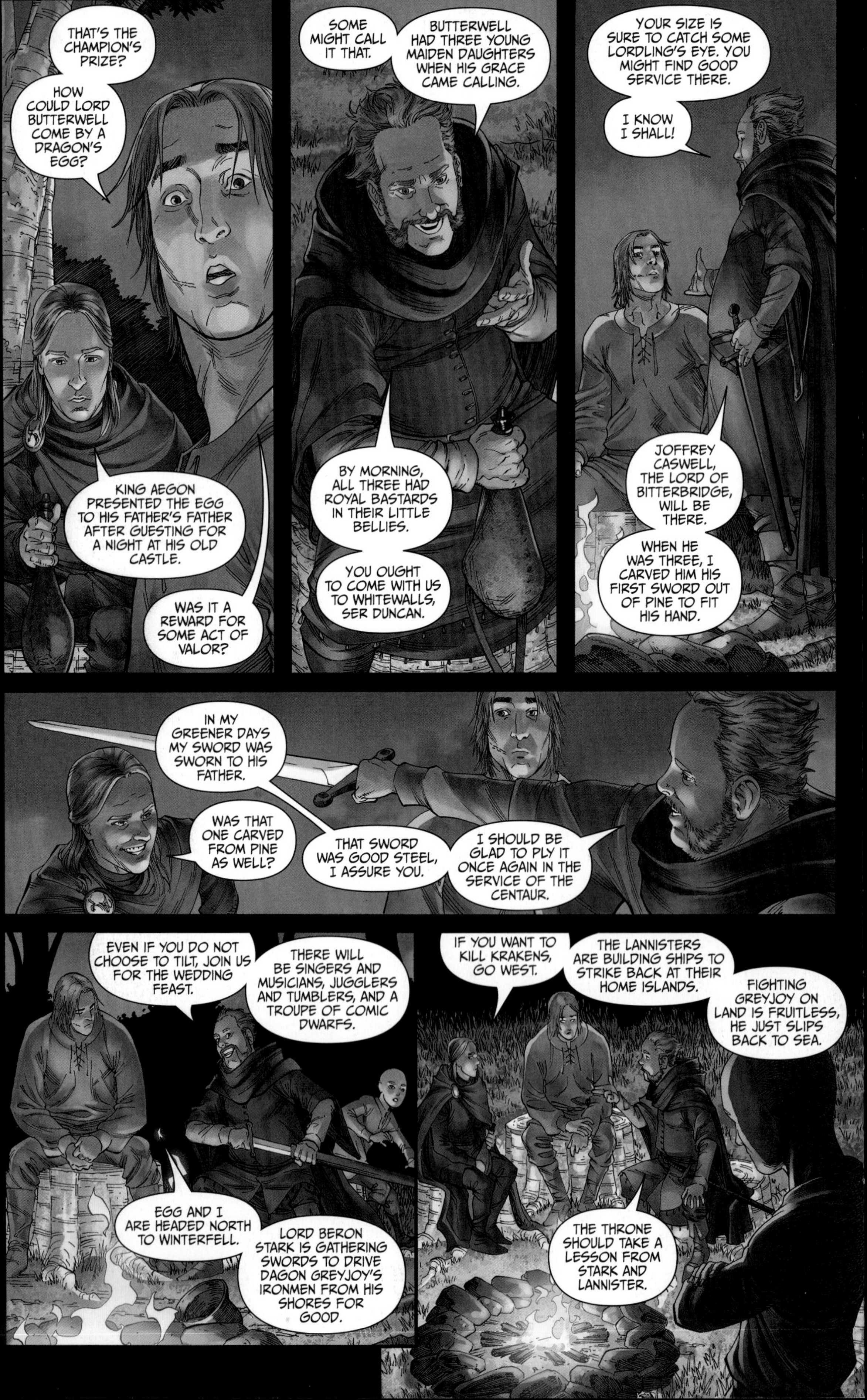
THAT'S THE CHAMPION'S PRIZE?
HOW COULD LORD BUTTERWELL COME BY A DRAGON'S EGG?
KING AEGON PRESENTED THE EGG TO HIS FATHER'S FATHER AFTER GUESTING FOR A NIGHT AT HIS OLD CASTLE.
WAS IT A REWARD FOR SOME ACT OF VALOR?
SOME MIGHT CALL IT THAT.
BUTTERWELL HAD THREE YOUNG MAIDEN DAUGHTERS WHEN HIS GRACE CAME CALLING.
BY MORNING, ALL THREE HAD ROYAL BASTARDS IN THEIR LITTLE BELLIES.
YOU OUGHT TO COME WITH US TO WHITEWALLS, SER DUNCAN.
YOUR SIZE IS SURE TO CATCH SOME LORDLING'S EYE. YOU MIGHT FIND GOOD SERVICE THERE.
I KNOW I SHALL!
JOFFREY CASWELL, THE LORD OF BITTERBRIDGE, WILL BE THERE.
WHEN HE WAS THREE, I CARVED HIM HIS FIRST SWORD OUT OF PINE TO FIT HIS HAND.
IN MY GREENER DAYS MY SWORD WAS SWORN TO HIS FATHER.
WAS THAT ONE CARVED FROM PINE AS WELL?
THAT SWORD WAS GOOD STEEL, I ASSURE YOU.
I SHOULD BE GLAD TO PLY IT ONCE AGAIN IN THE SERVICE OF THE CENTAUR.
EVEN IF YOU DO NOT CHOOSE TO TILT, JOIN US FOR THE WEDDING FEAST.
THERE WILL BE SINGERS AND MUSICIANS, JUGGLERS AND TUMBLERS, AND A TROUPE OF COMIC DWARFS.
EGG AND I ARE HEADED NORTH TO WINTERFELL.
LORD BERON STARK IS GATHERING SWORDS TO DRIVE DAGON GREYJOY'S IRONMEN FROM HIS SHORES FOR GOOD.
IF YOU WANT TO KILL KRAKENS, GO WEST.
THE LANNISTERS ARE BUILDING SHIPS TO STRIKE BACK AT THEIR HOME ISLANDS.
FIGHTING GREYJOY ON LAND IS FRUITLESS, HE JUST SLIPS BACK TO SEA.
THE THRONE SHOULD TAKE A LESSON FROM STARK AND LANNISTER.

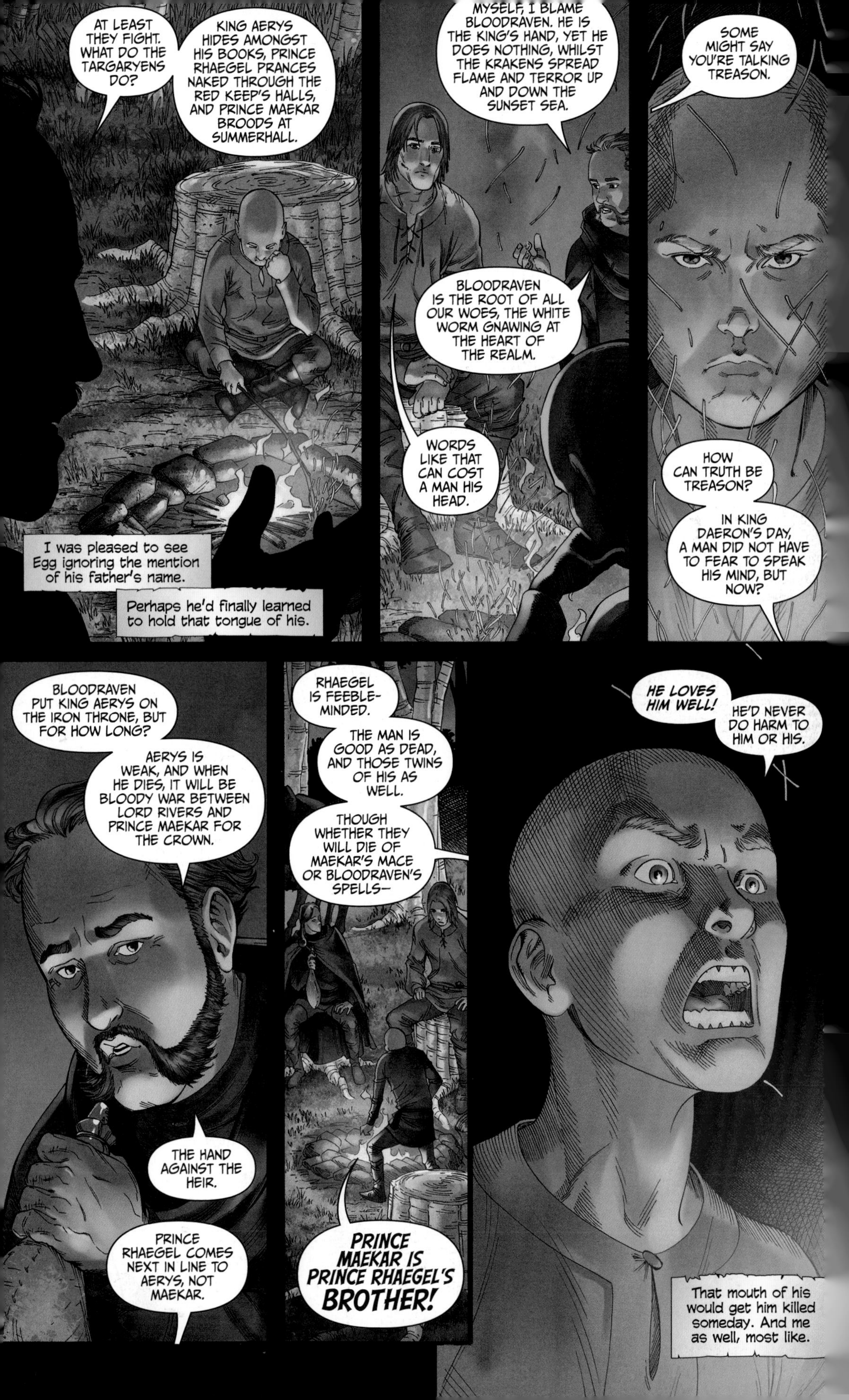

AT LEAST THEY FIGHT. WHAT DO THE TARGARYENS DO?
KING AERYS HIDES AMONGST HIS BOOKS, PRINCE RHAEGEL PRANCES NAKED THROUGH THE RED KEEP'S HALLS, AND PRINCE MAEKAR BROODS AT SUMMERHALL.
I was pleased to see Egg ignoring the mention of his father's name.
Perhaps he'd finally learned to hold that tongue of his.
MYSELF, I BLAME BLOODRAVEN. HE IS THE KING'S HAND, YET HE DOES NOTHING, WHILST THE KRAKENS SPREAD FLAME AND TERROR UP AND DOWN THE SUNSET SEA.
BLOODRAVEN IS THE ROOT OF ALL OUR WOES, THE WHITE WORM GNAWING AT THE HEART OF THE REALM.
WORDS LIKE THAT CAN COST A MAN HIS HEAD.
SOME MIGHT SAY YOU'RE TALKING TREASON.
HOW CAN TRUTH BE TREASON?
IN KING DAERON'S DAY, A MAN DID NOT HAVE TO FEAR TO SPEAK HIS MIND, BUT NOW?
BLOODRAVEN PUT KING AERYS ON THE IRON THRONE, BUT FOR HOW LONG?
AERYS IS WEAK, AND WHEN HE DIES, IT WILL BE BLOODY WAR BETWEEN LORD RIVERS AND PRINCE MAEKAR FOR THE CROWN.
THE HAND AGAINST THE HEIR.
PRINCE RHAEGEL COMES NEXT IN LINE TO AERYS, NOT MAEKAR.
RHAEGEL IS FEEBLE-MINDED.
THE MAN IS GOOD AS DEAD, AND THOSE TWINS OF HIS AS WELL.
THOUGH WHETHER THEY WILL DIE OF MAEKAR'S MACE OR BLOODRAVEN'S SPELLS—
PRINCE MAEKAR IS PRINCE RHAEGEL'S BROTHER!
HE LOVES HIM WELL!
HE'D NEVER DO HARM TO HIM OR HIS.
That mouth of his would get him killed someday. And me as well, most like.

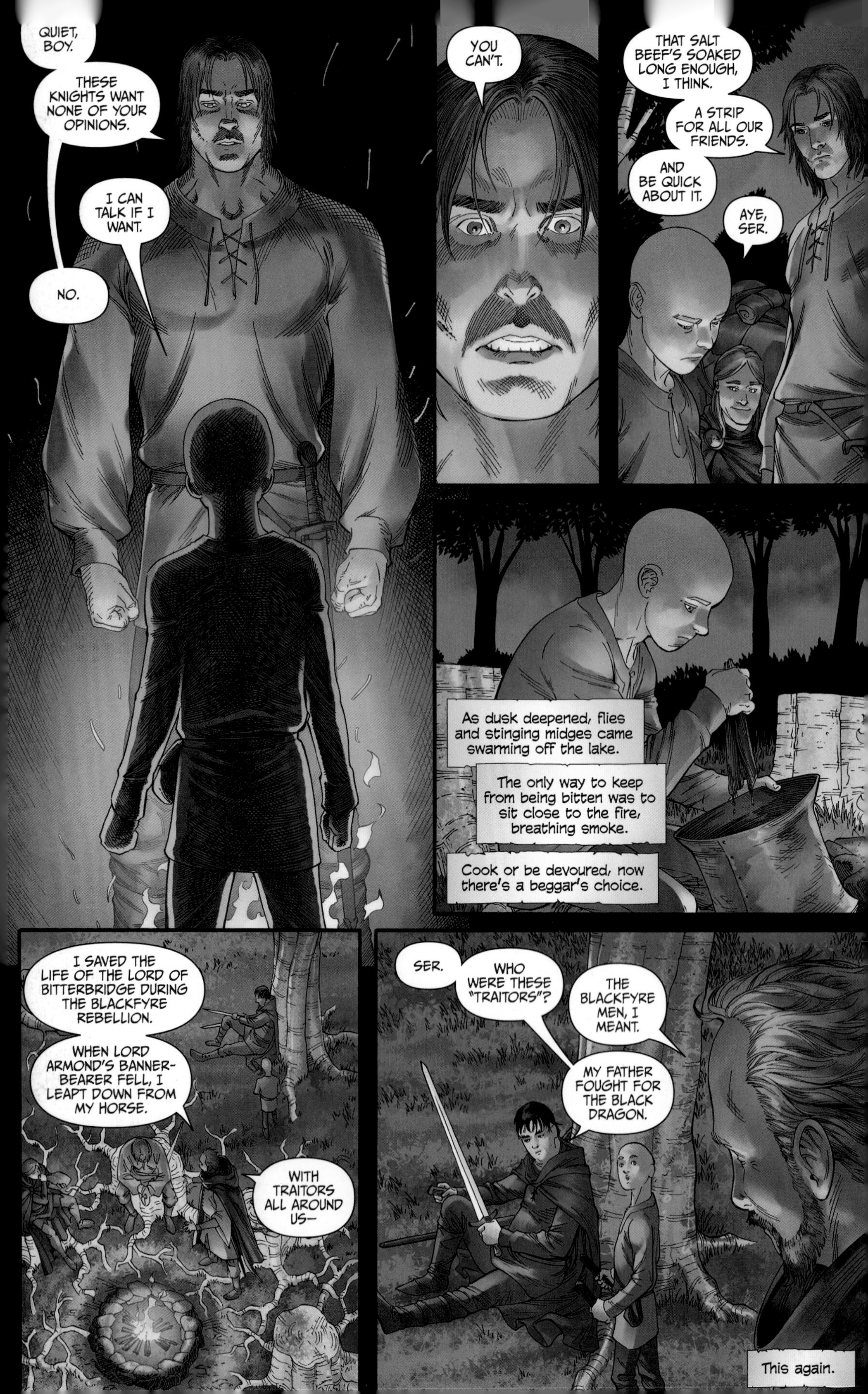
QUIET, BOY.
THESE KNIGHTS WANT NONE OF YOUR OPINIONS.
I CAN TALK IF I WANT.
NO.
YOU CAN'T.
THAT SALT BEEF'S SOAKED LONG ENOUGH, I THINK.
A STRIP FOR ALL OUR FRIENDS.
AND BE QUICK ABOUT IT.
AYE, SER.
As dusk deepened, flies and stinging midges came swarming off the lake.
The only way to keep from being bitten was to sit close to the fire, breathing smoke.
Cook or be devoured, now there's a beggar's choice.
I SAVED THE LIFE OF THE LORD OF BITTERBRIDGE DURING THE BLACKFYRE REBELLION.
WHEN LORD ARMOND'S BANNER-BEARER FELL, I LEAPT DOWN FROM MY HORSE.
WITH TRAITORS ALL AROUND US—
SER.
WHO WERE THESE "TRAITORS"?
THE BLACKFYRE MEN, I MEANT.
MY FATHER FOUGHT FOR THE BLACK DRAGON.
This again.

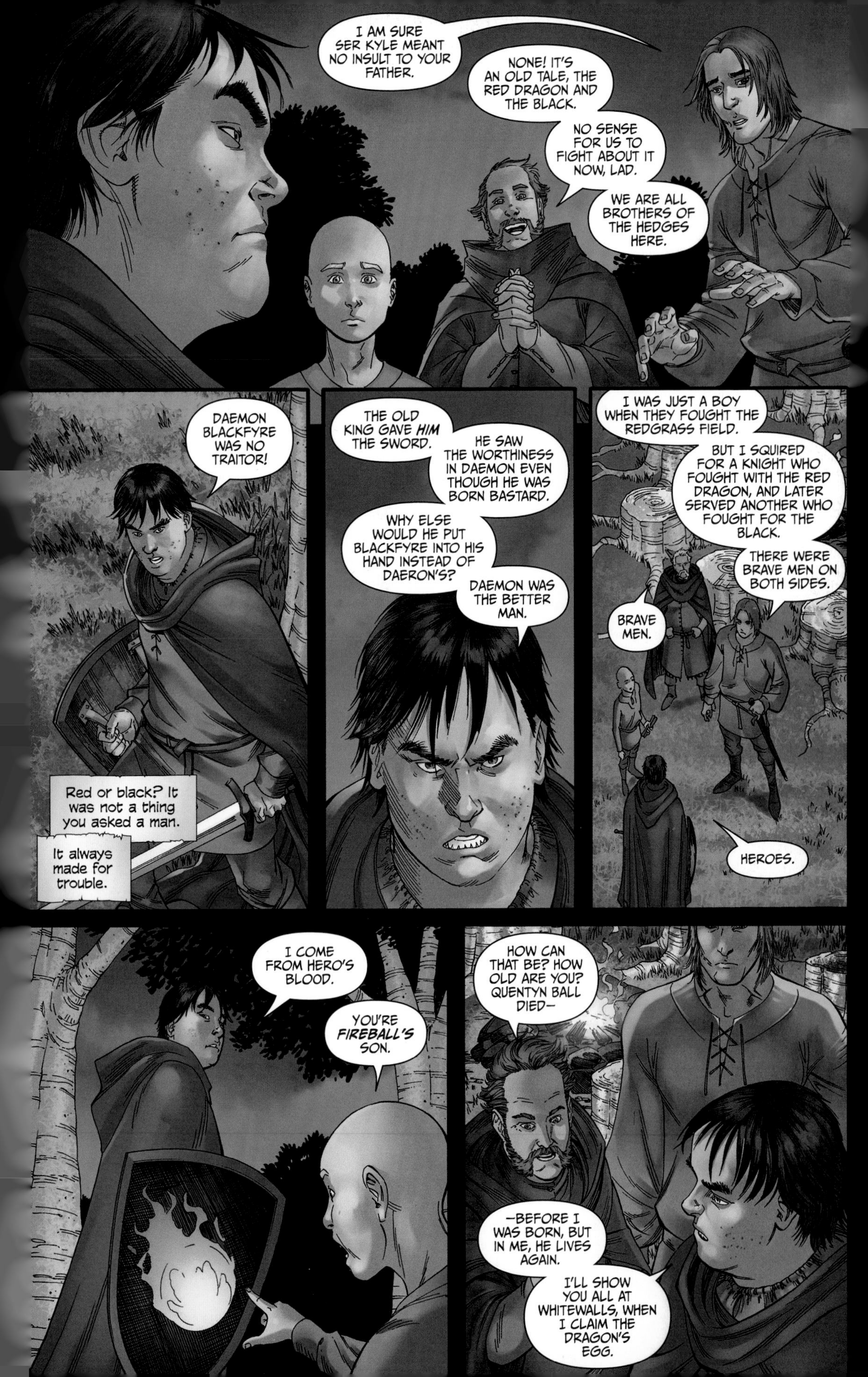
I AM SURE SER KYLE MEANT NO INSULT TO YOUR FATHER.
NONE! IT'S AN OLD TALE, THE RED DRAGON AND THE BLACK.
NO SENSE FOR US TO FIGHT ABOUT IT NOW, LAD.
WE ARE ALL BROTHERS OF THE HEDGES HERE.
DAEMON BLACKFYRE WAS NO TRAITOR!
Red or black? It was not a thing you asked a man.
It always made for trouble.
THE OLD KING GAVE *HIM* THE SWORD.
HE SAW THE WORTHINESS IN DAEMON EVEN THOUGH HE WAS BORN BASTARD.
WHY ELSE WOULD HE PUT BLACKFYRE INTO HIS HAND INSTEAD OF DAERON'S?
DAEMON WAS THE BETTER MAN.
I WAS JUST A BOY WHEN THEY FOUGHT THE REDGRASS FIELD.
BUT I SQUIRED FOR A KNIGHT WHO FOUGHT WITH THE RED DRAGON, AND LATER SERVED ANOTHER WHO FOUGHT FOR THE BLACK.
THERE WERE BRAVE MEN ON BOTH SIDES.
BRAVE MEN.
HEROES.
I COME FROM HERO'S BLOOD.
YOU'RE *FIREBALL'S* SON.
HOW CAN THAT BE? HOW OLD ARE YOU? QUENTYN BALL DIED—
—BEFORE I WAS BORN, BUT IN ME, HE LIVES AGAIN.
I'LL SHOW YOU ALL AT WHITEWALLS, WHEN I CLAIM THE DRAGON'S EGG.

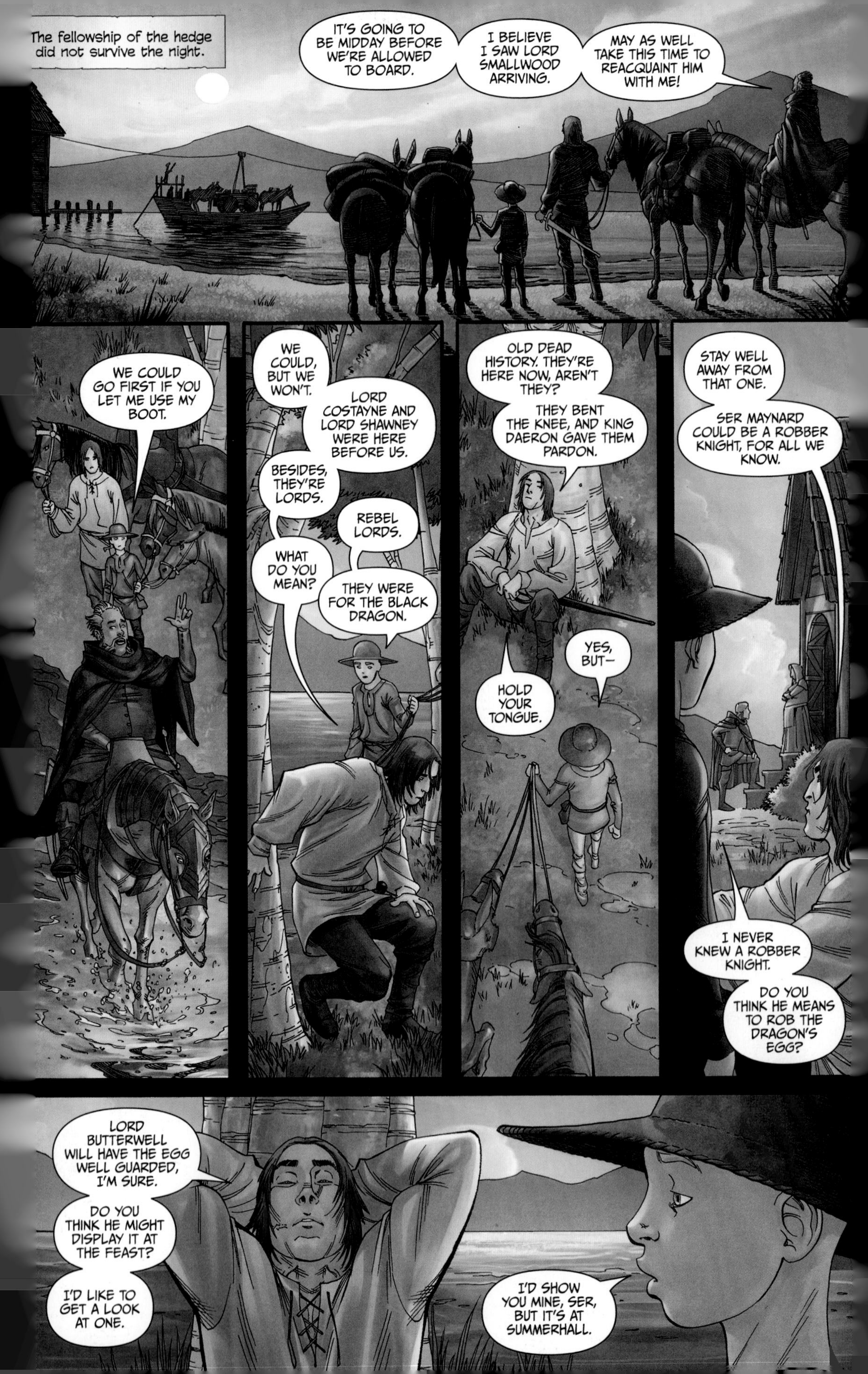

The fellowship of the hedge did not survive the night.
IT'S GOING TO BE MIDDAY BEFORE WE'RE ALLOWED TO BOARD.
I BELIEVE I SAW LORD SMALLWOOD ARRIVING.
MAY AS WELL TAKE THIS TIME TO REACQUAINT HIM WITH ME!
WE COULD GO FIRST IF YOU LET ME USE MY BOOT.
WE COULD, BUT WE WON'T.
LORD COSTAYNE AND LORD SHAWNEY WERE HERE BEFORE US.
BESIDES, THEY'RE LORDS.
REBEL LORDS.
WHAT DO YOU MEAN?
THEY WERE FOR THE BLACK DRAGON.
OLD DEAD HISTORY. THEY'RE HERE NOW, AREN'T THEY?
THEY BENT THE KNEE, AND KING DAERON GAVE THEM PARDON.
YES, BUT—
HOLD YOUR TONGUE.
STAY WELL AWAY FROM THAT ONE.
SER MAYNARD COULD BE A ROBBER KNIGHT, FOR ALL WE KNOW.
I NEVER KNEW A ROBBER KNIGHT.
DO YOU THINK HE MEANS TO ROB THE DRAGON'S EGG?
LORD BUTTERWELL WILL HAVE THE EGG WELL GUARDED, I'M SURE.
DO YOU THINK HE MIGHT DISPLAY IT AT THE FEAST?
I'D LIKE TO GET A LOOK AT ONE.
I'D SHOW YOU MINE, SER, BUT IT'S AT SUMMERHALL.

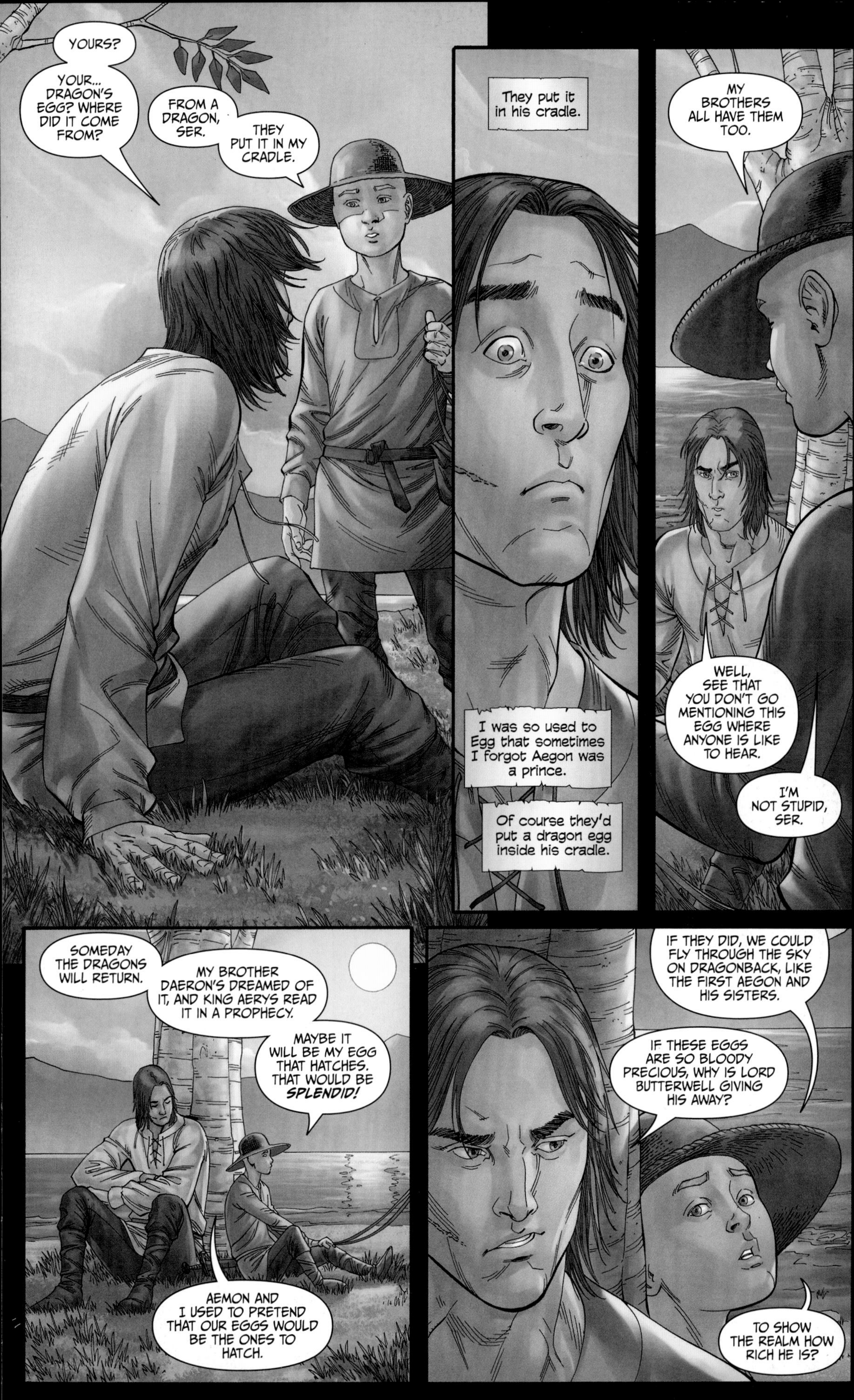
YOURS?
YOUR... DRAGON'S EGG? WHERE DID IT COME FROM?
FROM A DRAGON, SER.
THEY PUT IT IN MY CRADLE.
They put it in his cradle.
I was so used to Egg that sometimes I forgot Aegon was a prince.
Of course they'd put a dragon egg inside his cradle.
MY BROTHERS ALL HAVE THEM TOO.
WELL, SEE THAT YOU DON'T GO MENTIONING THIS EGG WHERE ANYONE IS LIKE TO HEAR.
I'M NOT STUPID, SER.
SOMEDAY THE DRAGONS WILL RETURN.
MY BROTHER DAERON'S DREAMED OF IT, AND KING AERYS READ IT IN A PROPHECY.
MAYBE IT WILL BE MY EGG THAT HATCHES. THAT WOULD BE *SPLENDID!*
AEMON AND I USED TO PRETEND THAT OUR EGGS WOULD BE THE ONES TO HATCH.
IF THEY DID, WE COULD FLY THROUGH THE SKY ON DRAGONBACK, LIKE THE FIRST AEGON AND HIS SISTERS.
IF THESE EGGS ARE SO BLOODY PRECIOUS, WHY IS LORD BUTTERWELL GIVING HIS AWAY?
TO SHOW THE REALM HOW RICH HE IS?

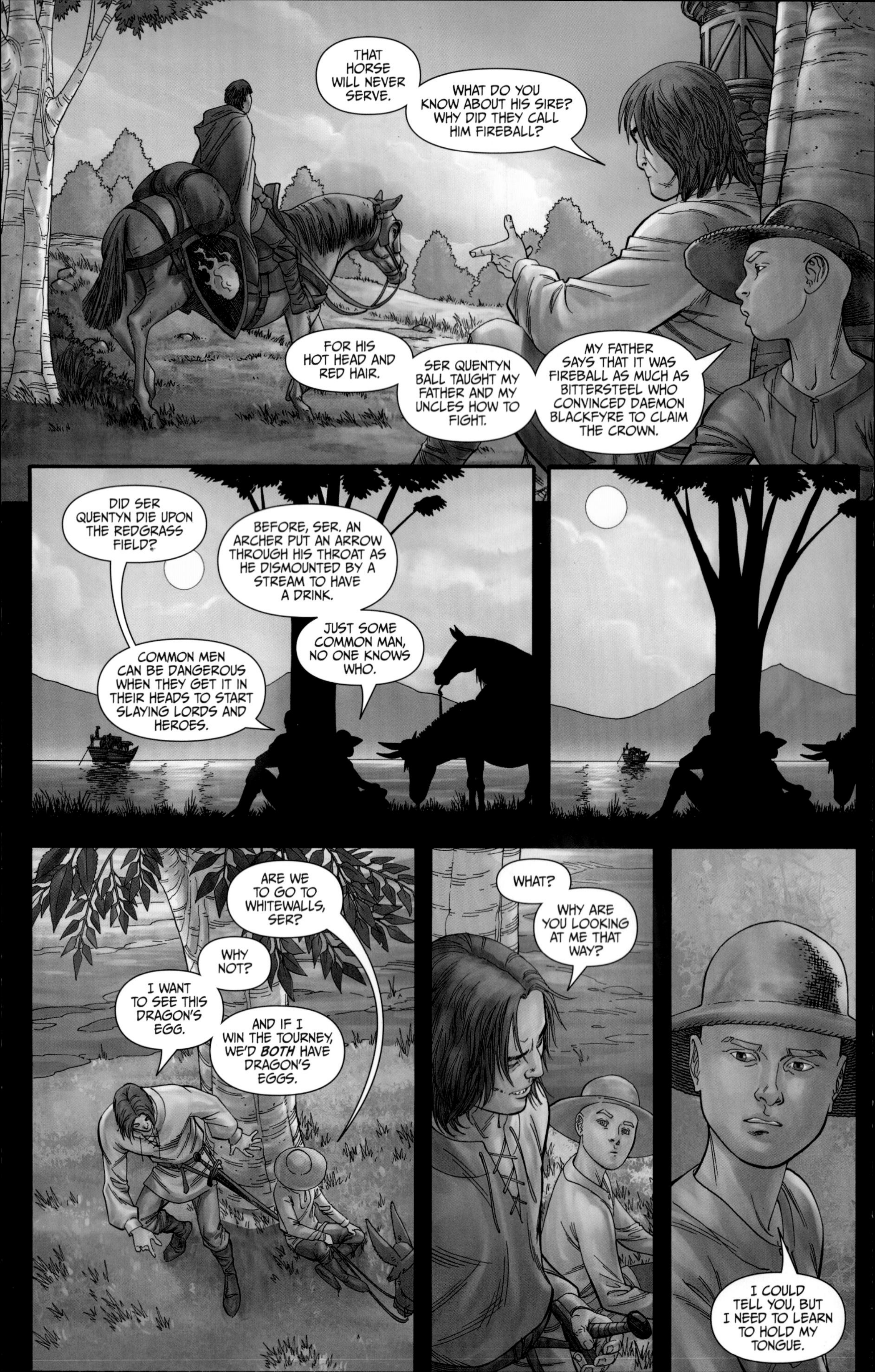
THAT HORSE WILL NEVER SERVE.
WHAT DO YOU KNOW ABOUT HIS SIRE? WHY DID THEY CALL HIM FIREBALL?
FOR HIS HOT HEAD AND RED HAIR.
SER QUENTYN BALL TAUGHT MY FATHER AND MY UNCLES HOW TO FIGHT.
MY FATHER SAYS THAT IT WAS FIREBALL AS MUCH AS BITTERSTEEL WHO CONVINCED DAEMON BLACKFYRE TO CLAIM THE CROWN.
DID SER QUENTYN DIE UPON THE REDGRASS FIELD?
BEFORE, SER. AN ARCHER PUT AN ARROW THROUGH HIS THROAT AS HE DISMOUNTED BY A STREAM TO HAVE A DRINK.
JUST SOME COMMON MAN, NO ONE KNOWS WHO.
COMMON MEN CAN BE DANGEROUS WHEN THEY GET IT IN THEIR HEADS TO START SLAYING LORDS AND HEROES.
ARE WE TO GO TO WHITEWALLS, SER?
WHY NOT?
I WANT TO SEE THIS DRAGON'S EGG.
AND IF I WIN THE TOURNEY, WE'D *BOTH* HAVE DRAGON'S EGGS.
WHAT?
WHY ARE YOU LOOKING AT ME THAT WAY?
I COULD TELL YOU, BUT I NEED TO LEARN TO HOLD MY TONGUE.

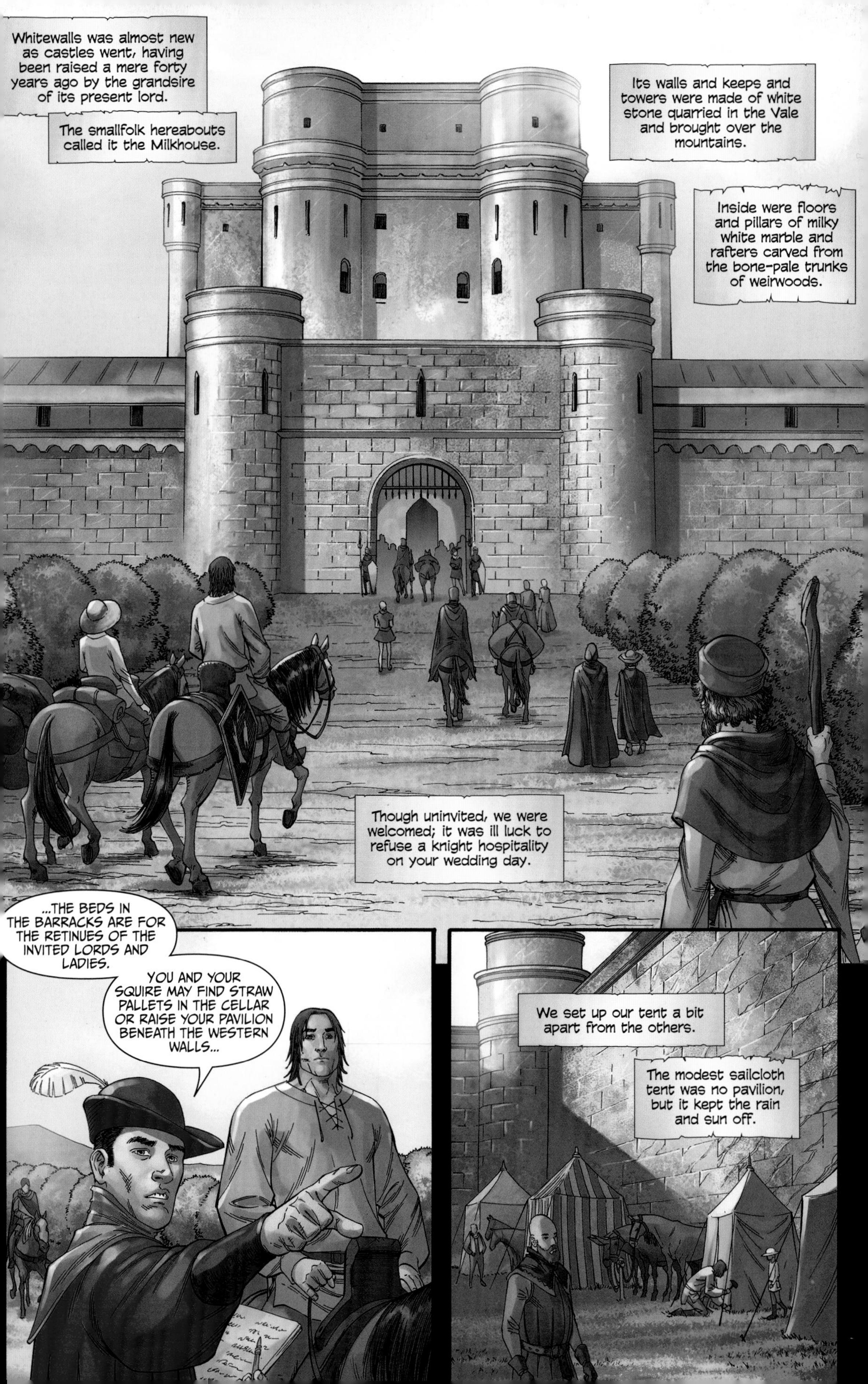
Whitewalls was almost new as castles went, having been raised a mere forty years ago by the grandsire of its present lord.
The smallfolk hereabouts called it the Milkhouse.
Its walls and keeps and towers were made of white stone quarried in the Vale and brought over the mountains.
Inside were floors and pillars of milky white marble and rafters carved from the bone-pale trunks of weirwoods.
Though uninvited, we were welcomed; it was ill luck to refuse a knight hospitality on your wedding day.
...THE BEDS IN THE BARRACKS ARE FOR THE RETINUES OF THE INVITED LORDS AND LADIES.
YOU AND YOUR SQUIRE MAY FIND STRAW PALLETS IN THE CELLAR OR RAISE YOUR PAVILION BENEATH THE WESTERN WALLS...
We set up our tent a bit apart from the others.
The modest sailcloth tent was no pavilion, but it kept the rain and sun off.

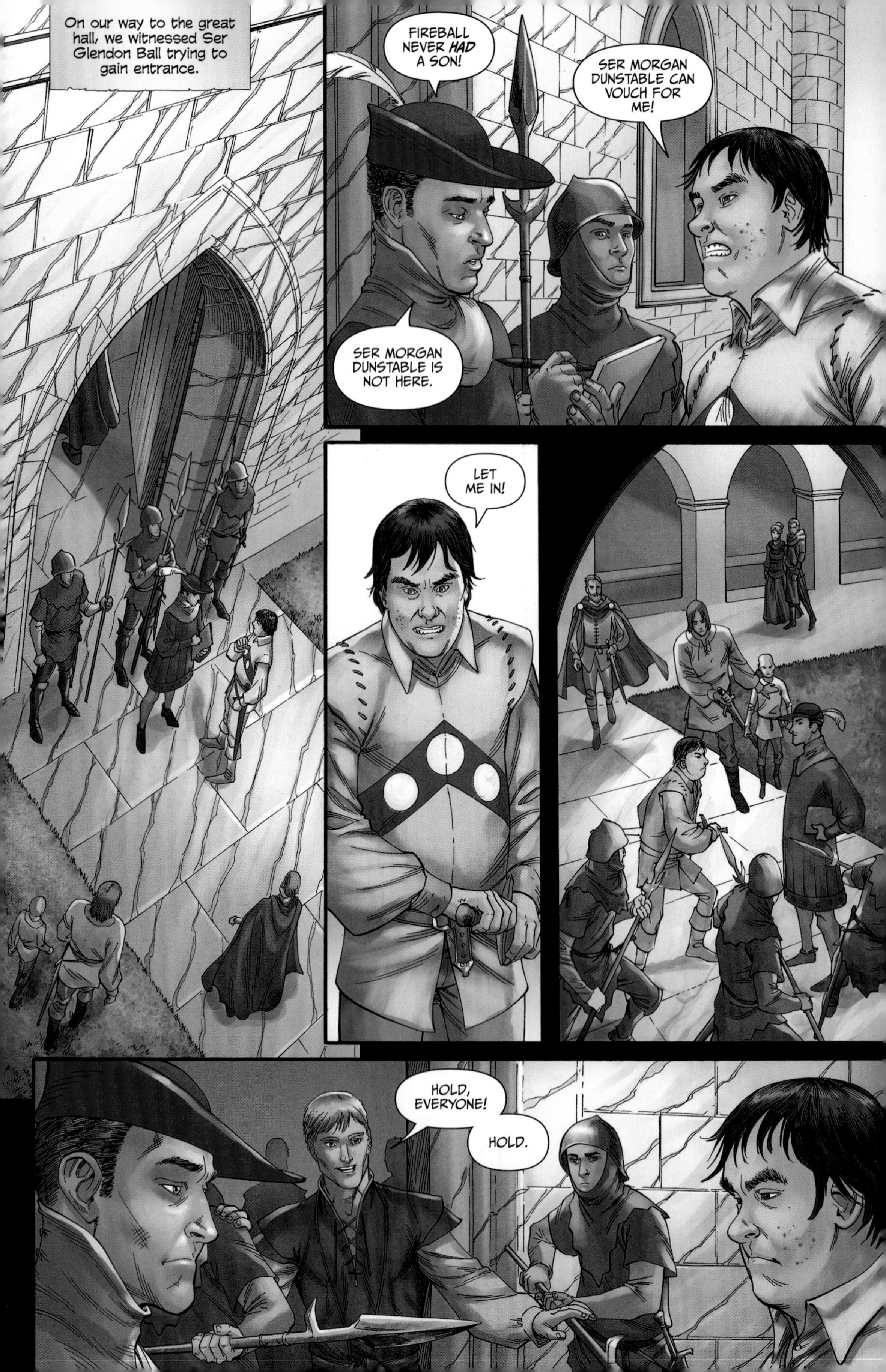
On our way to the great hall, we witnessed Ser Glendon Ball trying to gain entrance.
FIREBALL NEVER HAD A SON!
SER MORGAN DUNSTABLE CAN VOUCH FOR ME!
SER MORGAN DUNSTABLE IS NOT HERE.
LET ME IN!
HOLD, EVERYONE!
HOLD.

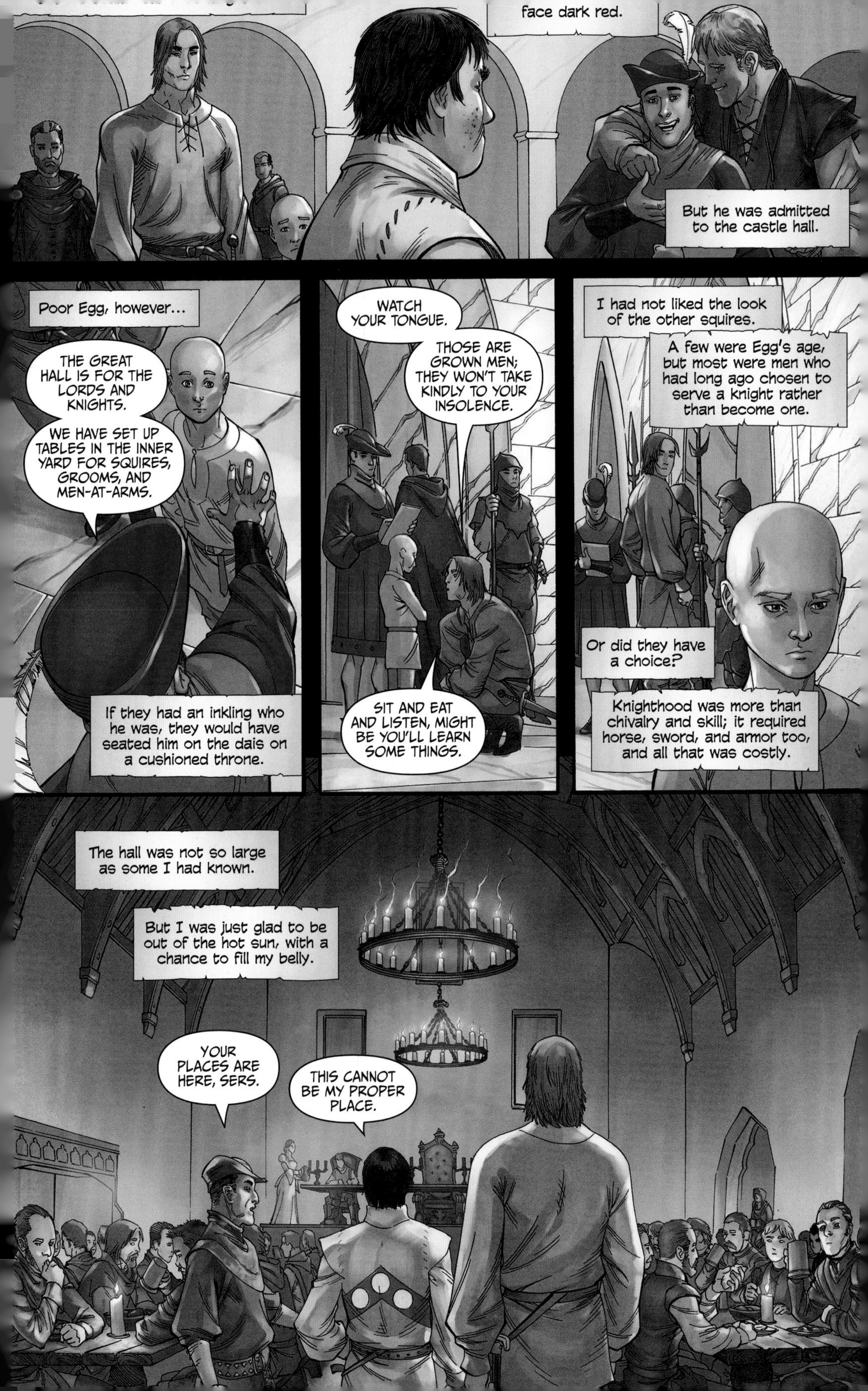
face dark red.
But he was admitted to the castle hall.
Poor Egg, however...
THE GREAT HALL IS FOR THE LORDS AND KNIGHTS.
WE HAVE SET UP TABLES IN THE INNER YARD FOR SQUIRES, GROOMS, AND MEN-AT-ARMS.
If they had an inkling who he was, they would have seated him on the dais on a cushioned throne.
WATCH YOUR TONGUE.
THOSE ARE GROWN MEN; THEY WON'T TAKE KINDLY TO YOUR INSOLENCE.
SIT AND EAT AND LISTEN, MIGHT BE YOU'LL LEARN SOME THINGS.
I had not liked the look of the other squires.
A few were Egg's age, but most were men who had long ago chosen to serve a knight rather than become one.
Or did they have a choice?
Knighthood was more than chivalry and skill; it required horse, sword, and armor too, and all that was costly.
The hall was not so large as some I had known.
But I was just glad to be out of the hot sun, with a chance to fill my belly.
YOUR PLACES ARE HERE, SERS.
THIS CANNOT BE MY PROPER PLACE.

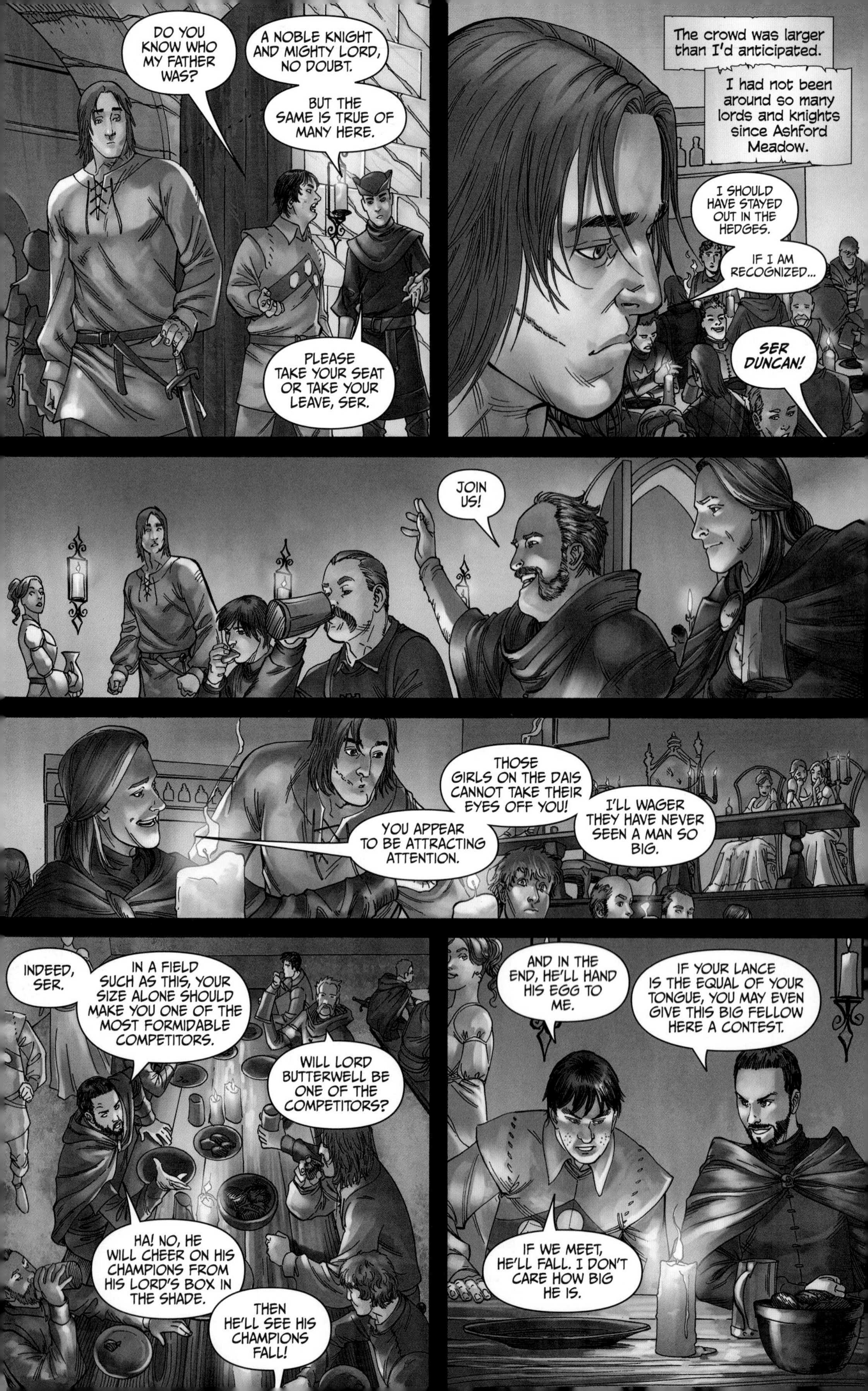
DO YOU KNOW WHO MY FATHER WAS?
A NOBLE KNIGHT AND MIGHTY LORD, NO DOUBT.
BUT THE SAME IS TRUE OF MANY HERE.
PLEASE TAKE YOUR SEAT OR TAKE YOUR LEAVE, SER.
The crowd was larger than I'd anticipated.
I had not been around so many lords and knights since Ashford Meadow.
I SHOULD HAVE STAYED OUT IN THE HEDGES.
IF I AM RECOGNIZED...
SER DUNCAN!
JOIN US!
THOSE GIRLS ON THE DAIS CANNOT TAKE THEIR EYES OFF YOU!
YOU APPEAR TO BE ATTRACTING ATTENTION.
I'LL WAGER THEY HAVE NEVER SEEN A MAN SO BIG.
INDEED, SER.
IN A FIELD SUCH AS THIS, YOUR SIZE ALONE SHOULD MAKE YOU ONE OF THE MOST FORMIDABLE COMPETITORS.
WILL LORD BUTTERWELL BE ONE OF THE COMPETITORS?
HA! NO, HE WILL CHEER ON HIS CHAMPIONS FROM HIS LORD'S BOX IN THE SHADE.
THEN HE'LL SEE HIS CHAMPIONS FALL!
AND IN THE END, HE'LL HAND HIS EGG TO ME.
IF YOUR LANCE IS THE EQUAL OF YOUR TONGUE, YOU MAY EVEN GIVE THIS BIG FELLOW HERE A CONTEST.
IF WE MEET, HE'LL FALL. I DON'T CARE HOW BIG HE IS.

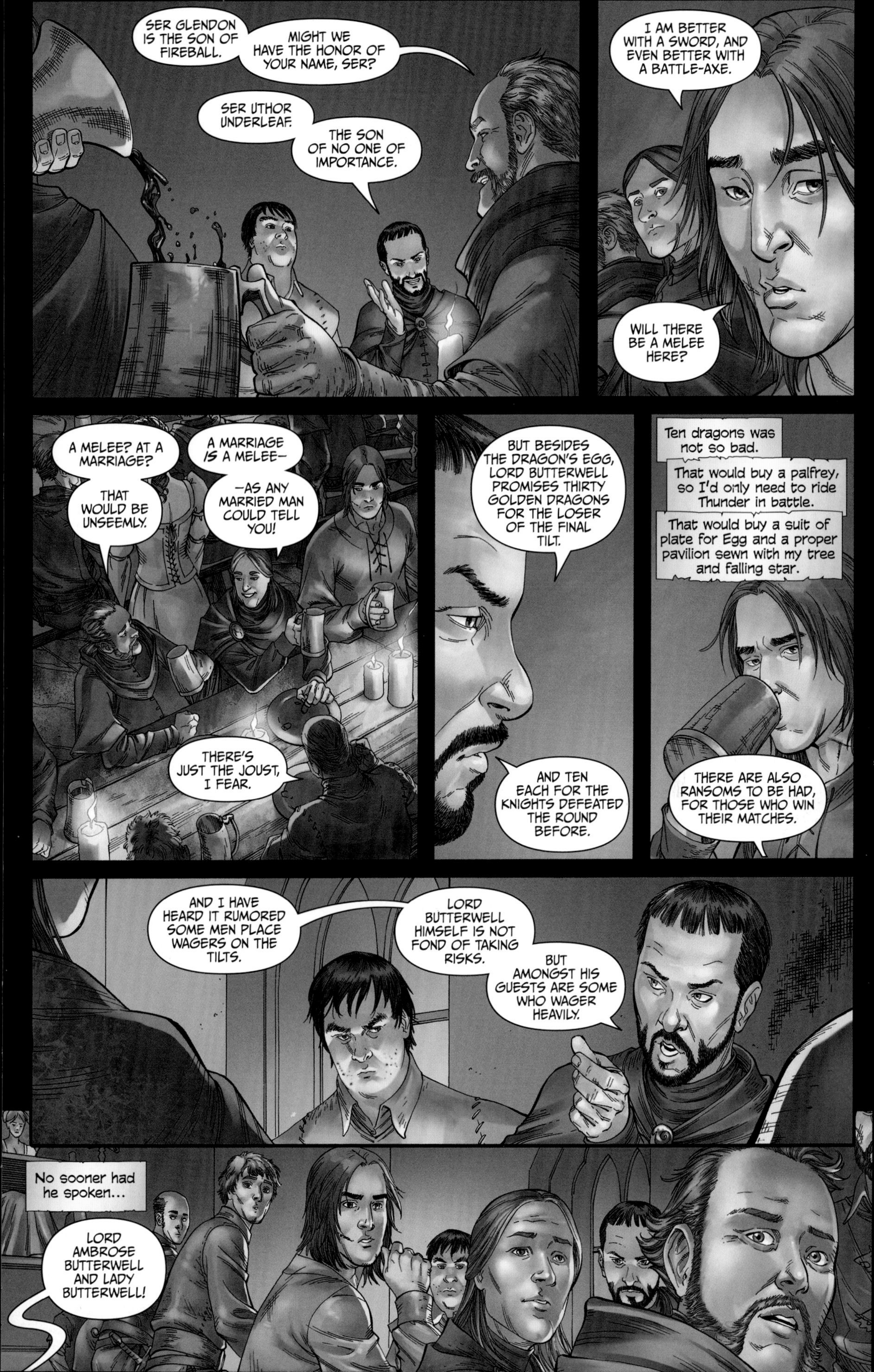
SER GLENDON IS THE SON OF FIREBALL.
MIGHT WE HAVE THE HONOR OF YOUR NAME, SER?
SER UTHOR UNDERLEAF.
THE SON OF NO ONE OF IMPORTANCE.
I AM BETTER WITH A SWORD, AND EVEN BETTER WITH A BATTLE-AXE.
WILL THERE BE A MELEE HERE?
A MELEE? AT A MARRIAGE?
THAT WOULD BE UNSEEMLY.
A MARRIAGE IS A MELEE—
—AS ANY MARRIED MAN COULD TELL YOU!
THERE'S JUST THE JOUST, I FEAR.
BUT BESIDES THE DRAGON'S EGG, LORD BUTTERWELL PROMISES THIRTY GOLDEN DRAGONS FOR THE LOSER OF THE FINAL TILT.
AND TEN EACH FOR THE KNIGHTS DEFEATED THE ROUND BEFORE.
Ten dragons was not so bad.
That would buy a palfrey, so I'd only need to ride Thunder in battle.
That would buy a suit of plate for Egg and a proper pavilion sewn with my tree and falling star.
THERE ARE ALSO RANSOMS TO BE HAD, FOR THOSE WHO WIN THEIR MATCHES.
AND I HAVE HEARD IT RUMORED SOME MEN PLACE WAGERS ON THE TILTS.
LORD BUTTERWELL HIMSELF IS NOT FOND OF TAKING RISKS.
BUT AMONGST HIS GUESTS ARE SOME WHO WAGER HEAVILY.
No sooner had he spoken...
LORD AMBROSE BUTTERWELL AND LADY BUTTERWELL!

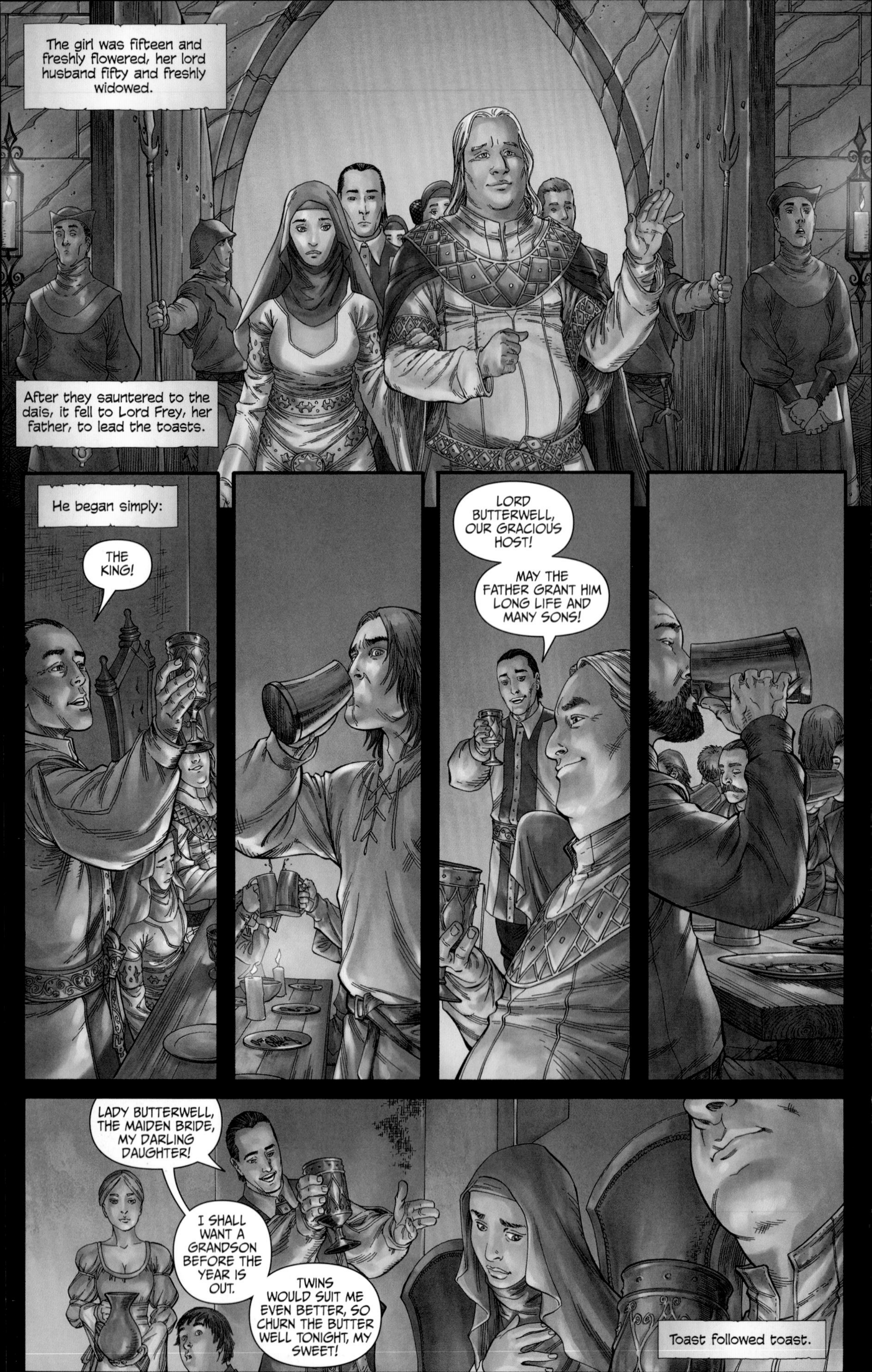

The girl was fifteen and freshly flowered, her lord husband fifty and freshly widowed.
After they sauntered to the dais, it fell to Lord Frey, her father, to lead the toasts.
He began simply:
THE KING!
LORD BUTTERWELL, OUR GRACIOUS HOST!
MAY THE FATHER GRANT HIM LONG LIFE AND MANY SONS!
LADY BUTTERWELL, THE MAIDEN BRIDE, MY DARLING DAUGHTER!
I SHALL WANT A GRANDSON BEFORE THE YEAR IS OUT.
TWINS WOULD SUIT ME EVEN BETTER, SO CHURN THE BUTTER WELL TONIGHT, MY SWEET!
Toast followed toast.

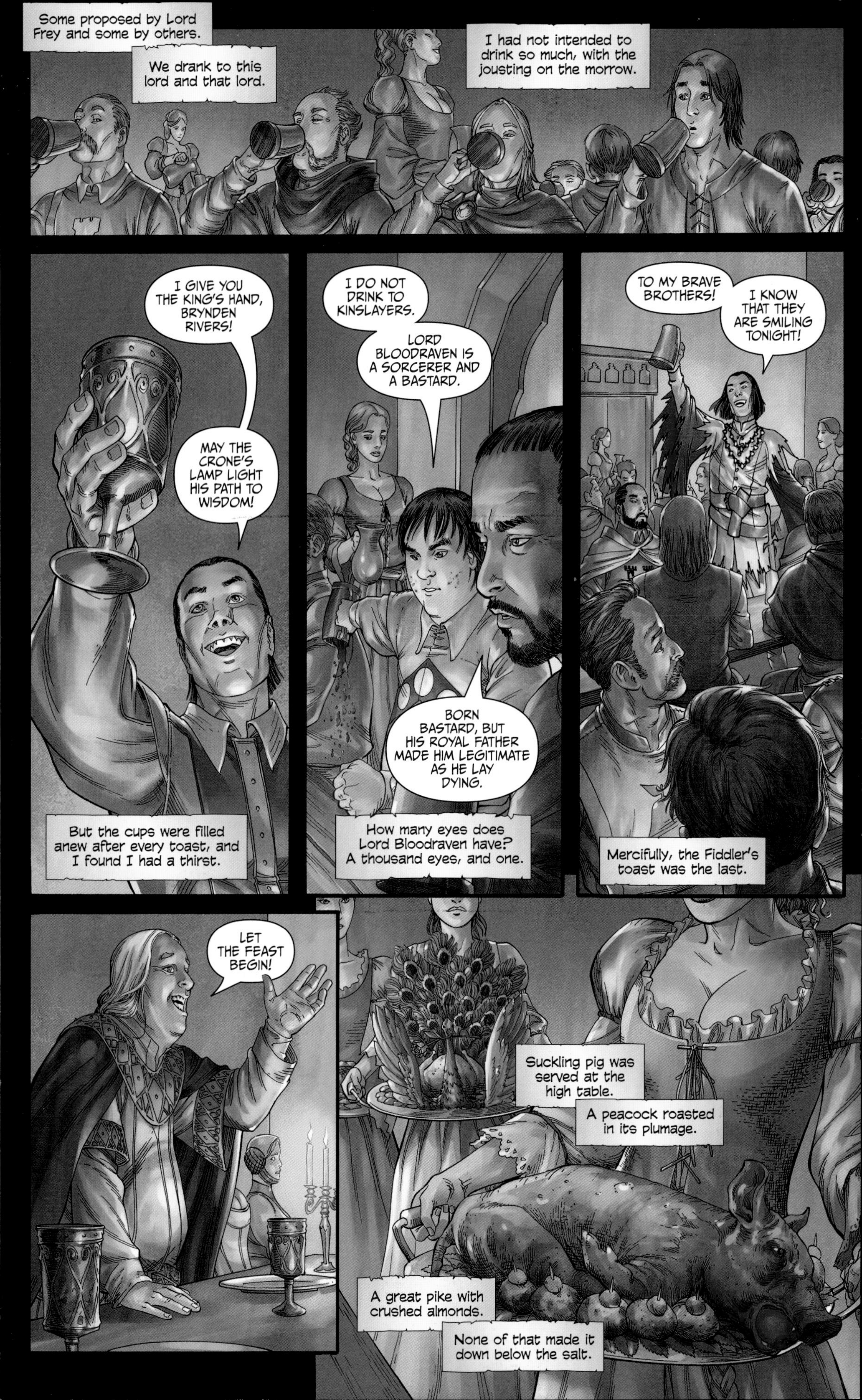
Some proposed by Lord Frey and some by others.
We drank to this lord and that lord.
I had not intended to drink so much, with the jousting on the morrow.
I GIVE YOU THE KING'S HAND, BRYNDEN RIVERS!
MAY THE CRONE'S LAMP LIGHT HIS PATH TO WISDOM!
But the cups were filled anew after every toast, and I found I had a thirst.
I DO NOT DRINK TO KINSLAYERS.
LORD BLOODRAVEN IS A SORCERER AND A BASTARD.
BORN BASTARD, BUT HIS ROYAL FATHER MADE HIM LEGITIMATE AS HE LAY DYING.
How many eyes does Lord Bloodraven have? A thousand eyes, and one.
TO MY BRAVE BROTHERS!
I KNOW THAT THEY ARE SMILING TONIGHT!
Mercifully, the Fiddler's toast was the last.
LET THE FEAST BEGIN!
Suckling pig was served at the high table.
A peacock roasted in its plumage.
A great pike with crushed almonds.
None of that made it down below the salt.

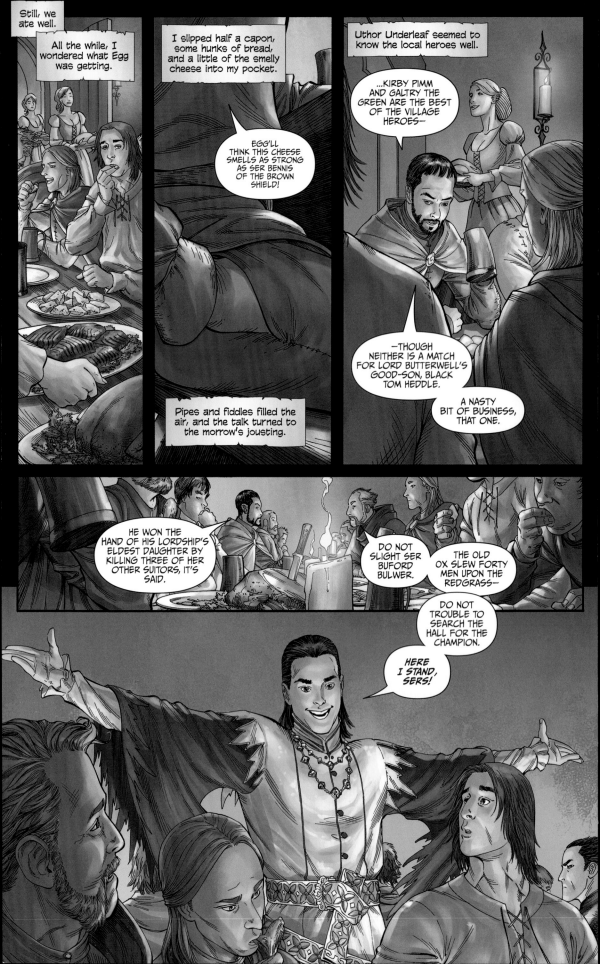

Still, we ate well.

All the while, I wondered what Egg was getting.

I slipped half a capon, some hunks of bread, and a little of the smelly cheese into my pocket.

EGG'LL THINK THIS CHEESE SMELLS AS STRONG AS SER BENNIS OF THE BROWN SHIELD!

Pipes and fiddles filled the air, and the talk turned to the morrow's jousting.

Uthor Underleaf seemed to know the local heroes well.

...KIRBY PIMM AND GALTRY THE GREEN ARE THE BEST OF THE VILLAGE HEROES—

—THOUGH NEITHER IS A MATCH FOR LORD BUTTERWELL'S GOOD-SON, BLACK TOM HEDDLE.

A NASTY BIT OF BUSINESS, THAT ONE.

HE WON THE HAND OF HIS LORDSHIP'S ELDEST DAUGHTER BY KILLING THREE OF HER OTHER SUITORS, IT'S SAID.

DO NOT SLIGHT SER BUFORD BULWER.

THE OLD OX SLEW FORTY MEN UPON THE REDGRASS—

DO NOT TROUBLE TO SEARCH THE HALL FOR THE CHAMPION.

HERE I STAND, SERS!

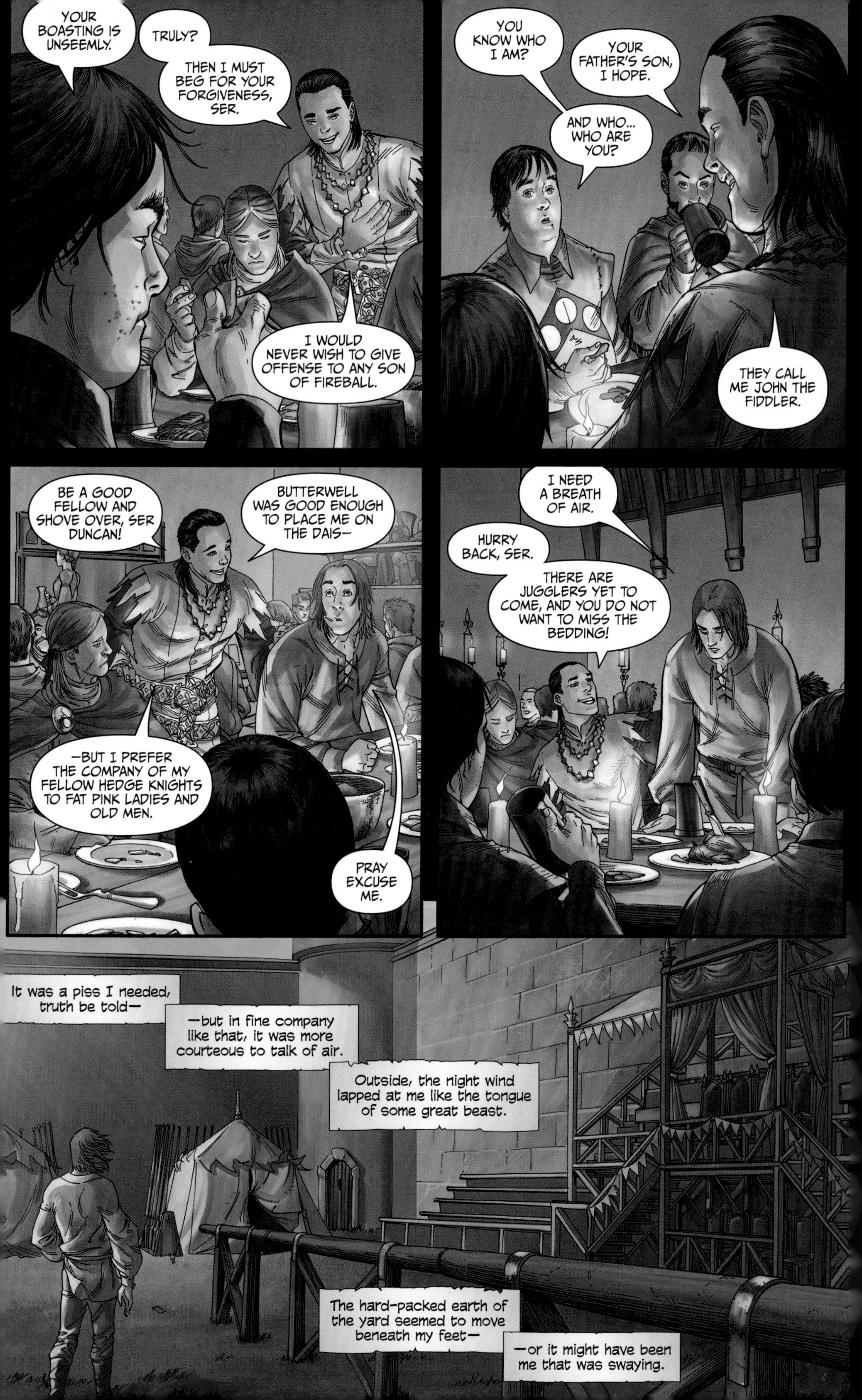
YOUR BOASTING IS UNSEEMLY.
TRULY?
THEN I MUST BEG FOR YOUR FORGIVENESS, SER.
I WOULD NEVER WISH TO GIVE OFFENSE TO ANY SON OF FIREBALL.
YOU KNOW WHO I AM?
YOUR FATHER'S SON, I HOPE.
AND WHO... WHO ARE YOU?
THEY CALL ME JOHN THE FIDDLER.
BE A GOOD FELLOW AND SHOVE OVER, SER DUNCAN!
BUTTERWELL WAS GOOD ENOUGH TO PLACE ME ON THE DAIS—
—BUT I PREFER THE COMPANY OF MY FELLOW HEDGE KNIGHTS TO FAT PINK LADIES AND OLD MEN.
PRAY EXCUSE ME.
I NEED A BREATH OF AIR.
HURRY BACK, SER.
THERE ARE JUGGLERS YET TO COME, AND YOU DO NOT WANT TO MISS THE BEDDING!
It was a piss I needed, truth be told—
—but in fine company like that, it was more courteous to talk of air.
Outside, the night wind lapped at me like the tongue of some great beast.
The hard-packed earth of the yard seemed to move beneath my feet—
—or it might have been me that was swaying.

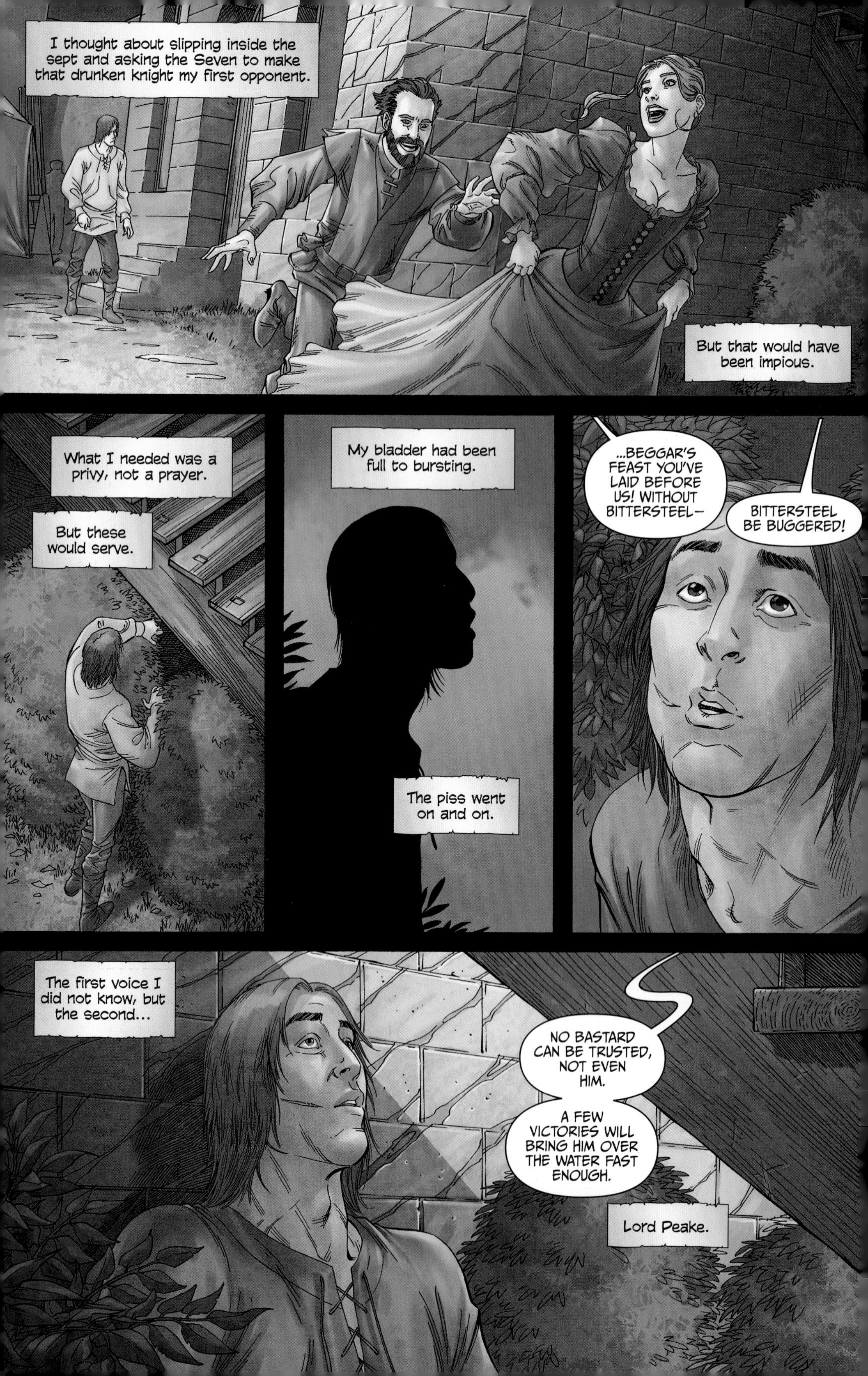
I thought about slipping inside the sept and asking the Seven to make that drunken knight my first opponent.
But that would have been impious.
What I needed was a privy, not a prayer.
But these would serve.
My bladder had been full to bursting.
The piss went on and on.
...BEGGAR'S FEAST YOU'VE LAID BEFORE US! WITHOUT BITTERSTEEL—
BITTERSTEEL BE BUGGERED!
The first voice I did not know, but the second...
NO BASTARD CAN BE TRUSTED, NOT EVEN HIM.
A FEW VICTORIES WILL BRING HIM OVER THE WATER FAST ENOUGH.
Lord Peake.

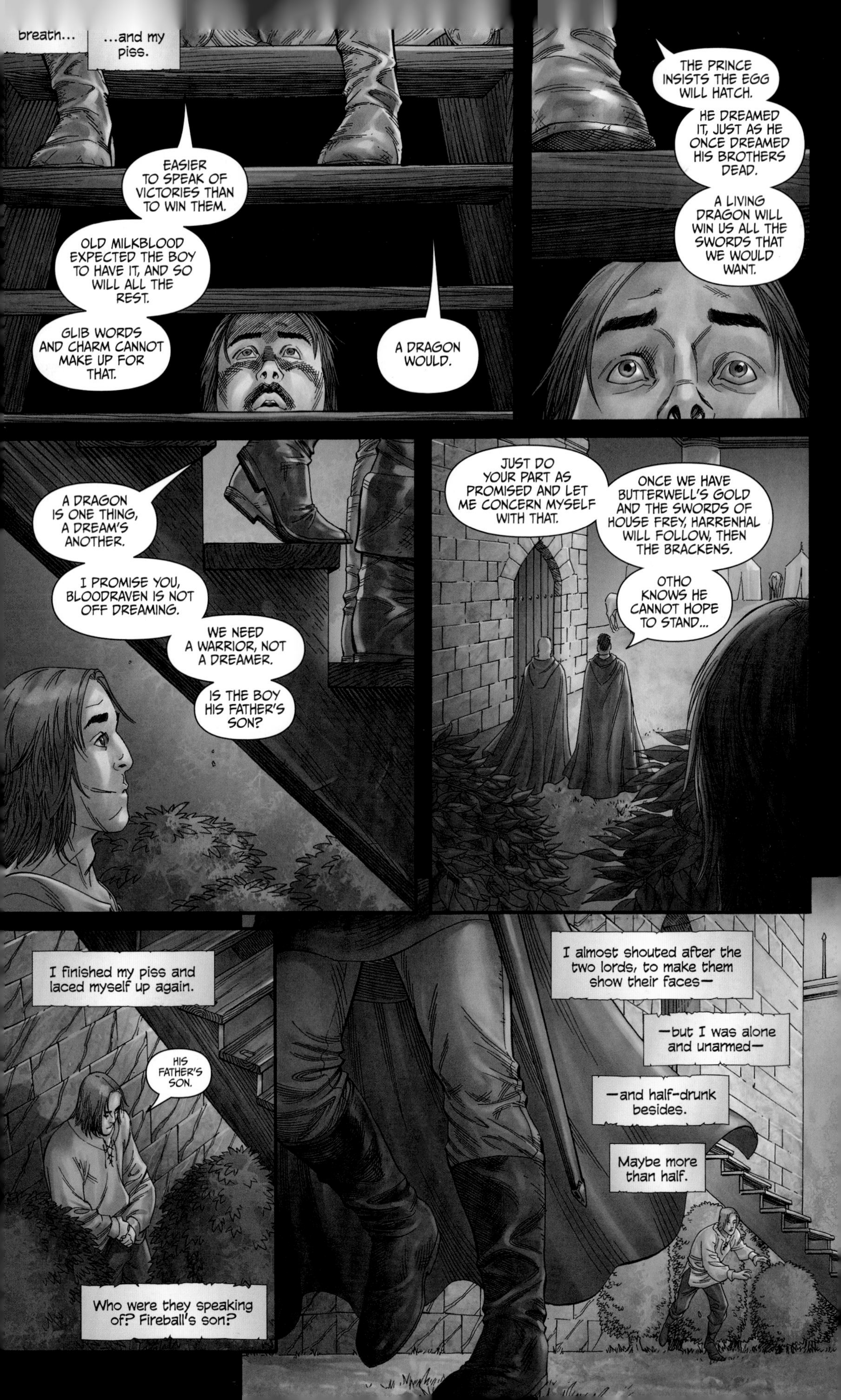
breath...
...and my piss.
EASIER TO SPEAK OF VICTORIES THAN TO WIN THEM.
OLD MILKBLOOD EXPECTED THE BOY TO HAVE IT, AND SO WILL ALL THE REST.
GLIB WORDS AND CHARM CANNOT MAKE UP FOR THAT.
A DRAGON WOULD.
THE PRINCE INSISTS THE EGG WILL HATCH.
HE DREAMED IT, JUST AS HE ONCE DREAMED HIS BROTHERS DEAD.
A LIVING DRAGON WILL WIN US ALL THE SWORDS THAT WE WOULD WANT.
A DRAGON IS ONE THING, A DREAM'S ANOTHER.
I PROMISE YOU, BLOODRAVEN IS NOT OFF DREAMING.
WE NEED A WARRIOR, NOT A DREAMER.
IS THE BOY HIS FATHER'S SON?
JUST DO YOUR PART AS PROMISED AND LET ME CONCERN MYSELF WITH THAT.
ONCE WE HAVE BUTTERWELL'S GOLD AND THE SWORDS OF HOUSE FREY, HARRENHAL WILL FOLLOW, THEN THE BRACKENS.
OTHO KNOWS HE CANNOT HOPE TO STAND...
I finished my piss and laced myself up again.
HIS FATHER'S SON.
Who were they speaking of? Fireball's son?
I almost shouted after the two lords, to make them show their faces—
—but I was alone and unarmed—
—and half-drunk besides.
Maybe more than half.

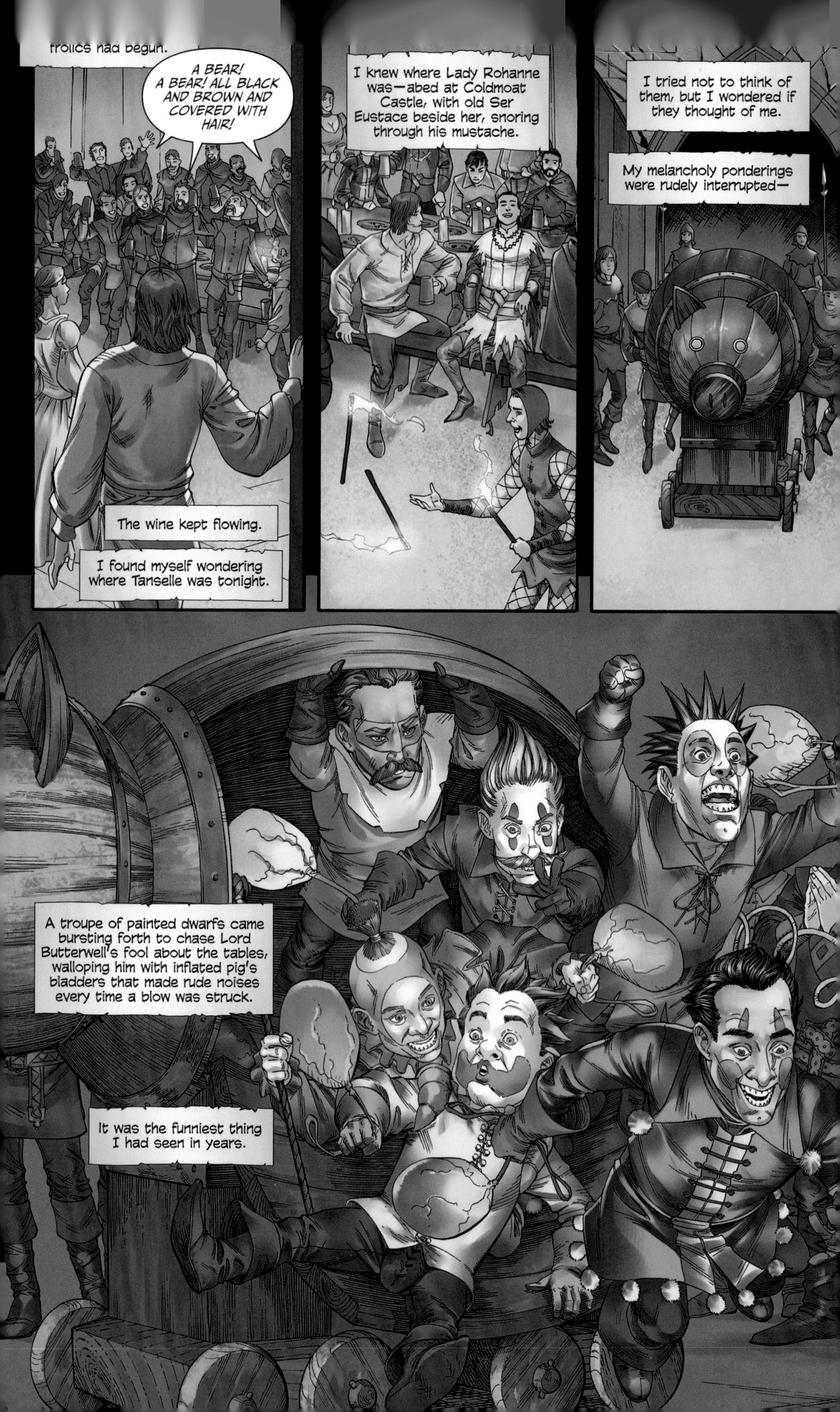

frolics had begun.
A BEAR! A BEAR! ALL BLACK AND BROWN AND COVERED WITH HAIR!
The wine kept flowing.
I found myself wondering where Tanselle was tonight.
I knew where Lady Rohanne was—abed at Coldmoat Castle, with old Ser Eustace beside her, snoring through his mustache.
I tried not to think of them, but I wondered if they thought of me.
My melancholy ponderings were rudely interrupted—
A troupe of painted dwarfs came bursting forth to chase Lord Butterwell's fool about the tables, walloping him with inflated pig's bladders that made rude noises every time a blow was struck.
It was the funniest thing I had seen in years.

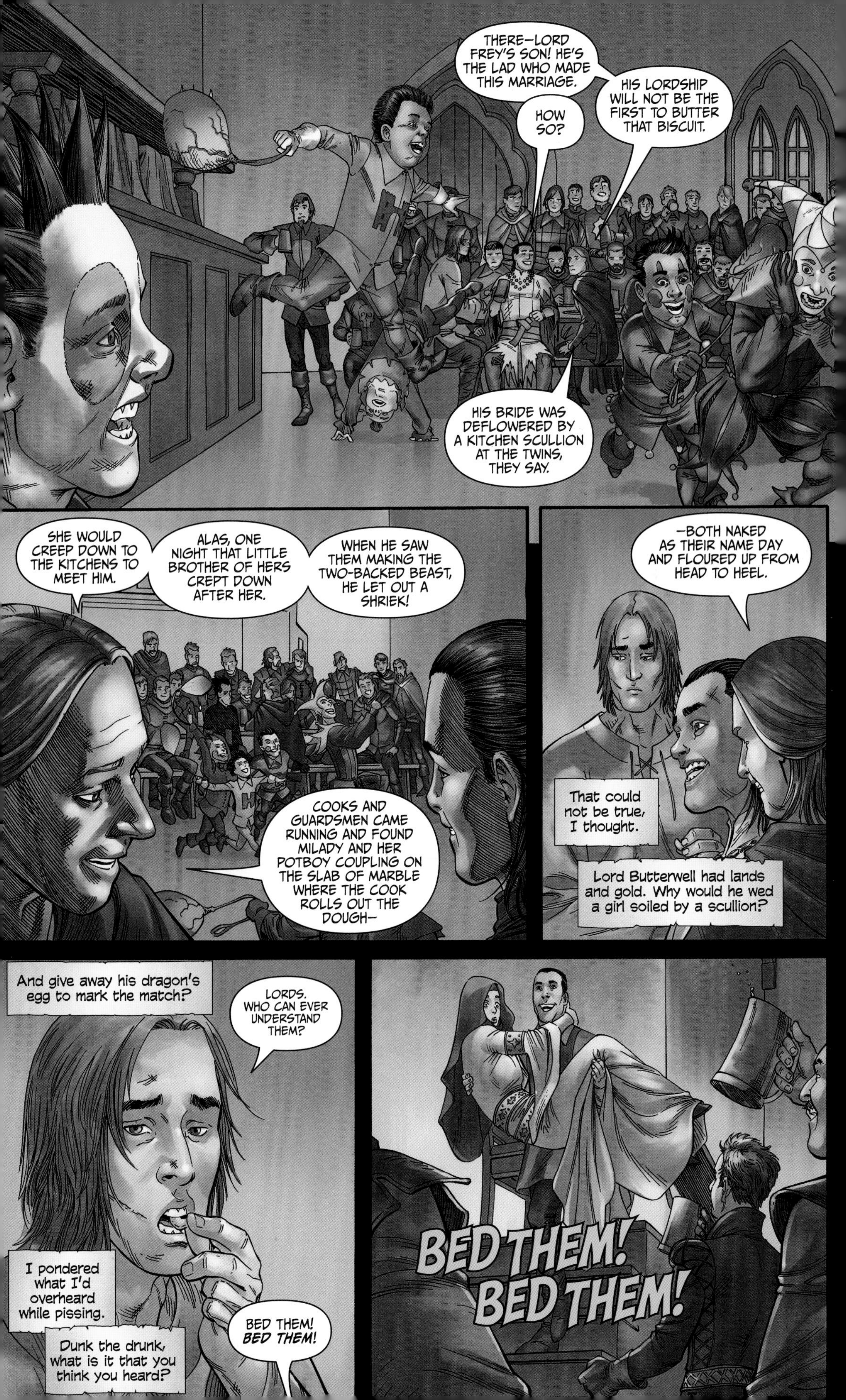
THERE—LORD FREY'S SON! HE'S THE LAD WHO MADE THIS MARRIAGE.
HOW SO?
HIS LORDSHIP WILL NOT BE THE FIRST TO BUTTER THAT BISCUIT.
HIS BRIDE WAS DEFLOWERED BY A KITCHEN SCULLION AT THE TWINS, THEY SAY.
SHE WOULD CREEP DOWN TO THE KITCHENS TO MEET HIM.
ALAS, ONE NIGHT THAT LITTLE BROTHER OF HERS CREPT DOWN AFTER HER.
WHEN HE SAW THEM MAKING THE TWO-BACKED BEAST, HE LET OUT A SHRIEK!
COOKS AND GUARDSMEN CAME RUNNING AND FOUND MILADY AND HER POTBOY COUPLING ON THE SLAB OF MARBLE WHERE THE COOK ROLLS OUT THE DOUGH—
—BOTH NAKED AS THEIR NAME DAY AND FLOURED UP FROM HEAD TO HEEL.
That could not be true, I thought.
Lord Butterwell had lands and gold. Why would he wed a girl soiled by a scullion?
And give away his dragon's egg to mark the match?
LORDS. WHO CAN EVER UNDERSTAND THEM?
I pondered what I'd overheard while pissing.
Dunk the drunk, what is it that you think you heard?
BED THEM! *BED THEM!*
BED THEM! BED THEM!

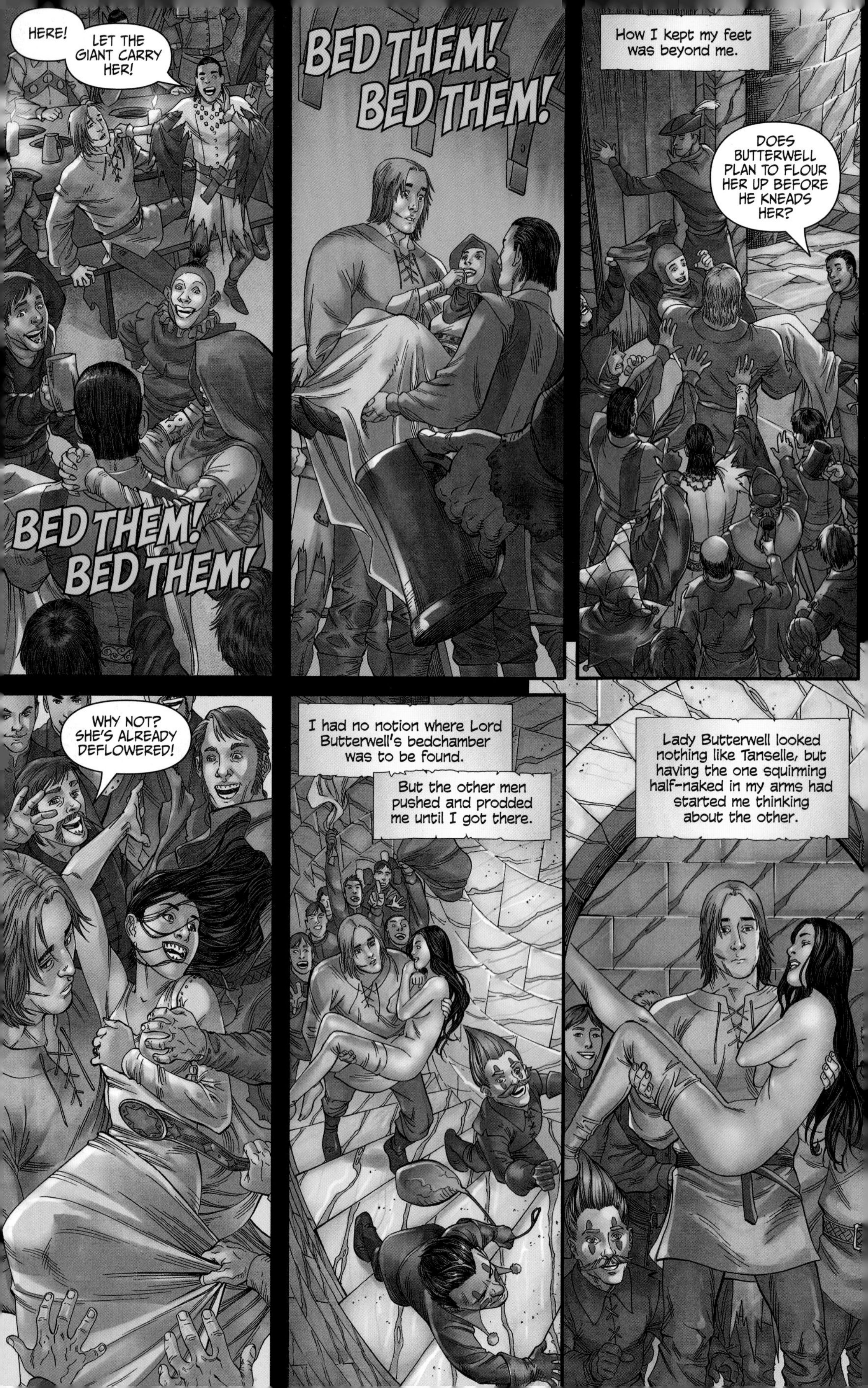
HERE!
LET THE GIANT CARRY HER!
BED THEM! BED THEM!
BED THEM! BED THEM!
How I kept my feet was beyond me.
DOES BUTTERWELL PLAN TO FLOUR HER UP BEFORE HE KNEADS HER?
WHY NOT? SHE'S ALREADY DEFLOWERED!
I had no notion where Lord Butterwell's bedchamber was to be found.
But the other men pushed and prodded me until I got there.
Lady Butterwell looked nothing like Tanselle, but having the one squirming half-naked in my arms had started me thinking about the other.

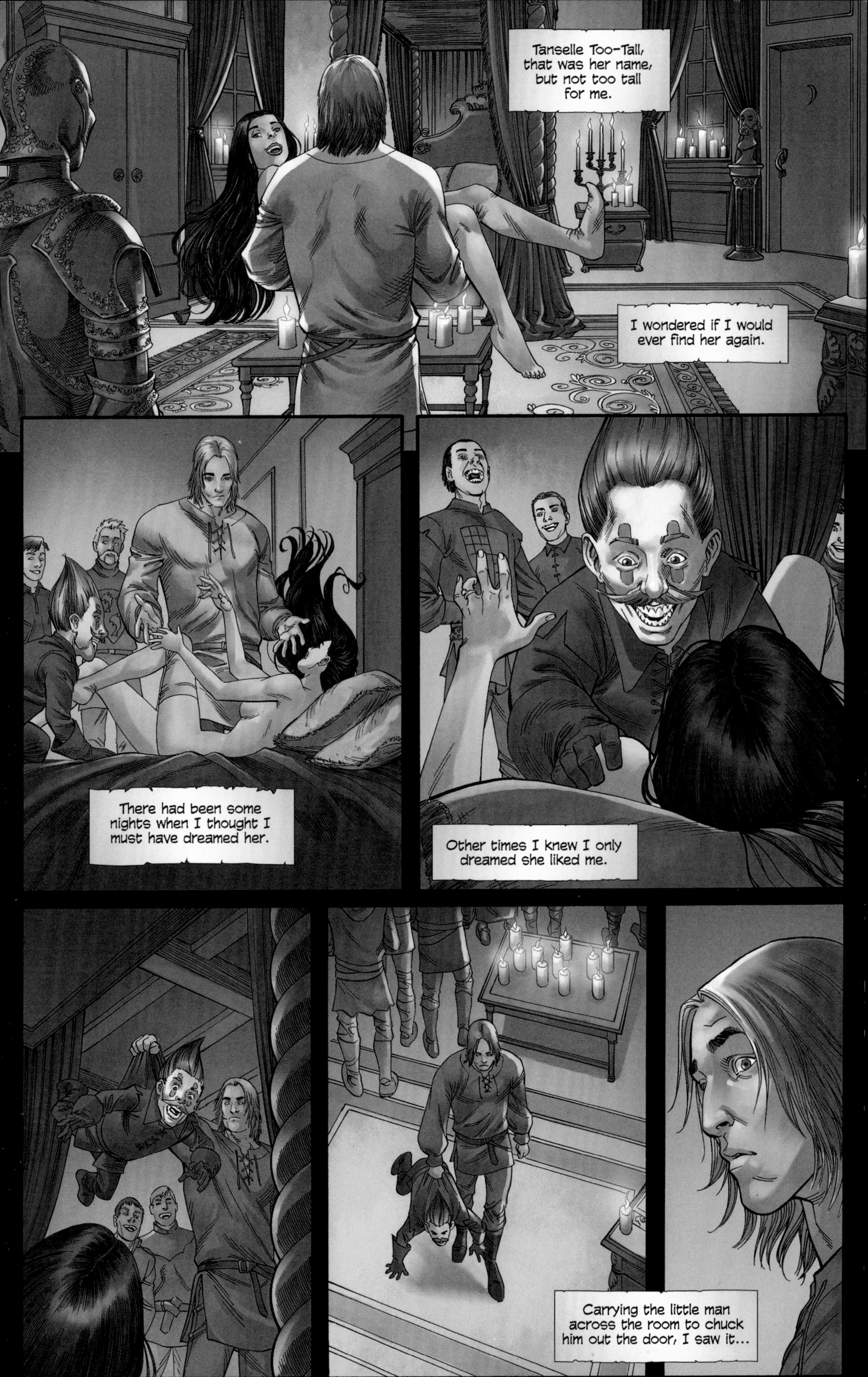
Tanselle Too-Tall, that was her name, but not too tall for me.
I wondered if I would ever find her again.
There had been some nights when I thought I must have dreamed her.
Other times I knew I only dreamed she liked me.
Carrying the little man across the room to chuck him out the door, I saw it...

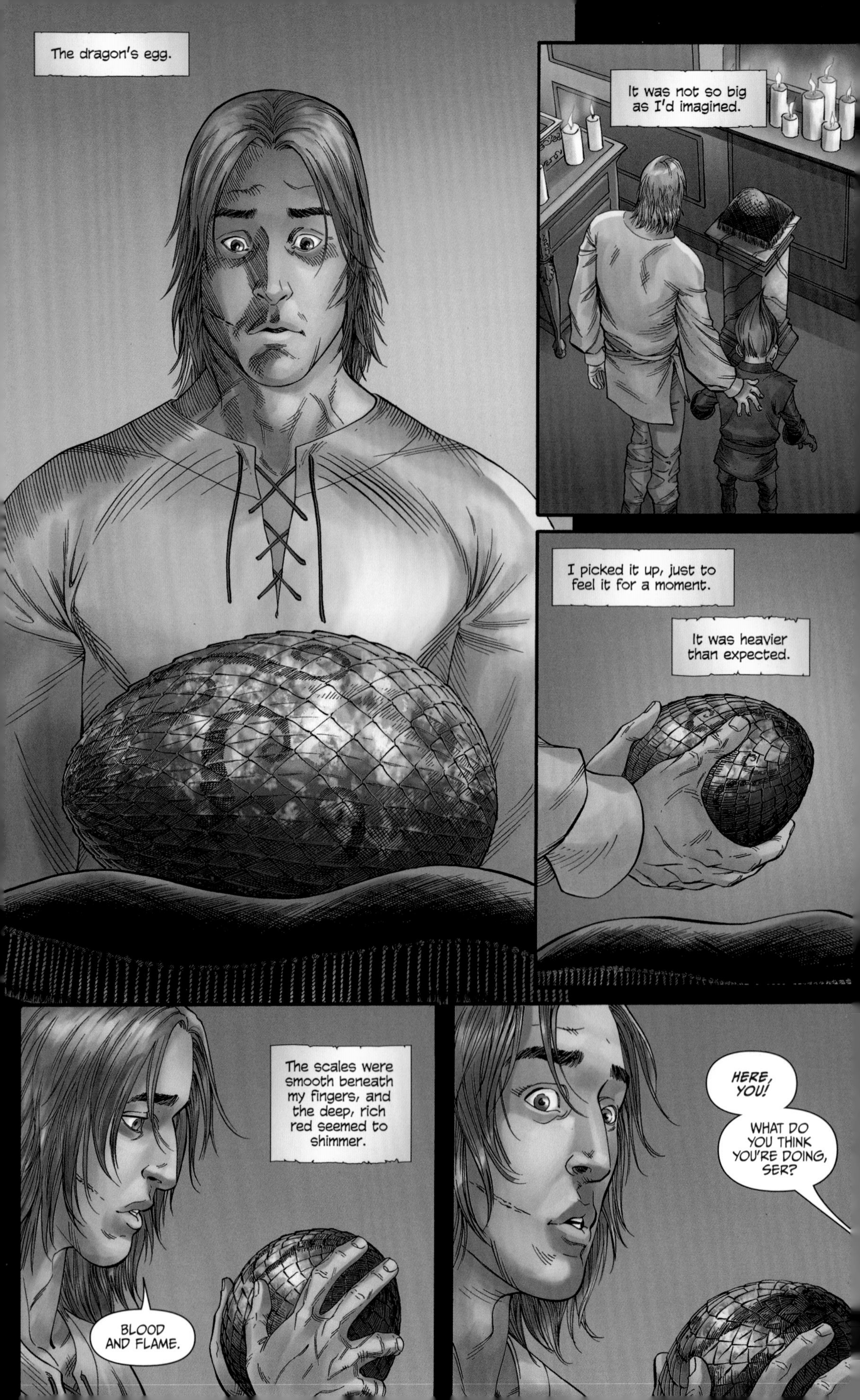
The dragon's egg.
It was not so big as I'd imagined.
I picked it up, just to feel it for a moment.
It was heavier than expected.
The scales were smooth beneath my fingers, and the deep, rich red seemed to shimmer.
BLOOD AND FLAME.
HERE, YOU!
WHAT DO YOU THINK YOU'RE DOING, SER?

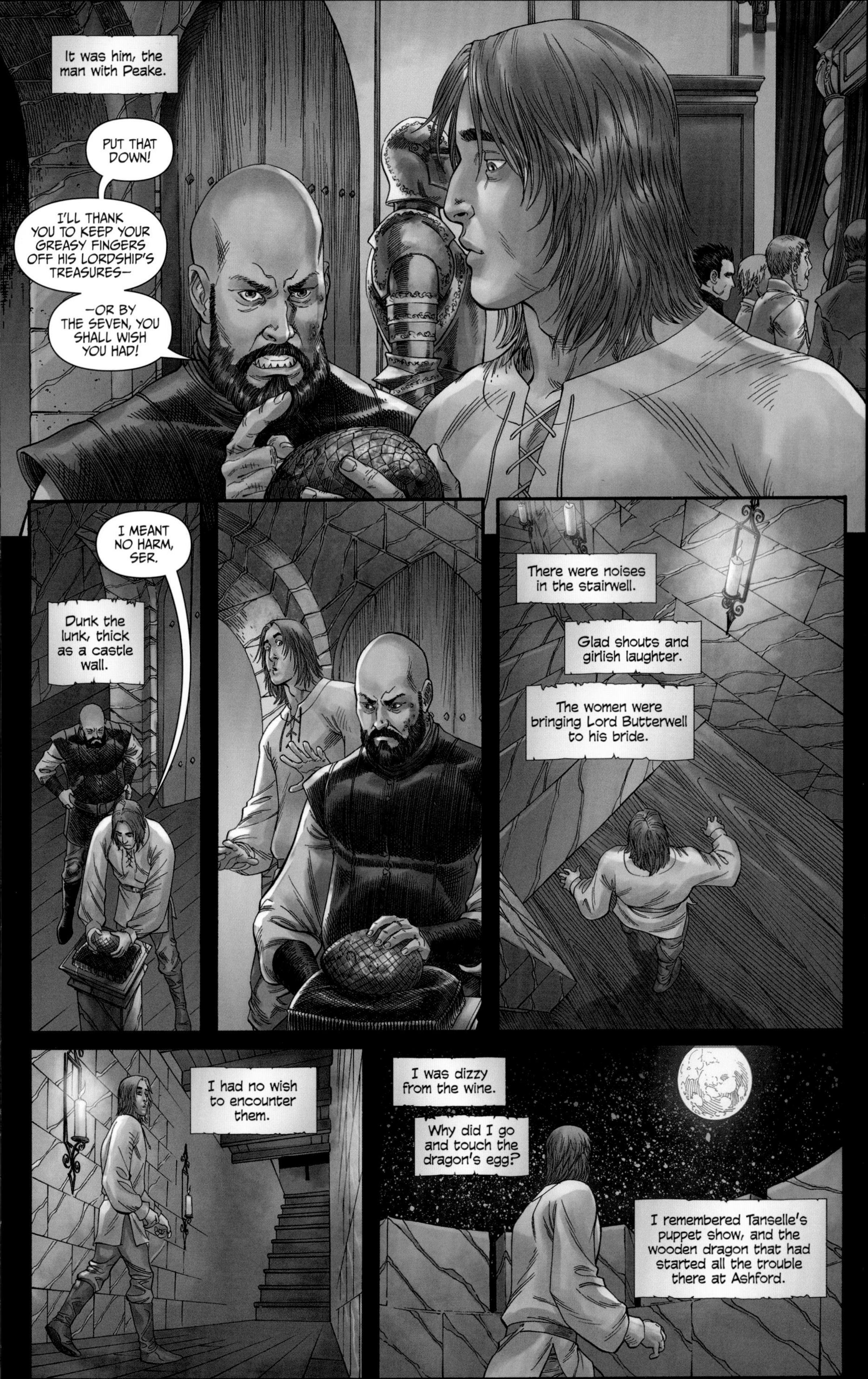
It was him, the man with Peake.
PUT THAT DOWN!
I'LL THANK YOU TO KEEP YOUR GREASY FINGERS OFF HIS LORDSHIP'S TREASURES—
—OR BY THE SEVEN, YOU SHALL WISH YOU HAD!
I MEANT NO HARM, SER.
Dunk the lunk, thick as a castle wall.
There were noises in the stairwell.
Glad shouts and girlish laughter.
The women were bringing Lord Butterwell to his bride.
I had no wish to encounter them.
I was dizzy from the wine.
Why did I go and touch the dragon's egg?
I remembered Tanselle's puppet show, and the wooden dragon that had started all the trouble there at Ashford.

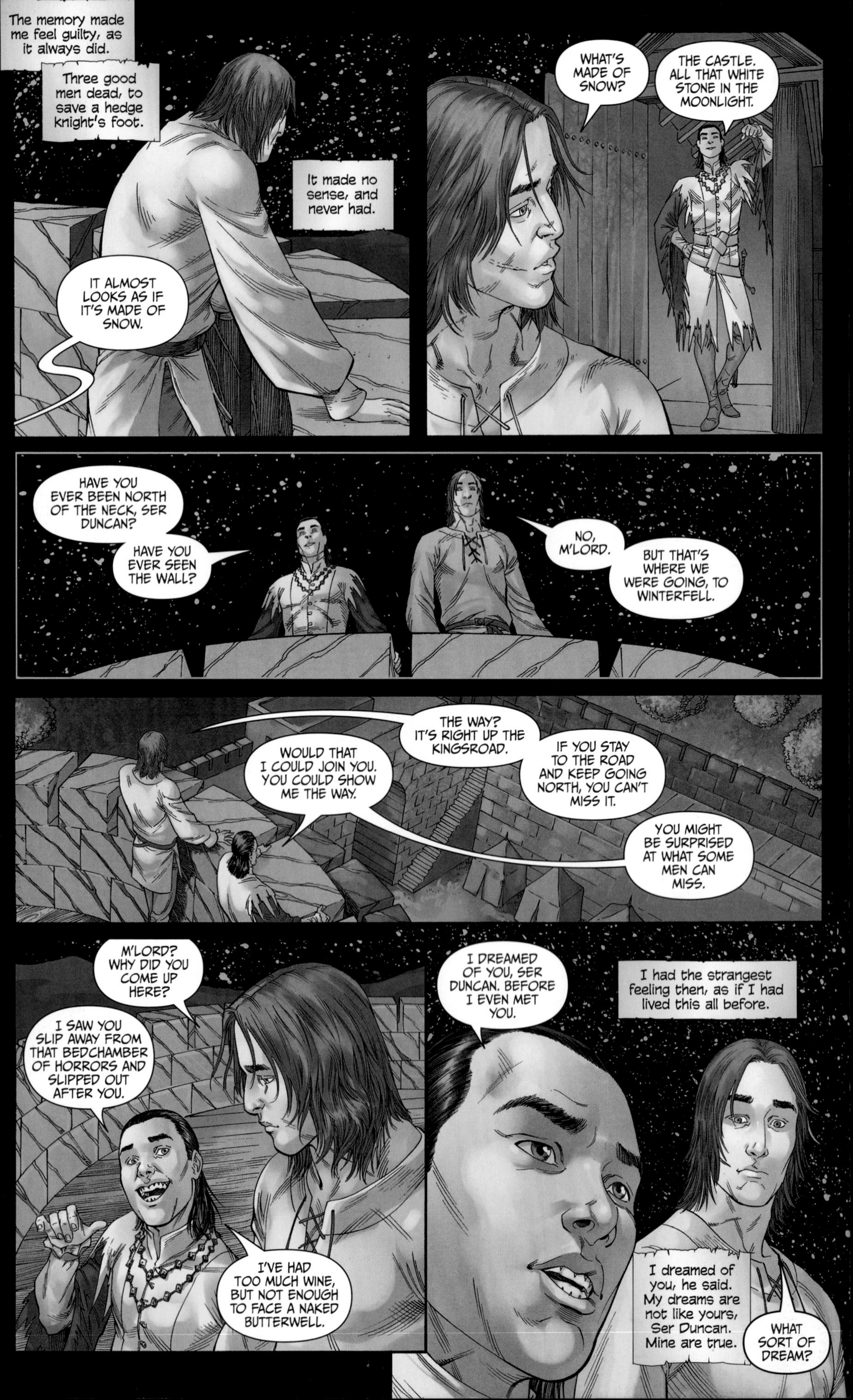
The memory made me feel guilty, as it always did.
Three good men dead, to save a hedge knight's foot.
It made no sense, and never had.
IT ALMOST LOOKS AS IF IT'S MADE OF SNOW.
WHAT'S MADE OF SNOW?
THE CASTLE. ALL THAT WHITE STONE IN THE MOONLIGHT.
HAVE YOU EVER BEEN NORTH OF THE NECK, SER DUNCAN?
HAVE YOU EVER SEEN THE WALL?
NO, M'LORD.
BUT THAT'S WHERE WE WERE GOING, TO WINTERFELL.
WOULD THAT I COULD JOIN YOU. YOU COULD SHOW ME THE WAY.
THE WAY? IT'S RIGHT UP THE KINGSROAD.
IF YOU STAY TO THE ROAD AND KEEP GOING NORTH, YOU CAN'T MISS IT.
YOU MIGHT BE SURPRISED AT WHAT SOME MEN CAN MISS.
M'LORD? WHY DID YOU COME UP HERE?
I SAW YOU SLIP AWAY FROM THAT BEDCHAMBER OF HORRORS AND SLIPPED OUT AFTER YOU.
I'VE HAD TOO MUCH WINE, BUT NOT ENOUGH TO FACE A NAKED BUTTERWELL.
I DREAMED OF YOU, SER DUNCAN. BEFORE I EVEN MET YOU.
I had the strangest feeling then, as if I had lived this all before.
I dreamed of you, he said. My dreams are not like yours, Ser Duncan. Mine are true.
WHAT SORT OF DREAM?

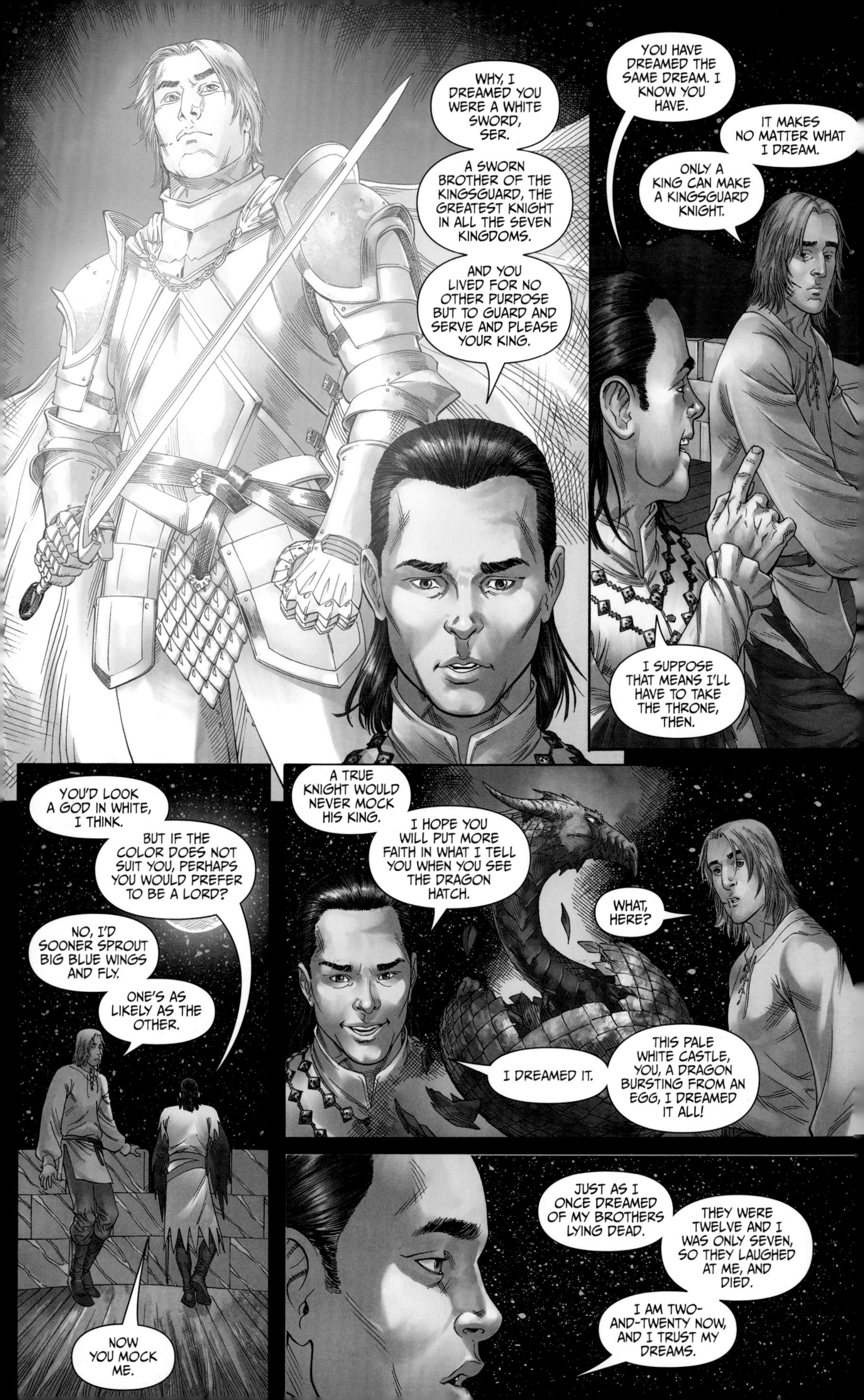
WHY, I DREAMED YOU WERE A WHITE SWORD, SER.
A SWORN BROTHER OF THE KINGSGUARD, THE GREATEST KNIGHT IN ALL THE SEVEN KINGDOMS.
AND YOU LIVED FOR NO OTHER PURPOSE BUT TO GUARD AND SERVE AND PLEASE YOUR KING.
YOU HAVE DREAMED THE SAME DREAM. I KNOW YOU HAVE.
IT MAKES NO MATTER WHAT I DREAM.
ONLY A KING CAN MAKE A KINGSGUARD KNIGHT.
I SUPPOSE THAT MEANS I'LL HAVE TO TAKE THE THRONE, THEN.
YOU'D LOOK A GOD IN WHITE, I THINK.
BUT IF THE COLOR DOES NOT SUIT YOU, PERHAPS YOU WOULD PREFER TO BE A LORD?
NO, I'D SOONER SPROUT BIG BLUE WINGS AND FLY.
ONE'S AS LIKELY AS THE OTHER.
NOW YOU MOCK ME.
A TRUE KNIGHT WOULD NEVER MOCK HIS KING.
I HOPE YOU WILL PUT MORE FAITH IN WHAT I TELL YOU WHEN YOU SEE THE DRAGON HATCH.
WHAT, HERE?
I DREAMED IT.
THIS PALE WHITE CASTLE, YOU, A DRAGON BURSTING FROM AN EGG, I DREAMED IT ALL!
JUST AS I ONCE DREAMED OF MY BROTHERS LYING DEAD.
THEY WERE TWELVE AND I WAS ONLY SEVEN, SO THEY LAUGHED AT ME, AND DIED.
I AM TWO-AND-TWENTY NOW, AND I TRUST MY DREAMS.

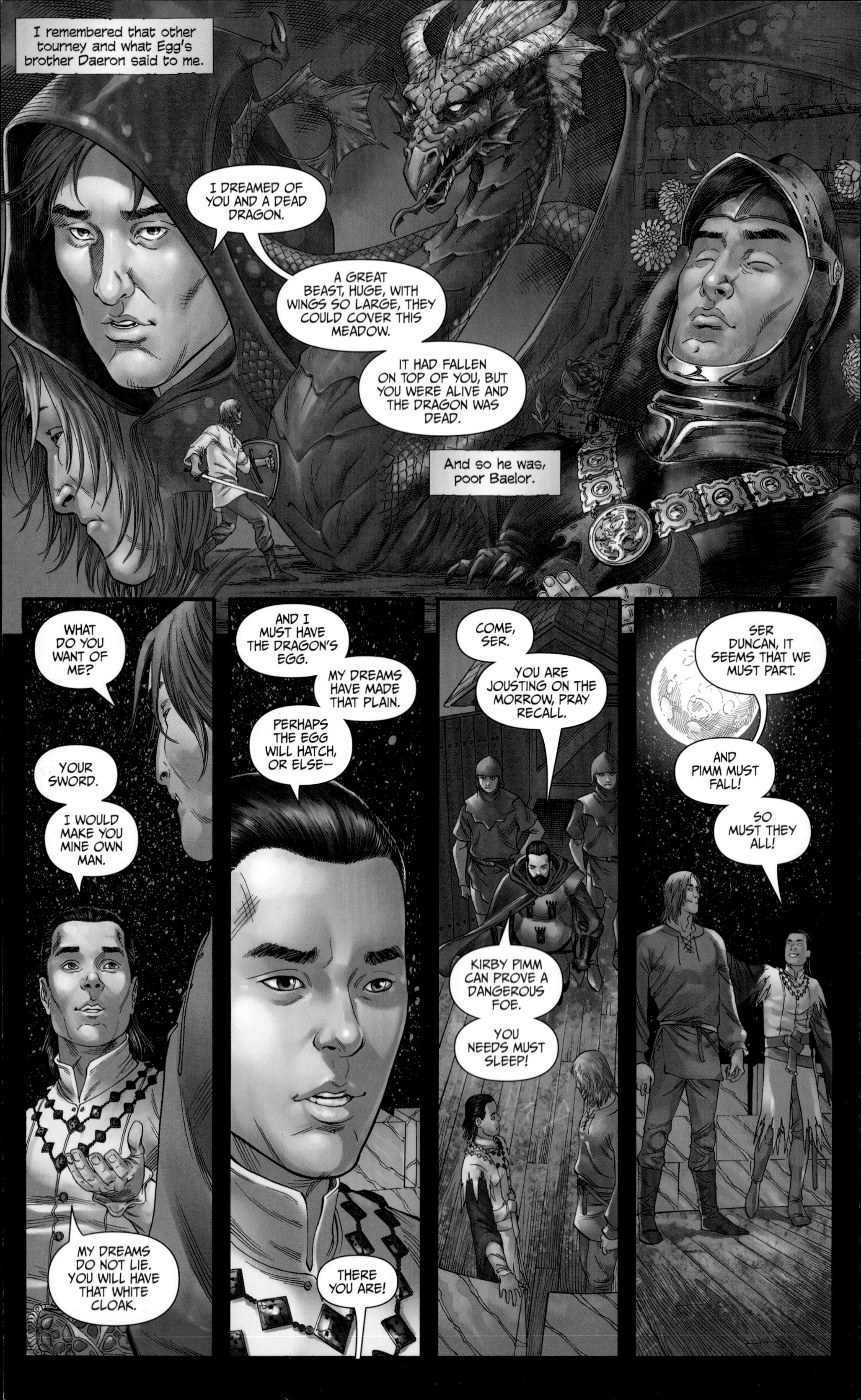
I remembered that other tourney and what Egg's brother Daeron said to me.
I DREAMED OF YOU AND A DEAD DRAGON.
A GREAT BEAST, HUGE, WITH WINGS SO LARGE, THEY COULD COVER THIS MEADOW.
IT HAD FALLEN ON TOP OF YOU, BUT YOU WERE ALIVE AND THE DRAGON WAS DEAD.
And so he was, poor Baelor.
WHAT DO YOU WANT OF ME?
YOUR SWORD.
I WOULD MAKE YOU MINE OWN MAN.
MY DREAMS DO NOT LIE. YOU WILL HAVE THAT WHITE CLOAK.
AND I MUST HAVE THE DRAGON'S EGG.
MY DREAMS HAVE MADE THAT PLAIN.
PERHAPS THE EGG WILL HATCH, OR ELSE–
THERE YOU ARE!
COME, SER.
YOU ARE JOUSTING ON THE MORROW, PRAY RECALL.
KIRBY PIMM CAN PROVE A DANGEROUS FOE.
YOU NEEDS MUST SLEEP!
SER DUNCAN, IT SEEMS THAT WE MUST PART.
AND PIMM MUST FALL!
SO MUST THEY ALL!

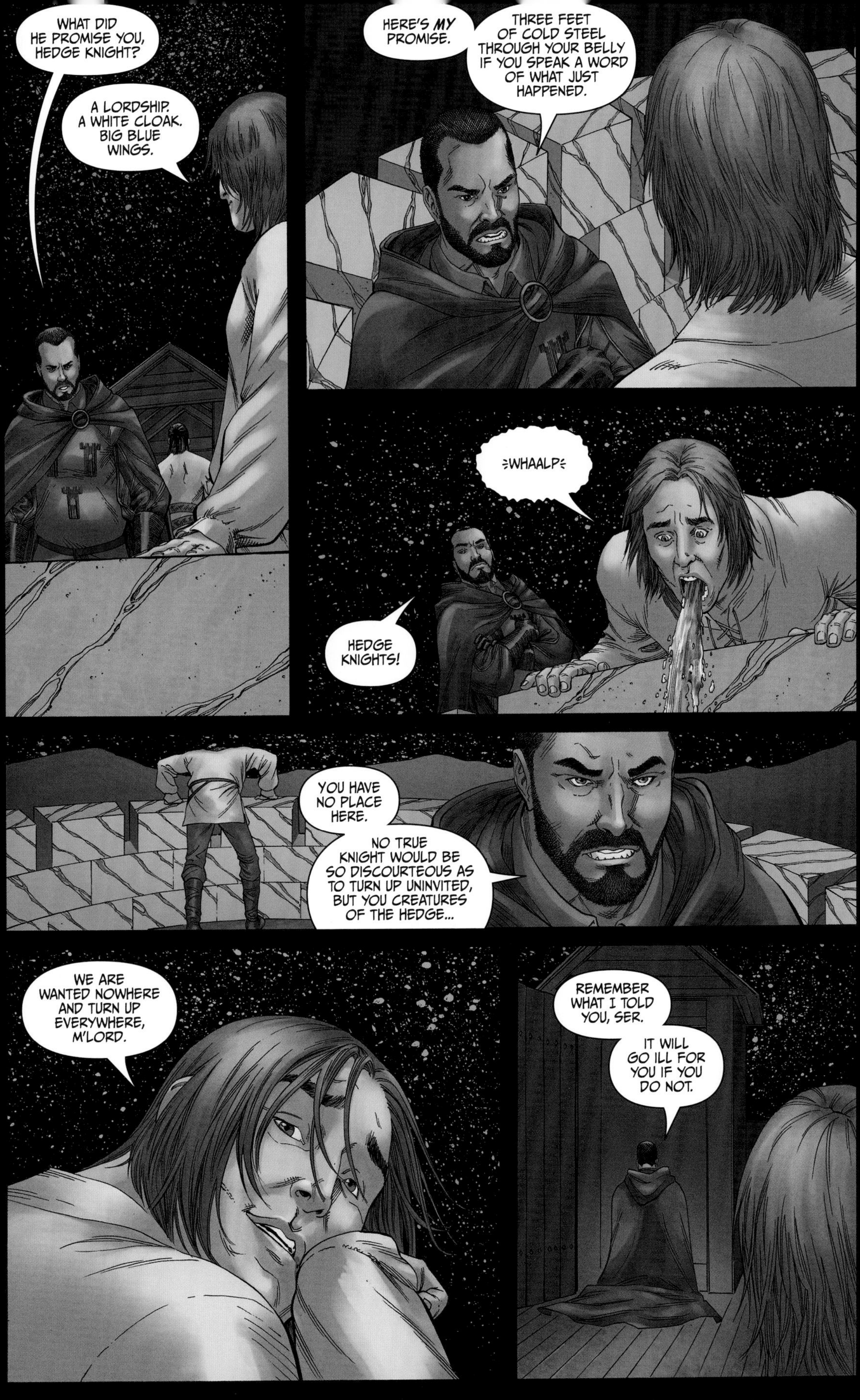
WHAT DID HE PROMISE YOU, HEDGE KNIGHT?
A LORDSHIP. A WHITE CLOAK. BIG BLUE WINGS.
HERE'S MY PROMISE.
THREE FEET OF COLD STEEL THROUGH YOUR BELLY IF YOU SPEAK A WORD OF WHAT JUST HAPPENED.
WHAALP
HEDGE KNIGHTS!
YOU HAVE NO PLACE HERE.
NO TRUE KNIGHT WOULD BE SO DISCOURTEOUS AS TO TURN UP UNINVITED, BUT YOU CREATURES OF THE HEDGE...
WE ARE WANTED NOWHERE AND TURN UP EVERYWHERE, M'LORD.
REMEMBER WHAT I TOLD YOU, SER.
IT WILL GO ILL FOR YOU IF YOU DO NOT.

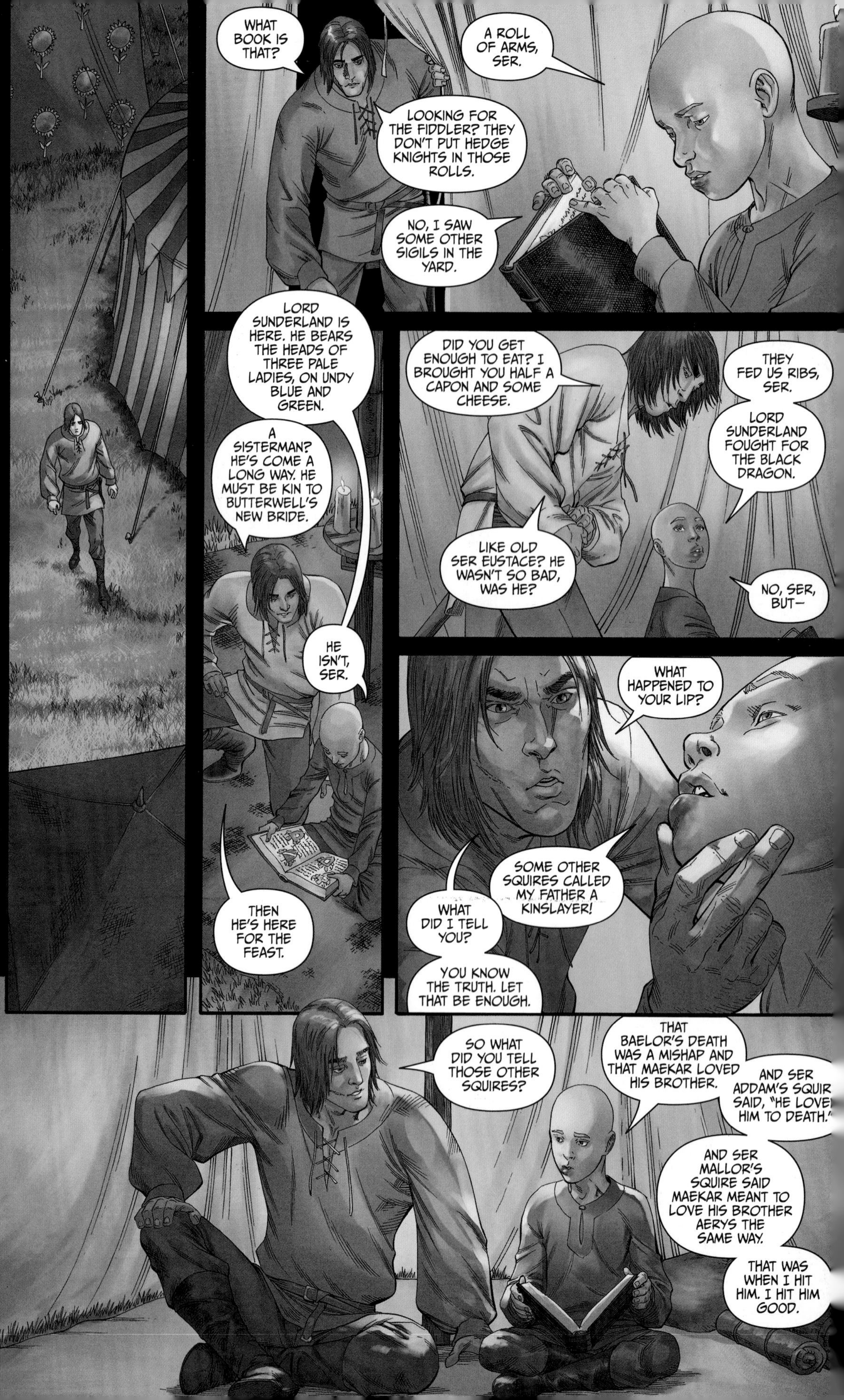

WHAT BOOK IS THAT?
A ROLL OF ARMS, SER.
LOOKING FOR THE FIDDLER? THEY DON'T PUT HEDGE KNIGHTS IN THOSE ROLLS.
NO, I SAW SOME OTHER SIGILS IN THE YARD.
LORD SUNDERLAND IS HERE. HE BEARS THE HEADS OF THREE PALE LADIES, ON UNDY BLUE AND GREEN.
A SISTERMAN? HE'S COME A LONG WAY. HE MUST BE KIN TO BUTTERWELL'S NEW BRIDE.
HE ISN'T, SER.
THEN HE'S HERE FOR THE FEAST.
DID YOU GET ENOUGH TO EAT? I BROUGHT YOU HALF A CAPON AND SOME CHEESE.
THEY FED US RIBS, SER.
LORD SUNDERLAND FOUGHT FOR THE BLACK DRAGON.
LIKE OLD SER EUSTACE? HE WASN'T SO BAD, WAS HE?
NO, SER, BUT—
WHAT HAPPENED TO YOUR LIP?
SOME OTHER SQUIRES CALLED MY FATHER A KINSLAYER!
WHAT DID I TELL YOU?
YOU KNOW THE TRUTH. LET THAT BE ENOUGH.
SO WHAT DID YOU TELL THOSE OTHER SQUIRES?
THAT BAELOR'S DEATH WAS A MISHAP AND THAT MAEKAR LOVED HIS BROTHER.
AND SER ADDAM'S SQUIR SAID, "HE LOVE HIM TO DEATH."
AND SER MALLOR'S SQUIRE SAID MAEKAR MEANT TO LOVE HIS BROTHER AERYS THE SAME WAY.
THAT WAS WHEN I HIT HIM. I HIT HIM GOOD.

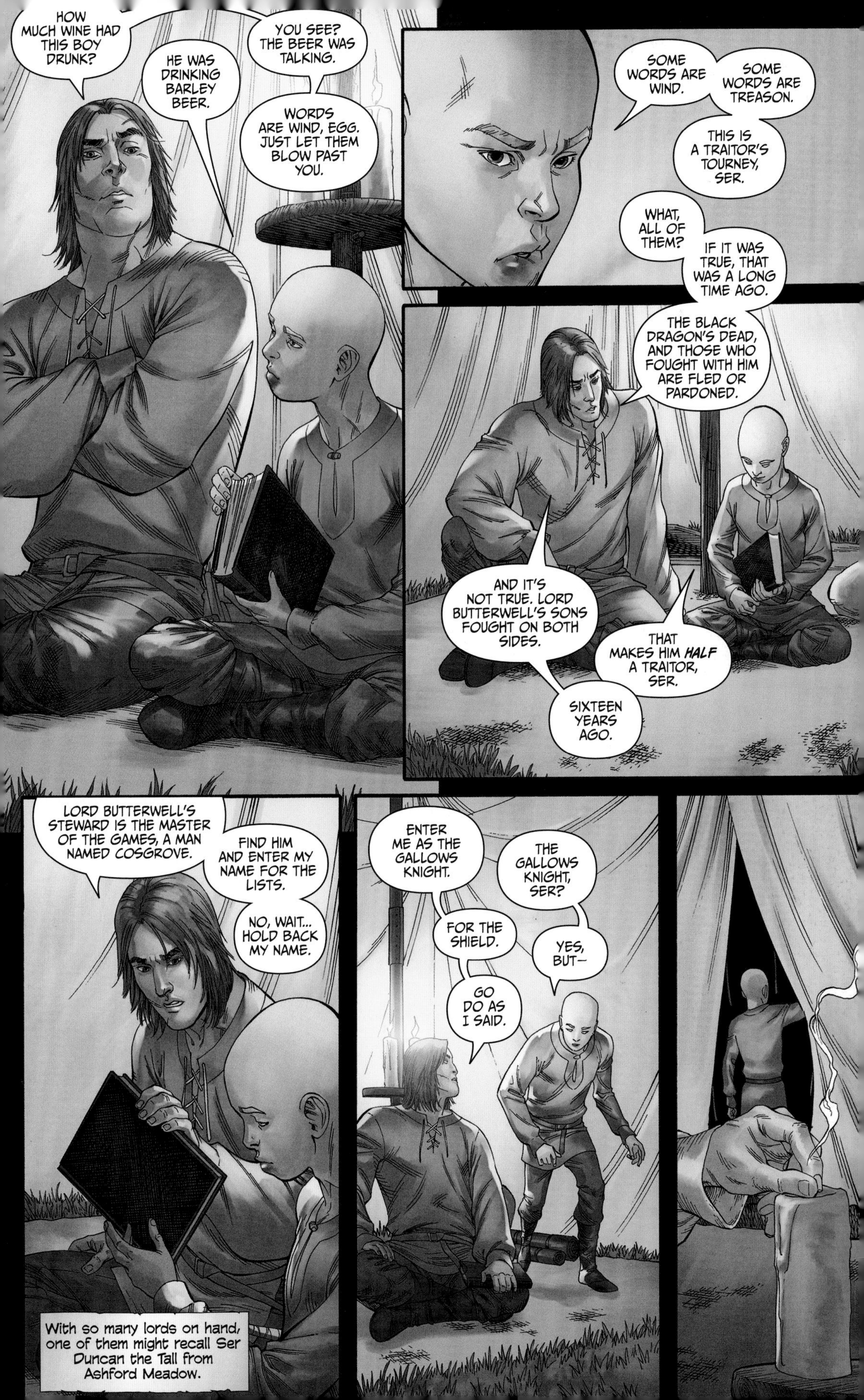
HOW MUCH WINE HAD THIS BOY DRUNK?
HE WAS DRINKING BARLEY BEER.
YOU SEE? THE BEER WAS TALKING.
WORDS ARE WIND, EGG. JUST LET THEM BLOW PAST YOU.
SOME WORDS ARE WIND.
SOME WORDS ARE TREASON.
THIS IS A TRAITOR'S TOURNEY, SER.
WHAT, ALL OF THEM?
IF IT WAS TRUE, THAT WAS A LONG TIME AGO.
THE BLACK DRAGON'S DEAD, AND THOSE WHO FOUGHT WITH HIM ARE FLED OR PARDONED.
AND IT'S NOT TRUE. LORD BUTTERWELL'S SONS FOUGHT ON BOTH SIDES.
THAT MAKES HIM HALF A TRAITOR, SER.
SIXTEEN YEARS AGO.
LORD BUTTERWELL'S STEWARD IS THE MASTER OF THE GAMES, A MAN NAMED COSGROVE.
FIND HIM AND ENTER MY NAME FOR THE LISTS.
NO, WAIT... HOLD BACK MY NAME.
With so many lords on hand, one of them might recall Ser Duncan the Tall from Ashford Meadow.
ENTER ME AS THE GALLOWS KNIGHT.
THE GALLOWS KNIGHT, SER?
FOR THE SHIELD.
YES, BUT—
GO DO AS I SAID.

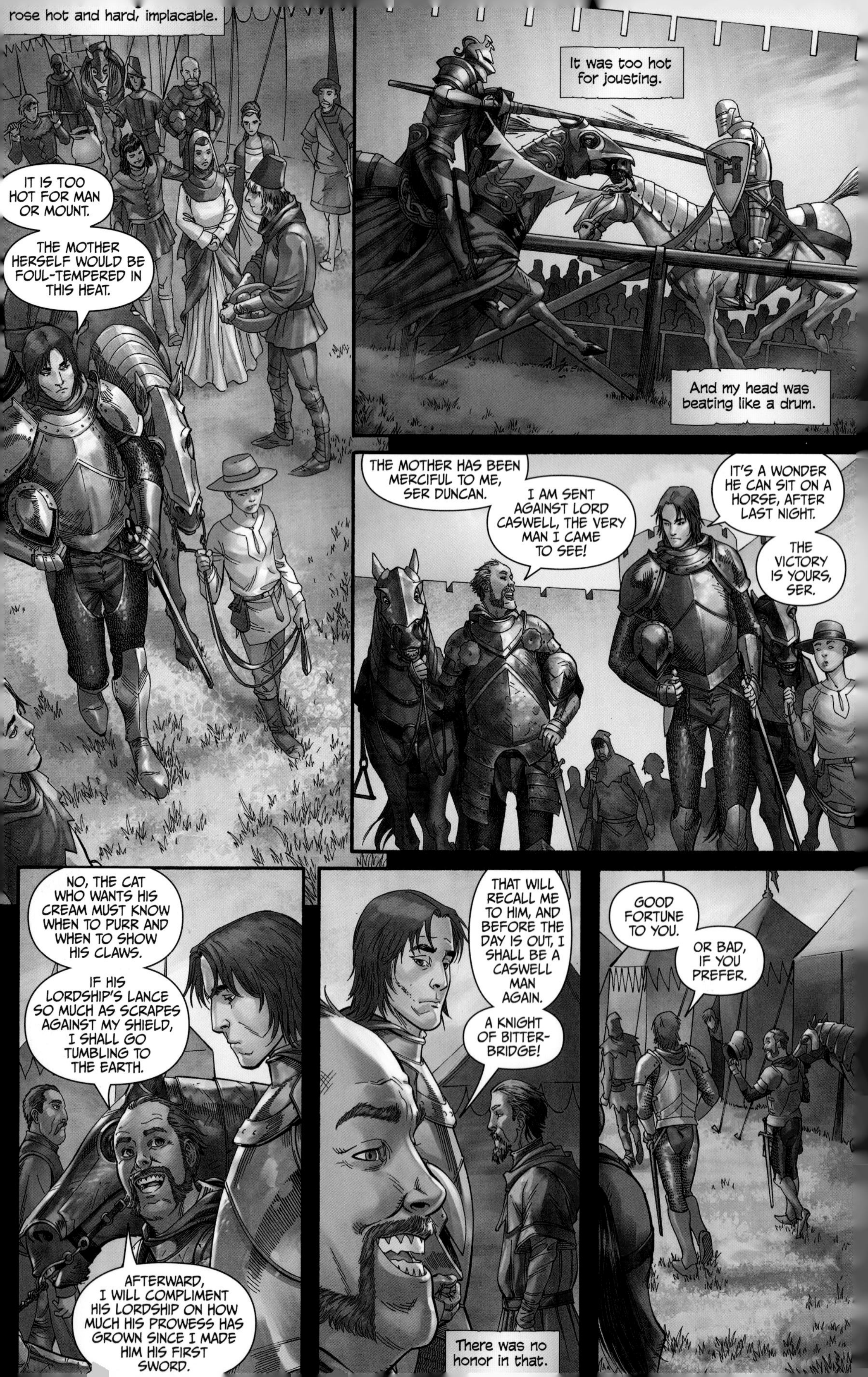

rose hot and hard, implacable.
IT IS TOO HOT FOR MAN OR MOUNT.
THE MOTHER HERSELF WOULD BE FOUL-TEMPERED IN THIS HEAT.
It was too hot for jousting.
And my head was beating like a drum.
THE MOTHER HAS BEEN MERCIFUL TO ME, SER DUNCAN.
I AM SENT AGAINST LORD CASWELL, THE VERY MAN I CAME TO SEE!
IT'S A WONDER HE CAN SIT ON A HORSE, AFTER LAST NIGHT.
THE VICTORY IS YOURS, SER.
NO, THE CAT WHO WANTS HIS CREAM MUST KNOW WHEN TO PURR AND WHEN TO SHOW HIS CLAWS.
IF HIS LORDSHIP'S LANCE SO MUCH AS SCRAPES AGAINST MY SHIELD, I SHALL GO TUMBLING TO THE EARTH.
AFTERWARD, I WILL COMPLIMENT HIS LORDSHIP ON HOW MUCH HIS PROWESS HAS GROWN SINCE I MADE HIM HIS FIRST SWORD.
THAT WILL RECALL ME TO HIM, AND BEFORE THE DAY IS OUT, I SHALL BE A CASWELL MAN AGAIN.
A KNIGHT OF BITTER-BRIDGE!
There was no honor in that.
GOOD FORTUNE TO YOU.
OR BAD, IF YOU PREFER.

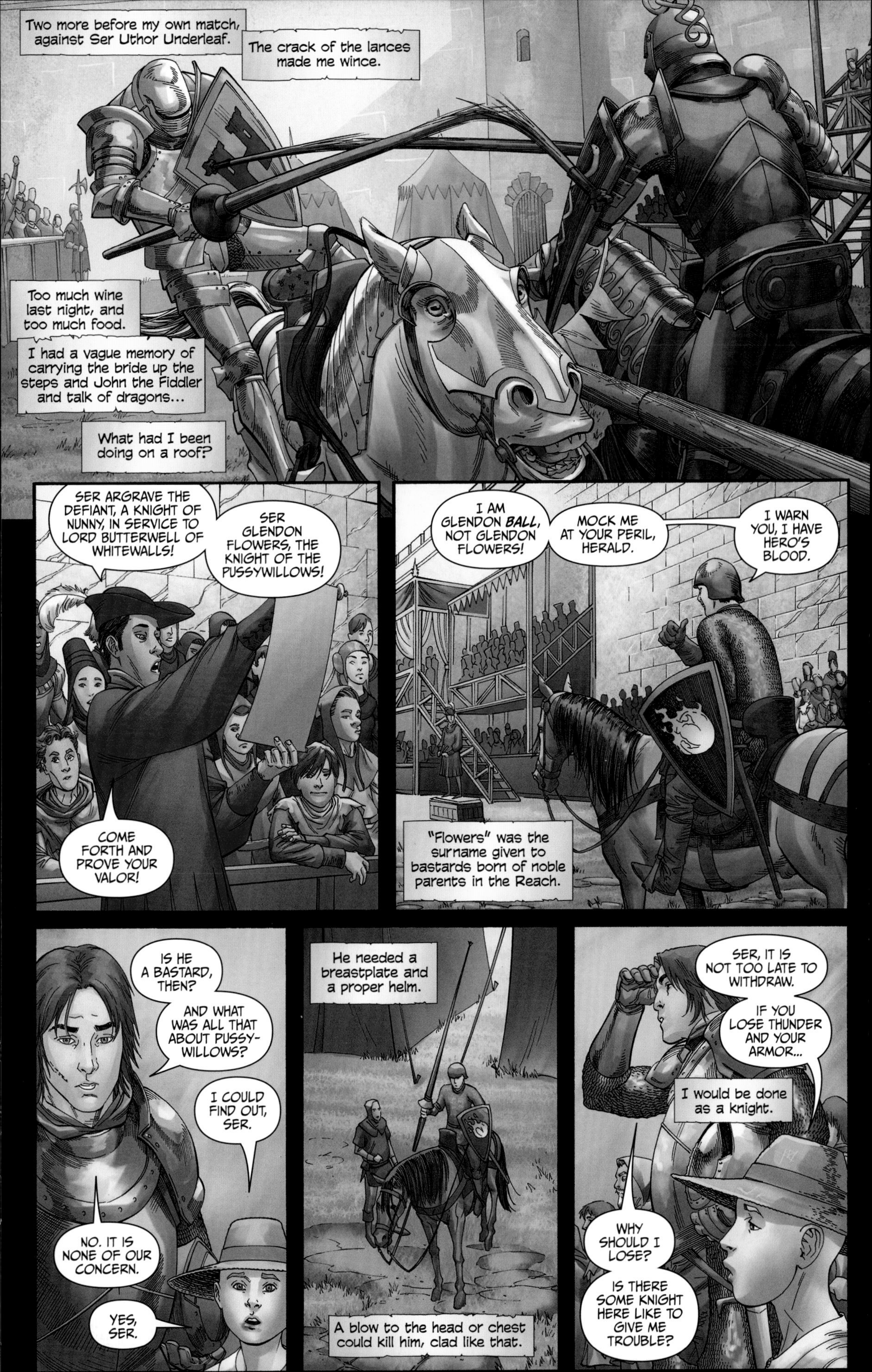

Two more before my own match, against Ser Uthor Underleaf.
The crack of the lances made me wince.
Too much wine last night, and too much food.
I had a vague memory of carrying the bride up the steps and John the Fiddler and talk of dragons...
What had I been doing on a roof?
SER ARGRAVE THE DEFIANT, A KNIGHT OF NUNNY, IN SERVICE TO LORD BUTTERWELL OF WHITEWALLS!
SER GLENDON FLOWERS, THE KNIGHT OF THE PUSSYWILLOWS!
COME FORTH AND PROVE YOUR VALOR!
I AM GLENDON **BALL**, NOT GLENDON FLOWERS!
MOCK ME AT YOUR PERIL, HERALD.
I WARN YOU, I HAVE HERO'S BLOOD.
"Flowers" was the surname given to bastards born of noble parents in the Reach.
IS HE A BASTARD, THEN?
AND WHAT WAS ALL THAT ABOUT PUSSY-WILLOWS?
I COULD FIND OUT, SER.
NO. IT IS NONE OF OUR CONCERN.
YES, SER.
He needed a breastplate and a proper helm.
A blow to the head or chest could kill him, clad like that.
SER, IT IS NOT TOO LATE TO WITHDRAW.
IF YOU LOSE THUNDER AND YOUR ARMOR...
I would be done as a knight.
WHY SHOULD I LOSE?
IS THERE SOME KNIGHT HERE LIKE TO GIVE ME TROUBLE?

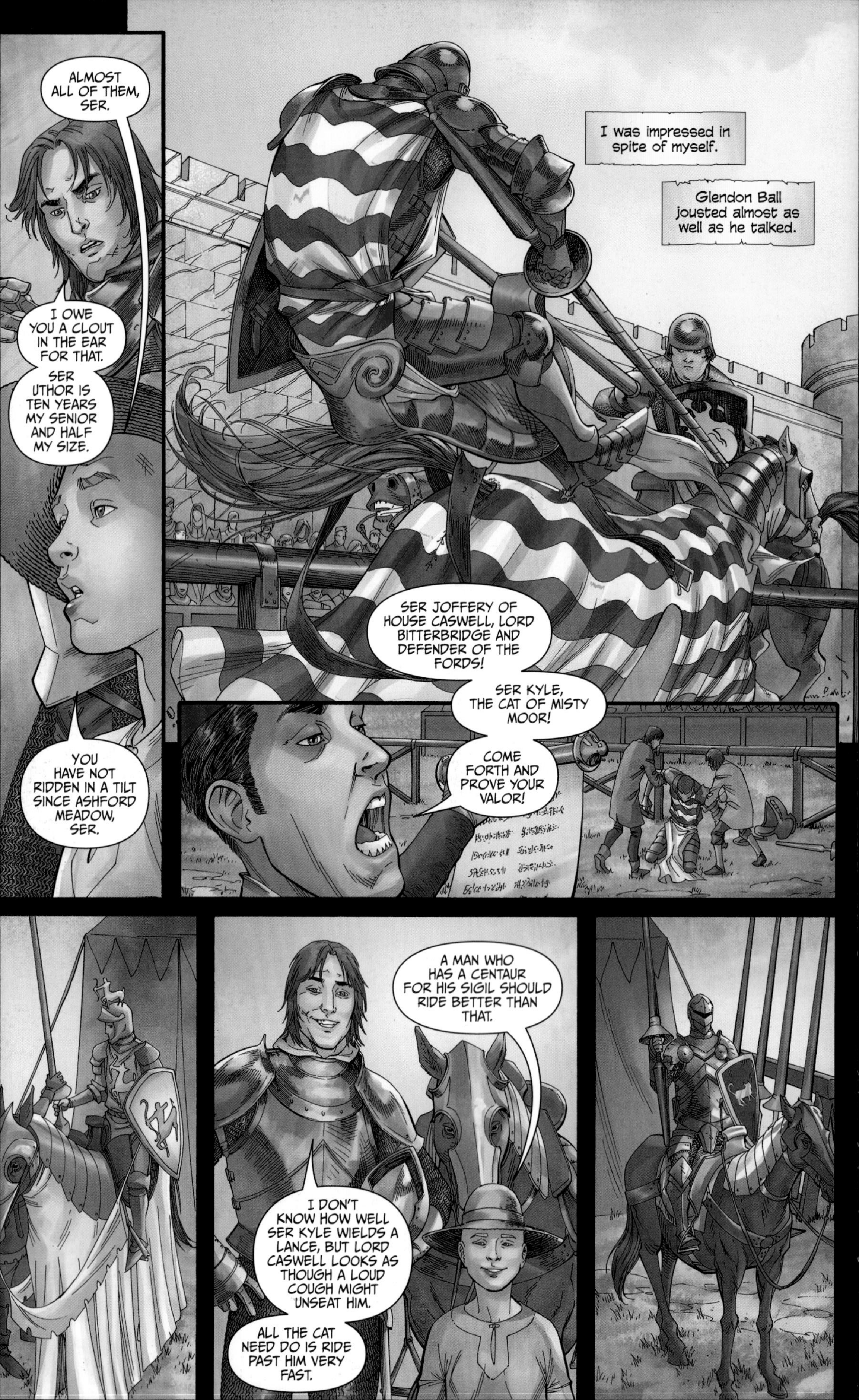
ALMOST ALL OF THEM, SER.
I was impressed in spite of myself.
Glendon Ball jousted almost as well as he talked.
I OWE YOU A CLOUT IN THE EAR FOR THAT.
SER UTHOR IS TEN YEARS MY SENIOR AND HALF MY SIZE.
YOU HAVE NOT RIDDEN IN A TILT SINCE ASHFORD MEADOW, SER.
SER JOFFERY OF HOUSE CASWELL, LORD BITTERBRIDGE AND DEFENDER OF THE FORDS!
SER KYLE, THE CAT OF MISTY MOOR!
COME FORTH AND PROVE YOUR VALOR!
A MAN WHO HAS A CENTAUR FOR HIS SIGIL SHOULD RIDE BETTER THAN THAT.
I DON'T KNOW HOW WELL SER KYLE WIELDS A LANCE, BUT LORD CASWELL LOOKS AS THOUGH A LOUD COUGH MIGHT UNSEAT HIM.
ALL THE CAT NEED DO IS RIDE PAST HIM VERY FAST.

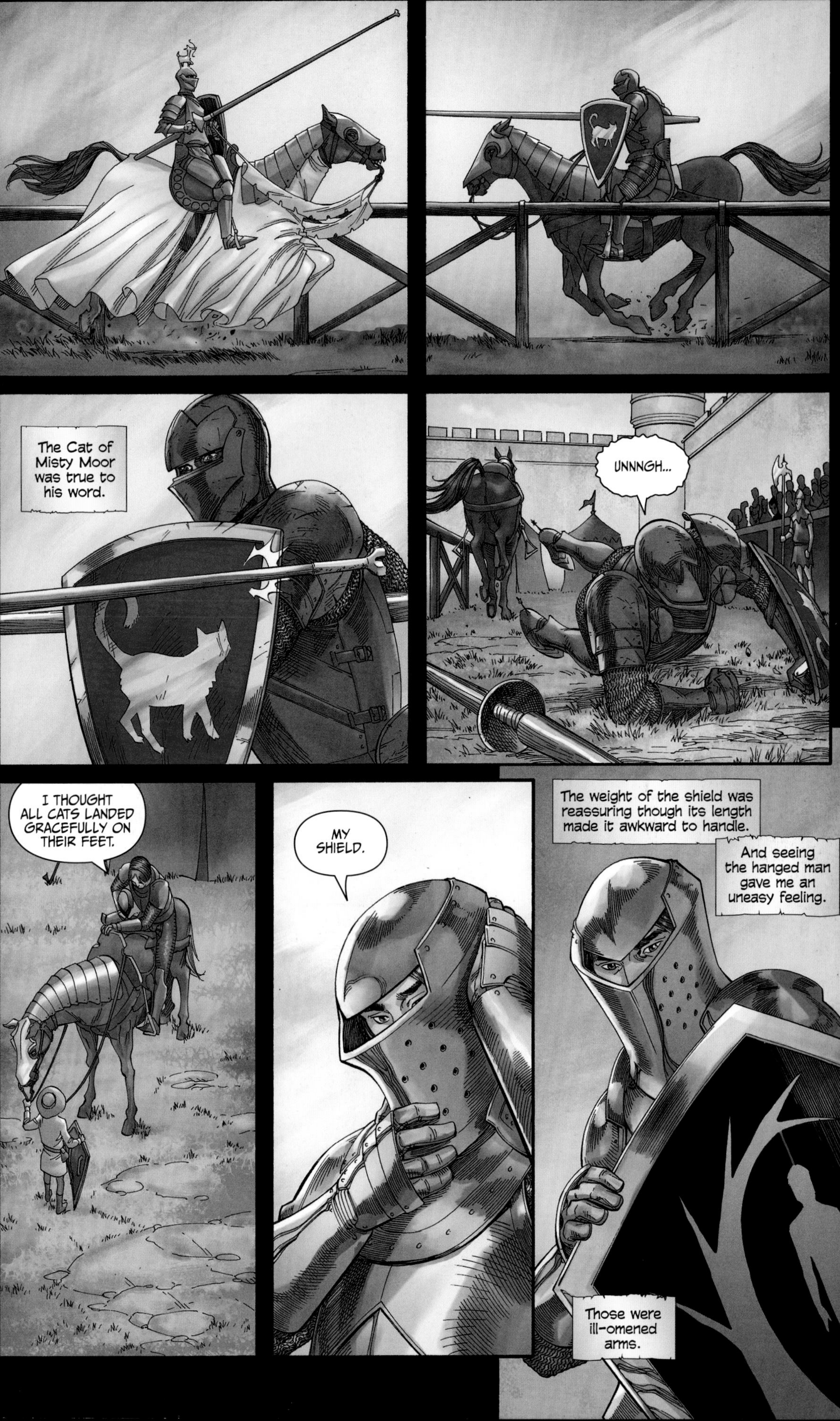
The Cat of Misty Moor was true to his word.
UNNNGH...
I THOUGHT ALL CATS LANDED GRACEFULLY ON THEIR FEET.
MY SHIELD.
The weight of the shield was reassuring though its length made it awkward to handle.
And seeing the hanged man gave me an uneasy feeling.
Those were ill-omened arms.

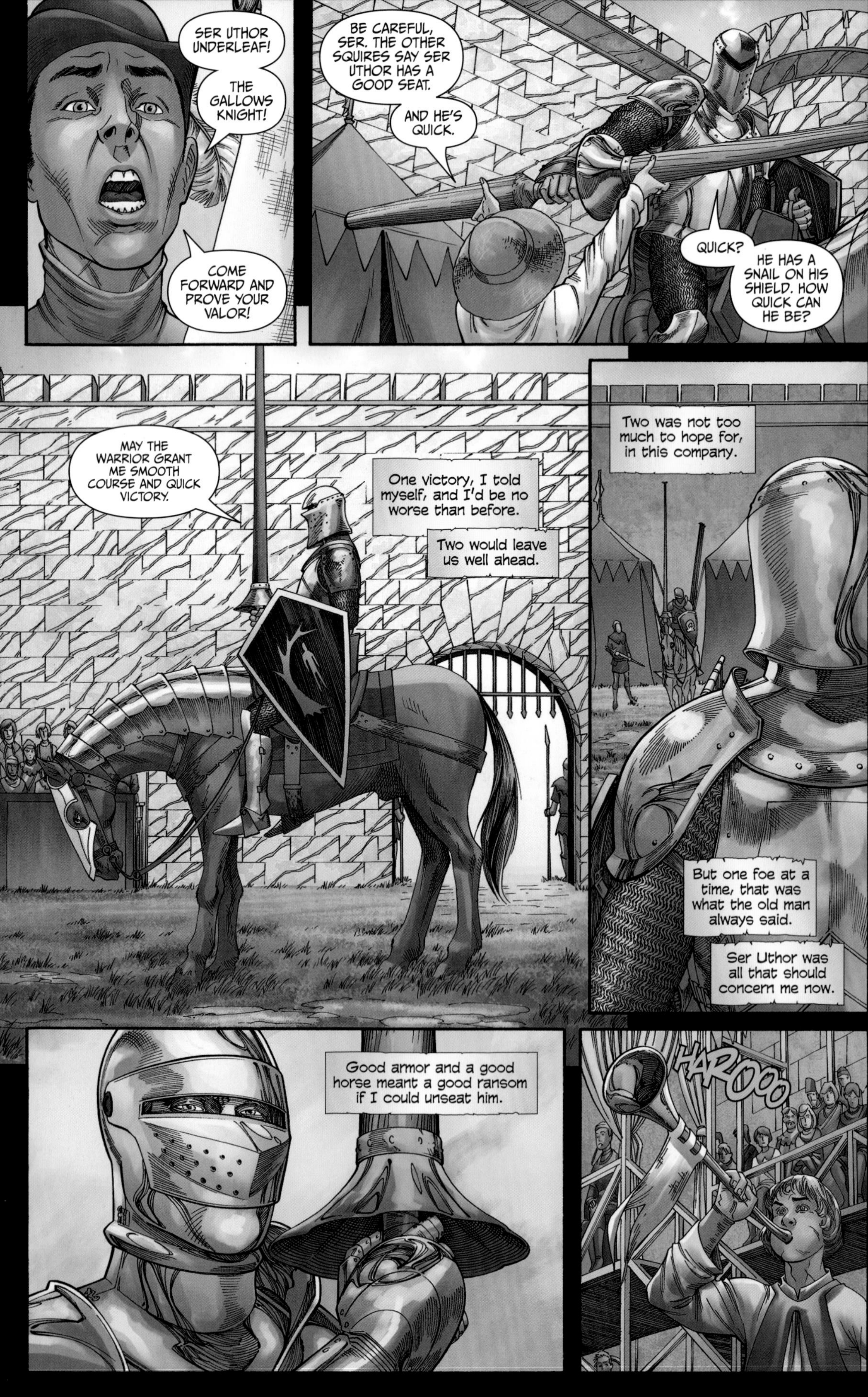

SER UTHOR UNDERLEAF!
THE GALLOWS KNIGHT!
COME FORWARD AND PROVE YOUR VALOR!
BE CAREFUL, SER. THE OTHER SQUIRES SAY SER UTHOR HAS A GOOD SEAT.
AND HE'S QUICK.
QUICK?
HE HAS A SNAIL ON HIS SHIELD. HOW QUICK CAN HE BE?
MAY THE WARRIOR GRANT ME SMOOTH COURSE AND QUICK VICTORY.
One victory, I told myself, and I'd be no worse than before.
Two would leave us well ahead.
Two was not too much to hope for, in this company.
But one foe at a time, that was what the old man always said.
Ser Uthor was all that should concern me now.
Good armor and a good horse meant a good ransom if I could unseat him.
HAROOO

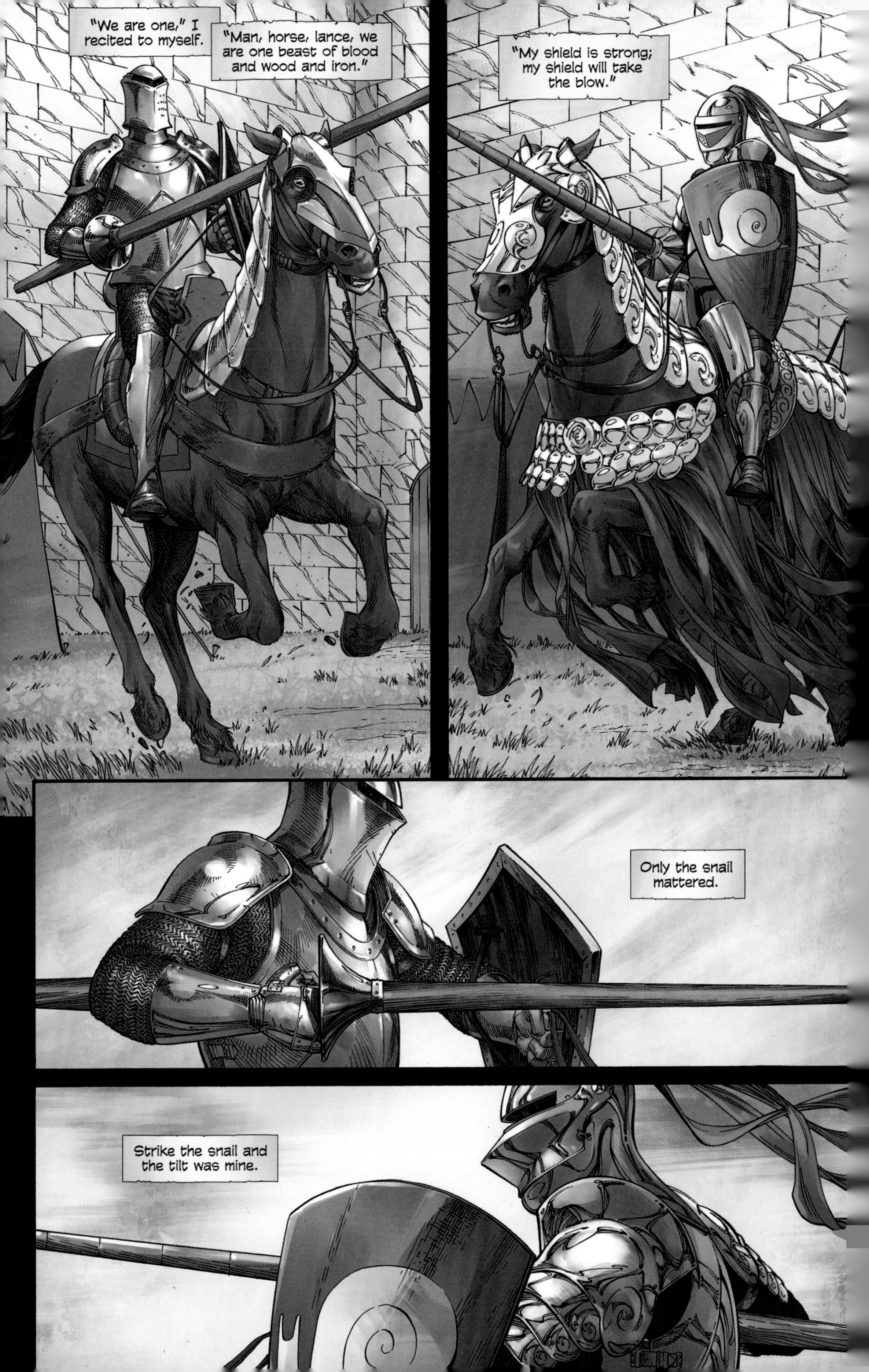
"We are one," I recited to myself.
"Man, horse, lance, we are one beast of blood and wood and iron."
"My shield is strong; my shield will take the blow."
Only the snail mattered.
Strike the snail and the tilt was mine.

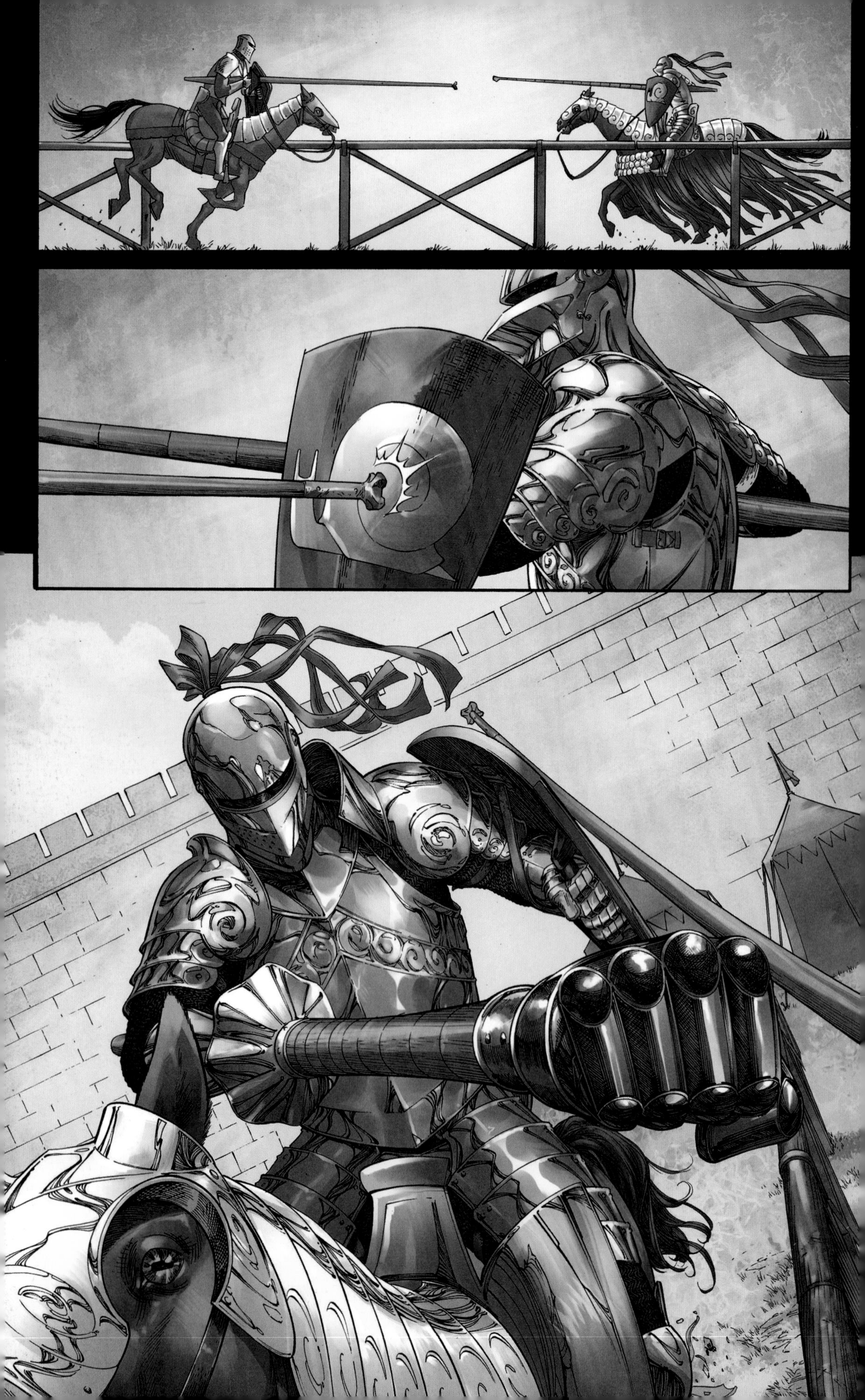

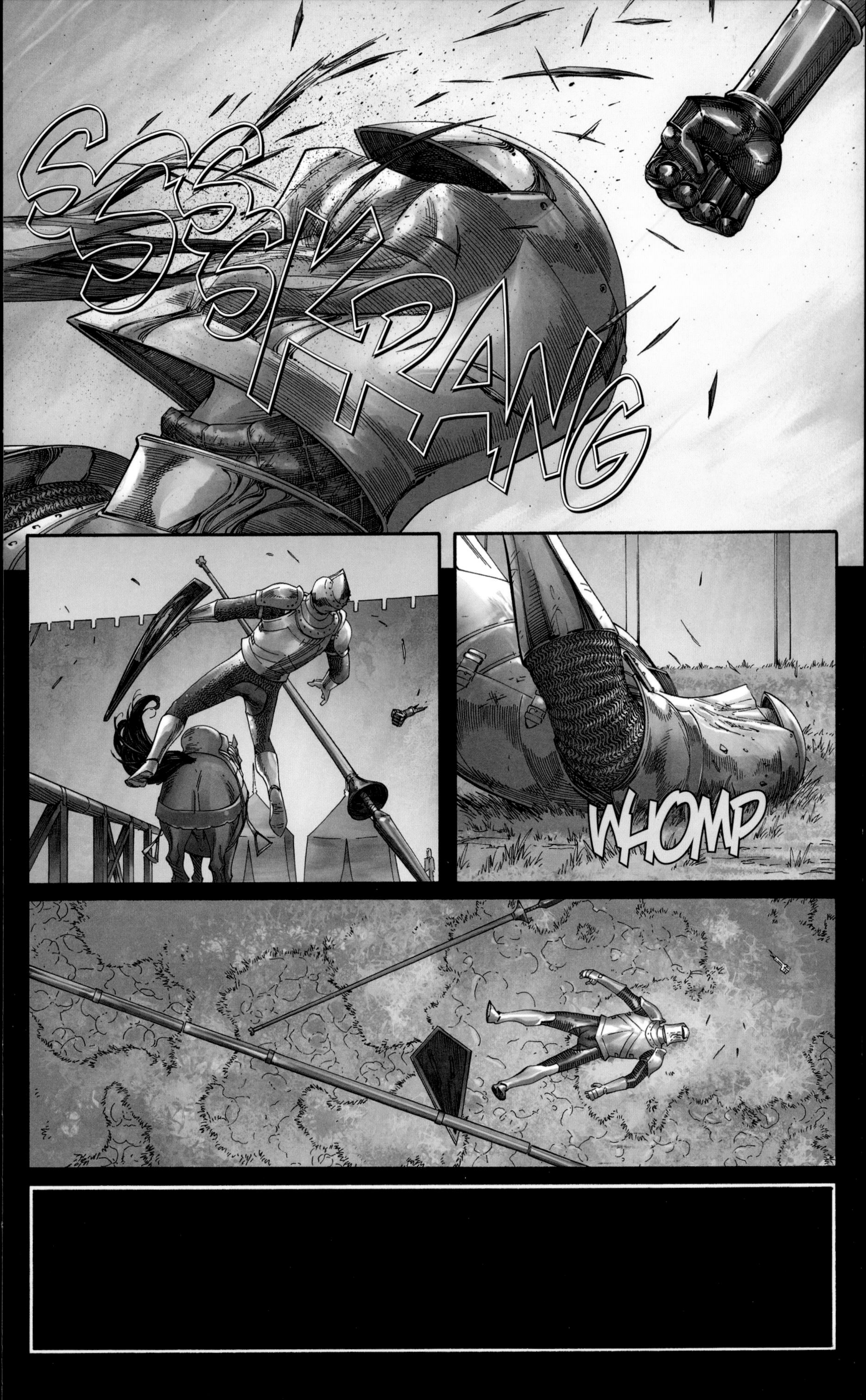
SSSSSSKRANG
WHOMP

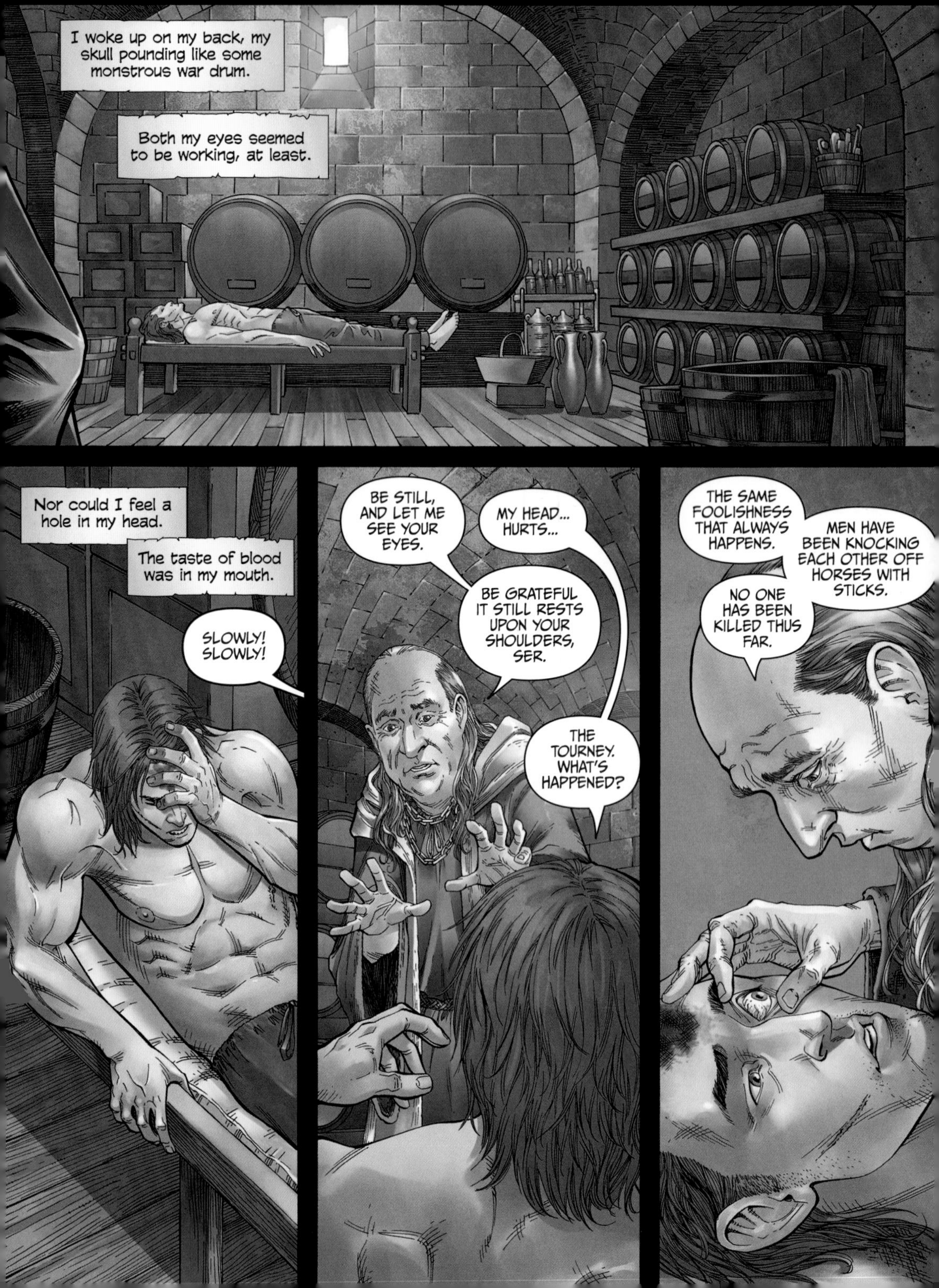
I woke up on my back, my skull pounding like some monstrous war drum.
Both my eyes seemed to be working, at least.
Nor could I feel a hole in my head.
The taste of blood was in my mouth.
SLOWLY! SLOWLY!
BE STILL, AND LET ME SEE YOUR EYES.
MY HEAD... HURTS...
BE GRATEFUL IT STILL RESTS UPON YOUR SHOULDERS, SER.
THE TOURNEY. WHAT'S HAPPENED?
THE SAME FOOLISHNESS THAT ALWAYS HAPPENS.
MEN HAVE BEEN KNOCKING EACH OTHER OFF HORSES WITH STICKS.
NO ONE HAS BEEN KILLED THUS FAR.

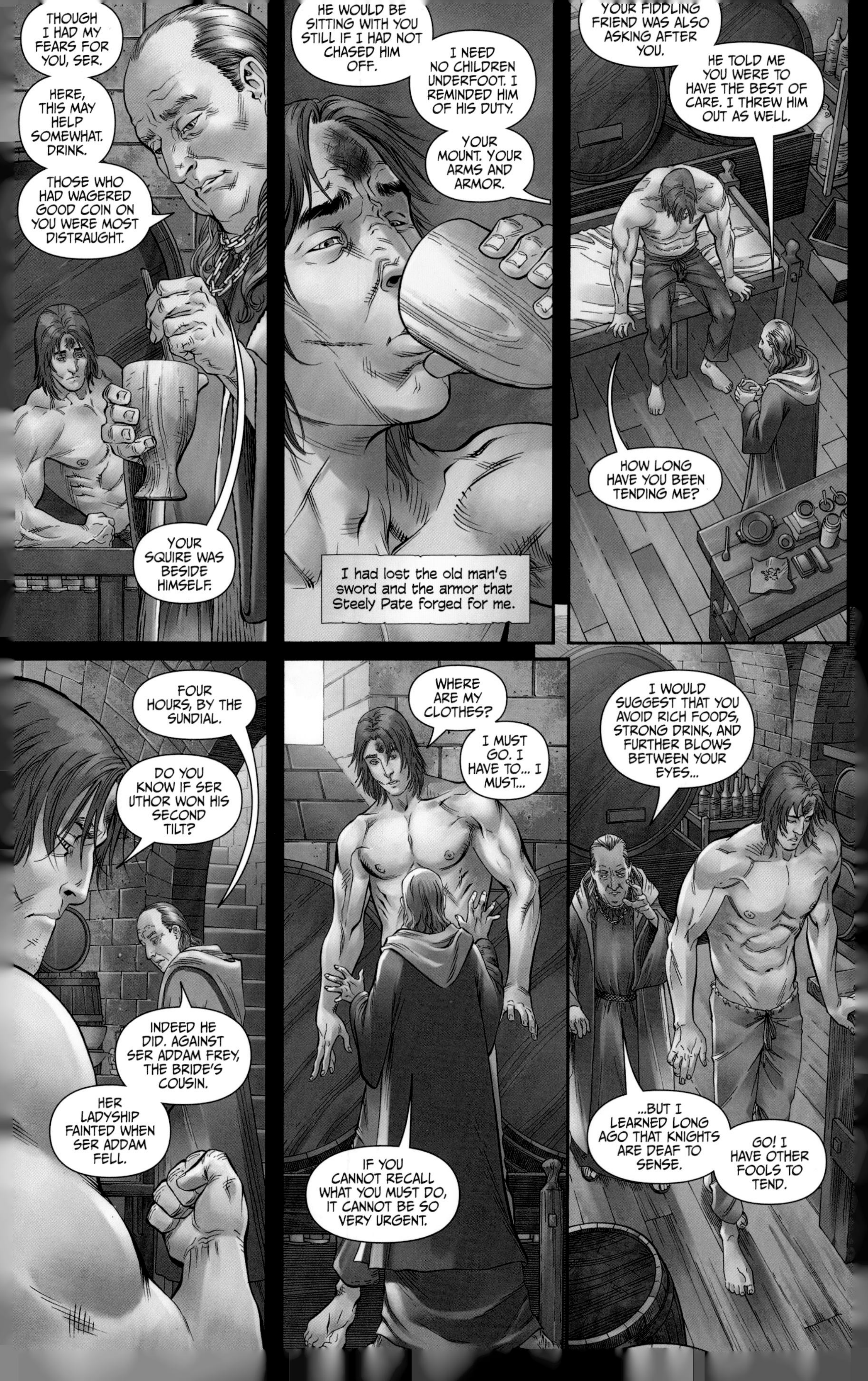
THOUGH I HAD MY FEARS FOR YOU, SER.
HERE, THIS MAY HELP SOMEWHAT. DRINK.
THOSE WHO HAD WAGERED GOOD COIN ON YOU WERE MOST DISTRAUGHT.
YOUR SQUIRE WAS BESIDE HIMSELF.
HE WOULD BE SITTING WITH YOU STILL IF I HAD NOT CHASED HIM OFF.
I NEED NO CHILDREN UNDERFOOT. I REMINDED HIM OF HIS DUTY.
YOUR MOUNT. YOUR ARMS AND ARMOR.
I had lost the old man's sword and the armor that Steely Pate forged for me.
YOUR FIDDLING FRIEND WAS ALSO ASKING AFTER YOU.
HE TOLD ME YOU WERE TO HAVE THE BEST OF CARE. I THREW HIM OUT AS WELL.
HOW LONG HAVE YOU BEEN TENDING ME?
FOUR HOURS, BY THE SUNDIAL.
DO YOU KNOW IF SER UTHOR WON HIS SECOND TILT?
INDEED HE DID. AGAINST SER ADDAM FREY, THE BRIDE'S COUSIN.
HER LADYSHIP FAINTED WHEN SER ADDAM FELL.
WHERE ARE MY CLOTHES?
I MUST GO. I HAVE TO... I MUST...
IF YOU CANNOT RECALL WHAT YOU MUST DO, IT CANNOT BE SO VERY URGENT.
I WOULD SUGGEST THAT YOU AVOID RICH FOODS, STRONG DRINK, AND FURTHER BLOWS BETWEEN YOUR EYES...
...BUT I LEARNED LONG AGO THAT KNIGHTS ARE DEAF TO SENSE.
GO! I HAVE OTHER FOOLS TO TEND.

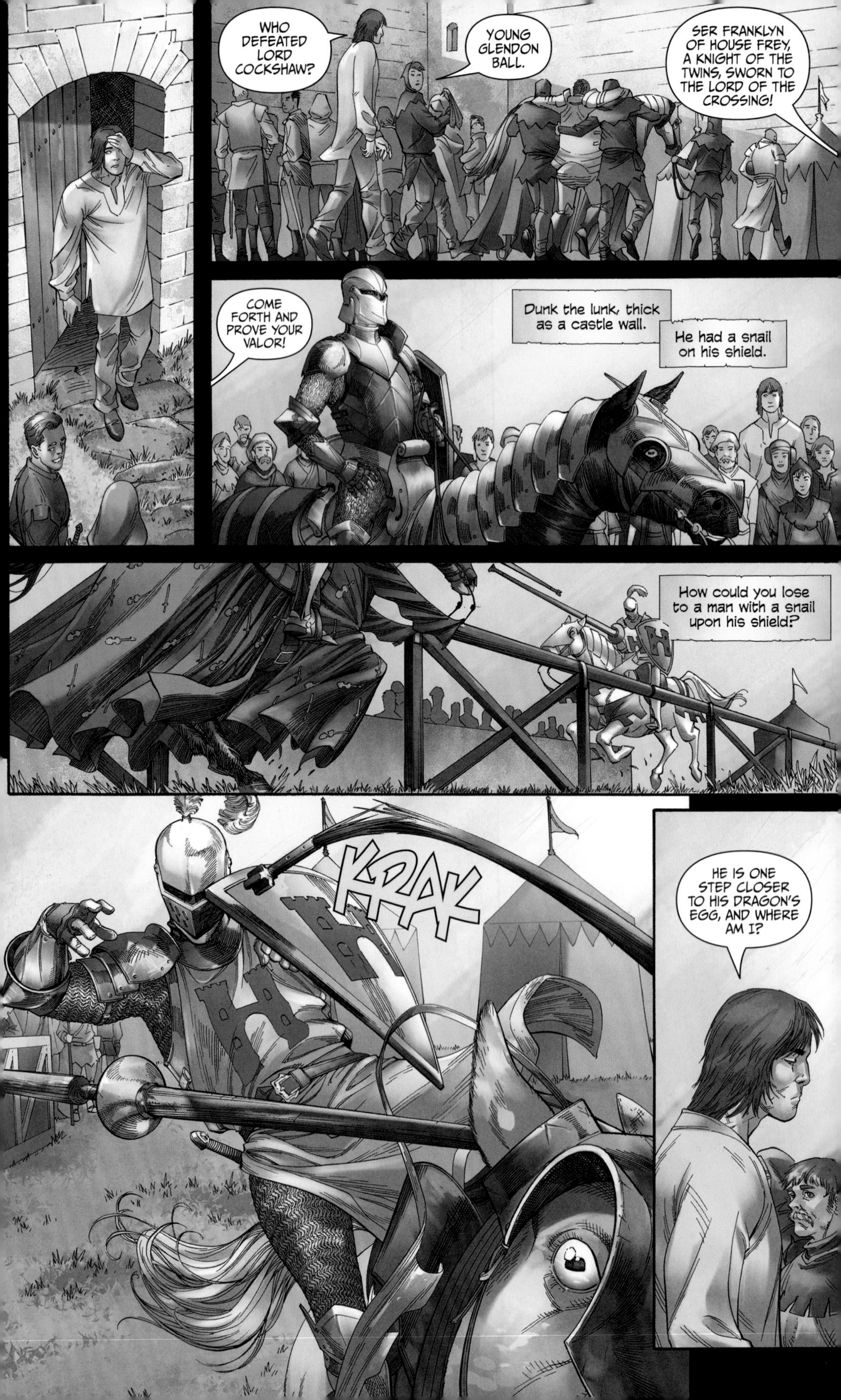
WHO DEFEATED LORD COCKSHAW?
YOUNG GLENDON BALL.
SER FRANKLYN OF HOUSE FREY, A KNIGHT OF THE TWINS, SWORN TO THE LORD OF THE CROSSING!
COME FORTH AND PROVE YOUR VALOR!
Dunk the lunk, thick as a castle wall.
He had a snail on his shield.
How could you lose to a man with a snail upon his shield?
KRAK
HE IS ONE STEP CLOSER TO HIS DRAGON'S EGG, AND WHERE AM I?

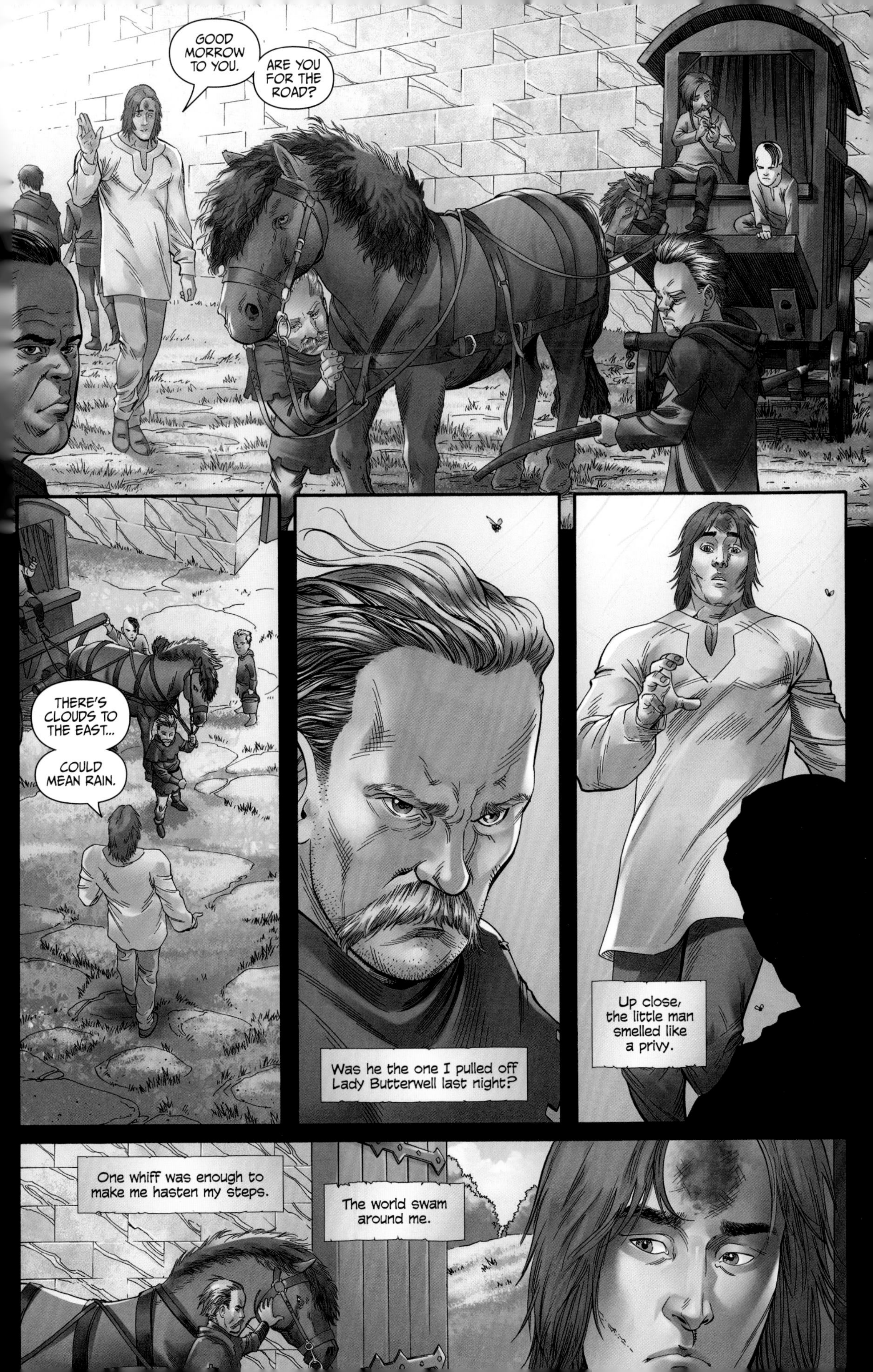
GOOD MORROW TO YOU.
ARE YOU FOR THE ROAD?
THERE'S CLOUDS TO THE EAST...
COULD MEAN RAIN.
Was he the one I pulled off Lady Butterwell last night?
Up close, the little man smelled like a privy.
One whiff was enough to make me hasten my steps.
The world swam around me.

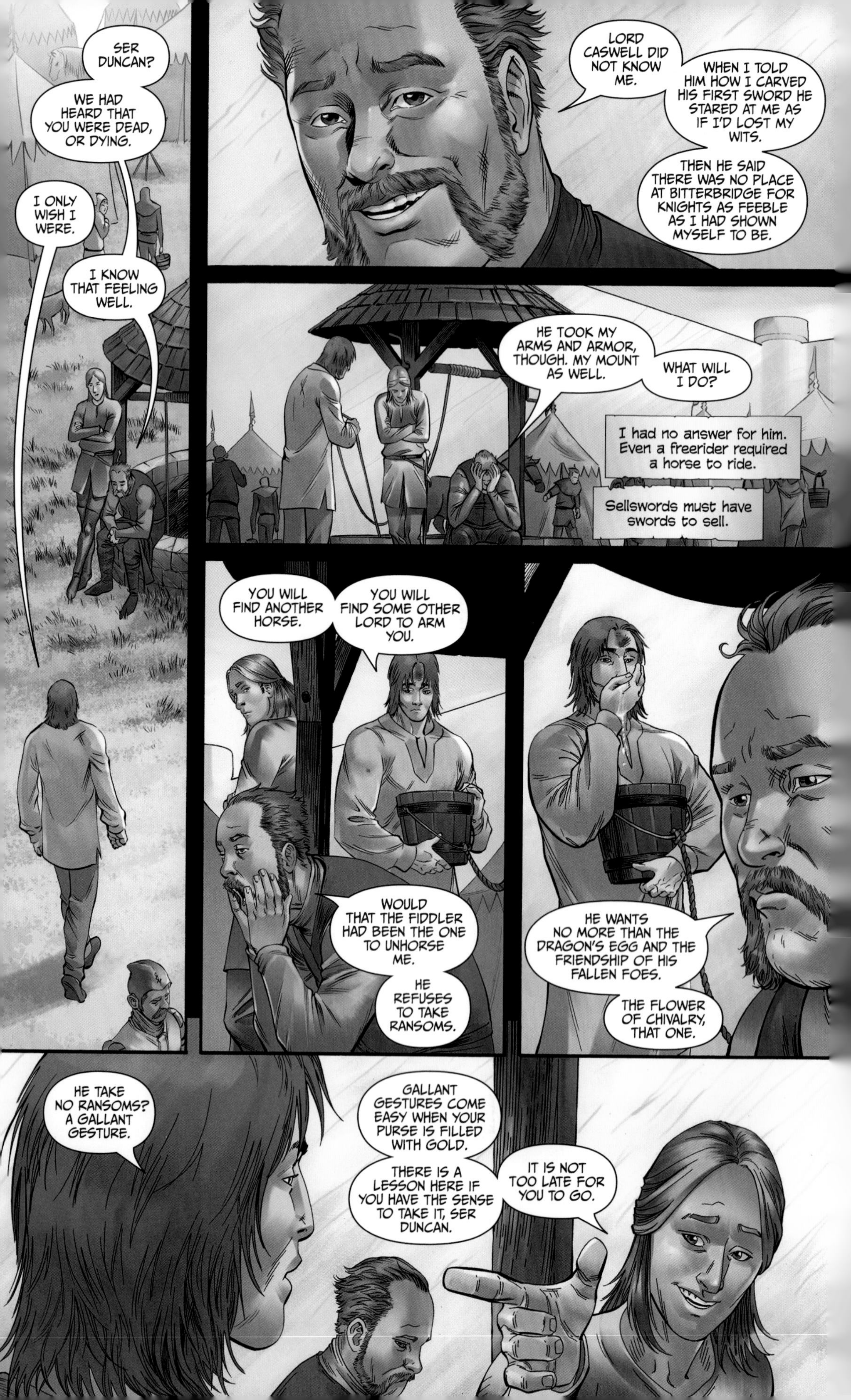
SER DUNCAN?
WE HAD HEARD THAT YOU WERE DEAD, OR DYING.
I ONLY WISH I WERE.
I KNOW THAT FEELING WELL.
LORD CASWELL DID NOT KNOW ME.
WHEN I TOLD HIM HOW I CARVED HIS FIRST SWORD HE STARED AT ME AS IF I'D LOST MY WITS.
THEN HE SAID THERE WAS NO PLACE AT BITTERBRIDGE FOR KNIGHTS AS FEEBLE AS I HAD SHOWN MYSELF TO BE.
HE TOOK MY ARMS AND ARMOR, THOUGH. MY MOUNT AS WELL.
WHAT WILL I DO?
I had no answer for him. Even a freerider required a horse to ride.
Sellswords must have swords to sell.
YOU WILL FIND ANOTHER HORSE.
YOU WILL FIND SOME OTHER LORD TO ARM YOU.
WOULD THAT THE FIDDLER HAD BEEN THE ONE TO UNHORSE ME.
HE REFUSES TO TAKE RANSOMS.
HE WANTS NO MORE THAN THE DRAGON'S EGG AND THE FRIENDSHIP OF HIS FALLEN FOES.
THE FLOWER OF CHIVALRY, THAT ONE.
HE TAKE NO RANSOMS? A GALLANT GESTURE.
GALLANT GESTURES COME EASY WHEN YOUR PURSE IS FILLED WITH GOLD.
THERE IS A LESSON HERE IF YOU HAVE THE SENSE TO TAKE IT, SER DUNCAN.
IT IS NOT TOO LATE FOR YOU TO GO.

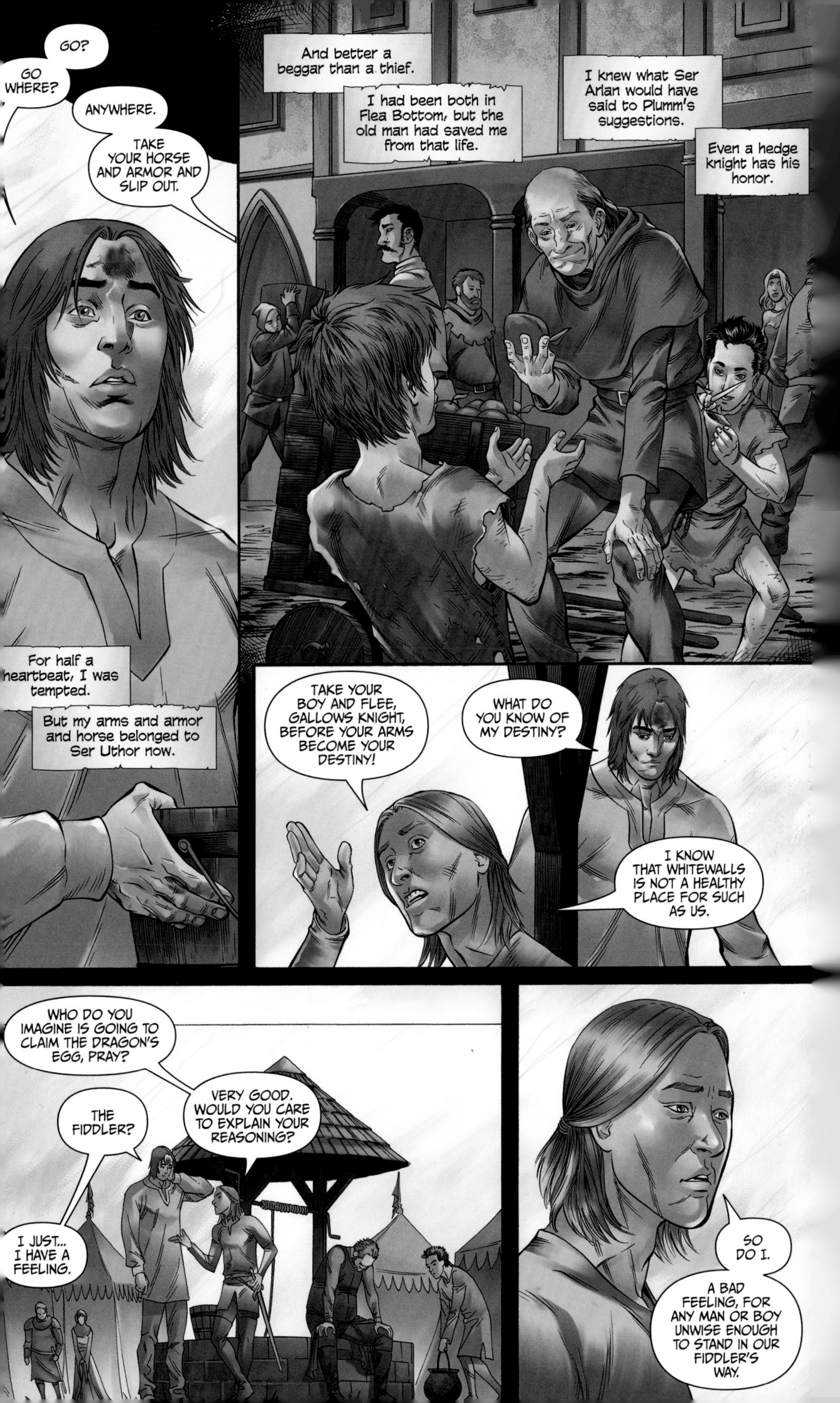
GO?
GO WHERE?
ANYWHERE.
TAKE YOUR HORSE AND ARMOR AND SLIP OUT.
And better a beggar than a thief.
I had been both in Flea Bottom, but the old man had saved me from that life.
I knew what Ser Arlan would have said to Plumm's suggestions.
Even a hedge knight has his honor.
For half a heartbeat, I was tempted.
But my arms and armor and horse belonged to Ser Uthor now.
TAKE YOUR BOY AND FLEE, GALLOWS KNIGHT, BEFORE YOUR ARMS BECOME YOUR DESTINY!
WHAT DO YOU KNOW OF MY DESTINY?
I KNOW THAT WHITEWALLS IS NOT A HEALTHY PLACE FOR SUCH AS US.
WHO DO YOU IMAGINE IS GOING TO CLAIM THE DRAGON'S EGG, PRAY?
THE FIDDLER?
VERY GOOD. WOULD YOU CARE TO EXPLAIN YOUR REASONING?
I JUST... I HAVE A FEELING.
SO DO I.
A BAD FEELING, FOR ANY MAN OR BOY UNWISE ENOUGH TO STAND IN OUR FIDDLER'S WAY.

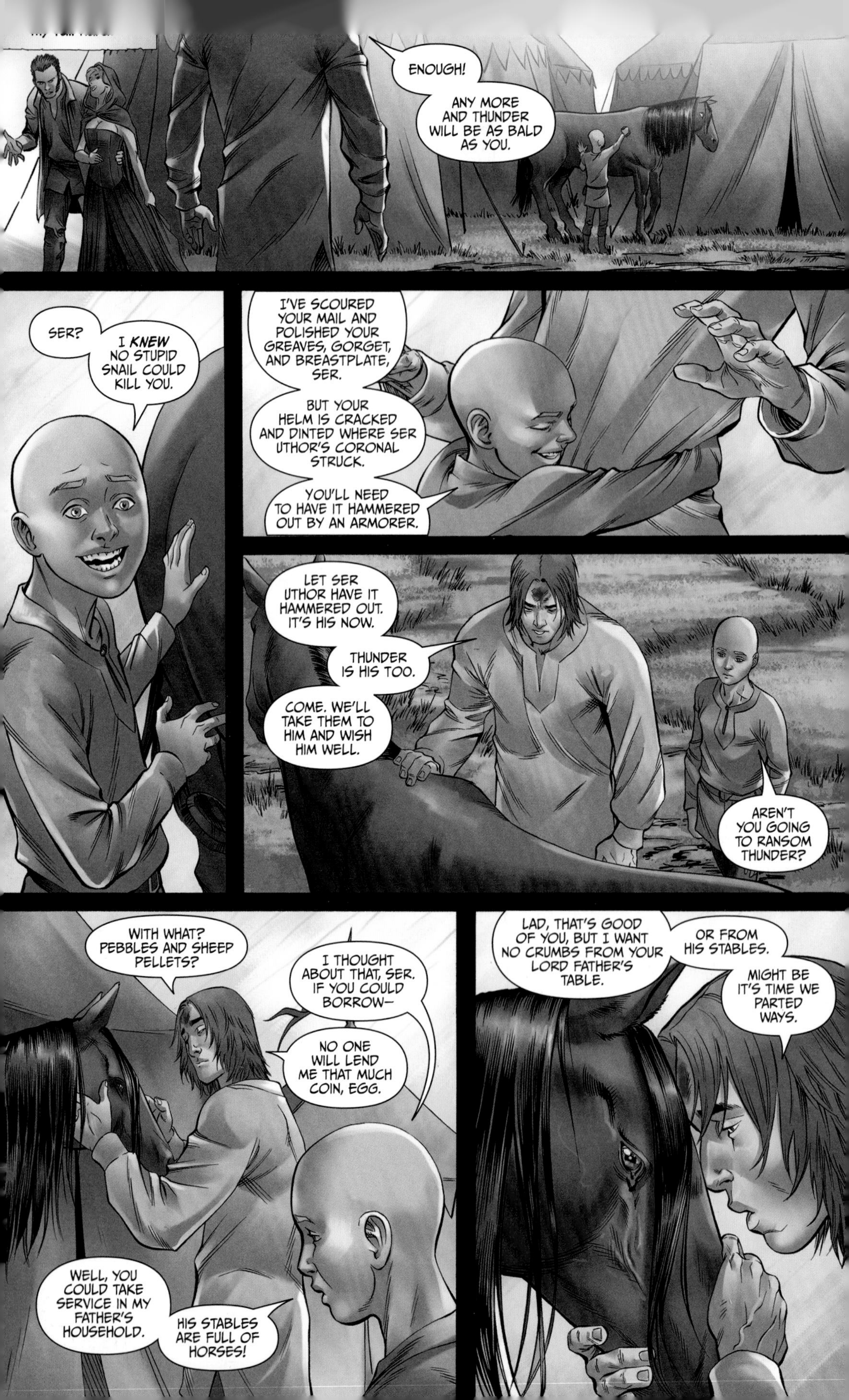
ENOUGH!
ANY MORE AND THUNDER WILL BE AS BALD AS YOU.
SER?
I KNEW NO STUPID SNAIL COULD KILL YOU.
I'VE SCOURED YOUR MAIL AND POLISHED YOUR GREAVES, GORGET, AND BREASTPLATE, SER.
BUT YOUR HELM IS CRACKED AND DINTED WHERE SER UTHOR'S CORONAL STRUCK.
YOU'LL NEED TO HAVE IT HAMMERED OUT BY AN ARMORER.
LET SER UTHOR HAVE IT HAMMERED OUT. IT'S HIS NOW.
THUNDER IS HIS TOO.
COME. WE'LL TAKE THEM TO HIM AND WISH HIM WELL.
AREN'T YOU GOING TO RANSOM THUNDER?
WITH WHAT? PEBBLES AND SHEEP PELLETS?
I THOUGHT ABOUT THAT, SER. IF YOU COULD BORROW—
NO ONE WILL LEND ME THAT MUCH COIN, EGG.
WELL, YOU COULD TAKE SERVICE IN MY FATHER'S HOUSEHOLD.
HIS STABLES ARE FULL OF HORSES!
LAD, THAT'S GOOD OF YOU, BUT I WANT NO CRUMBS FROM YOUR LORD FATHER'S TABLE.
OR FROM HIS STABLES.
MIGHT BE IT'S TIME WE PARTED WAYS.

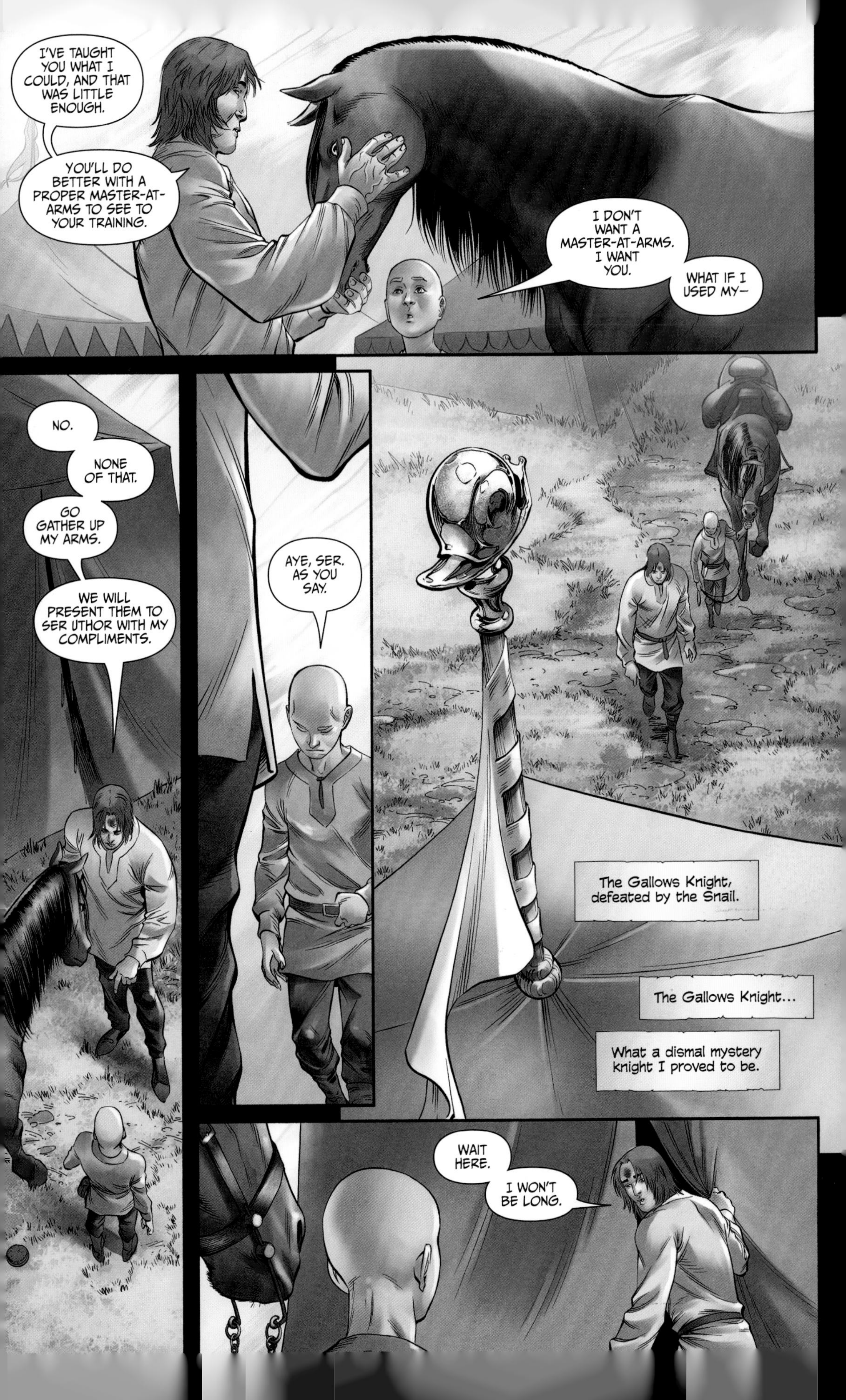
I'VE TAUGHT YOU WHAT I COULD, AND THAT WAS LITTLE ENOUGH.
YOU'LL DO BETTER WITH A PROPER MASTER-AT-ARMS TO SEE TO YOUR TRAINING.
I DON'T WANT A MASTER-AT-ARMS. I WANT YOU.
WHAT IF I USED MY—
NO.
NONE OF THAT.
GO GATHER UP MY ARMS.
WE WILL PRESENT THEM TO SER UTHOR WITH MY COMPLIMENTS.
AYE, SER. AS YOU SAY.
The Gallows Knight, defeated by the Snail.
The Gallows Knight...
What a dismal mystery knight I proved to be.
WAIT HERE.
I WON'T BE LONG.

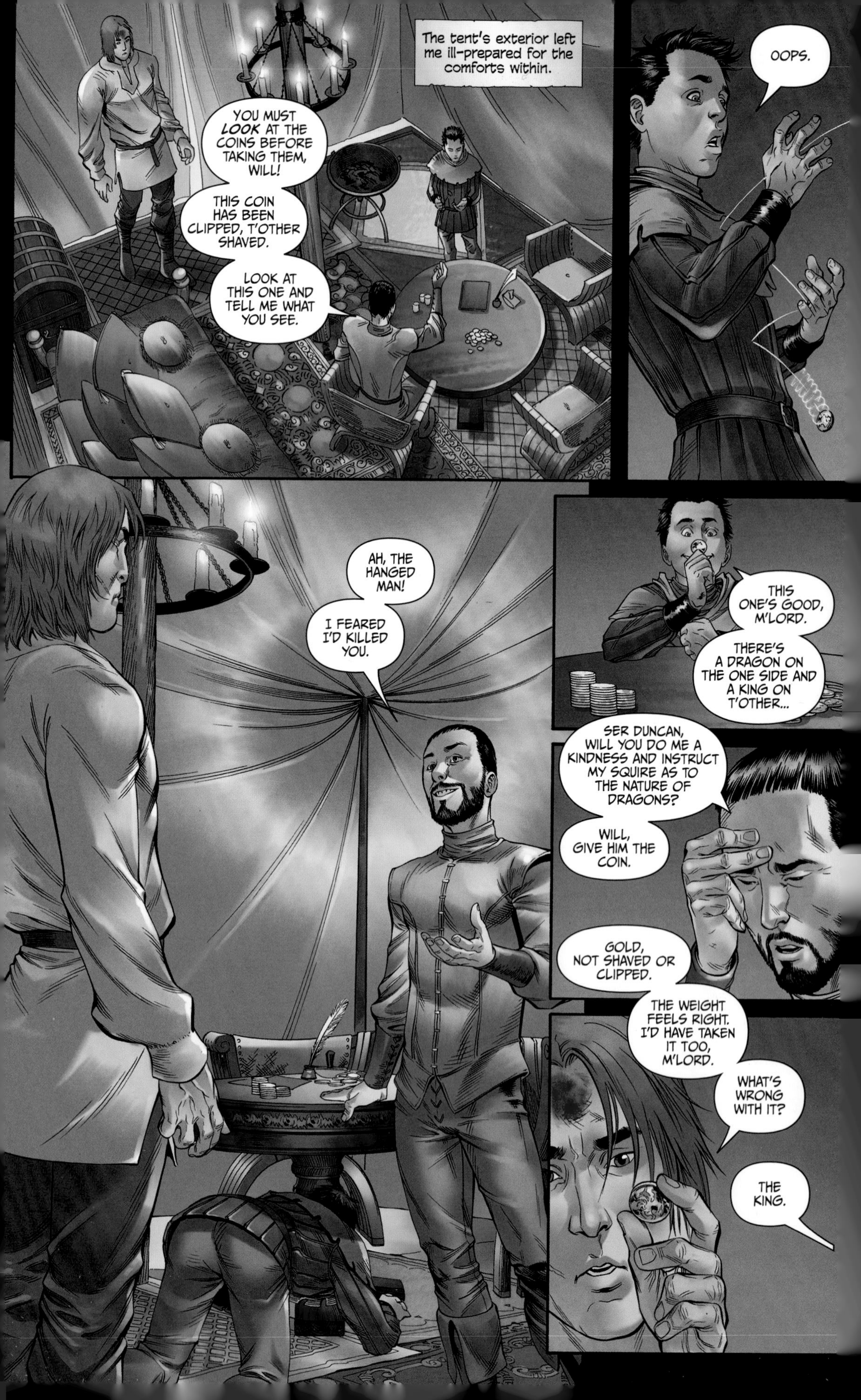
The tent's exterior left me ill-prepared for the comforts within.
YOU MUST *LOOK* AT THE COINS BEFORE TAKING THEM, WILL!
THIS COIN HAS BEEN CLIPPED, T'OTHER SHAVED.
LOOK AT THIS ONE AND TELL ME WHAT YOU SEE.
OOPS.
AH, THE HANGED MAN!
I FEARED I'D KILLED YOU.
THIS ONE'S GOOD, M'LORD.
THERE'S A DRAGON ON THE ONE SIDE AND A KING ON T'OTHER...
SER DUNCAN, WILL YOU DO ME A KINDNESS AND INSTRUCT MY SQUIRE AS TO THE NATURE OF DRAGONS?
WILL, GIVE HIM THE COIN.
GOLD, NOT SHAVED OR CLIPPED.
THE WEIGHT FEELS RIGHT. I'D HAVE TAKEN IT TOO, M'LORD.
WHAT'S WRONG WITH IT?
THE KING.

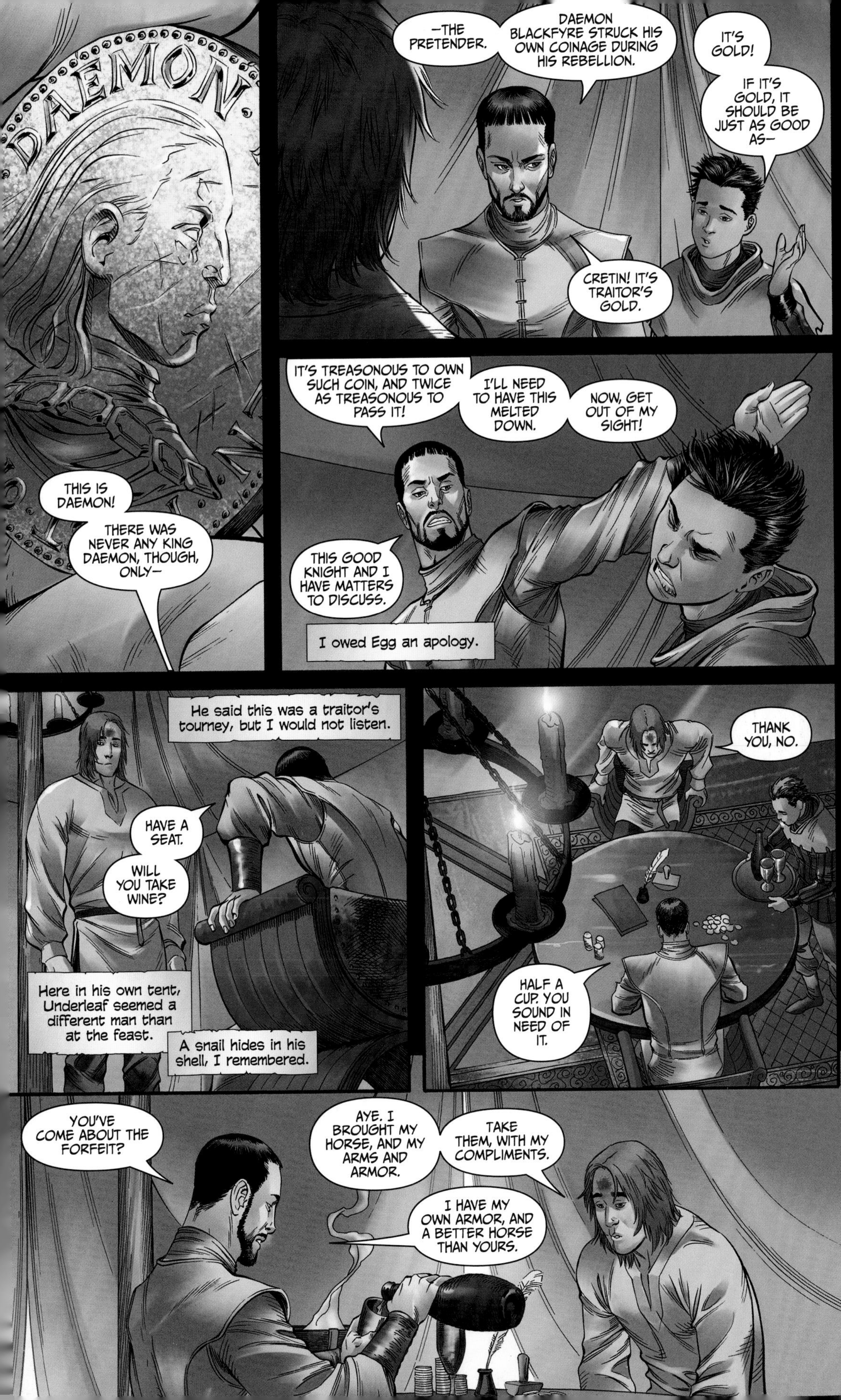
THIS IS DAEMON!
THERE WAS NEVER ANY KING DAEMON, THOUGH, ONLY—
—THE PRETENDER.
DAEMON BLACKFYRE STRUCK HIS OWN COINAGE DURING HIS REBELLION.
IT'S GOLD!
IF IT'S GOLD, IT SHOULD BE JUST AS GOOD AS—
CRETIN! IT'S TRAITOR'S GOLD.
IT'S TREASONOUS TO OWN SUCH COIN, AND TWICE AS TREASONOUS TO PASS IT!
I'LL NEED TO HAVE THIS MELTED DOWN.
NOW, GET OUT OF MY SIGHT!
THIS GOOD KNIGHT AND I HAVE MATTERS TO DISCUSS.
I owed Egg an apology.
He said this was a traitor's tourney, but I would not listen.
HAVE A SEAT.
WILL YOU TAKE WINE?
Here in his own tent, Underleaf seemed a different man than at the feast.
A snail hides in his shell, I remembered.
THANK YOU, NO.
HALF A CUP. YOU SOUND IN NEED OF IT.
YOU'VE COME ABOUT THE FORFEIT?
AYE. I BROUGHT MY HORSE, AND MY ARMS AND ARMOR.
TAKE THEM, WITH MY COMPLIMENTS.
I HAVE MY OWN ARMOR, AND A BETTER HORSE THAN YOURS.

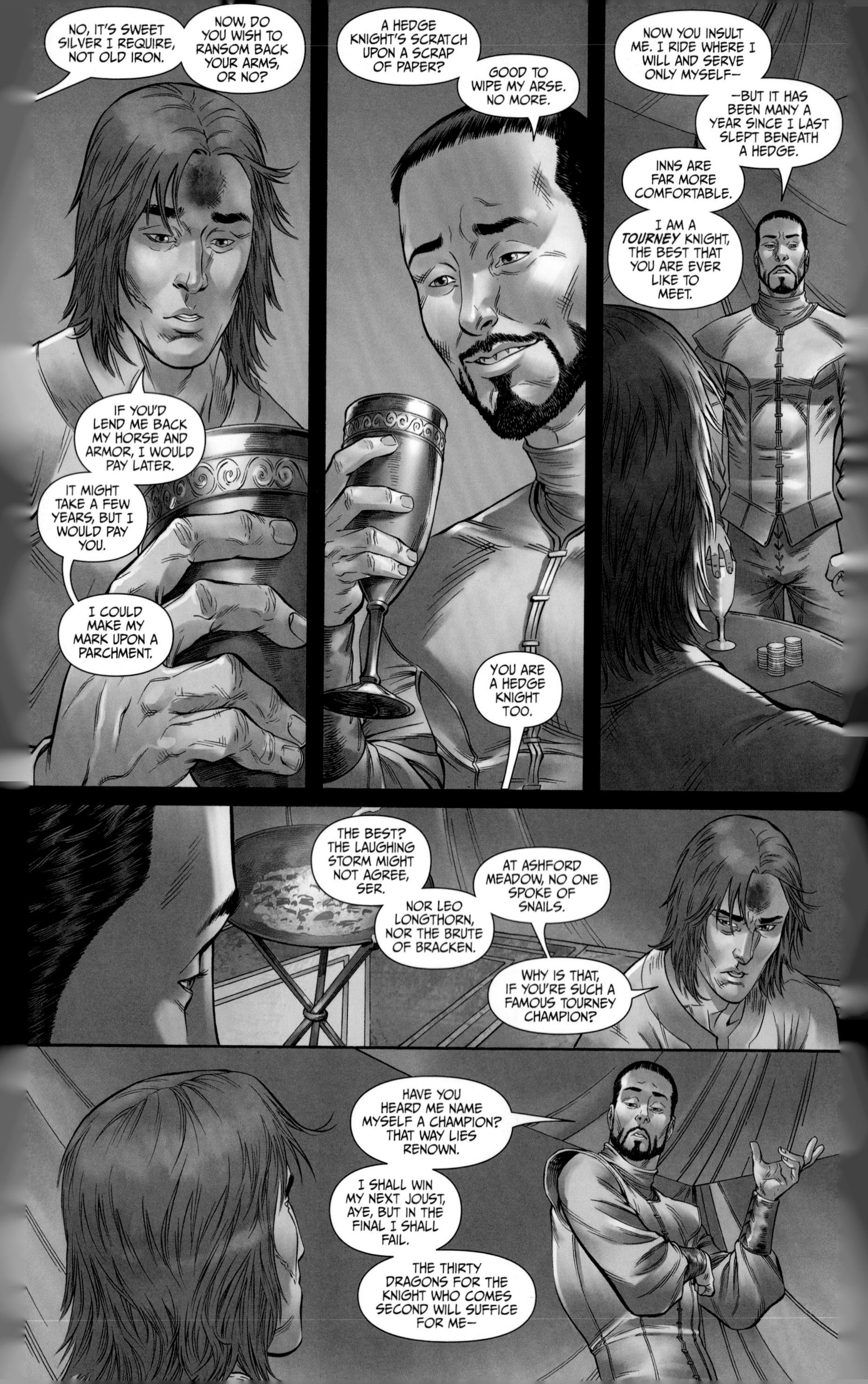
NO, IT'S SWEET SILVER I REQUIRE, NOT OLD IRON.
NOW, DO YOU WISH TO RANSOM BACK YOUR ARMS, OR NO?
IF YOU'D LEND ME BACK MY HORSE AND ARMOR, I WOULD PAY LATER.
IT MIGHT TAKE A FEW YEARS, BUT I WOULD PAY YOU.
I COULD MAKE MY MARK UPON A PARCHMENT.
A HEDGE KNIGHT'S SCRATCH UPON A SCRAP OF PAPER?
GOOD TO WIPE MY ARSE. NO MORE.
YOU ARE A HEDGE KNIGHT TOO.
NOW YOU INSULT ME. I RIDE WHERE I WILL AND SERVE ONLY MYSELF—
—BUT IT HAS BEEN MANY A YEAR SINCE I LAST SLEPT BENEATH A HEDGE.
INNS ARE FAR MORE COMFORTABLE.
I AM A *TOURNEY* KNIGHT, THE BEST THAT YOU ARE EVER LIKE TO MEET.
THE BEST? THE LAUGHING STORM MIGHT NOT AGREE, SER.
NOR LEO LONGTHORN, NOR THE BRUTE OF BRACKEN.
AT ASHFORD MEADOW, NO ONE SPOKE OF SNAILS.
WHY IS THAT, IF YOU'RE SUCH A FAMOUS TOURNEY CHAMPION?
HAVE YOU HEARD ME NAME MYSELF A CHAMPION? THAT WAY LIES RENOWN.
I SHALL WIN MY NEXT JOUST, AYE, BUT IN THE FINAL I SHALL FAIL.
THE THIRTY DRAGONS FOR THE KNIGHT WHO COMES SECOND WILL SUFFICE FOR ME—

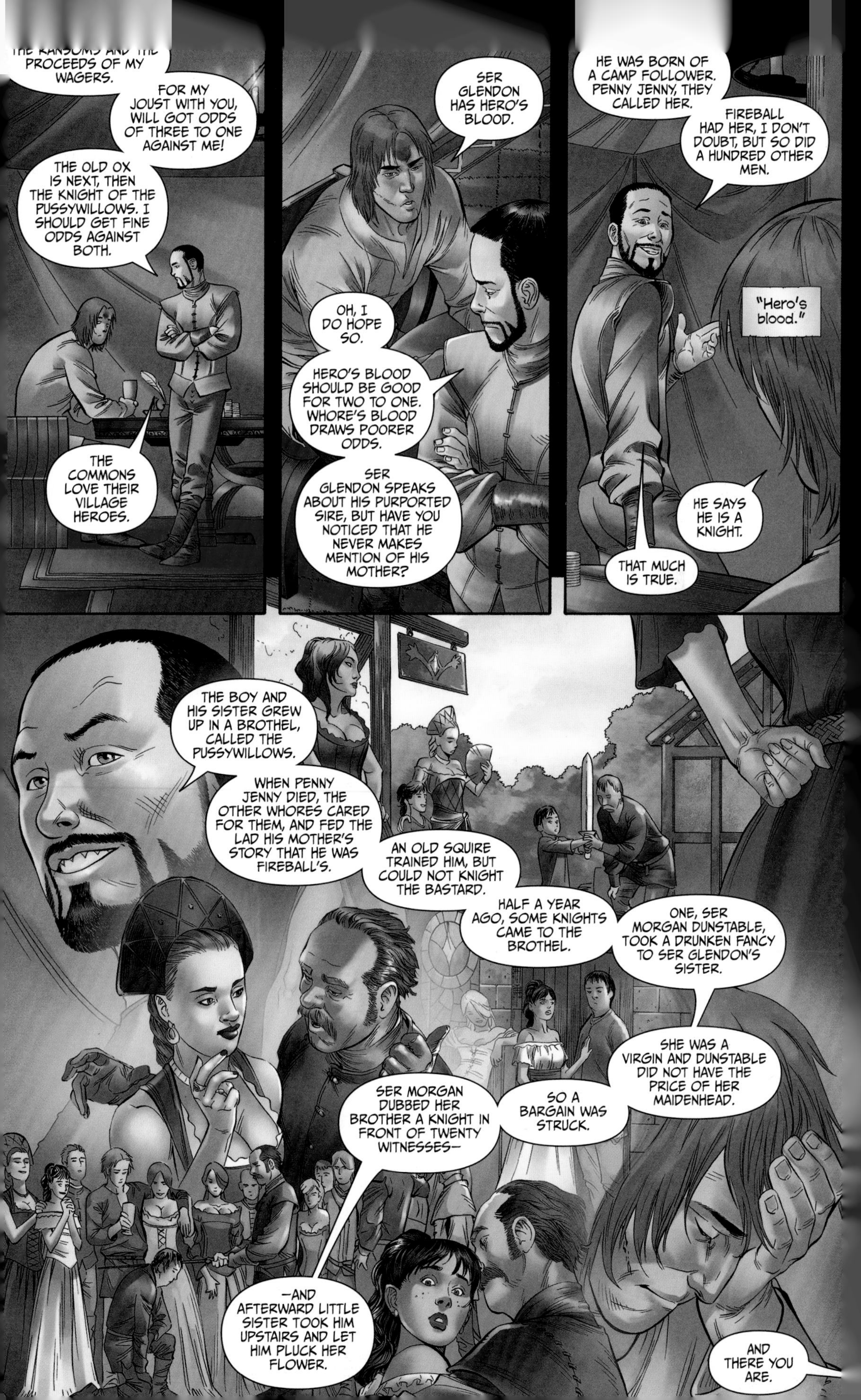

THE RANSOMS AND THE PROCEEDS OF MY WAGERS.
FOR MY JOUST WITH YOU, WILL GOT ODDS OF THREE TO ONE AGAINST ME!
THE OLD OX IS NEXT, THEN THE KNIGHT OF THE PUSSYWILLOWS. I SHOULD GET FINE ODDS AGAINST BOTH.
THE COMMONS LOVE THEIR VILLAGE HEROES.
SER GLENDON HAS HERO'S BLOOD.
OH, I DO HOPE SO.
HERO'S BLOOD SHOULD BE GOOD FOR TWO TO ONE. WHORE'S BLOOD DRAWS POORER ODDS.
SER GLENDON SPEAKS ABOUT HIS PURPORTED SIRE, BUT HAVE YOU NOTICED THAT HE NEVER MAKES MENTION OF HIS MOTHER?
HE WAS BORN OF A CAMP FOLLOWER. PENNY JENNY, THEY CALLED HER.
FIREBALL HAD HER, I DON'T DOUBT, BUT SO DID A HUNDRED OTHER MEN.
"Hero's blood."
HE SAYS HE IS A KNIGHT.
THAT MUCH IS TRUE.
THE BOY AND HIS SISTER GREW UP IN A BROTHEL, CALLED THE PUSSYWILLOWS.
WHEN PENNY JENNY DIED, THE OTHER WHORES CARED FOR THEM, AND FED THE LAD HIS MOTHER'S STORY THAT HE WAS FIREBALL'S.
AN OLD SQUIRE TRAINED HIM, BUT COULD NOT KNIGHT THE BASTARD.
HALF A YEAR AGO, SOME KNIGHTS CAME TO THE BROTHEL.
ONE, SER MORGAN DUNSTABLE, TOOK A DRUNKEN FANCY TO SER GLENDON'S SISTER.
SHE WAS A VIRGIN AND DUNSTABLE DID NOT HAVE THE PRICE OF HER MAIDENHEAD.
SO A BARGAIN WAS STRUCK.
SER MORGAN DUBBED HER BROTHER A KNIGHT IN FRONT OF TWENTY WITNESSES—
—AND AFTERWARD LITTLE SISTER TOOK HIM UPSTAIRS AND LET HIM PLUCK HER FLOWER.
AND THERE YOU ARE.

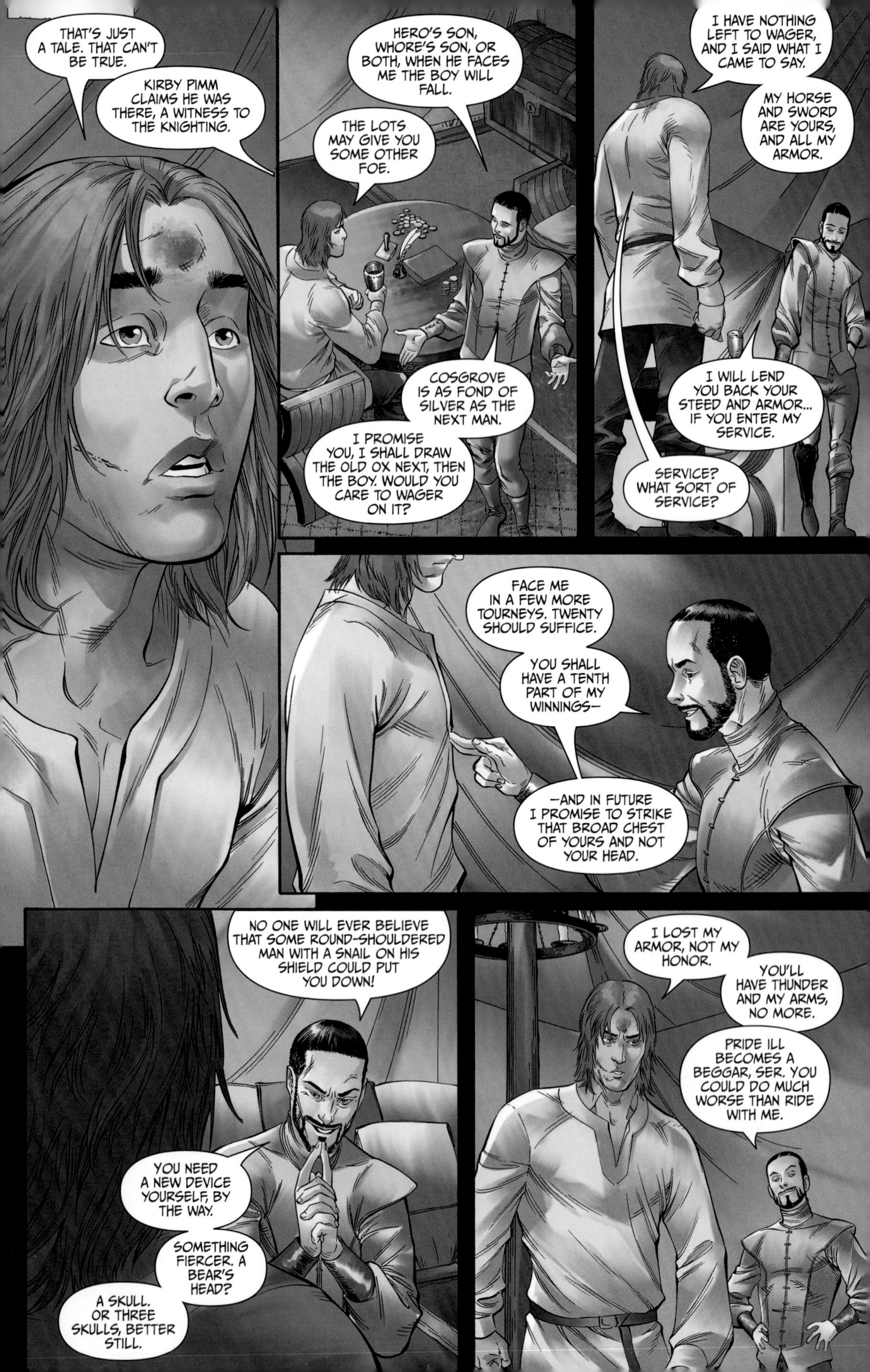
THAT'S JUST A TALE. THAT CAN'T BE TRUE.
KIRBY PIMM CLAIMS HE WAS THERE, A WITNESS TO THE KNIGHTING.
HERO'S SON, WHORE'S SON, OR BOTH, WHEN HE FACES ME THE BOY WILL FALL.
THE LOTS MAY GIVE YOU SOME OTHER FOE.
COSGROVE IS AS FOND OF SILVER AS THE NEXT MAN.
I PROMISE YOU, I SHALL DRAW THE OLD OX NEXT, THEN THE BOY. WOULD YOU CARE TO WAGER ON IT?
I HAVE NOTHING LEFT TO WAGER, AND I SAID WHAT I CAME TO SAY.
MY HORSE AND SWORD ARE YOURS, AND ALL MY ARMOR.
I WILL LEND YOU BACK YOUR STEED AND ARMOR... IF YOU ENTER MY SERVICE.
SERVICE? WHAT SORT OF SERVICE?
FACE ME IN A FEW MORE TOURNEYS. TWENTY SHOULD SUFFICE.
YOU SHALL HAVE A TENTH PART OF MY WINNINGS—
—AND IN FUTURE I PROMISE TO STRIKE THAT BROAD CHEST OF YOURS AND NOT YOUR HEAD.
NO ONE WILL EVER BELIEVE THAT SOME ROUND-SHOULDERED MAN WITH A SNAIL ON HIS SHIELD COULD PUT YOU DOWN!
YOU NEED A NEW DEVICE YOURSELF, BY THE WAY.
SOMETHING FIERCER. A BEAR'S HEAD?
A SKULL. OR THREE SKULLS, BETTER STILL.
I LOST MY ARMOR, NOT MY HONOR.
YOU'LL HAVE THUNDER AND MY ARMS, NO MORE.
PRIDE ILL BECOMES A BEGGAR, SER. YOU COULD DO MUCH WORSE THAN RIDE WITH ME.

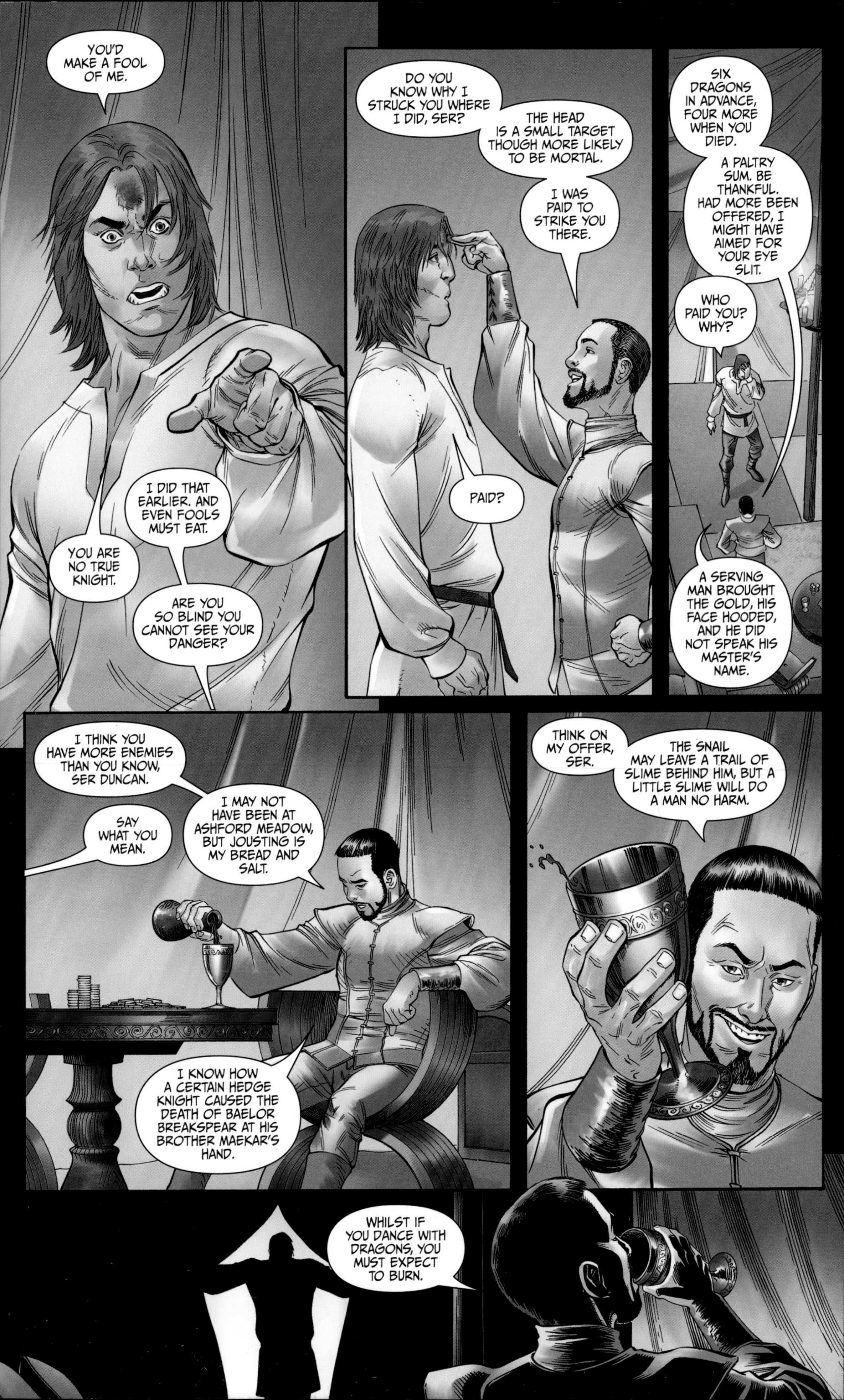
YOU'D MAKE A FOOL OF ME.
YOU ARE NO TRUE KNIGHT.
I DID THAT EARLIER. AND EVEN FOOLS MUST EAT.
ARE YOU SO BLIND YOU CANNOT SEE YOUR DANGER?
DO YOU KNOW WHY I STRUCK YOU WHERE I DID, SER?
THE HEAD IS A SMALL TARGET THOUGH MORE LIKELY TO BE MORTAL.
I WAS PAID TO STRIKE YOU THERE.
PAID?
SIX DRAGONS IN ADVANCE, FOUR MORE WHEN YOU DIED.
A PALTRY SUM. BE THANKFUL. HAD MORE BEEN OFFERED, I MIGHT HAVE AIMED FOR YOUR EYE SLIT.
WHO PAID YOU? WHY?
A SERVING MAN BROUGHT THE GOLD, HIS FACE HOODED, AND HE DID NOT SPEAK HIS MASTER'S NAME.
I THINK YOU HAVE MORE ENEMIES THAN YOU KNOW, SER DUNCAN.
SAY WHAT YOU MEAN.
I MAY NOT HAVE BEEN AT ASHFORD MEADOW, BUT JOUSTING IS MY BREAD AND SALT.
I KNOW HOW A CERTAIN HEDGE KNIGHT CAUSED THE DEATH OF BAELOR BREAKSPEAR AT HIS BROTHER MAEKAR'S HAND.
THINK ON MY OFFER, SER.
THE SNAIL MAY LEAVE A TRAIL OF SLIME BEHIND HIM, BUT A LITTLE SLIME WILL DO A MAN NO HARM.
WHILST IF YOU DANCE WITH DRAGONS, YOU MUST EXPECT TO BURN.

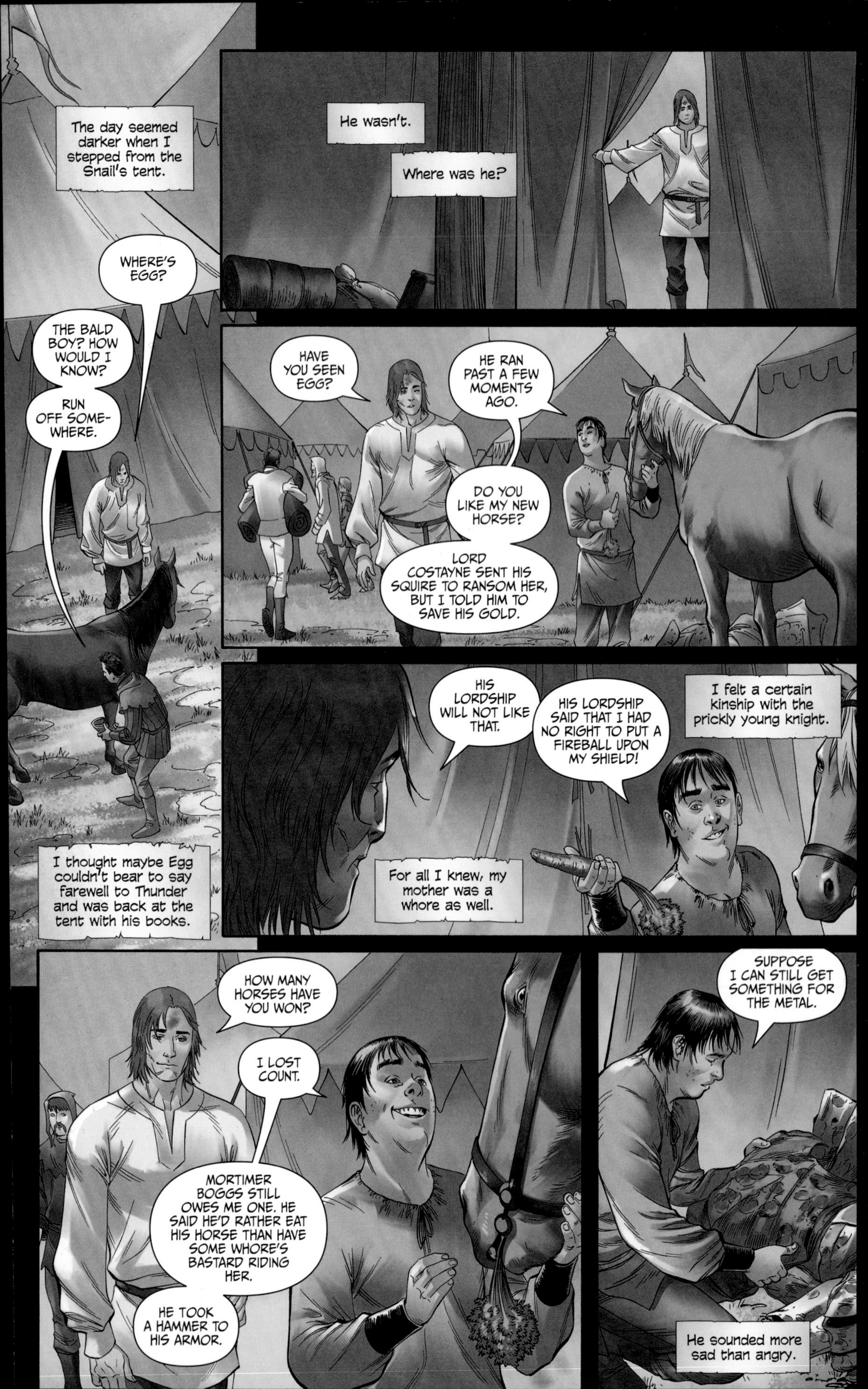
The day seemed darker when I stepped from the Snail's tent.
He wasn't.
Where was he?
WHERE'S EGG?
THE BALD BOY? HOW WOULD I KNOW?
RUN OFF SOME-WHERE.
I thought maybe Egg couldn't bear to say farewell to Thunder and was back at the tent with his books.
HAVE YOU SEEN EGG?
HE RAN PAST A FEW MOMENTS AGO.
DO YOU LIKE MY NEW HORSE?
LORD COSTAYNE SENT HIS SQUIRE TO RANSOM HER, BUT I TOLD HIM TO SAVE HIS GOLD.
HIS LORDSHIP WILL NOT LIKE THAT.
HIS LORDSHIP SAID THAT I HAD NO RIGHT TO PUT A FIREBALL UPON MY SHIELD!
I felt a certain kinship with the prickly young knight.
For all I knew, my mother was a whore as well.
HOW MANY HORSES HAVE YOU WON?
I LOST COUNT.
MORTIMER BOGGS STILL OWES ME ONE. HE SAID HE'D RATHER EAT HIS HORSE THAN HAVE SOME WHORE'S BASTARD RIDING HER.
HE TOOK A HAMMER TO HIS ARMOR.
SUPPOSE I CAN STILL GET SOMETHING FOR THE METAL.
He sounded more sad than angry.

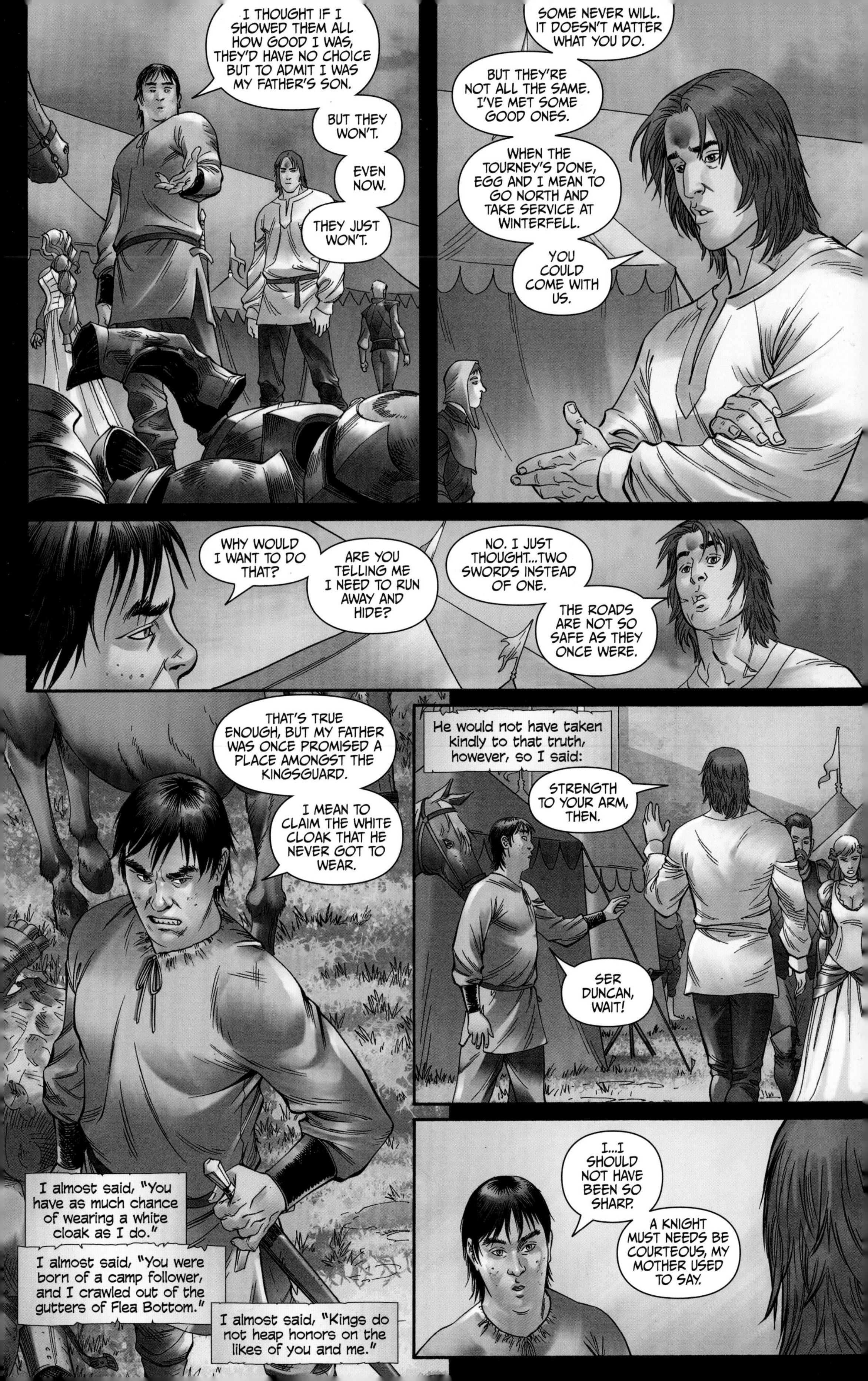
I THOUGHT IF I SHOWED THEM ALL HOW GOOD I WAS, THEY'D HAVE NO CHOICE BUT TO ADMIT I WAS MY FATHER'S SON.
BUT THEY WON'T.
EVEN NOW.
THEY JUST WON'T.
SOME NEVER WILL. IT DOESN'T MATTER WHAT YOU DO.
BUT THEY'RE NOT ALL THE SAME. I'VE MET SOME GOOD ONES.
WHEN THE TOURNEY'S DONE, EGG AND I MEAN TO GO NORTH AND TAKE SERVICE AT WINTERFELL.
YOU COULD COME WITH US.
WHY WOULD I WANT TO DO THAT?
ARE YOU TELLING ME I NEED TO RUN AWAY AND HIDE?
NO. I JUST THOUGHT...TWO SWORDS INSTEAD OF ONE.
THE ROADS ARE NOT SO SAFE AS THEY ONCE WERE.
THAT'S TRUE ENOUGH, BUT MY FATHER WAS ONCE PROMISED A PLACE AMONGST THE KINGSGUARD.
I MEAN TO CLAIM THE WHITE CLOAK THAT HE NEVER GOT TO WEAR.
I almost said, "You have as much chance of wearing a white cloak as I do."
I almost said, "You were born of a camp follower, and I crawled out of the gutters of Flea Bottom."
I almost said, "Kings do not heap honors on the likes of you and me."
He would not have taken kindly to that truth, however, so I said:
STRENGTH TO YOUR ARM, THEN.
SER DUNCAN, WAIT!
I...I SHOULD NOT HAVE BEEN SO SHARP.
A KNIGHT MUST NEEDS BE COURTEOUS, MY MOTHER USED TO SAY.

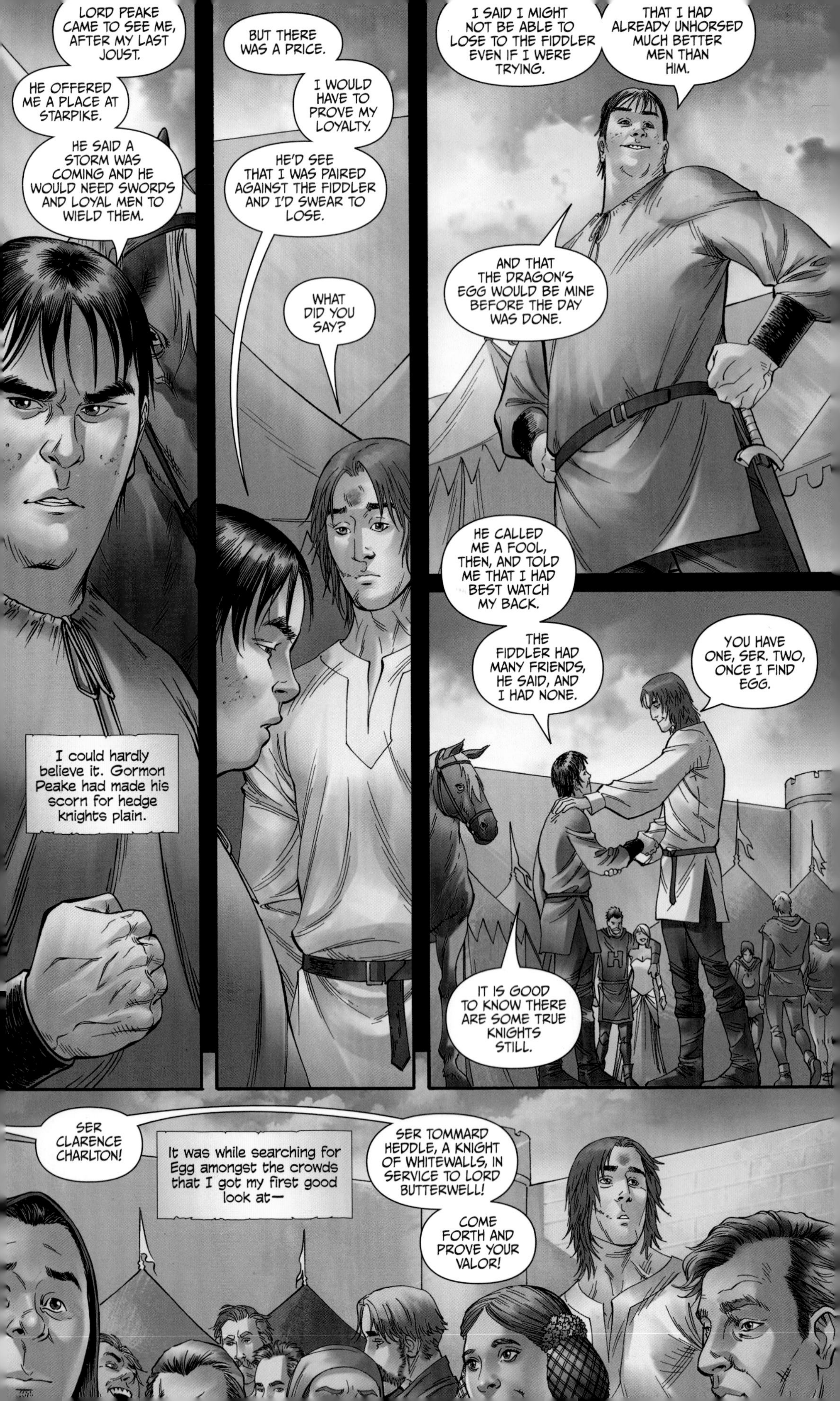
LORD PEAKE CAME TO SEE ME, AFTER MY LAST JOUST.
HE OFFERED ME A PLACE AT STARPIKE.
HE SAID A STORM WAS COMING AND HE WOULD NEED SWORDS AND LOYAL MEN TO WIELD THEM.
I could hardly believe it. Gormon Peake had made his scorn for hedge knights plain.
BUT THERE WAS A PRICE.
I WOULD HAVE TO PROVE MY LOYALTY.
HE'D SEE THAT I WAS PAIRED AGAINST THE FIDDLER AND I'D SWEAR TO LOSE.
WHAT DID YOU SAY?
I SAID I MIGHT NOT BE ABLE TO LOSE TO THE FIDDLER EVEN IF I WERE TRYING.
THAT I HAD ALREADY UNHORSED MUCH BETTER MEN THAN HIM.
AND THAT THE DRAGON'S EGG WOULD BE MINE BEFORE THE DAY WAS DONE.
HE CALLED ME A FOOL, THEN, AND TOLD ME THAT I HAD BEST WATCH MY BACK.
THE FIDDLER HAD MANY FRIENDS, HE SAID, AND I HAD NONE.
YOU HAVE ONE, SER. TWO, ONCE I FIND EGG.
IT IS GOOD TO KNOW THERE ARE SOME TRUE KNIGHTS STILL.
SER CLARENCE CHARLTON!
It was while searching for Egg amongst the crowds that I got my first good look at—
SER TOMMARD HEDDLE, A KNIGHT OF WHITEWALLS, IN SERVICE TO LORD BUTTERWELL!
COME FORTH AND PROVE YOUR VALOR!

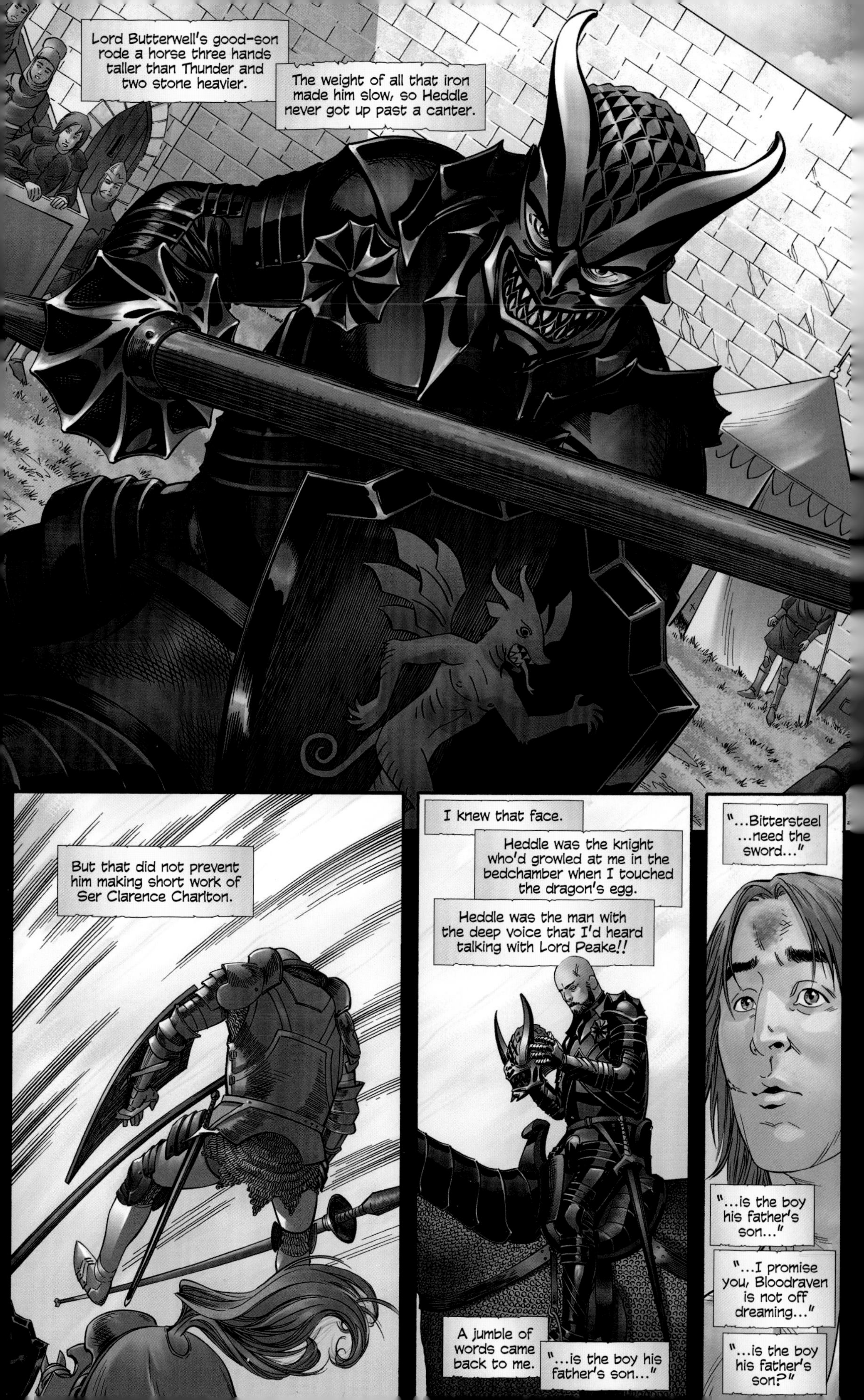
Lord Butterwell's good-son rode a horse three hands taller than Thunder and two stone heavier.
The weight of all that iron made him slow, so Heddle never got up past a canter.
But that did not prevent him making short work of Ser Clarence Charlton.
I knew that face.
Heddle was the knight who'd growled at me in the bedchamber when I touched the dragon's egg.
Heddle was the man with the deep voice that I'd heard talking with Lord Peake!!
A jumble of words came back to me.
"...is the boy his father's son..."
"...Bittersteel ...need the sword..."
"...is the boy his father's son..."
"...I promise you, Bloodraven is not off dreaming..."
"...is the boy his father's son?"

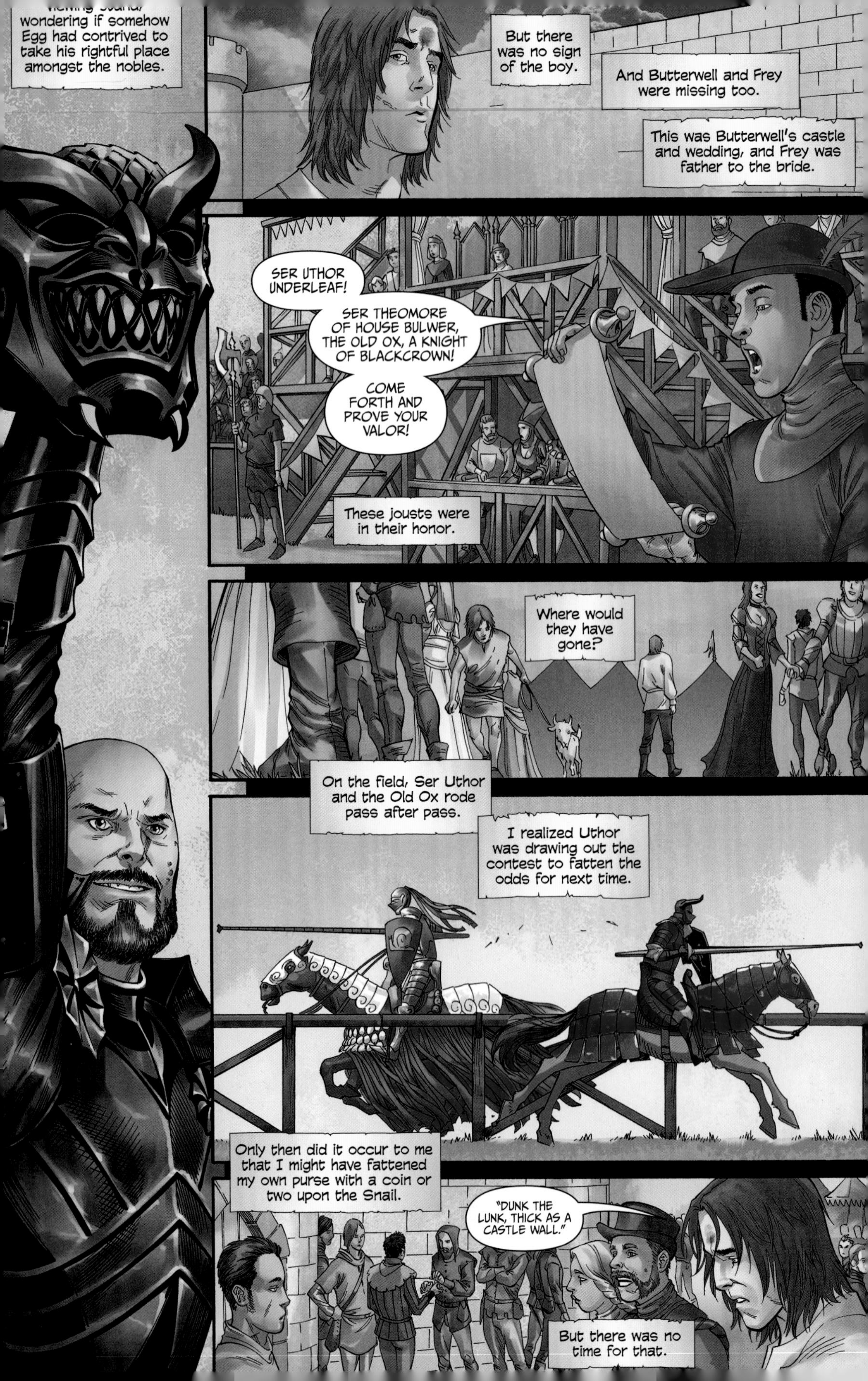
wondering if somehow Egg had contrived to take his rightful place amongst the nobles.
But there was no sign of the boy.
And Butterwell and Frey were missing too.
This was Butterwell's castle and wedding, and Frey was father to the bride.
SER UTHOR UNDERLEAF!
SER THEOMORE OF HOUSE BULWER, THE OLD OX, A KNIGHT OF BLACKCROWN!
COME FORTH AND PROVE YOUR VALOR!
These jousts were in their honor.
Where would they have gone?
On the field, Ser Uthor and the Old Ox rode pass after pass.
I realized Uthor was drawing out the contest to fatten the odds for next time.
Only then did it occur to me that I might have fattened my own purse with a coin or two upon the Snail.
"DUNK THE LUNK, THICK AS A CASTLE WALL."
But there was no time for that.

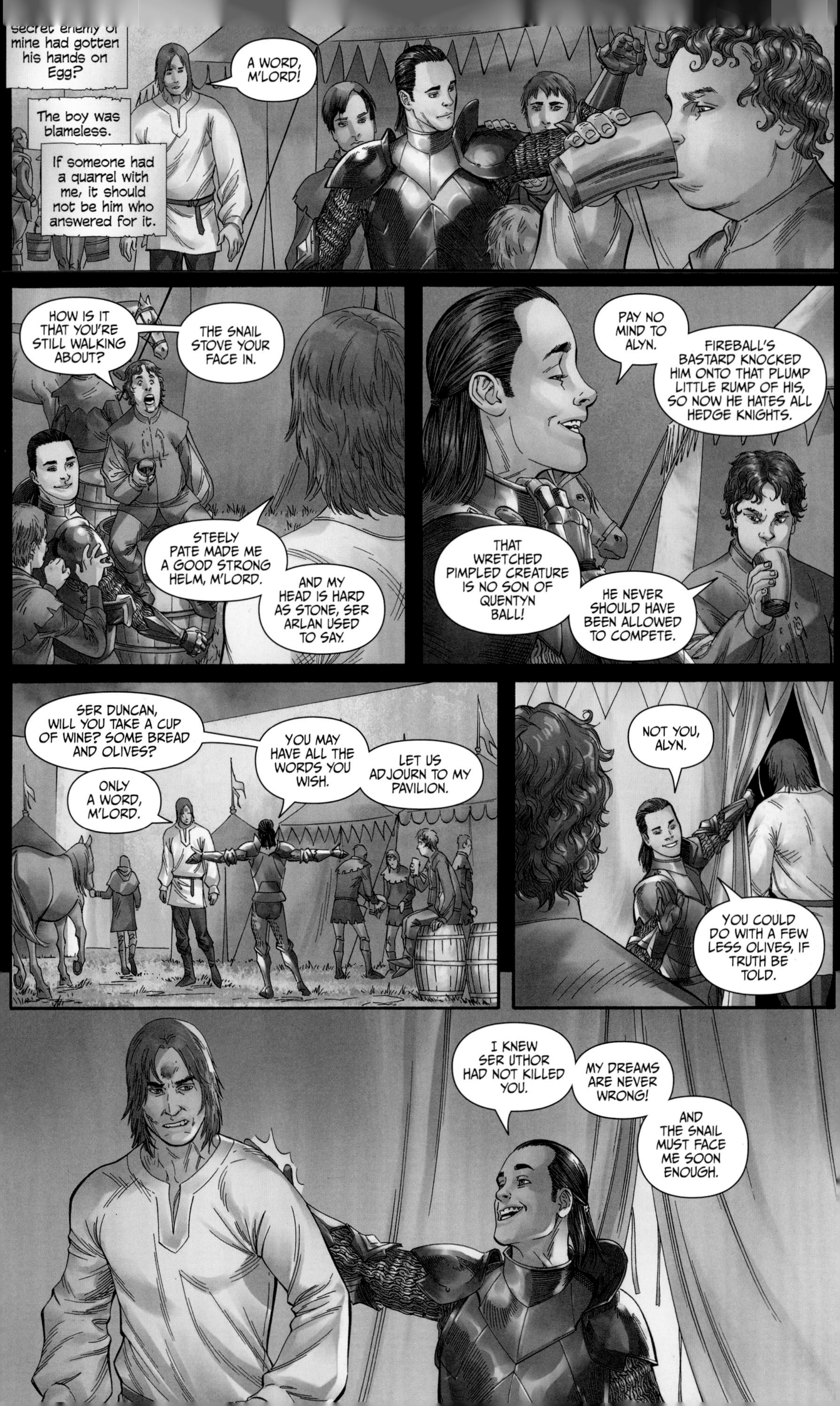
secret enemy of mine had gotten his hands on Egg?
The boy was blameless.
If someone had a quarrel with me, it should not be him who answered for it.
A WORD, M'LORD!
HOW IS IT THAT YOU'RE STILL WALKING ABOUT?
THE SNAIL STOVE YOUR FACE IN.
STEELY PATE MADE ME A GOOD STRONG HELM, M'LORD.
AND MY HEAD IS HARD AS STONE, SER ARLAN USED TO SAY.
PAY NO MIND TO ALYN.
FIREBALL'S BASTARD KNOCKED HIM ONTO THAT PLUMP LITTLE RUMP OF HIS, SO NOW HE HATES ALL HEDGE KNIGHTS.
THAT WRETCHED PIMPLED CREATURE IS NO SON OF QUENTYN BALL!
HE NEVER SHOULD HAVE BEEN ALLOWED TO COMPETE.
SER DUNCAN, WILL YOU TAKE A CUP OF WINE? SOME BREAD AND OLIVES?
ONLY A WORD, M'LORD.
YOU MAY HAVE ALL THE WORDS YOU WISH.
LET US ADJOURN TO MY PAVILION.
NOT YOU, ALYN.
YOU COULD DO WITH A FEW LESS OLIVES, IF TRUTH BE TOLD.
I KNEW SER UTHOR HAD NOT KILLED YOU.
MY DREAMS ARE NEVER WRONG!
AND THE SNAIL MUST FACE ME SOON ENOUGH.

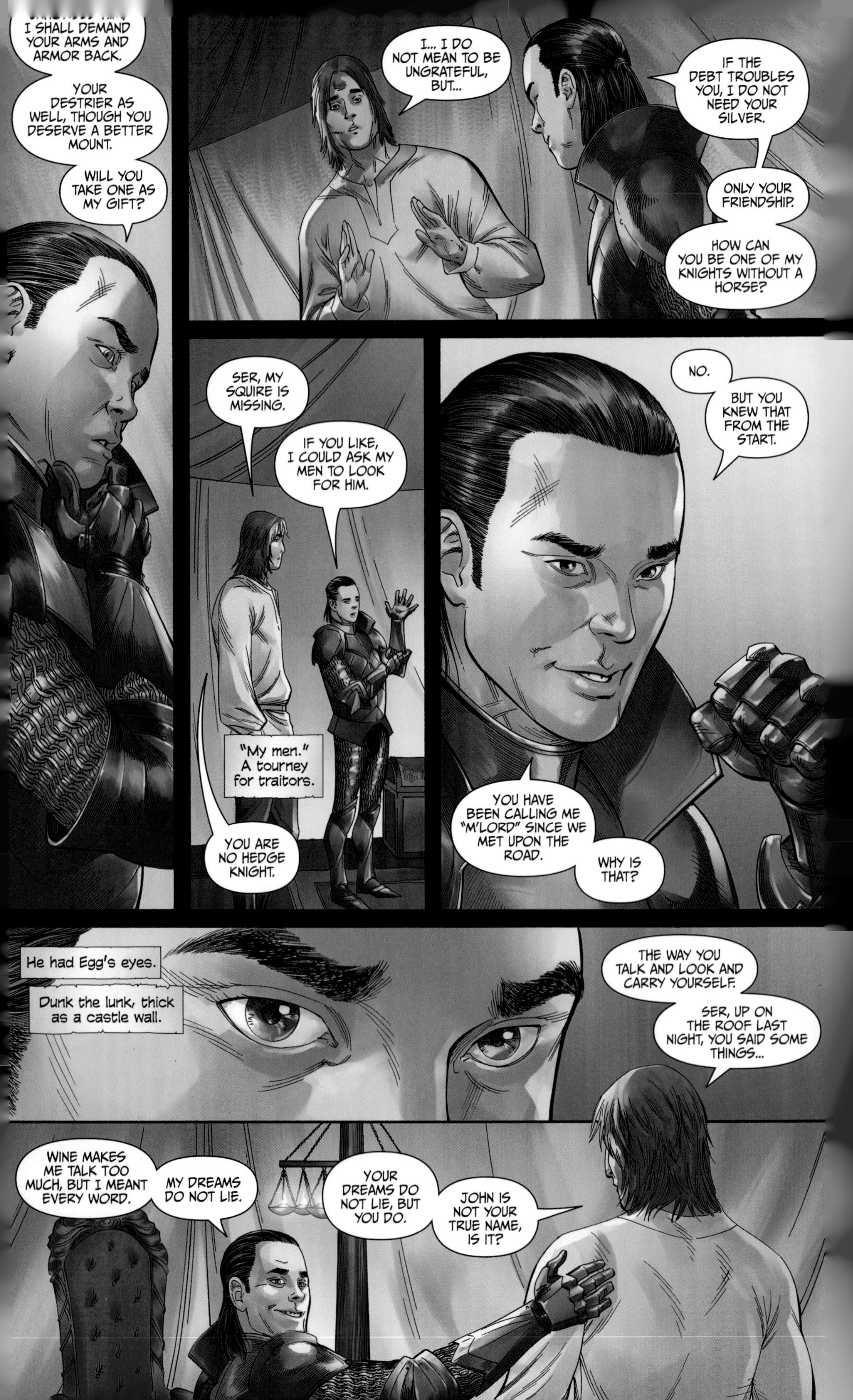
I SHALL DEMAND YOUR ARMS AND ARMOR BACK.
YOUR DESTRIER AS WELL, THOUGH YOU DESERVE A BETTER MOUNT.
WILL YOU TAKE ONE AS MY GIFT?
I... I DO NOT MEAN TO BE UNGRATEFUL, BUT...
IF THE DEBT TROUBLES YOU, I DO NOT NEED YOUR SILVER.
ONLY YOUR FRIENDSHIP.
HOW CAN YOU BE ONE OF MY KNIGHTS WITHOUT A HORSE?
SER, MY SQUIRE IS MISSING.
IF YOU LIKE, I COULD ASK MY MEN TO LOOK FOR HIM.
"My men." A tourney for traitors.
YOU ARE NO HEDGE KNIGHT.
NO.
BUT YOU KNEW THAT FROM THE START.
YOU HAVE BEEN CALLING ME "M'LORD" SINCE WE MET UPON THE ROAD.
WHY IS THAT?
He had Egg's eyes.
Dunk the lunk, thick as a castle wall.
THE WAY YOU TALK AND LOOK AND CARRY YOURSELF.
SER, UP ON THE ROOF LAST NIGHT, YOU SAID SOME THINGS...
WINE MAKES ME TALK TOO MUCH, BUT I MEANT EVERY WORD.
MY DREAMS DO NOT LIE.
YOUR DREAMS DO NOT LIE, BUT YOU DO.
JOHN IS NOT YOUR TRUE NAME, IS IT?

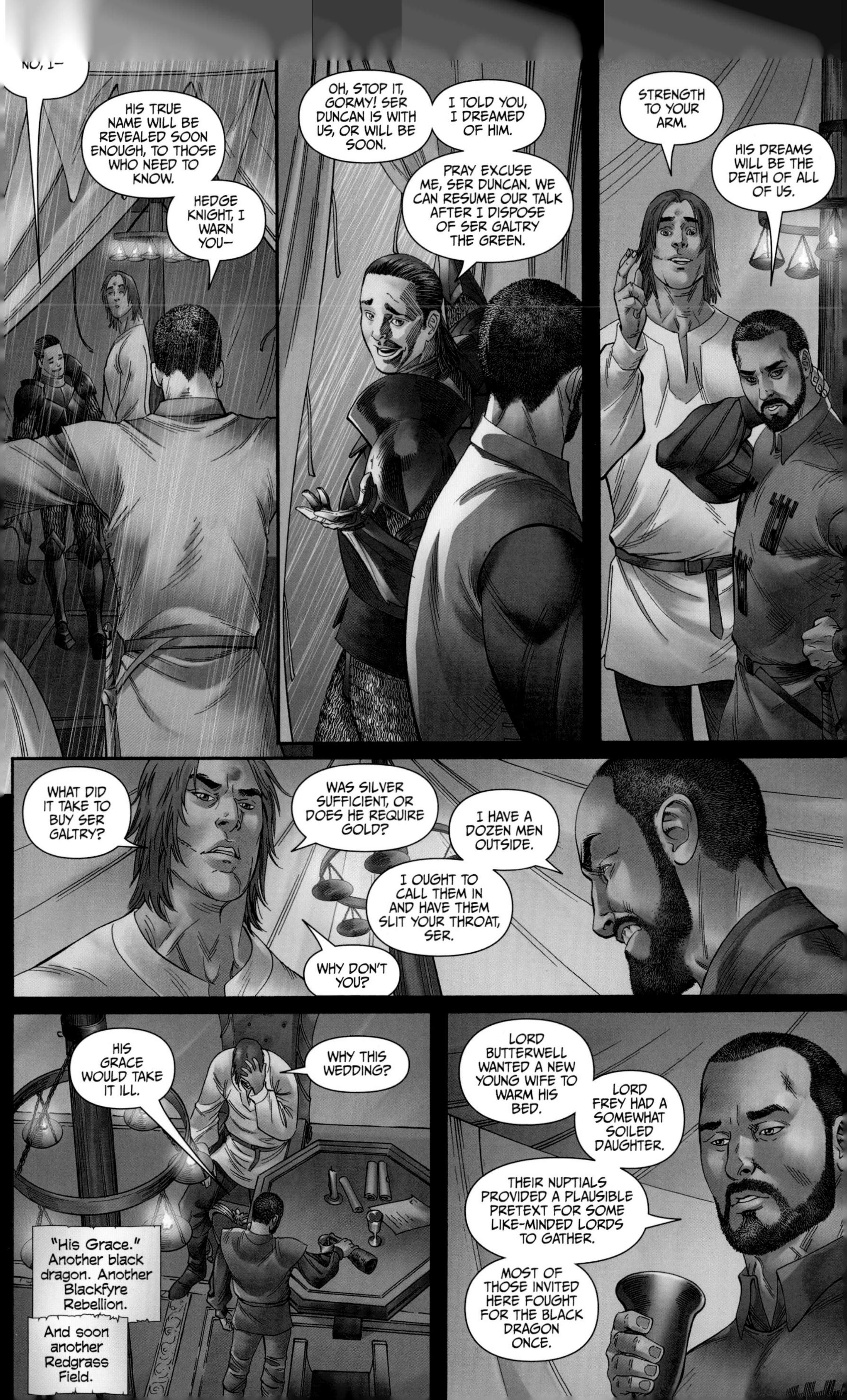
NO, I—
HIS TRUE NAME WILL BE REVEALED SOON ENOUGH, TO THOSE WHO NEED TO KNOW.
HEDGE KNIGHT, I WARN YOU—
OH, STOP IT, GORMY! SER DUNCAN IS WITH US, OR WILL BE SOON.
I TOLD YOU, I DREAMED OF HIM.
PRAY EXCUSE ME, SER DUNCAN. WE CAN RESUME OUR TALK AFTER I DISPOSE OF SER GALTRY THE GREEN.
STRENGTH TO YOUR ARM.
HIS DREAMS WILL BE THE DEATH OF ALL OF US.
WHAT DID IT TAKE TO BUY SER GALTRY?
WAS SILVER SUFFICIENT, OR DOES HE REQUIRE GOLD?
I HAVE A DOZEN MEN OUTSIDE.
I OUGHT TO CALL THEM IN AND HAVE THEM SLIT YOUR THROAT, SER.
WHY DON'T YOU?
HIS GRACE WOULD TAKE IT ILL.
WHY THIS WEDDING?
"His Grace." Another black dragon. Another Blackfyre Rebellion.
And soon another Redgrass Field.
LORD BUTTERWELL WANTED A NEW YOUNG WIFE TO WARM HIS BED.
LORD FREY HAD A SOMEWHAT SOILED DAUGHTER.
THEIR NUPTIALS PROVIDED A PLAUSIBLE PRETEXT FOR SOME LIKE-MINDED LORDS TO GATHER.
MOST OF THOSE INVITED HERE FOUGHT FOR THE BLACK DRAGON ONCE.

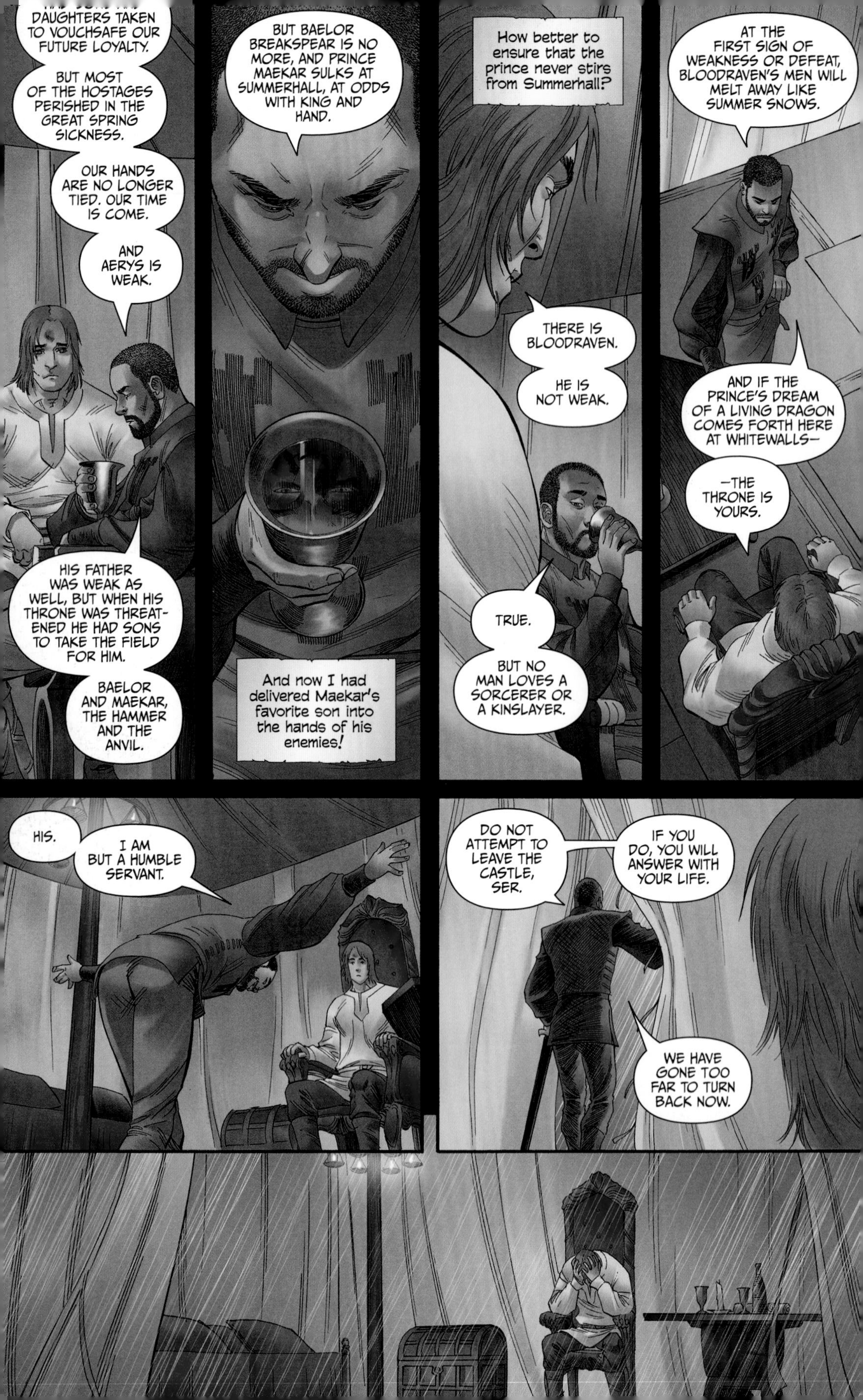
DAUGHTERS TAKEN TO VOUCHSAFE OUR FUTURE LOYALTY.
BUT MOST OF THE HOSTAGES PERISHED IN THE GREAT SPRING SICKNESS.
OUR HANDS ARE NO LONGER TIED. OUR TIME IS COME.
AND AERYS IS WEAK.
HIS FATHER WAS WEAK AS WELL, BUT WHEN HIS THRONE WAS THREAT-ENED HE HAD SONS TO TAKE THE FIELD FOR HIM.
BAELOR AND MAEKAR, THE HAMMER AND THE ANVIL.
BUT BAELOR BREAKSPEAR IS NO MORE, AND PRINCE MAEKAR SULKS AT SUMMERHALL, AT ODDS WITH KING AND HAND.
And now I had delivered Maekar's favorite son into the hands of his enemies!
How better to ensure that the prince never stirs from Summerhall?
THERE IS BLOODRAVEN.
HE IS NOT WEAK.
TRUE.
BUT NO MAN LOVES A SORCERER OR A KINSLAYER.
AT THE FIRST SIGN OF WEAKNESS OR DEFEAT, BLOODRAVEN'S MEN WILL MELT AWAY LIKE SUMMER SNOWS.
AND IF THE PRINCE'S DREAM OF A LIVING DRAGON COMES FORTH HERE AT WHITEWALLS—
—THE THRONE IS YOURS.
HIS.
I AM BUT A HUMBLE SERVANT.
DO NOT ATTEMPT TO LEAVE THE CASTLE, SER.
IF YOU DO, YOU WILL ANSWER WITH YOUR LIFE.
WE HAVE GONE TOO FAR TO TURN BACK NOW.

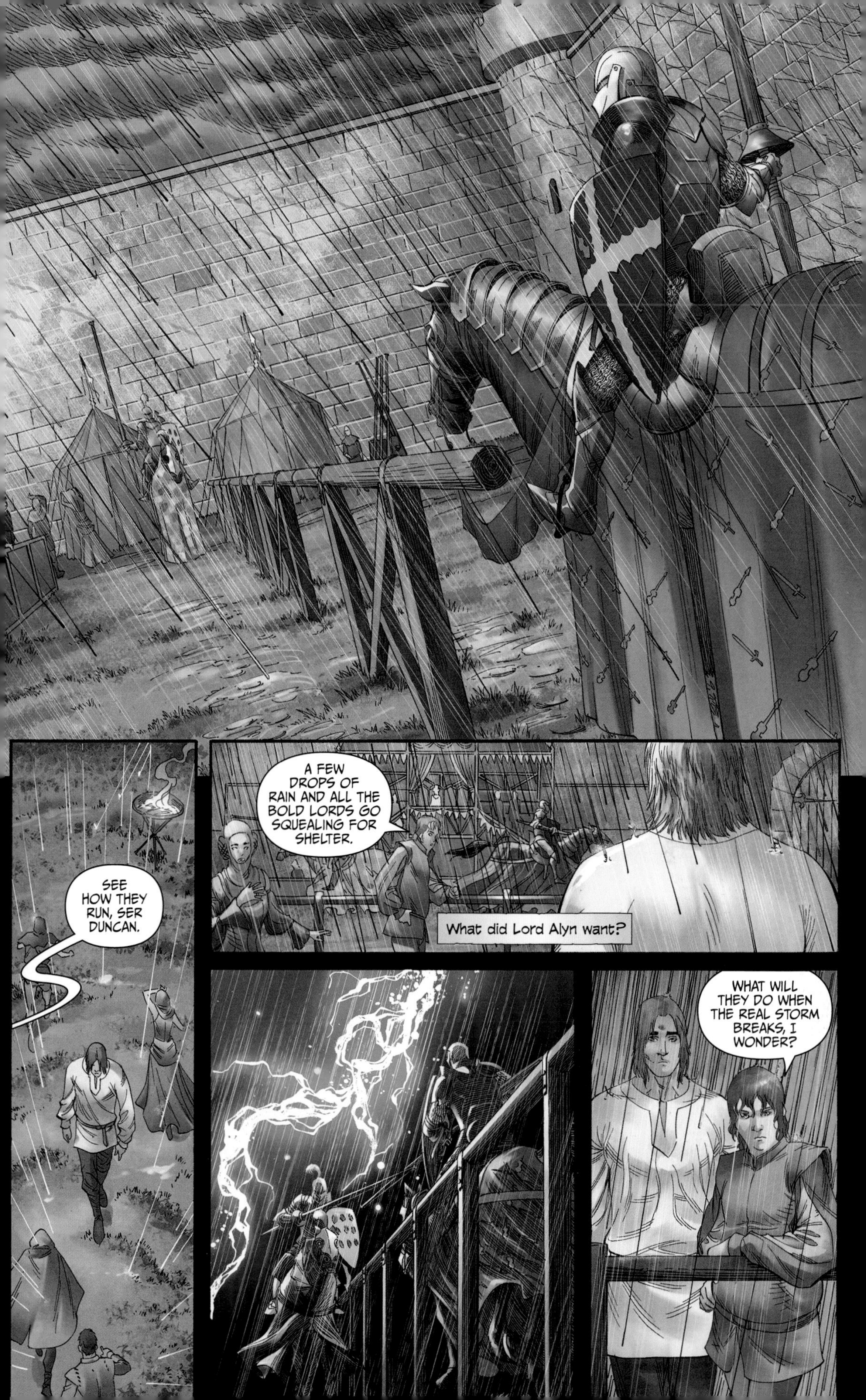
SEE HOW THEY RUN, SER DUNCAN.
A FEW DROPS OF RAIN AND ALL THE BOLD LORDS GO SQUEALING FOR SHELTER.
What did Lord Alyn want?
WHAT WILL THEY DO WHEN THE REAL STORM BREAKS, I WONDER?

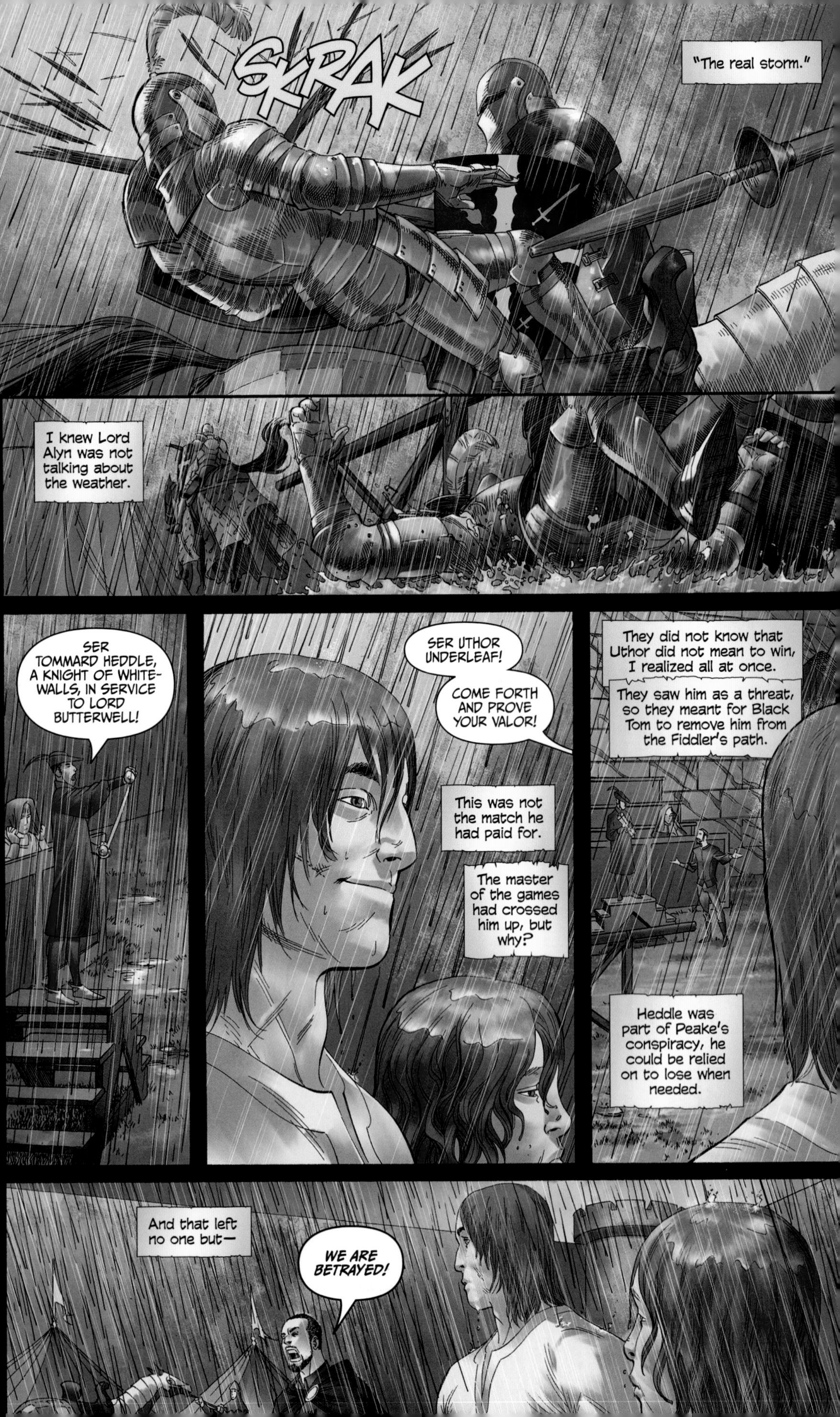
SKRAK
"The real storm."
I knew Lord Alyn was not talking about the weather.
SER TOMMARD HEDDLE, A KNIGHT OF WHITE-WALLS, IN SERVICE TO LORD BUTTERWELL!
SER UTHOR UNDERLEAF!
COME FORTH AND PROVE YOUR VALOR!
This was not the match he had paid for.
The master of the games had crossed him up, but why?
They did not know that Uthor did not mean to win, I realized all at once.
They saw him as a threat, so they meant for Black Tom to remove him from the Fiddler's path.
Heddle was part of Peake's conspiracy, he could be relied on to lose when needed.
And that left no one but—
WE ARE BETRAYED!

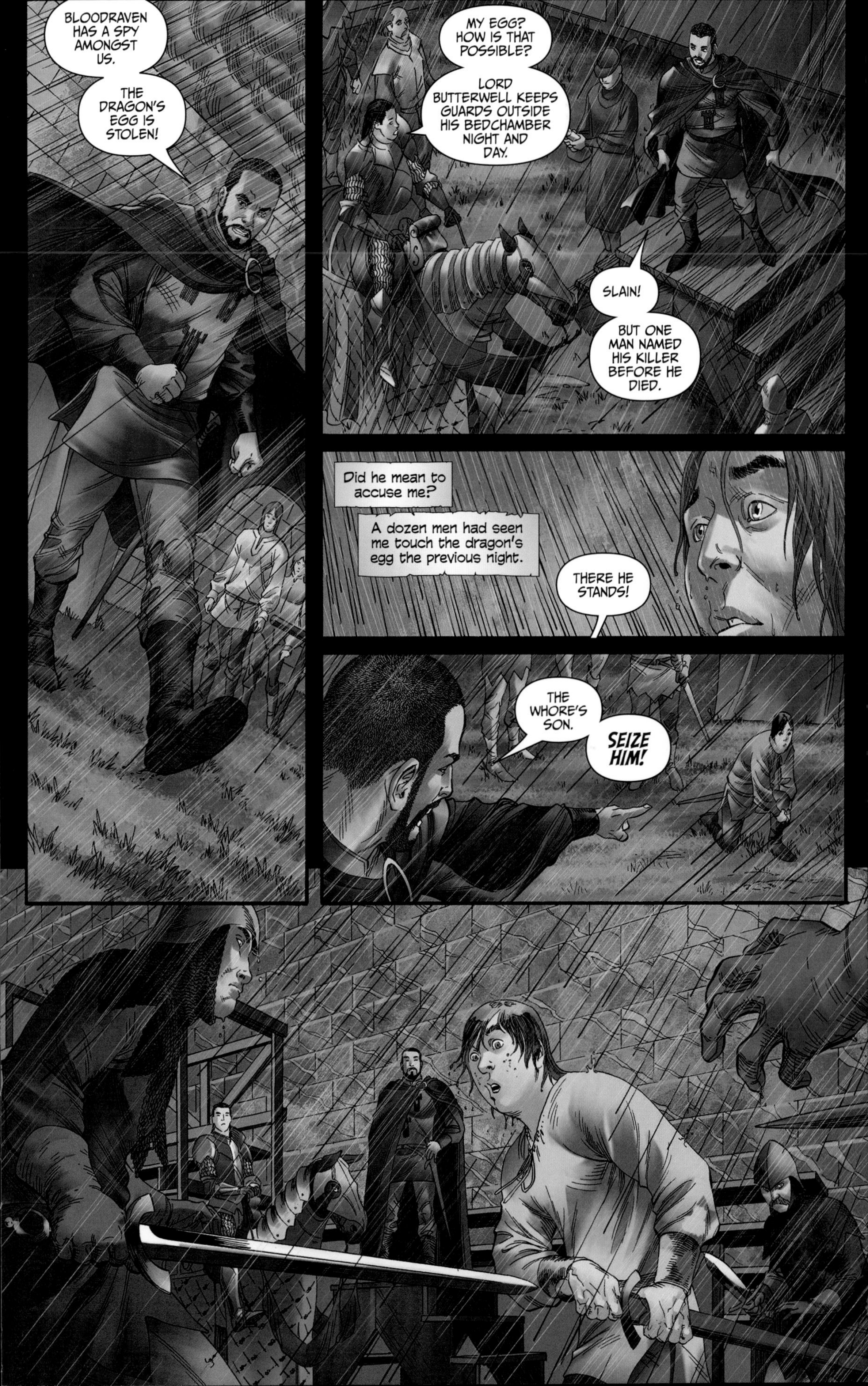
BLOODRAVEN HAS A SPY AMONGST US.
THE DRAGON'S EGG IS STOLEN!
MY EGG? HOW IS THAT POSSIBLE?
LORD BUTTERWELL KEEPS GUARDS OUTSIDE HIS BEDCHAMBER NIGHT AND DAY.
SLAIN!
BUT ONE MAN NAMED HIS KILLER BEFORE HE DIED.
Did he mean to accuse me?
A dozen men had seen me touch the dragon's egg the previous night.
THERE HE STANDS!
THE WHORE'S SON.
SEIZE HIM!

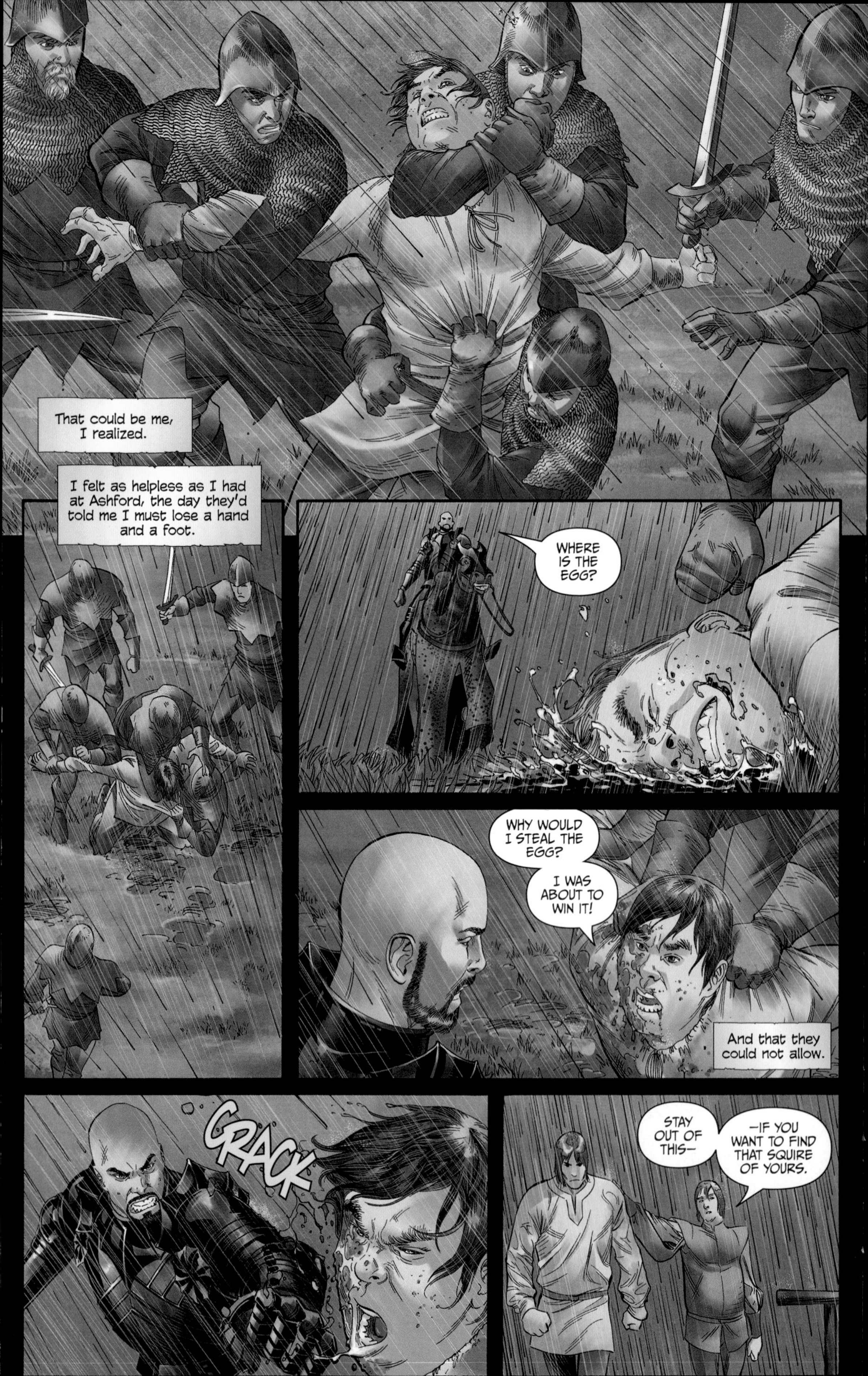
That could be me, I realized.
I felt as helpless as I had at Ashford, the day they'd told me I must lose a hand and a foot.
WHERE IS THE EGG?
WHY WOULD I STEAL THE EGG?
I WAS ABOUT TO WIN IT!
And that they could not allow.
CRACK
STAY OUT OF THIS—
—IF YOU WANT TO FIND THAT SQUIRE OF YOURS.

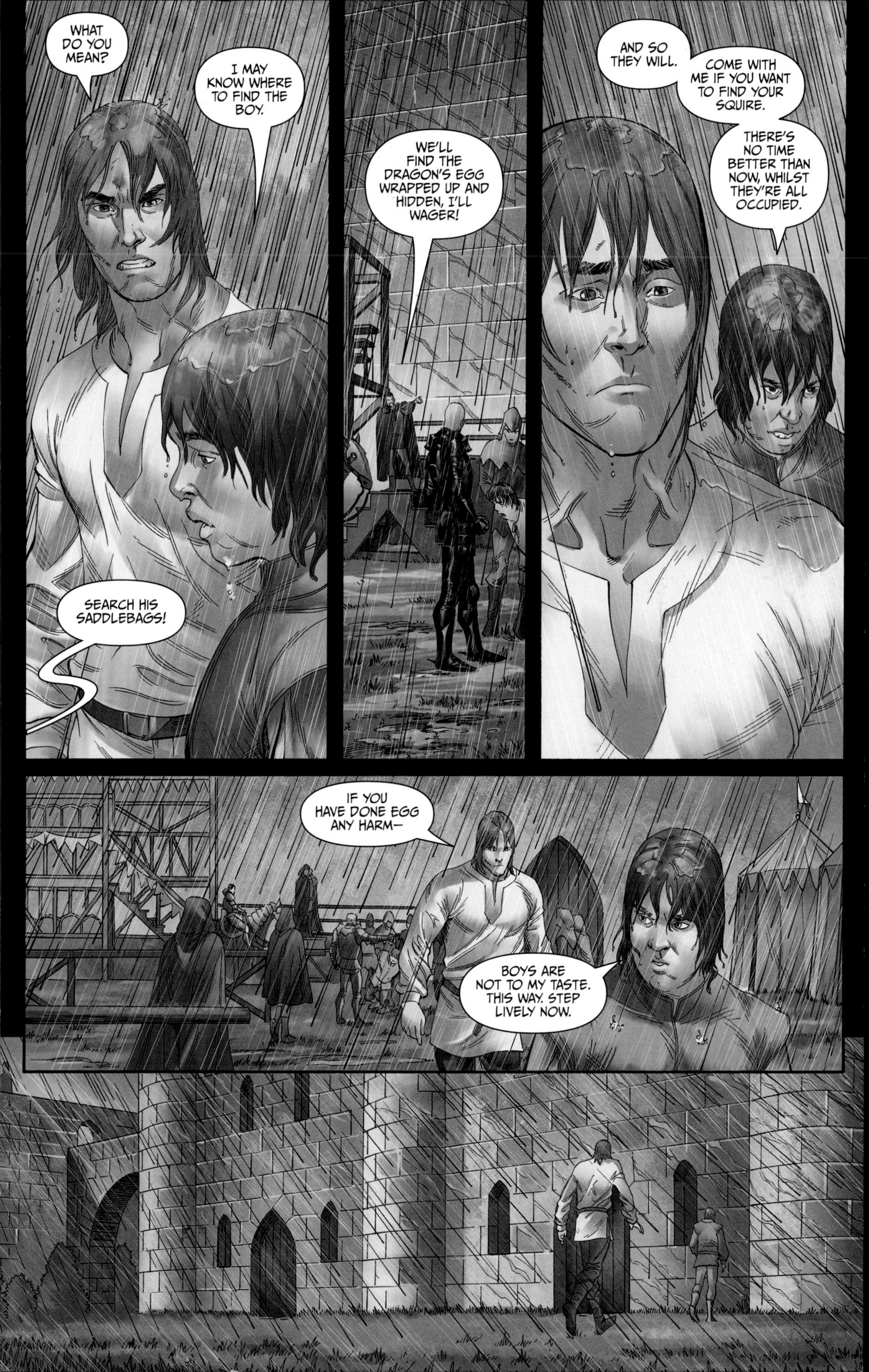
WHAT DO YOU MEAN?
I MAY KNOW WHERE TO FIND THE BOY.
SEARCH HIS SADDLEBAGS!
WE'LL FIND THE DRAGON'S EGG WRAPPED UP AND HIDDEN, I'LL WAGER!
AND SO THEY WILL.
COME WITH ME IF YOU WANT TO FIND YOUR SQUIRE.
THERE'S NO TIME BETTER THAN NOW, WHILST THEY'RE ALL OCCUPIED.
IF YOU HAVE DONE EGG ANY HARM—
BOYS ARE NOT TO MY TASTE. THIS WAY. STEP LIVELY NOW.

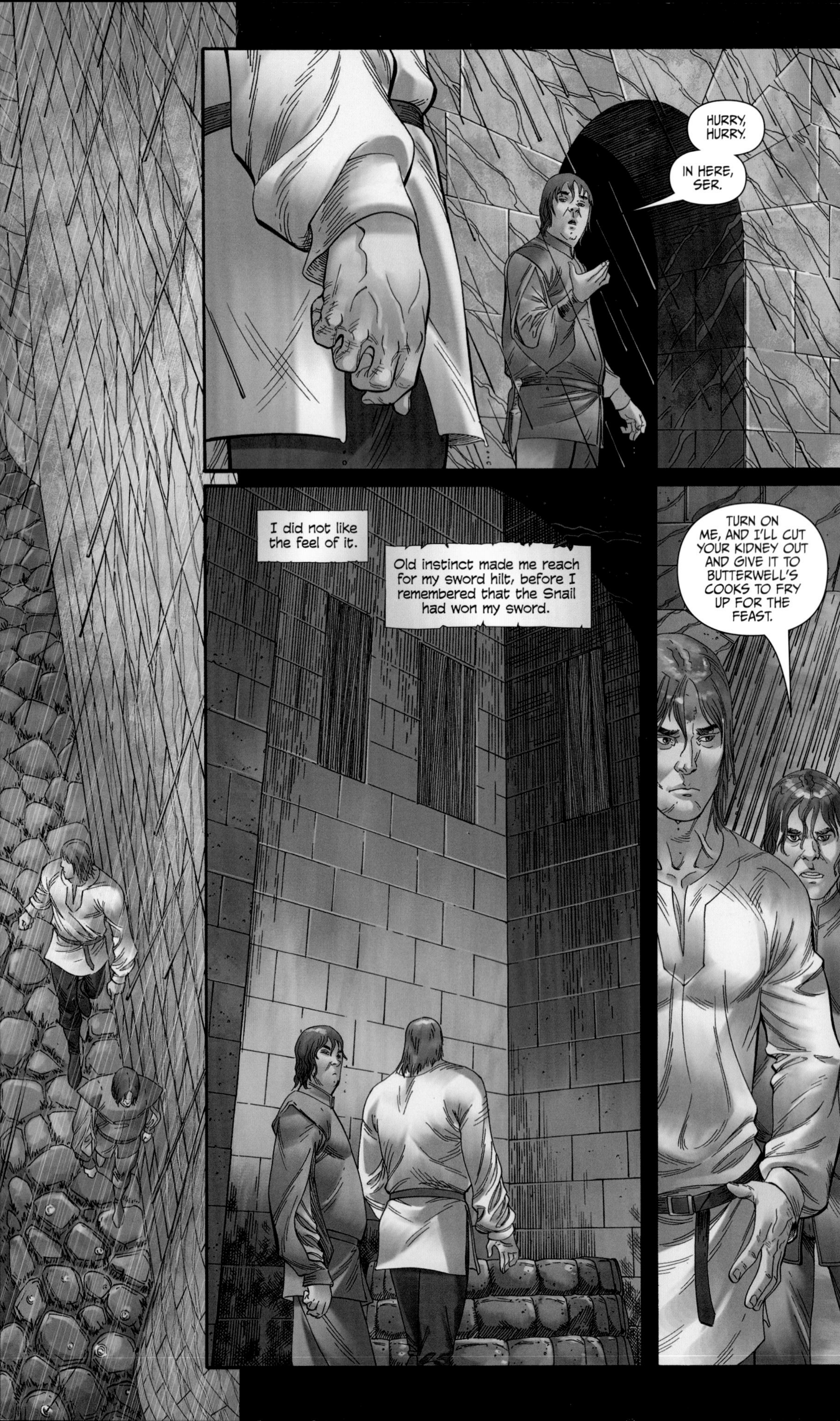
HURRY, HURRY.
IN HERE, SER.
I did not like the feel of it.
Old instinct made me reach for my sword hilt, before I remembered that the Snail had won my sword.
TURN ON ME, AND I'LL CUT YOUR KIDNEY OUT AND GIVE IT TO BUTTERWELL'S COOKS TO FRY UP FOR THE FEAST.

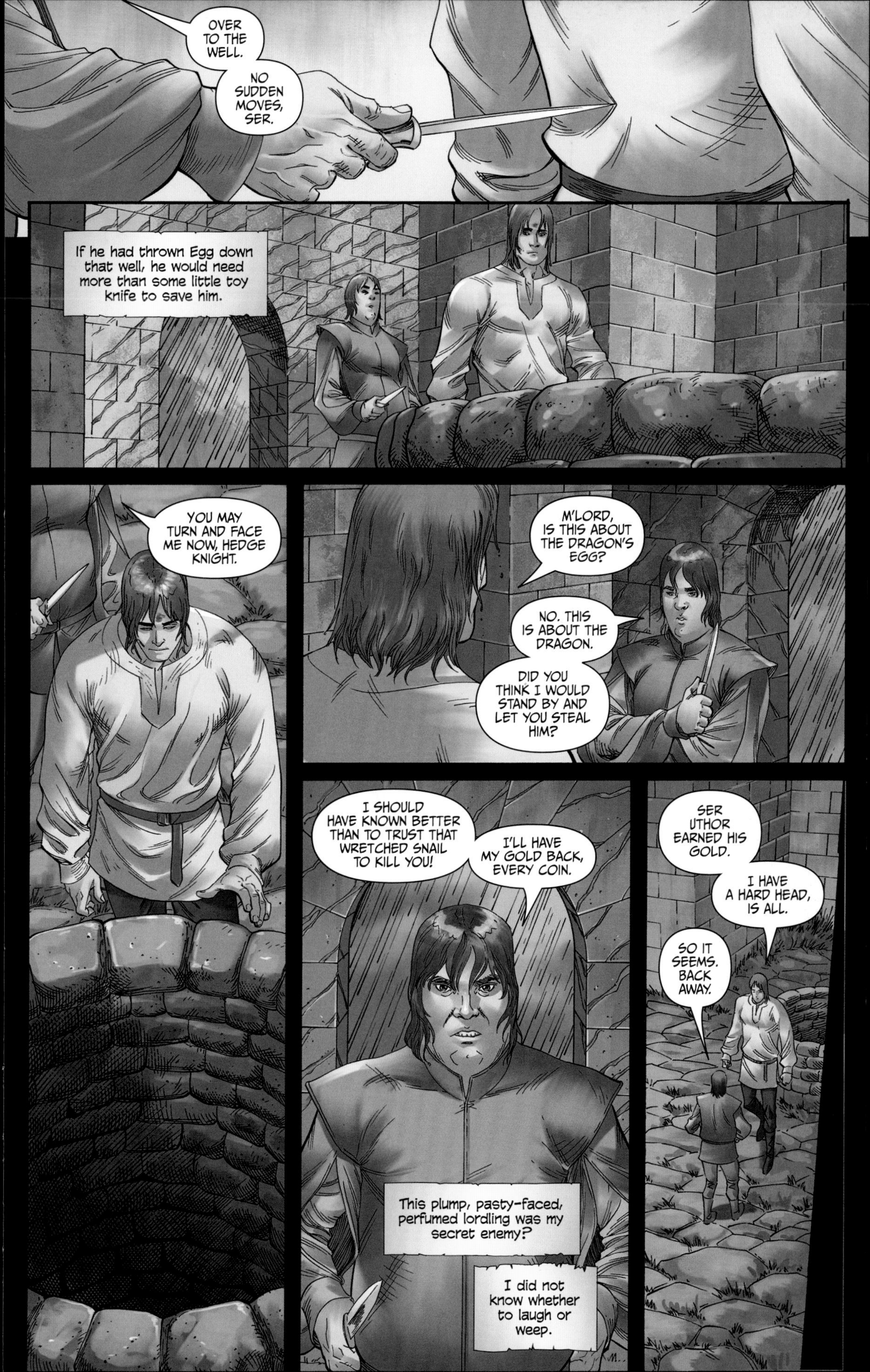
OVER TO THE WELL.
NO SUDDEN MOVES, SER.
If he had thrown Egg down that well, he would need more than some little toy knife to save him.
YOU MAY TURN AND FACE ME NOW, HEDGE KNIGHT.
M'LORD, IS THIS ABOUT THE DRAGON'S EGG?
NO. THIS IS ABOUT THE DRAGON.
DID YOU THINK I WOULD STAND BY AND LET YOU STEAL HIM?
I SHOULD HAVE KNOWN BETTER THAN TO TRUST THAT WRETCHED SNAIL TO KILL YOU!
I'LL HAVE MY GOLD BACK, EVERY COIN.
This plump, pasty-faced, perfumed lordling was my secret enemy?
I did not know whether to laugh or weep.
SER UTHOR EARNED HIS GOLD.
I HAVE A HARD HEAD, IS ALL.
SO IT SEEMS. BACK AWAY.

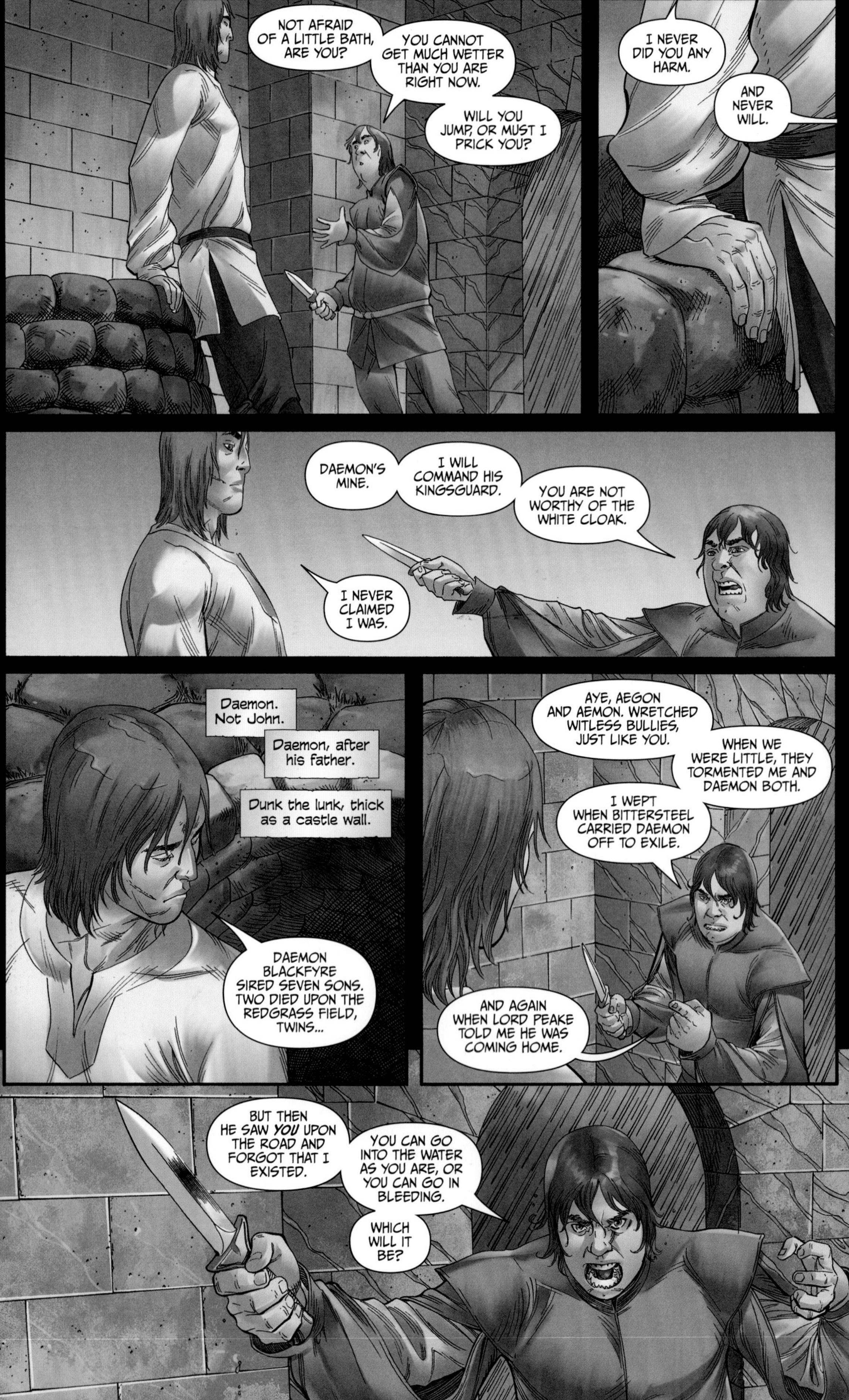

NOT AFRAID OF A LITTLE BATH, ARE YOU?
YOU CANNOT GET MUCH WETTER THAN YOU ARE RIGHT NOW.
WILL YOU JUMP, OR MUST I PRICK YOU?
I NEVER DID YOU ANY HARM.
AND NEVER WILL.
DAEMON'S MINE.
I WILL COMMAND HIS KINGSGUARD.
YOU ARE NOT WORTHY OF THE WHITE CLOAK.
I NEVER CLAIMED I WAS.
Daemon. Not John.
Daemon, after his father.
Dunk the lunk, thick as a castle wall.
DAEMON BLACKFYRE SIRED SEVEN SONS. TWO DIED UPON THE REDGRASS FIELD, TWINS...
AYE, AEGON AND AEMON. WRETCHED WITLESS BULLIES, JUST LIKE YOU.
WHEN WE WERE LITTLE, THEY TORMENTED ME AND DAEMON BOTH.
I WEPT WHEN BITTERSTEEL CARRIED DAEMON OFF TO EXILE.
AND AGAIN WHEN LORD PEAKE TOLD ME HE WAS COMING HOME.
BUT THEN HE SAW *YOU* UPON THE ROAD AND FORGOT THAT I EXISTED.
YOU CAN GO INTO THE WATER AS YOU ARE, OR YOU CAN GO IN BLEEDING.
WHICH WILL IT BE?

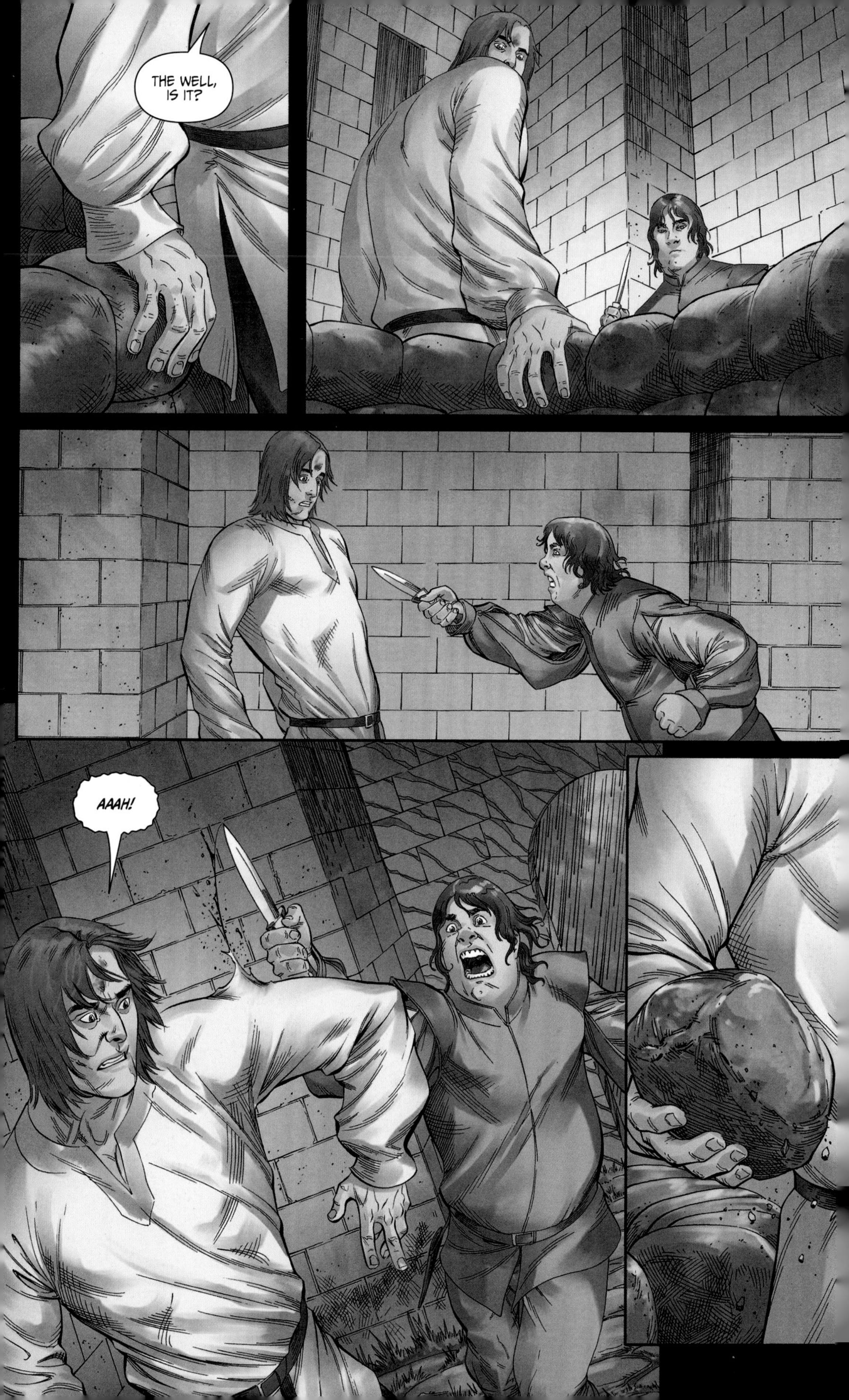
THE WELL, IS IT?
AAAH!

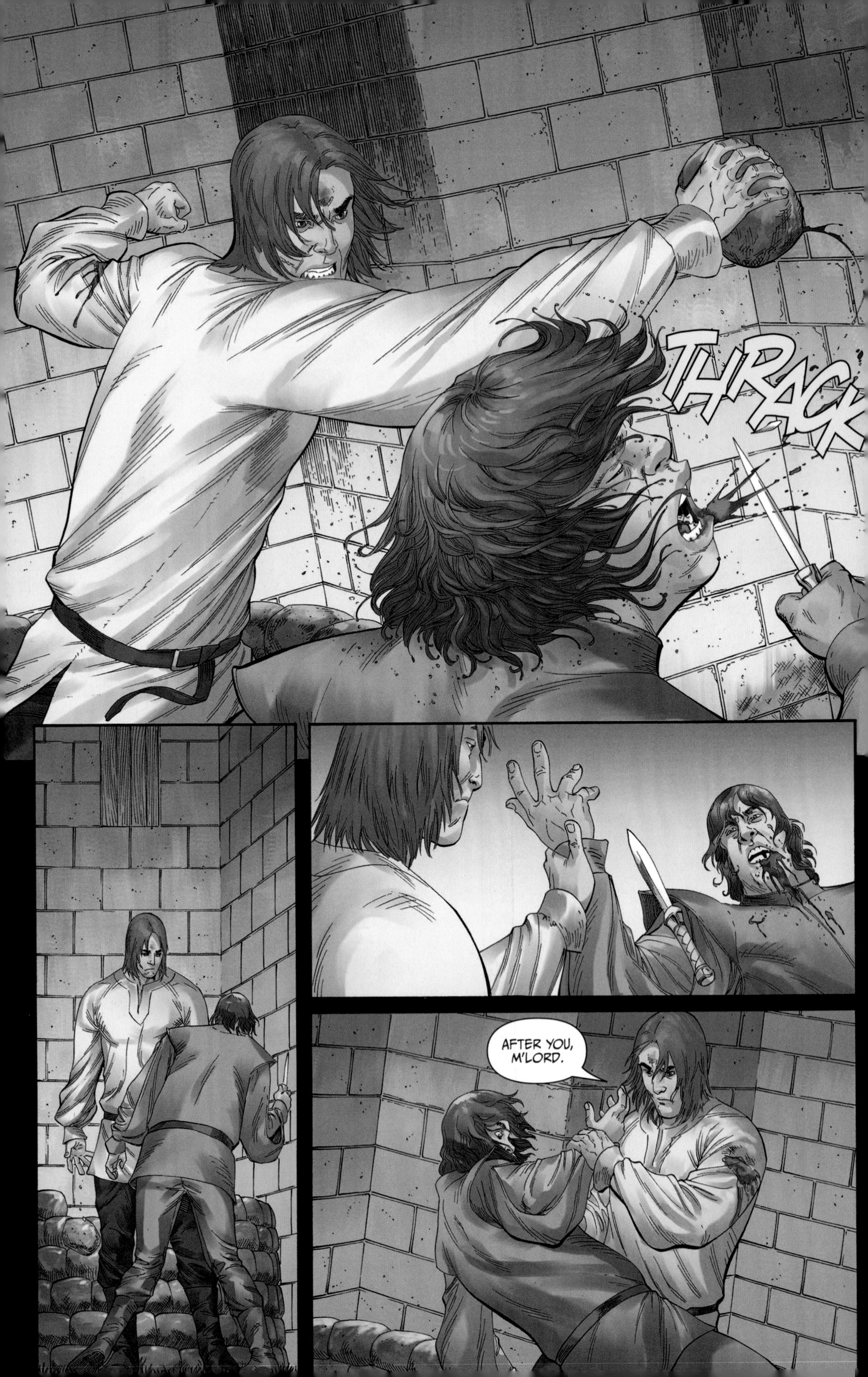
THRACK
AFTER YOU, M'LORD.

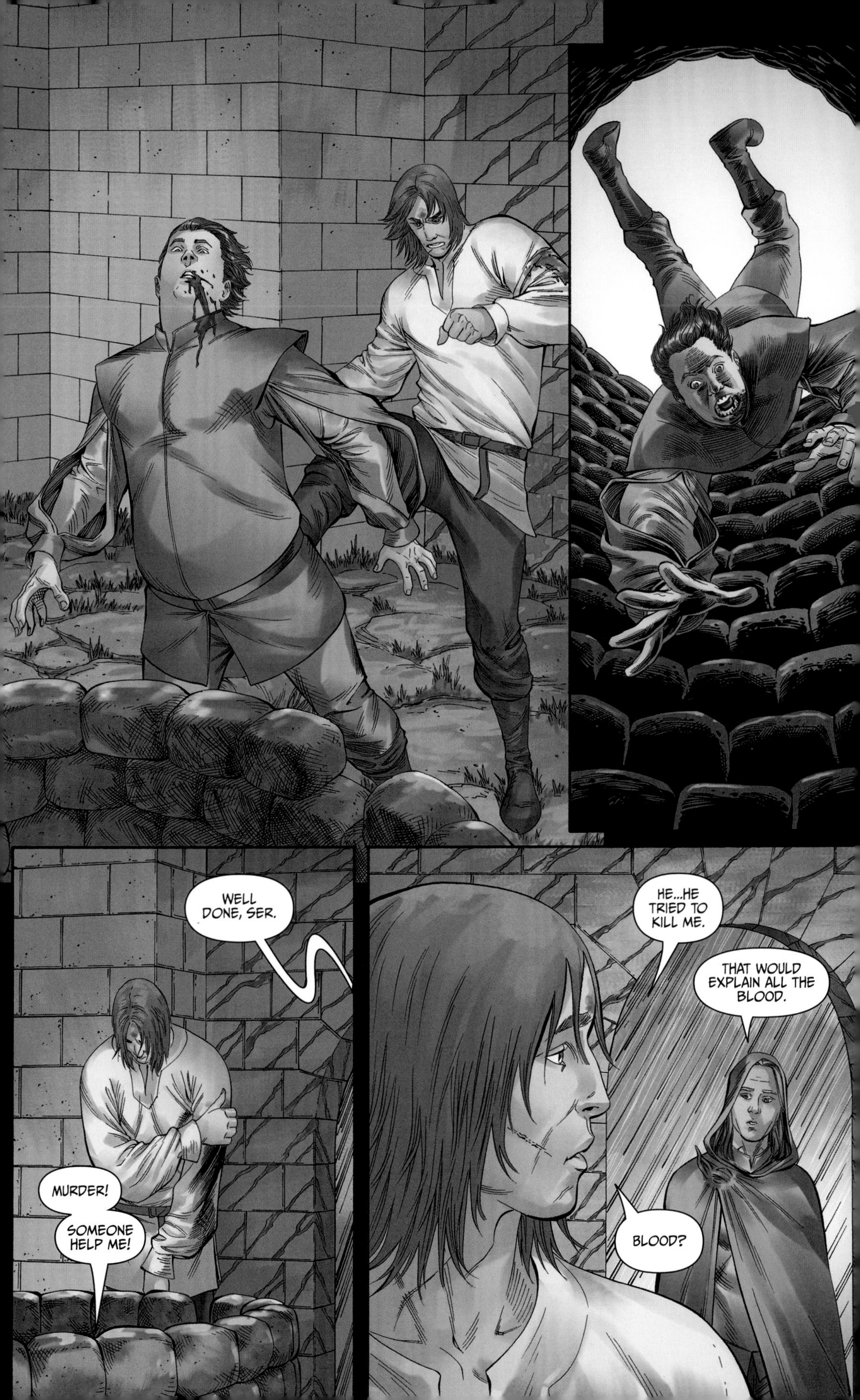
WELL DONE, SER.
MURDER!
SOMEONE HELP ME!
HE...HE TRIED TO KILL ME.
THAT WOULD EXPLAIN ALL THE BLOOD.
BLOOD?

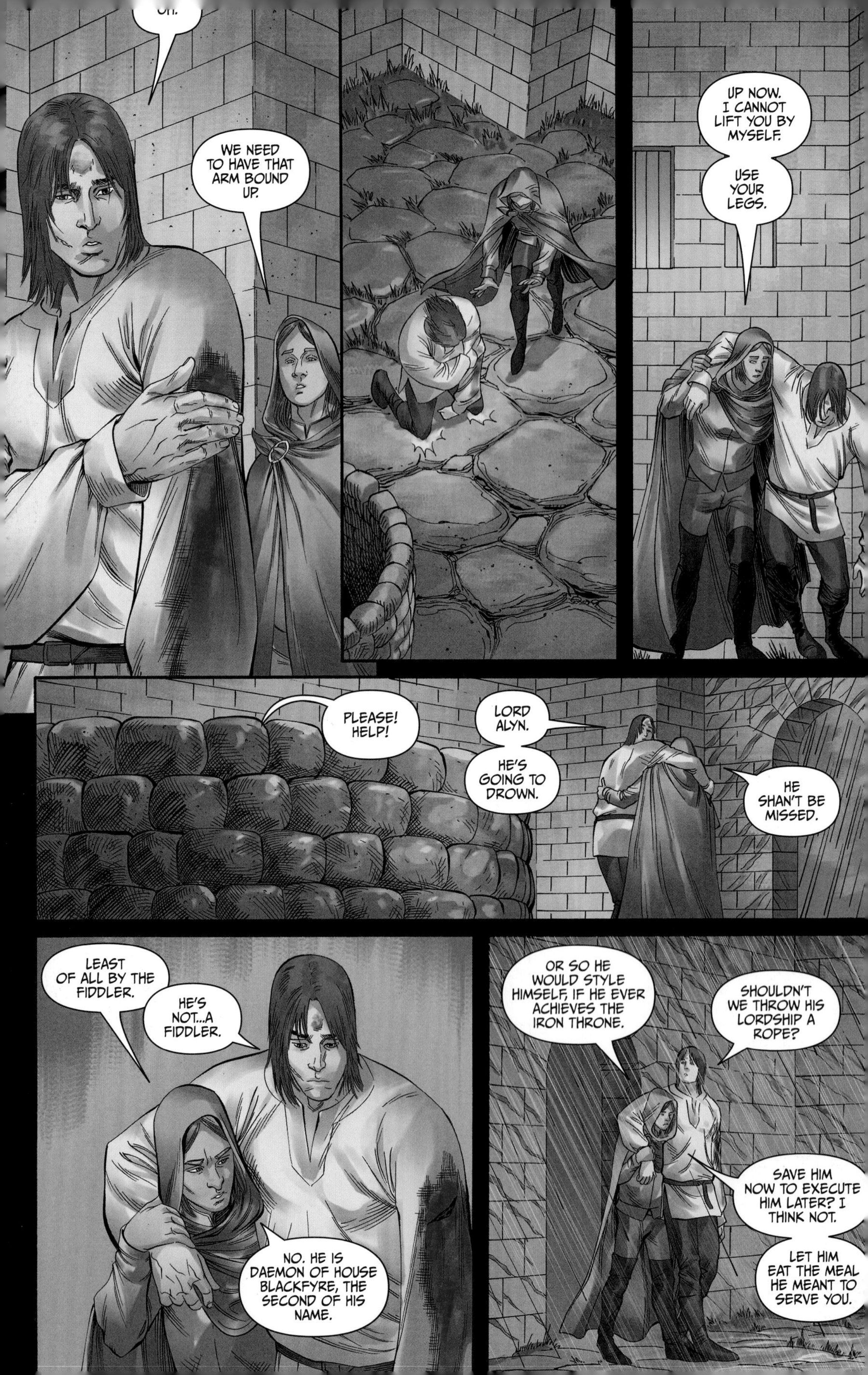
UH.
WE NEED TO HAVE THAT ARM BOUND UP.
UP NOW. I CANNOT LIFT YOU BY MYSELF.
USE YOUR LEGS.
PLEASE! HELP!
LORD ALYN.
HE'S GOING TO DROWN.
HE SHAN'T BE MISSED.
LEAST OF ALL BY THE FIDDLER.
HE'S NOT...A FIDDLER.
NO. HE IS DAEMON OF HOUSE BLACKFYRE, THE SECOND OF HIS NAME.
OR SO HE WOULD STYLE HIMSELF, IF HE EVER ACHIEVES THE IRON THRONE.
SHOULDN'T WE THROW HIS LORDSHIP A ROPE?
SAVE HIM NOW TO EXECUTE HIM LATER? I THINK NOT.
LET HIM EAT THE MEAL HE MEANT TO SERVE YOU.

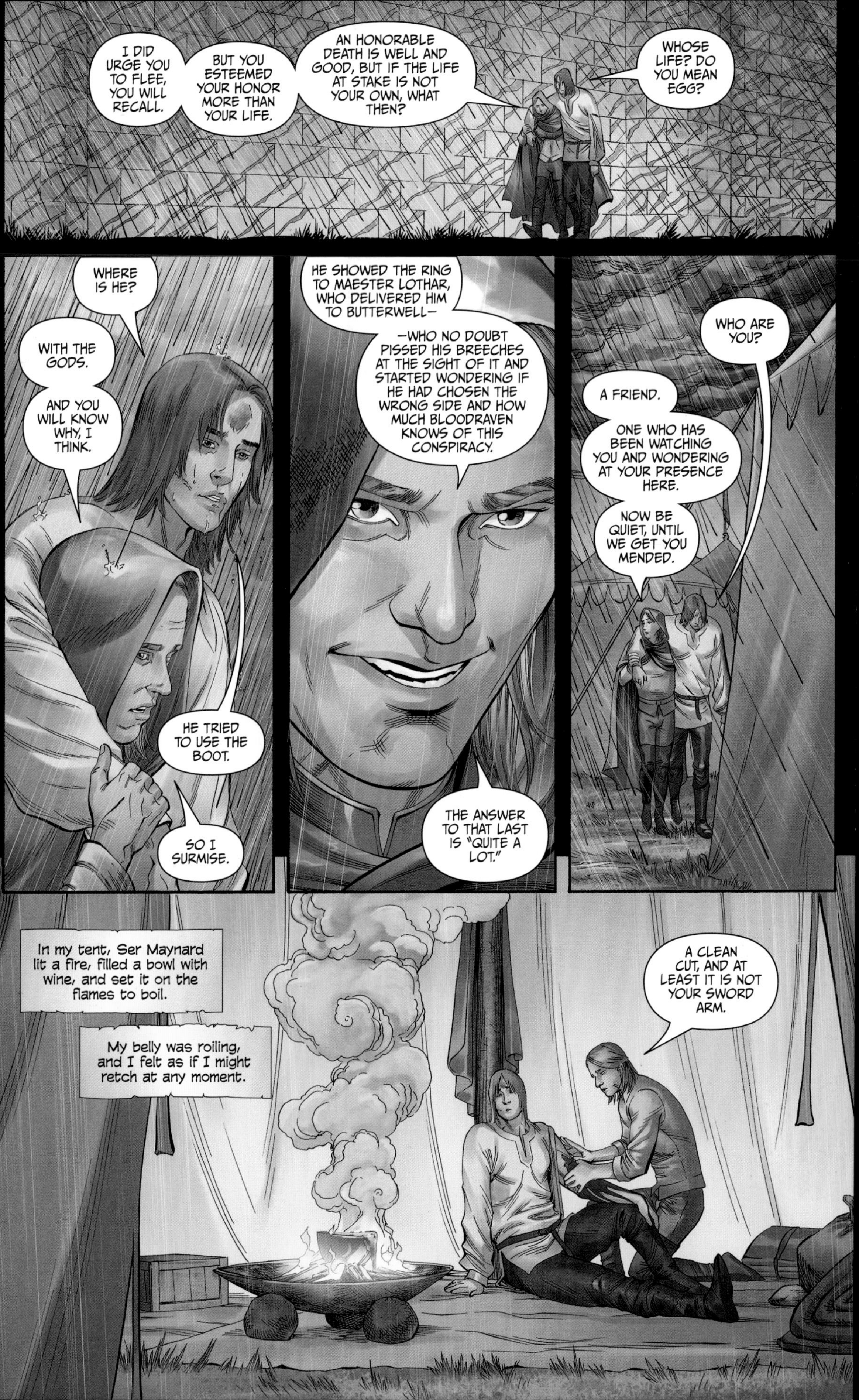
I DID URGE YOU TO FLEE, YOU WILL RECALL.
BUT YOU ESTEEMED YOUR HONOR MORE THAN YOUR LIFE.
AN HONORABLE DEATH IS WELL AND GOOD, BUT IF THE LIFE AT STAKE IS NOT YOUR OWN, WHAT THEN?
WHOSE LIFE? DO YOU MEAN EGG?
WHERE IS HE?
WITH THE GODS.
AND YOU WILL KNOW WHY, I THINK.
HE TRIED TO USE THE BOOT.
SO I SURMISE.
HE SHOWED THE RING TO MAESTER LOTHAR, WHO DELIVERED HIM TO BUTTERWELL—
—WHO NO DOUBT PISSED HIS BREECHES AT THE SIGHT OF IT AND STARTED WONDERING IF HE HAD CHOSEN THE WRONG SIDE AND HOW MUCH BLOODRAVEN KNOWS OF THIS CONSPIRACY.
THE ANSWER TO THAT LAST IS "QUITE A LOT."
WHO ARE YOU?
A FRIEND.
ONE WHO HAS BEEN WATCHING YOU AND WONDERING AT YOUR PRESENCE HERE.
NOW BE QUIET, UNTIL WE GET YOU MENDED.
In my tent, Ser Maynard lit a fire, filled a bowl with wine, and set it on the flames to boil.
My belly was roiling, and I felt as if I might retch at any moment.
A CLEAN CUT, AND AT LEAST IT IS NOT YOUR SWORD ARM.

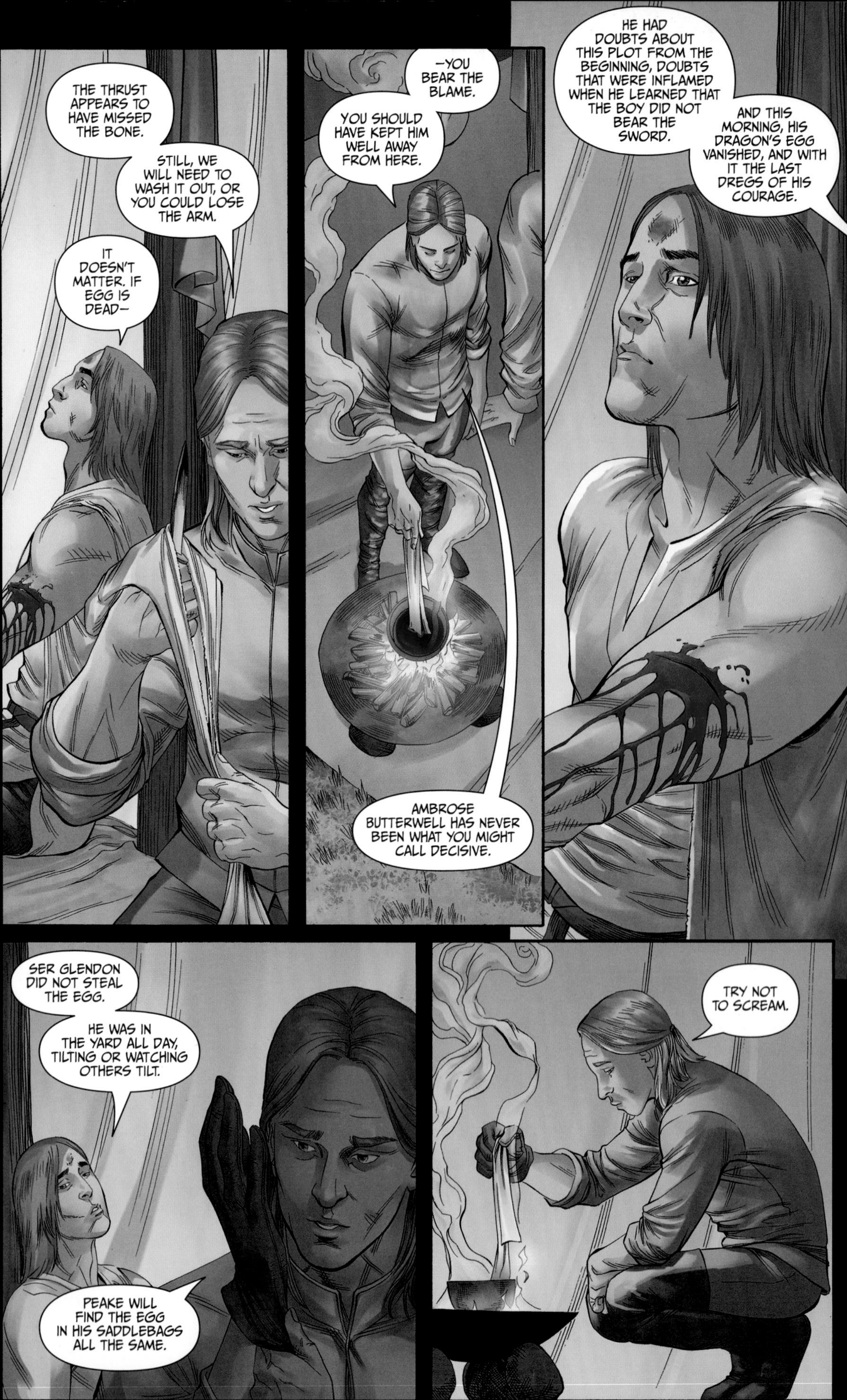
THE THRUST APPEARS TO HAVE MISSED THE BONE.
STILL, WE WILL NEED TO WASH IT OUT, OR YOU COULD LOSE THE ARM.
IT DOESN'T MATTER. IF EGG IS DEAD—
—YOU BEAR THE BLAME.
YOU SHOULD HAVE KEPT HIM WELL AWAY FROM HERE.
AMBROSE BUTTERWELL HAS NEVER BEEN WHAT YOU MIGHT CALL DECISIVE.
HE HAD DOUBTS ABOUT THIS PLOT FROM THE BEGINNING, DOUBTS THAT WERE INFLAMED WHEN HE LEARNED THAT THE BOY DID NOT BEAR THE SWORD.
AND THIS MORNING, HIS DRAGON'S EGG VANISHED, AND WITH IT THE LAST DREGS OF HIS COURAGE.
SER GLENDON DID NOT STEAL THE EGG.
HE WAS IN THE YARD ALL DAY, TILTING OR WATCHING OTHERS TILT.
PEAKE WILL FIND THE EGG IN HIS SADDLEBAGS ALL THE SAME.
TRY NOT TO SCREAM.

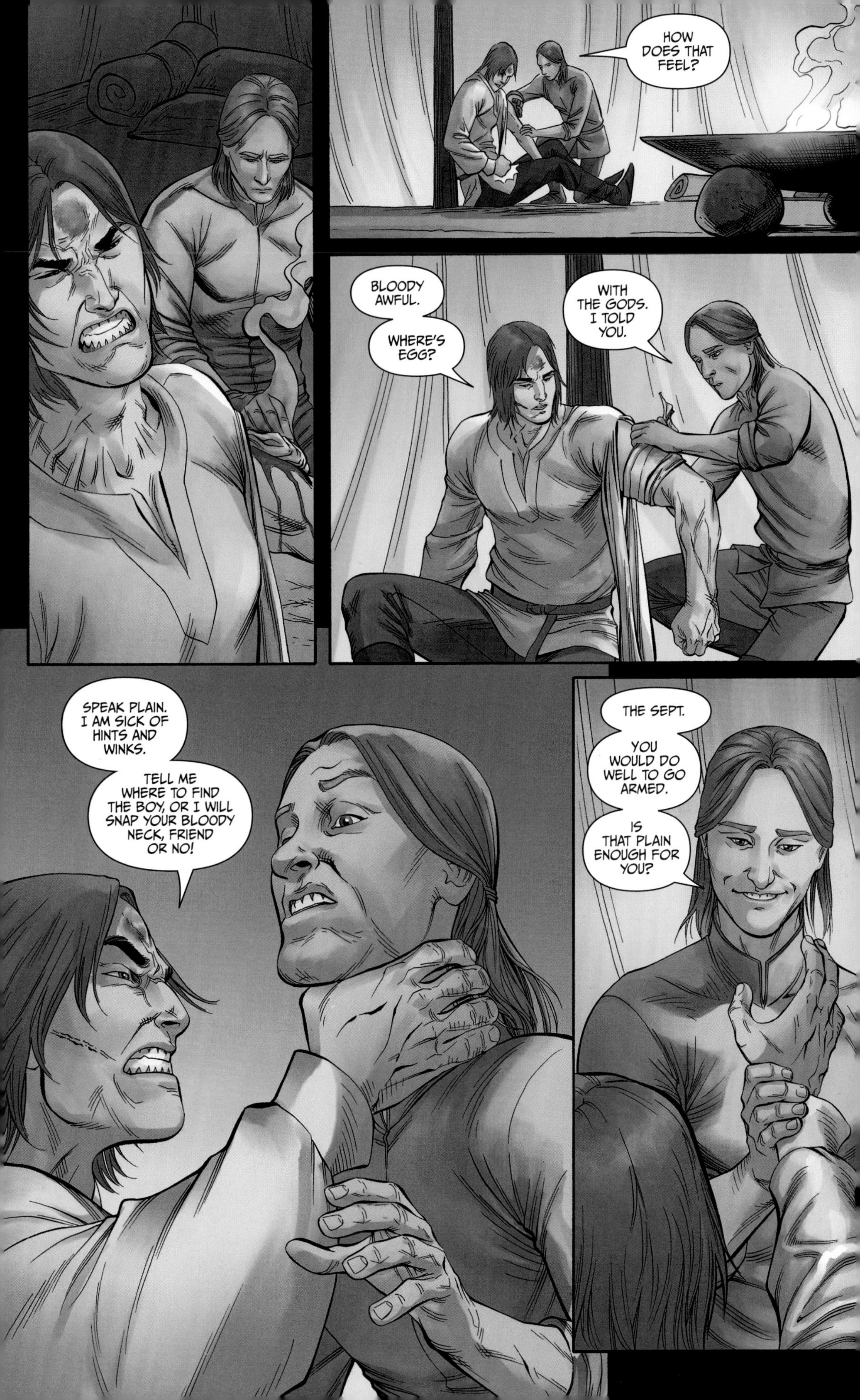
HOW DOES THAT FEEL?
BLOODY AWFUL.
WHERE'S EGG?
WITH THE GODS. I TOLD YOU.
SPEAK PLAIN. I AM SICK OF HINTS AND WINKS.
TELL ME WHERE TO FIND THE BOY, OR I WILL SNAP YOUR BLOODY NECK, FRIEND OR NO!
THE SEPT.
YOU WOULD DO WELL TO GO ARMED.
IS THAT PLAIN ENOUGH FOR YOU?

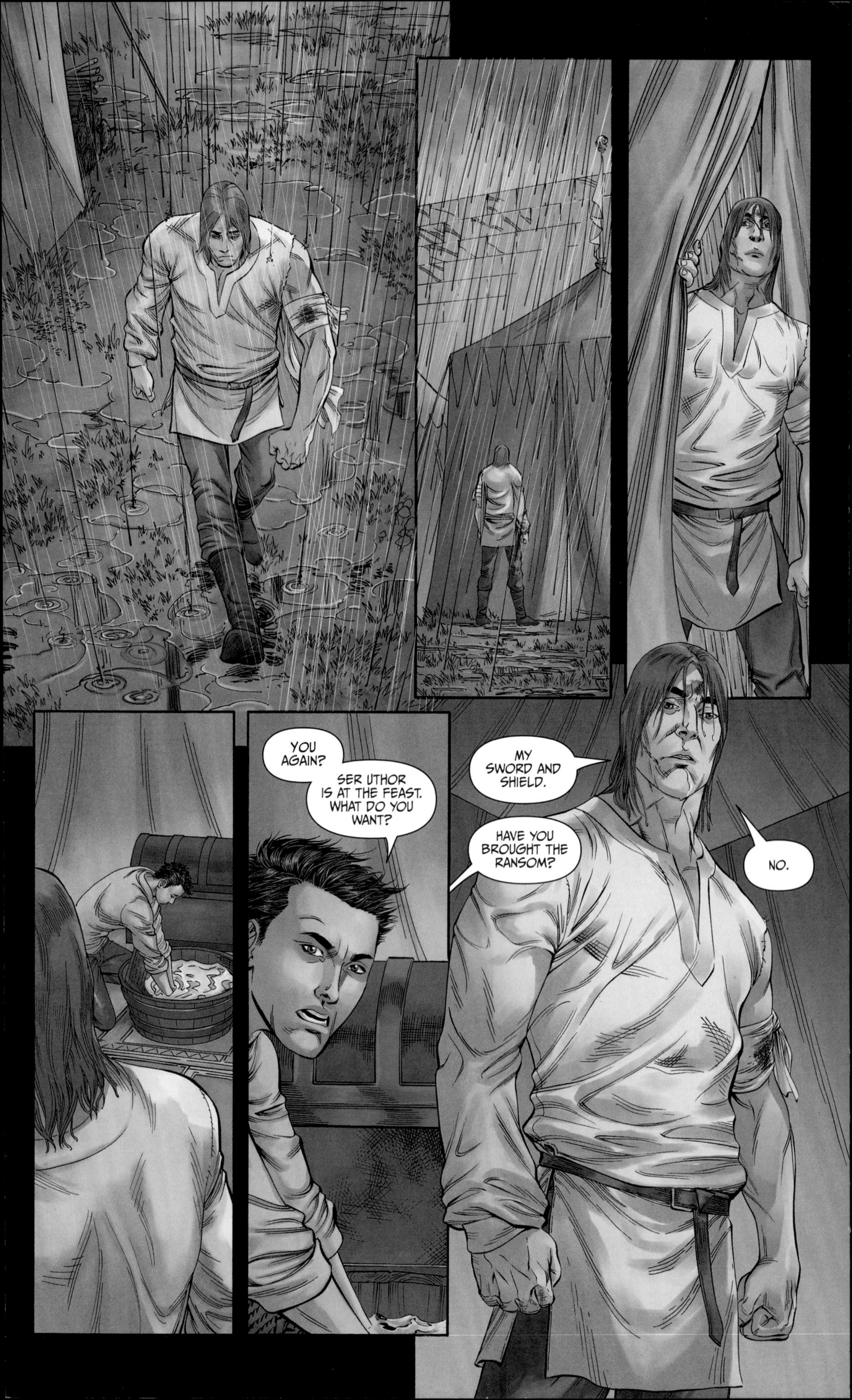
YOU AGAIN?
SER UTHOR IS AT THE FEAST. WHAT DO YOU WANT?
MY SWORD AND SHIELD.
HAVE YOU BROUGHT THE RANSOM?
NO.

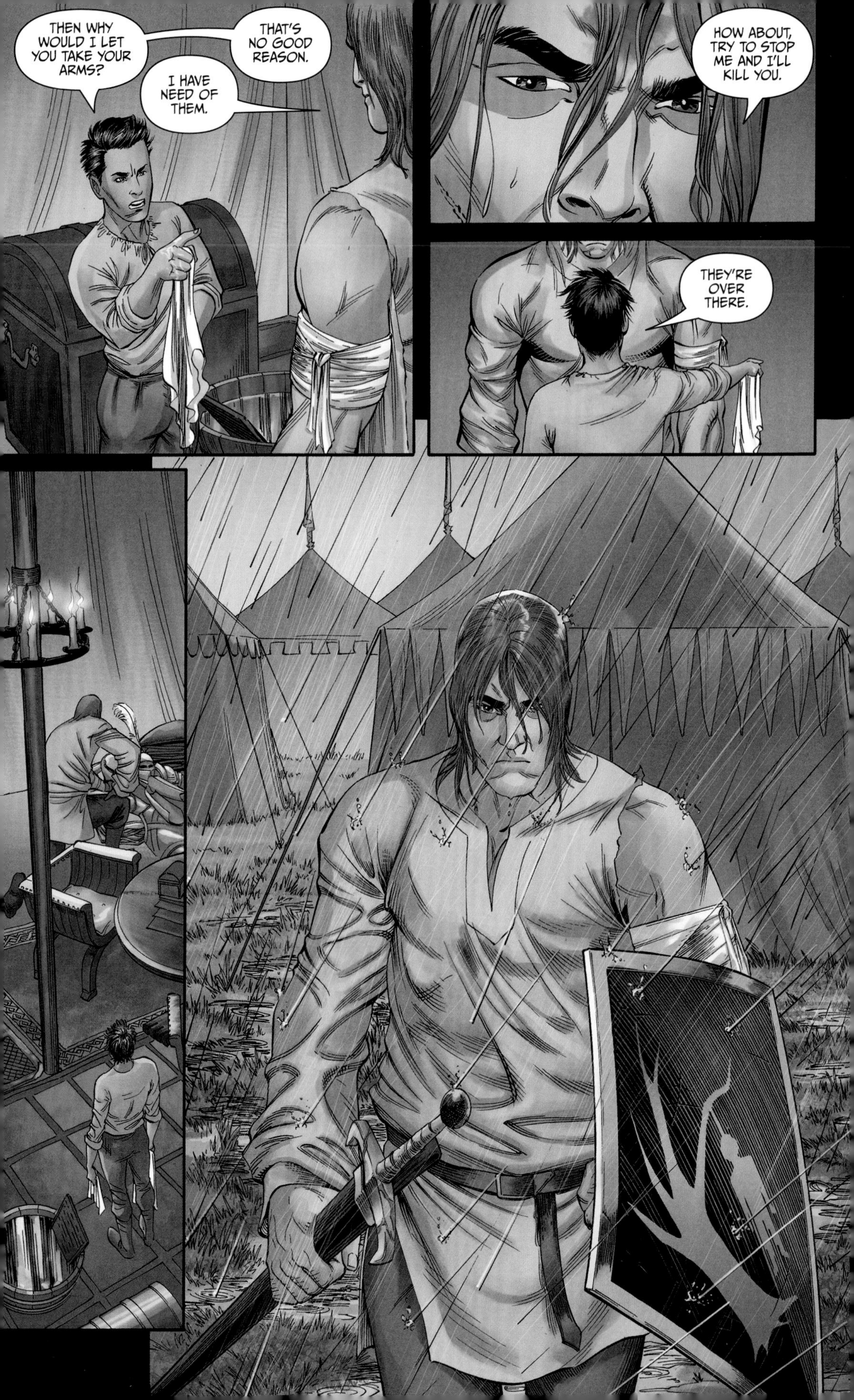
THEN WHY WOULD I LET YOU TAKE YOUR ARMS?
THAT'S NO GOOD REASON.
I HAVE NEED OF THEM.
HOW ABOUT, TRY TO STOP ME AND I'LL KILL YOU.
THEY'RE OVER THERE.

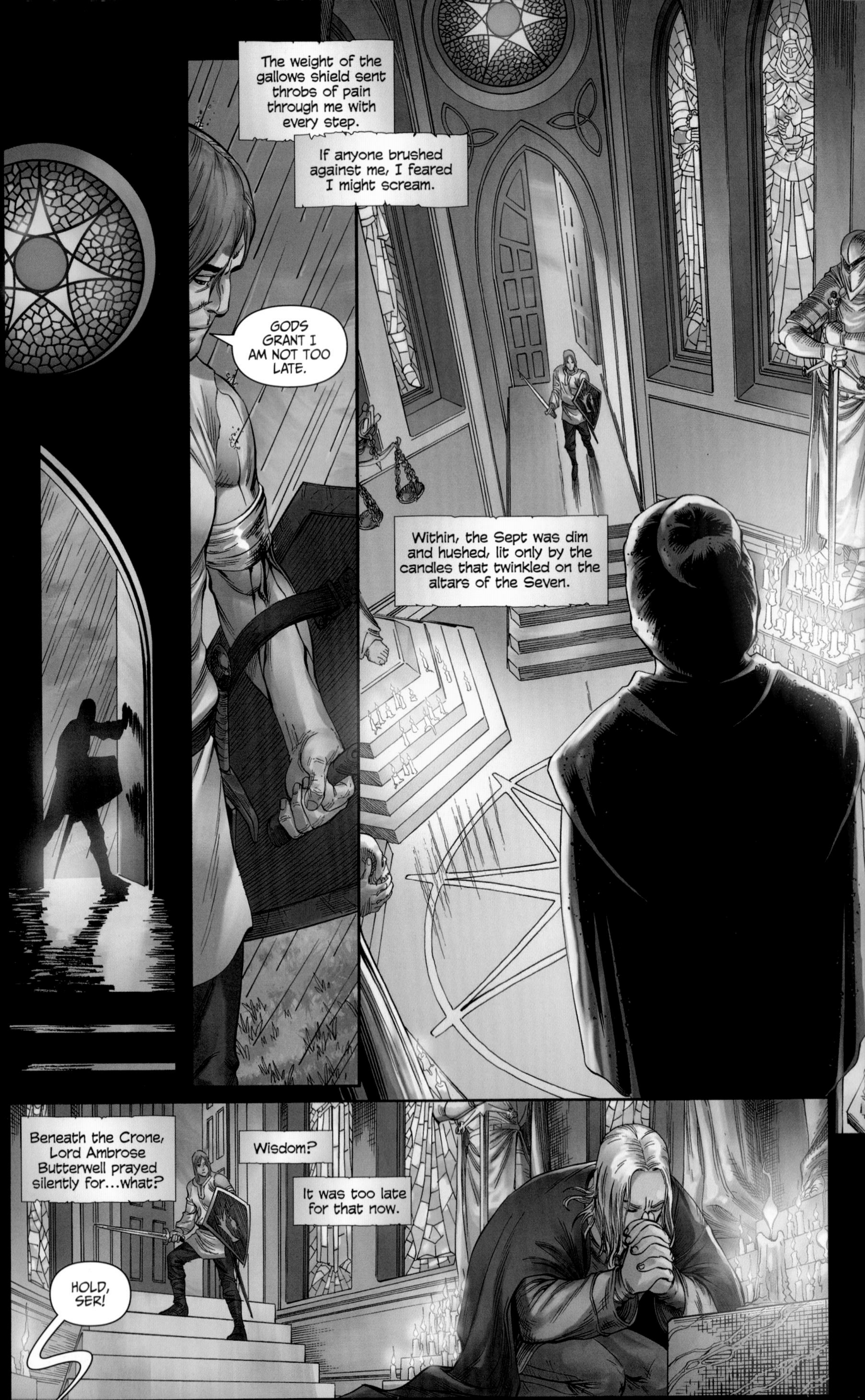

The weight of the gallows shield sent throbs of pain through me with every step.
If anyone brushed against me, I feared I might scream.
GODS GRANT I AM NOT TOO LATE.
Within, the Sept was dim and hushed, lit only by the candles that twinkled on the altars of the Seven.
Beneath the Crone, Lord Ambrose Butterwell prayed silently for...what?
Wisdom?
It was too late for that now.
HOLD, SER!

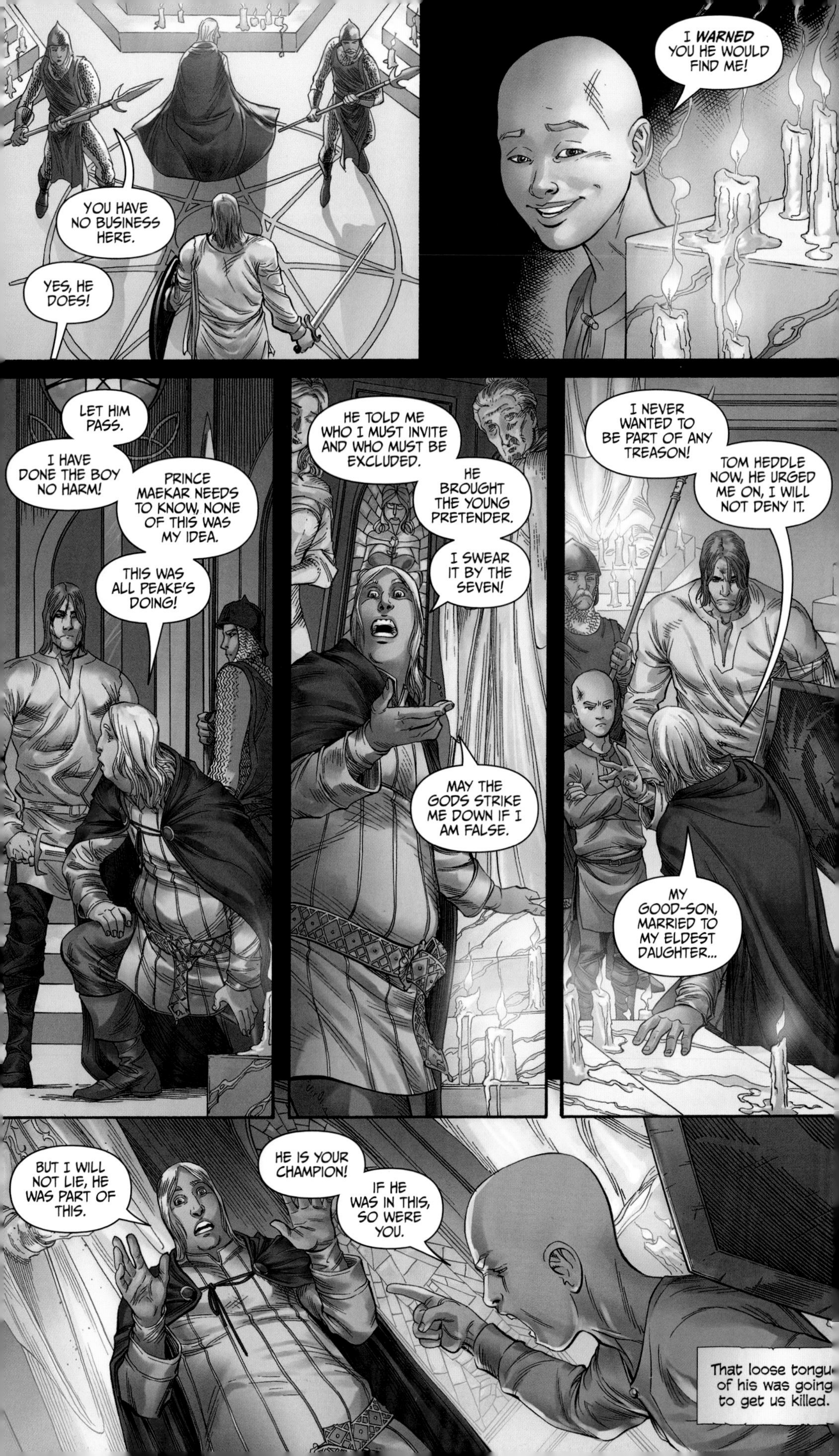
YOU HAVE NO BUSINESS HERE.
YES, HE DOES!
I WARNED YOU HE WOULD FIND ME!
LET HIM PASS.
I HAVE DONE THE BOY NO HARM!
PRINCE MAEKAR NEEDS TO KNOW, NONE OF THIS WAS MY IDEA.
THIS WAS ALL PEAKE'S DOING!
HE TOLD ME WHO I MUST INVITE AND WHO MUST BE EXCLUDED.
HE BROUGHT THE YOUNG PRETENDER.
I SWEAR IT BY THE SEVEN!
MAY THE GODS STRIKE ME DOWN IF I AM FALSE.
I NEVER WANTED TO BE PART OF ANY TREASON!
TOM HEDDLE NOW, HE URGED ME ON, I WILL NOT DENY IT.
MY GOOD-SON, MARRIED TO MY ELDEST DAUGHTER...
BUT I WILL NOT LIE, HE WAS PART OF THIS.
HE IS YOUR CHAMPION!
IF HE WAS IN THIS, SO WERE YOU.
That loose tongu
of his was going
to get us killed.

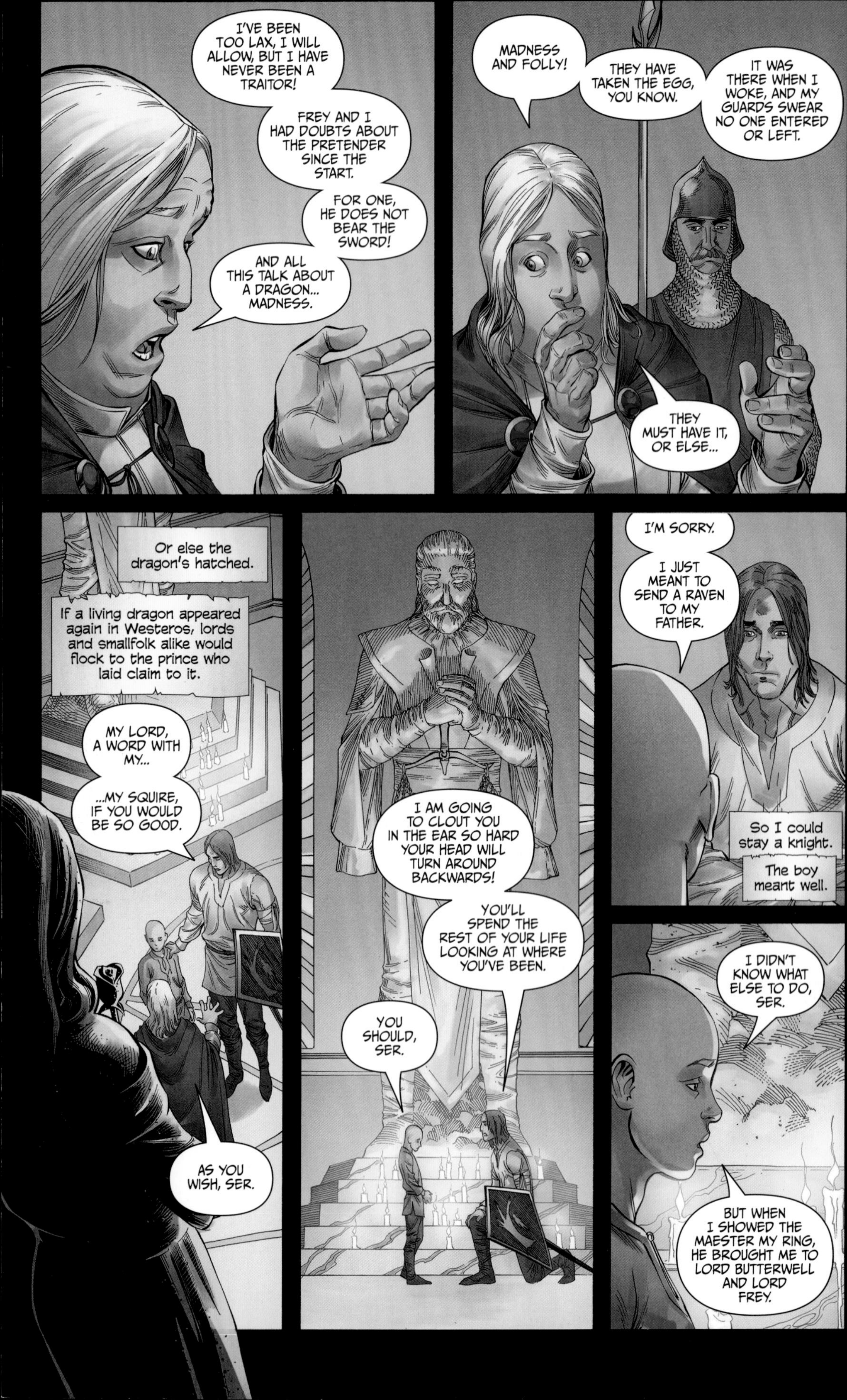
I'VE BEEN TOO LAX, I WILL ALLOW, BUT I HAVE NEVER BEEN A TRAITOR!
FREY AND I HAD DOUBTS ABOUT THE PRETENDER SINCE THE START.
FOR ONE, HE DOES NOT BEAR THE SWORD!
AND ALL THIS TALK ABOUT A DRAGON... MADNESS.
MADNESS AND FOLLY!
THEY HAVE TAKEN THE EGG, YOU KNOW.
IT WAS THERE WHEN I WOKE, AND MY GUARDS SWEAR NO ONE ENTERED OR LEFT.
THEY MUST HAVE IT, OR ELSE...
Or else the dragon's hatched.
If a living dragon appeared again in Westeros, lords and smallfolk alike would flock to the prince who laid claim to it.
MY LORD, A WORD WITH MY...
...MY SQUIRE, IF YOU WOULD BE SO GOOD.
AS YOU WISH, SER.
I AM GOING TO CLOUT YOU IN THE EAR SO HARD YOUR HEAD WILL TURN AROUND BACKWARDS!
YOU'LL SPEND THE REST OF YOUR LIFE LOOKING AT WHERE YOU'VE BEEN.
YOU SHOULD, SER.
I'M SORRY.
I JUST MEANT TO SEND A RAVEN TO MY FATHER.
So I could stay a knight.
The boy meant well.
I DIDN'T KNOW WHAT ELSE TO DO, SER.
BUT WHEN I SHOWED THE MAESTER MY RING, HE BROUGHT ME TO LORD BUTTERWELL AND LORD FREY.

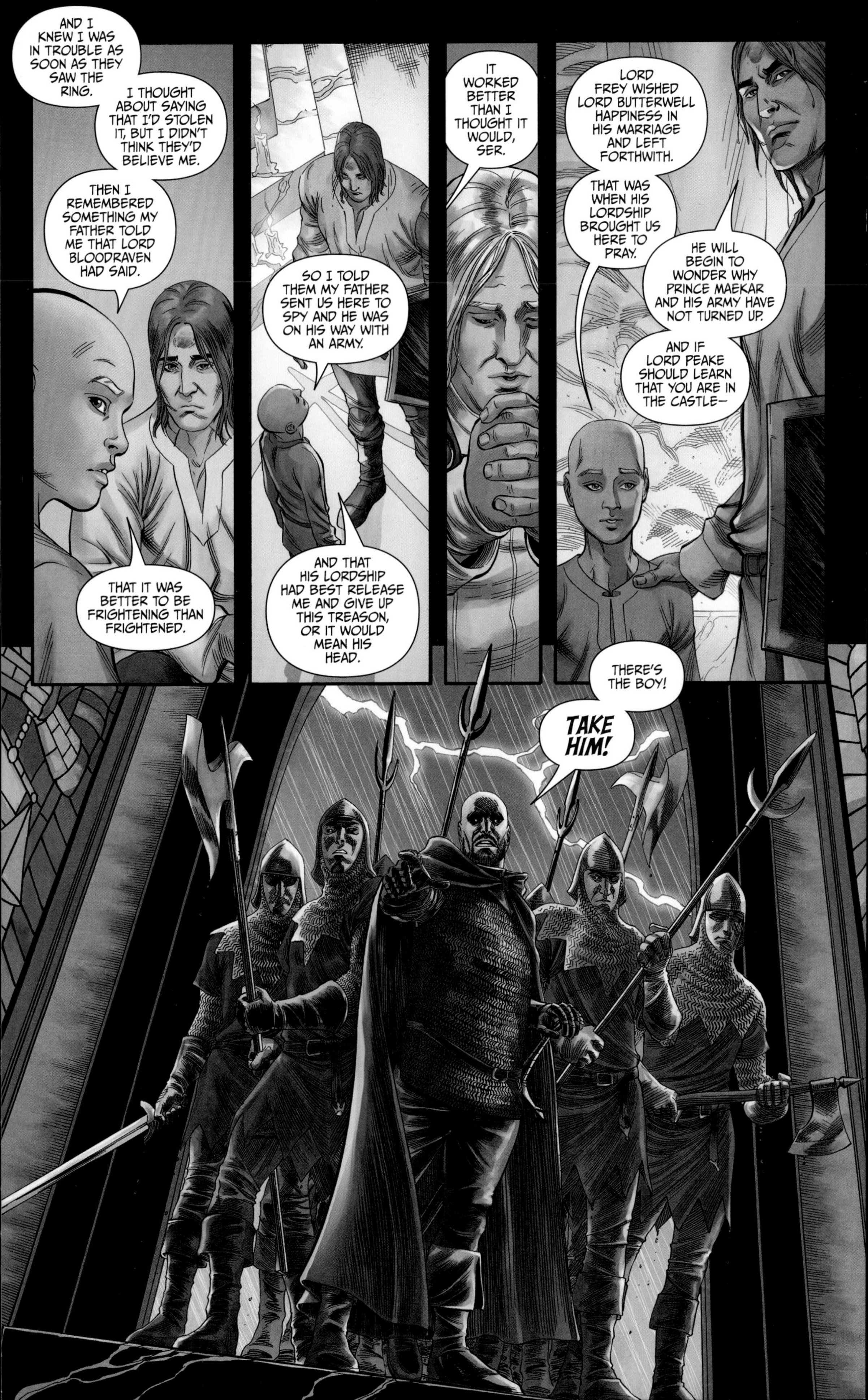
AND I KNEW I WAS IN TROUBLE AS SOON AS THEY SAW THE RING.
I THOUGHT ABOUT SAYING THAT I'D STOLEN IT, BUT I DIDN'T THINK THEY'D BELIEVE ME.
THEN I REMEMBERED SOMETHING MY FATHER TOLD ME THAT LORD BLOODRAVEN HAD SAID.
THAT IT WAS BETTER TO BE FRIGHTENING THAN FRIGHTENED.
SO I TOLD THEM MY FATHER SENT US HERE TO SPY AND HE WAS ON HIS WAY WITH AN ARMY.
AND THAT HIS LORDSHIP HAD BEST RELEASE ME AND GIVE UP THIS TREASON, OR IT WOULD MEAN HIS HEAD.
IT WORKED BETTER THAN I THOUGHT IT WOULD, SER.
LORD FREY WISHED LORD BUTTERWELL HAPPINESS IN HIS MARRIAGE AND LEFT FORTHWITH.
THAT WAS WHEN HIS LORDSHIP BROUGHT US HERE TO PRAY.
HE WILL BEGIN TO WONDER WHY PRINCE MAEKAR AND HIS ARMY HAVE NOT TURNED UP.
AND IF LORD PEAKE SHOULD LEARN THAT YOU ARE IN THE CASTLE—
THERE'S THE BOY!
TAKE HIM!

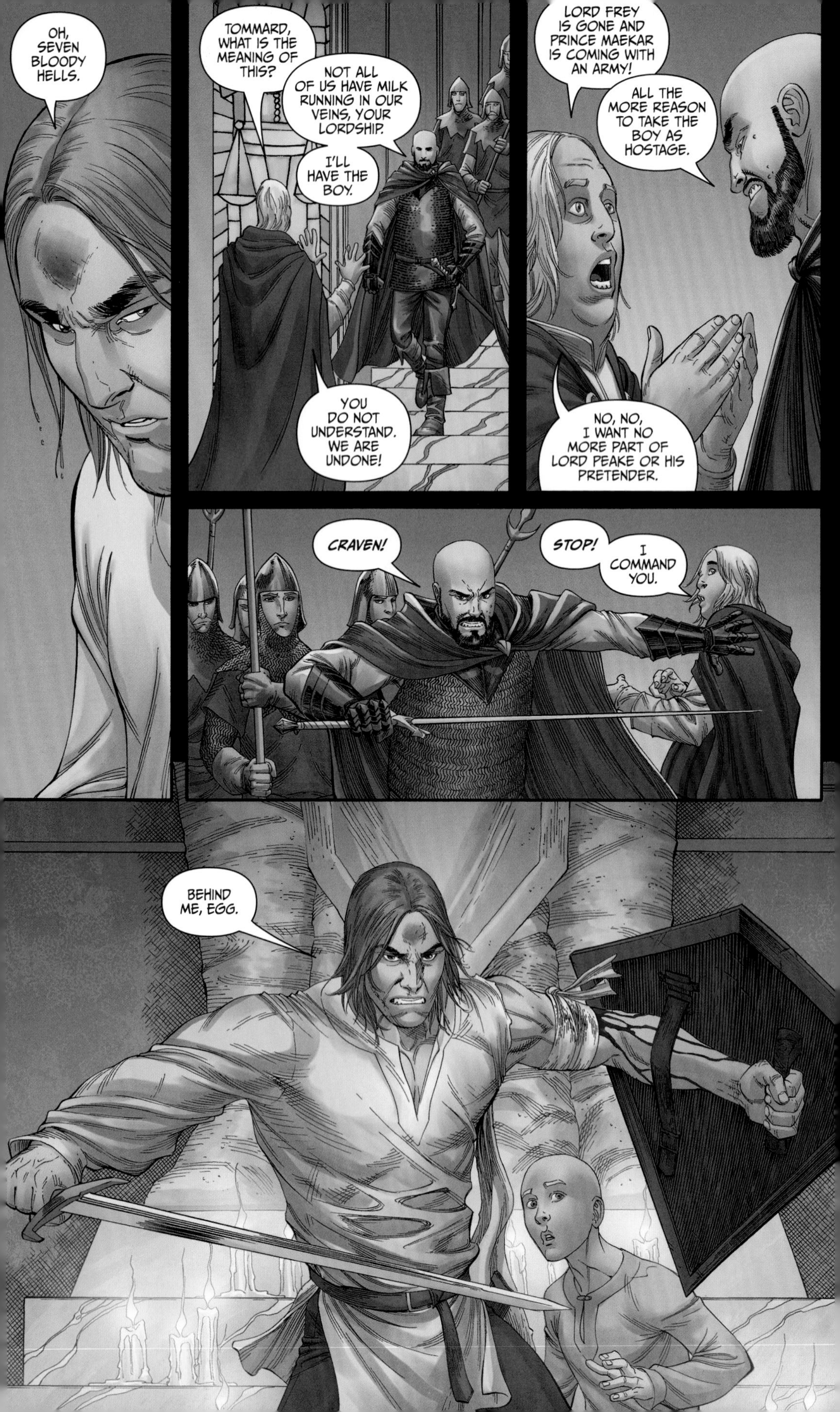
OH, SEVEN BLOODY HELLS.
TOMMARD, WHAT IS THE MEANING OF THIS?
NOT ALL OF US HAVE MILK RUNNING IN OUR VEINS, YOUR LORDSHIP.
I'LL HAVE THE BOY.
YOU DO NOT UNDERSTAND. WE ARE UNDONE!
LORD FREY IS GONE AND PRINCE MAEKAR IS COMING WITH AN ARMY!
ALL THE MORE REASON TO TAKE THE BOY AS HOSTAGE.
NO, NO, I WANT NO MORE PART OF LORD PEAKE OR HIS PRETENDER.
CRAVEN!
STOP!
I COMMAND YOU.
BEHIND ME, EGG.

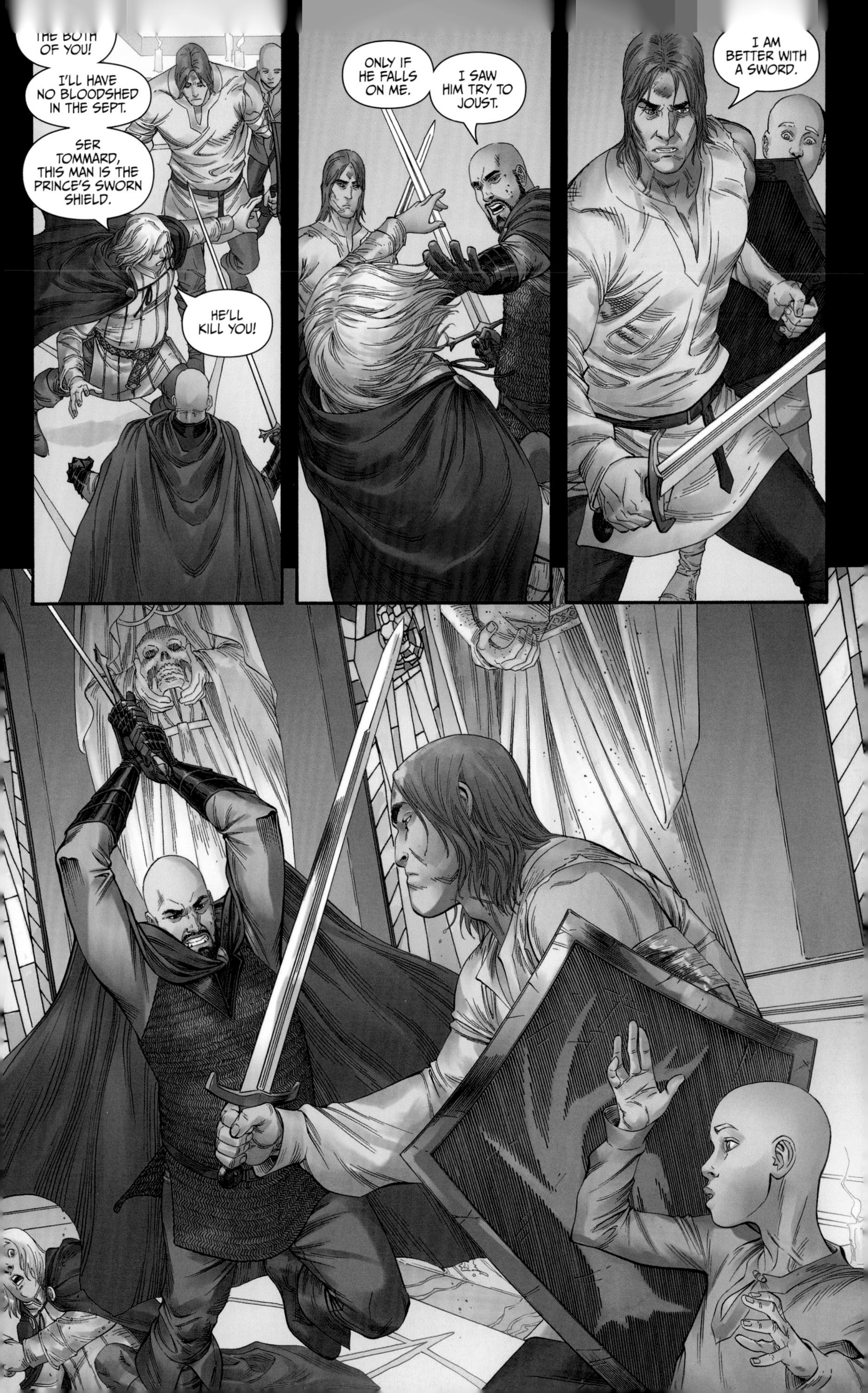
THE BOTH OF YOU!
I'LL HAVE NO BLOODSHED IN THE SEPT.
SER TOMMARD, THIS MAN IS THE PRINCE'S SWORN SHIELD.
HE'LL KILL YOU!
ONLY IF HE FALLS ON ME.
I SAW HIM TRY TO JOUST.
I AM BETTER WITH A SWORD.

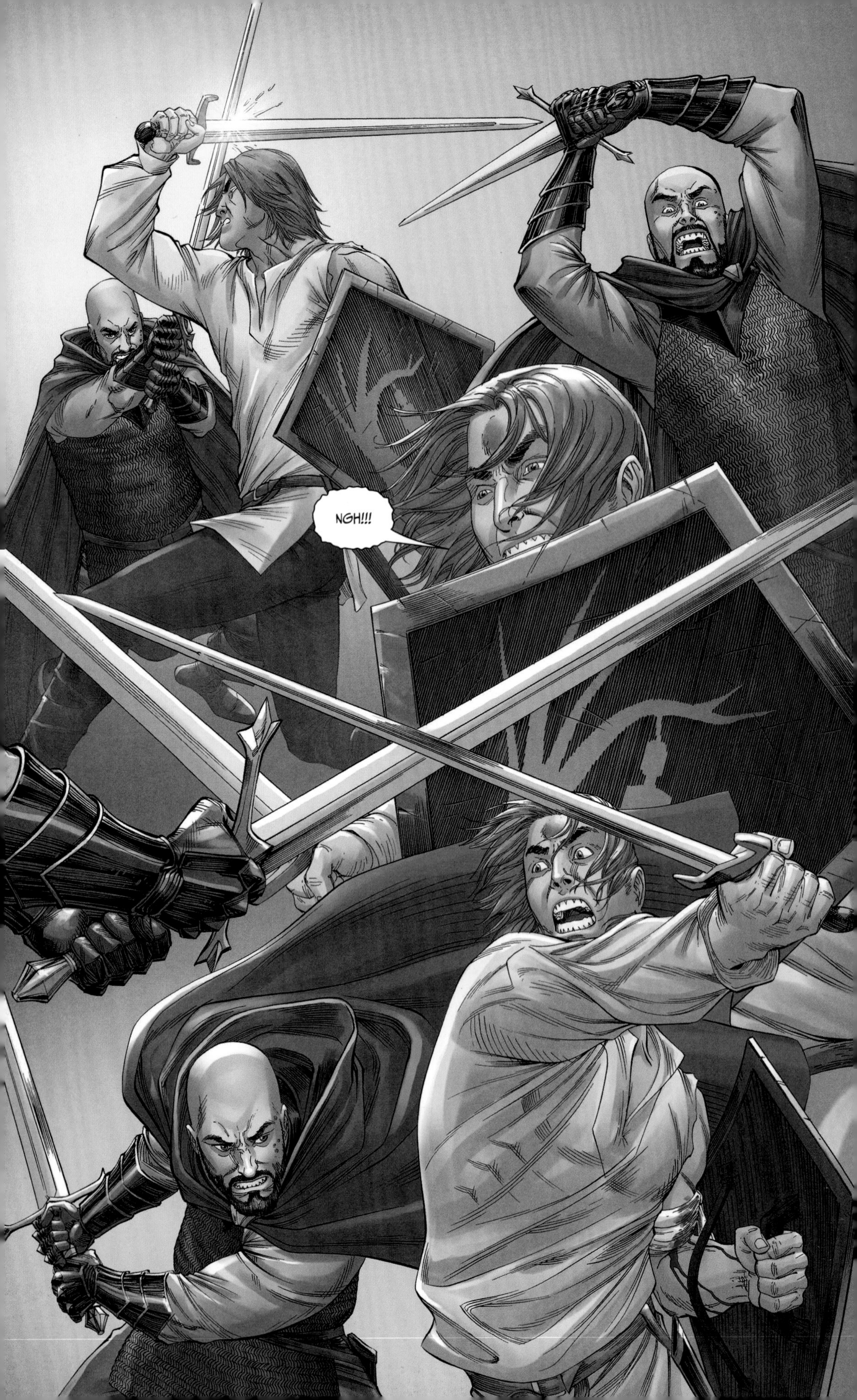
NGH!!!

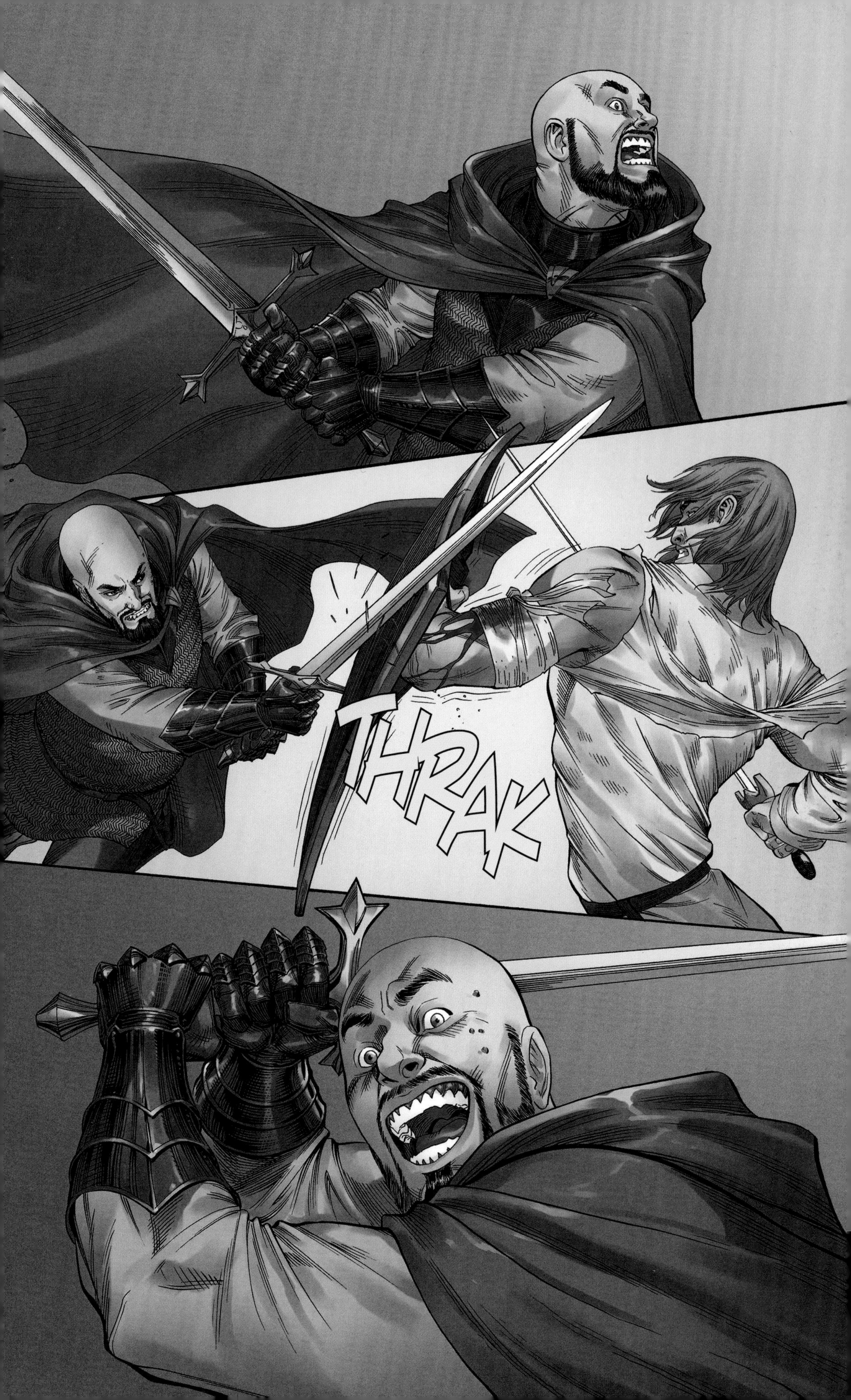
THRAK

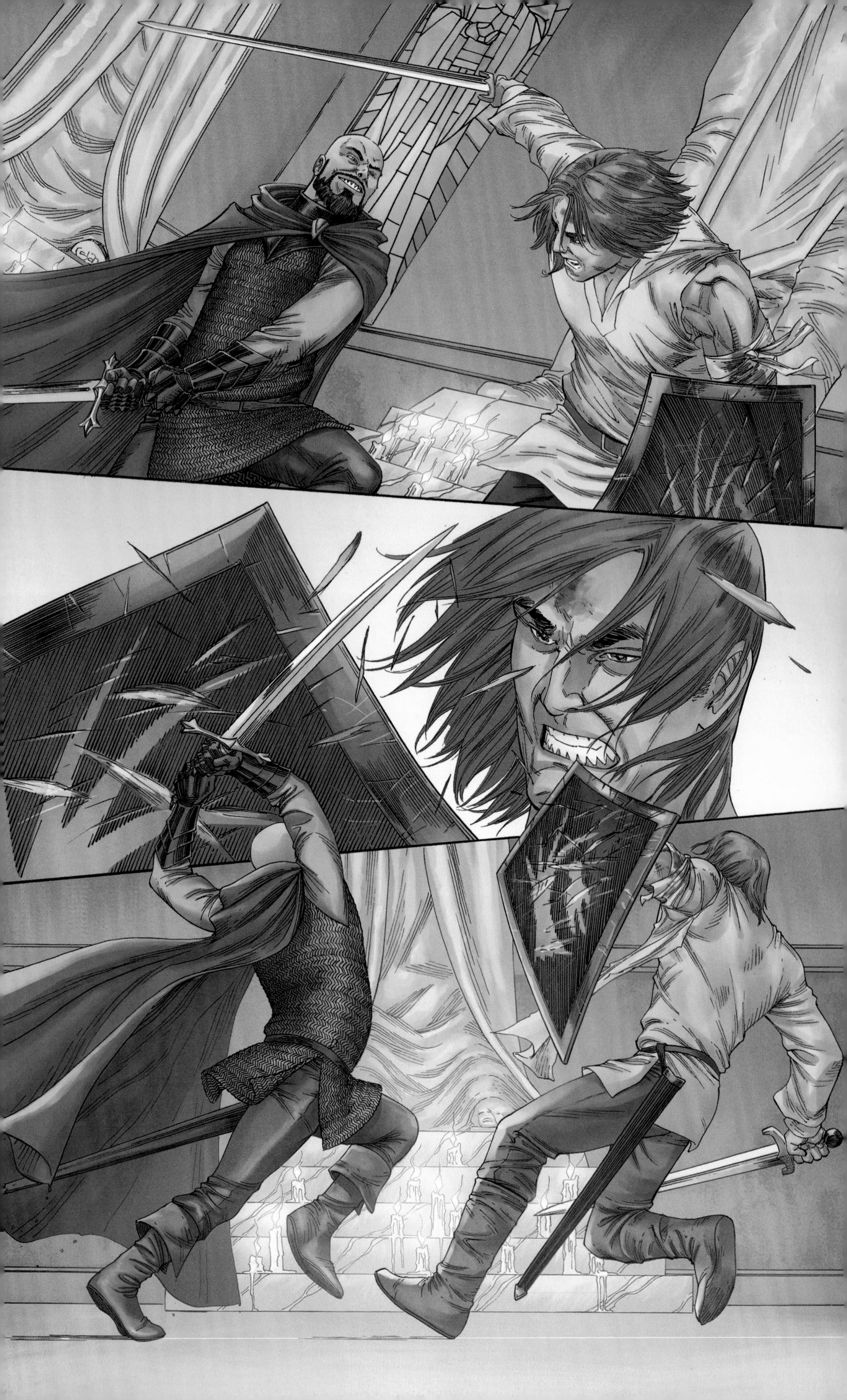

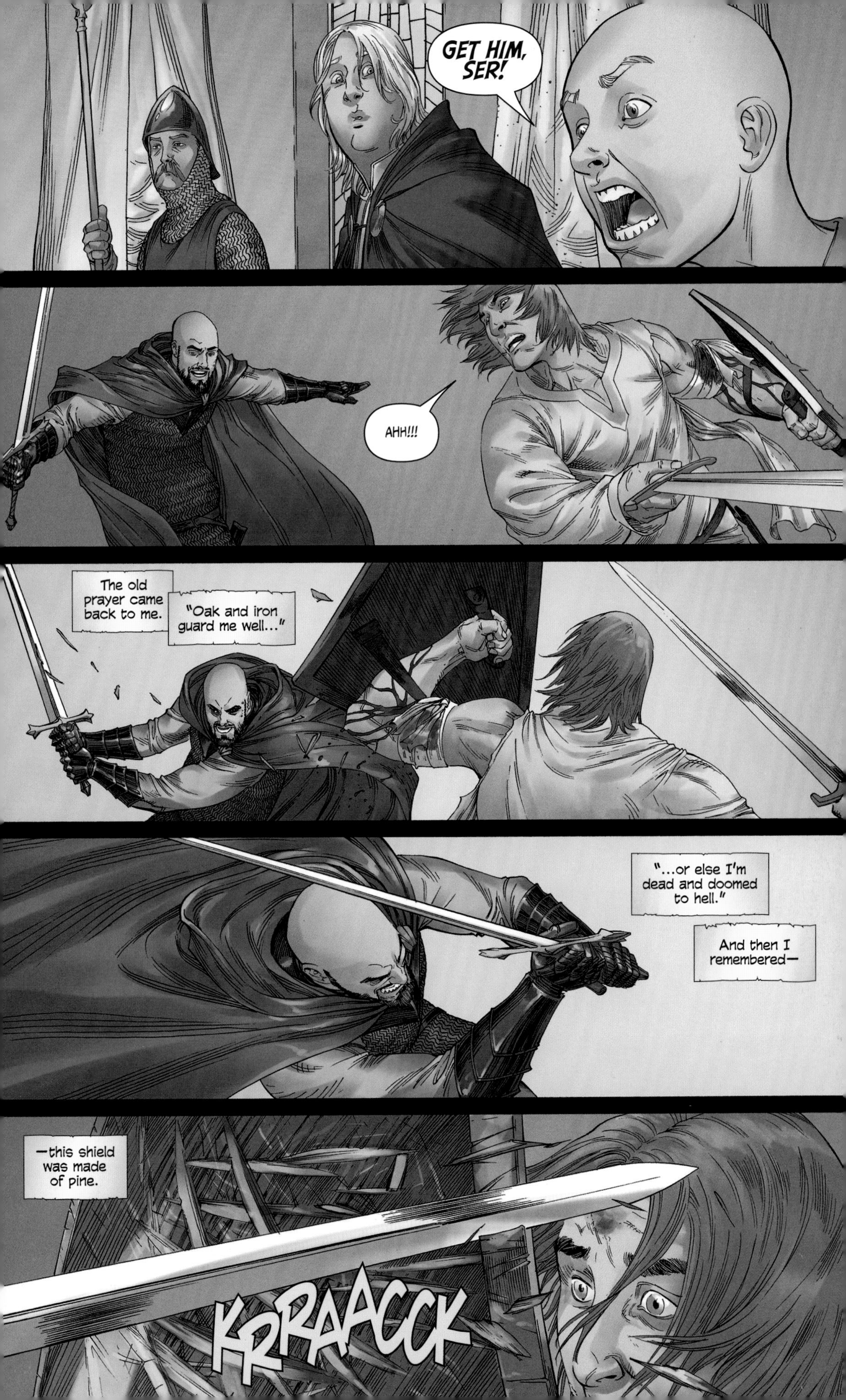
GET HIM, SER!
AHH!!!
The old prayer came back to me.
"Oak and iron guard me well..."
"...or else I'm dead and doomed to hell."
And then I remembered—
—this shield was made of pine.
KRRAACCK

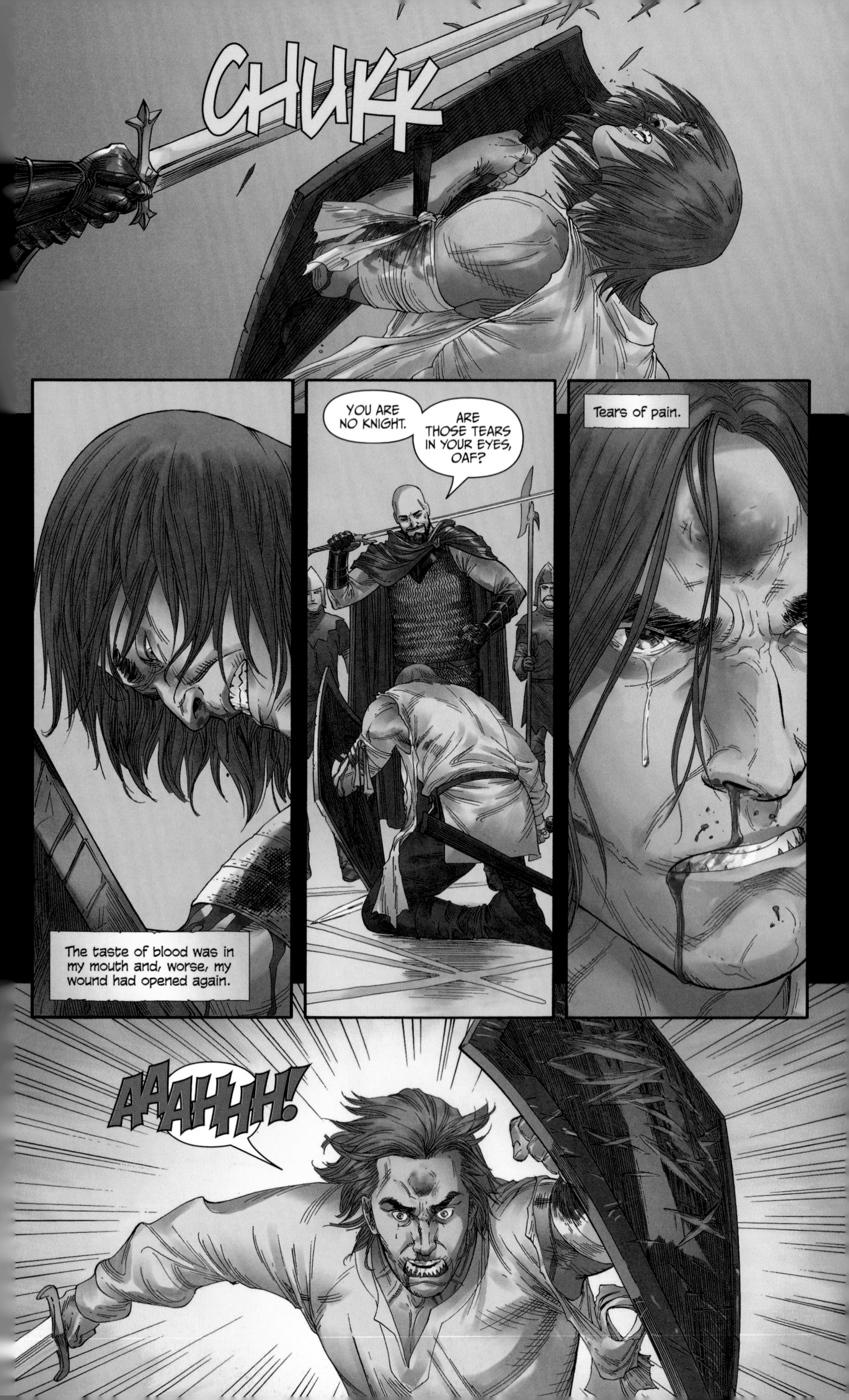
CHUKK
The taste of blood was in my mouth and, worse, my wound had opened again.
YOU ARE NO KNIGHT.
ARE THOSE TEARS IN YOUR EYES, OAF?
Tears of pain.
AAAHHH!

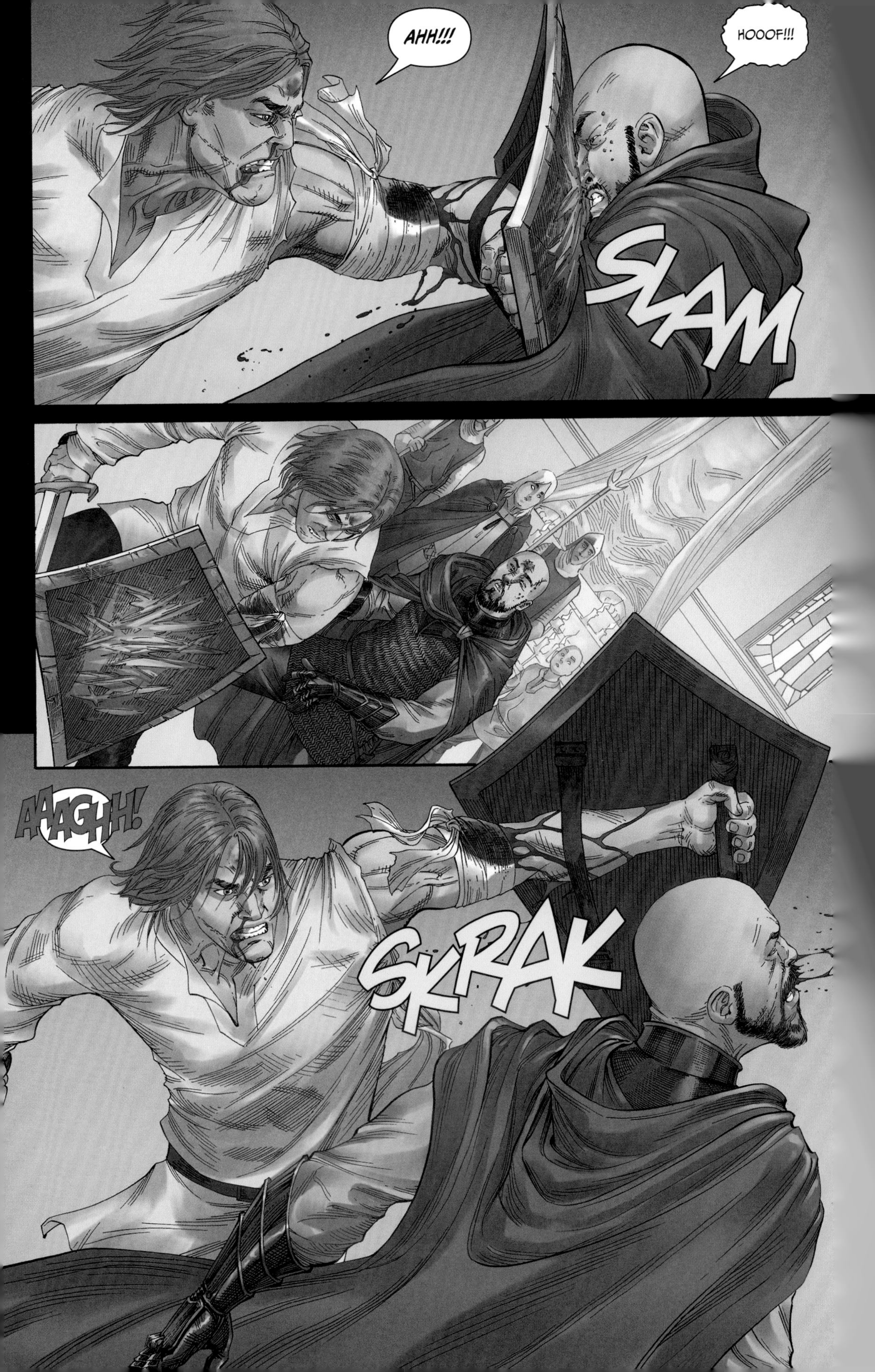

AHH!!!
HOOOF!!!
SLAM
AAAGHH!
SKRAK

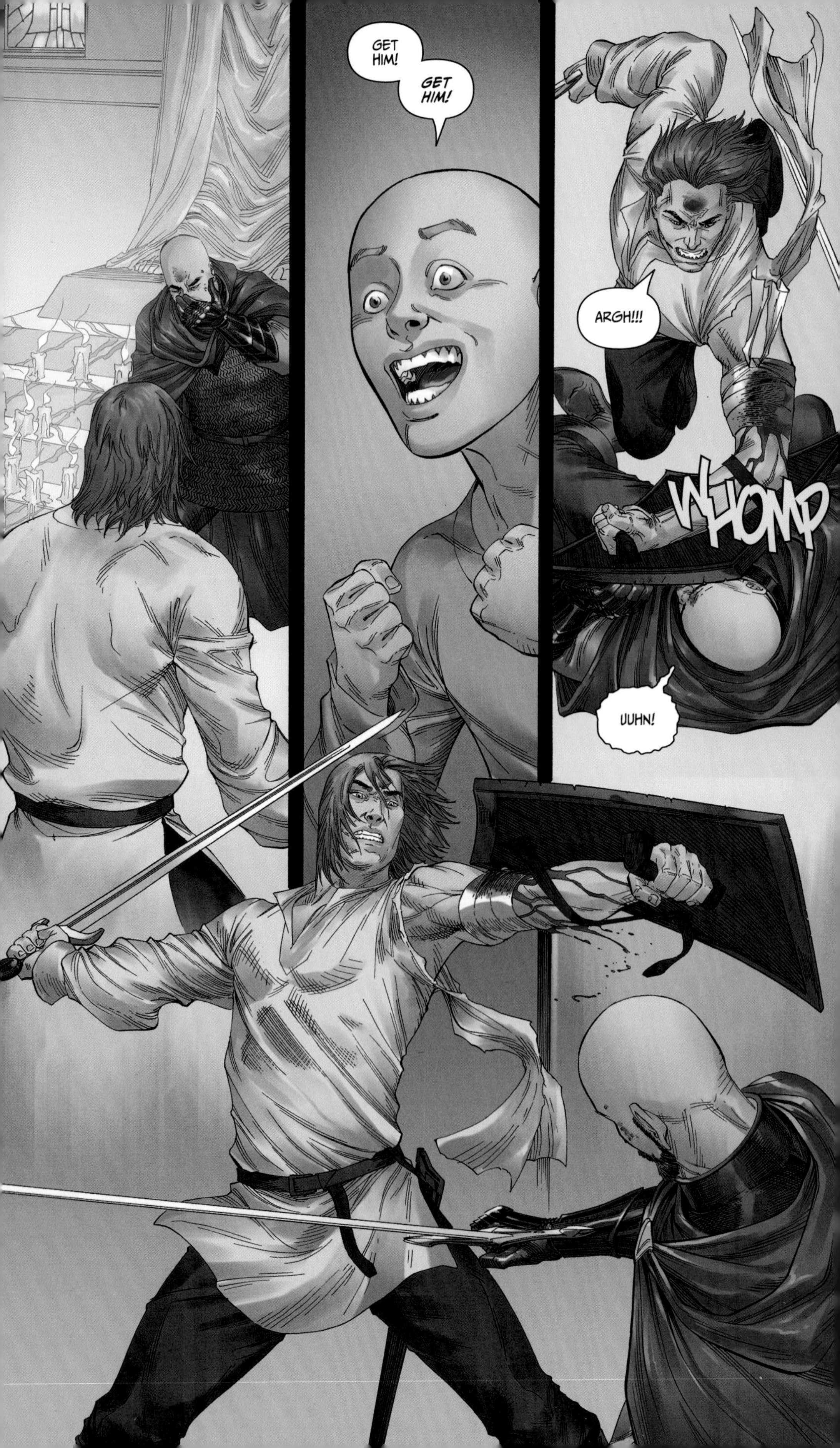
GET HIM!
GET HIM!
ARGH!!!
WHOMP
UUHN!

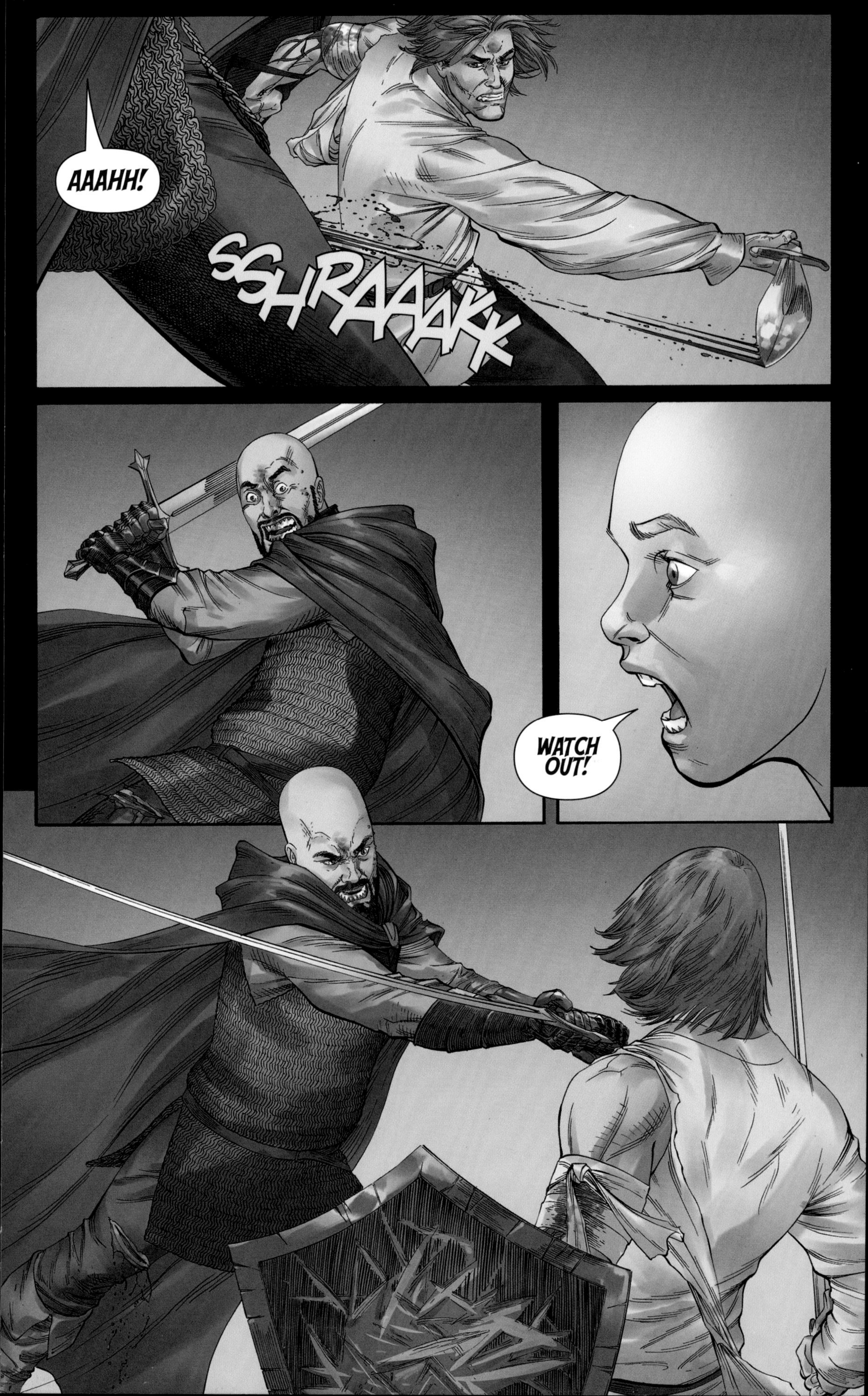
AAAHH!
SSHRAAAKK
WATCH OUT!

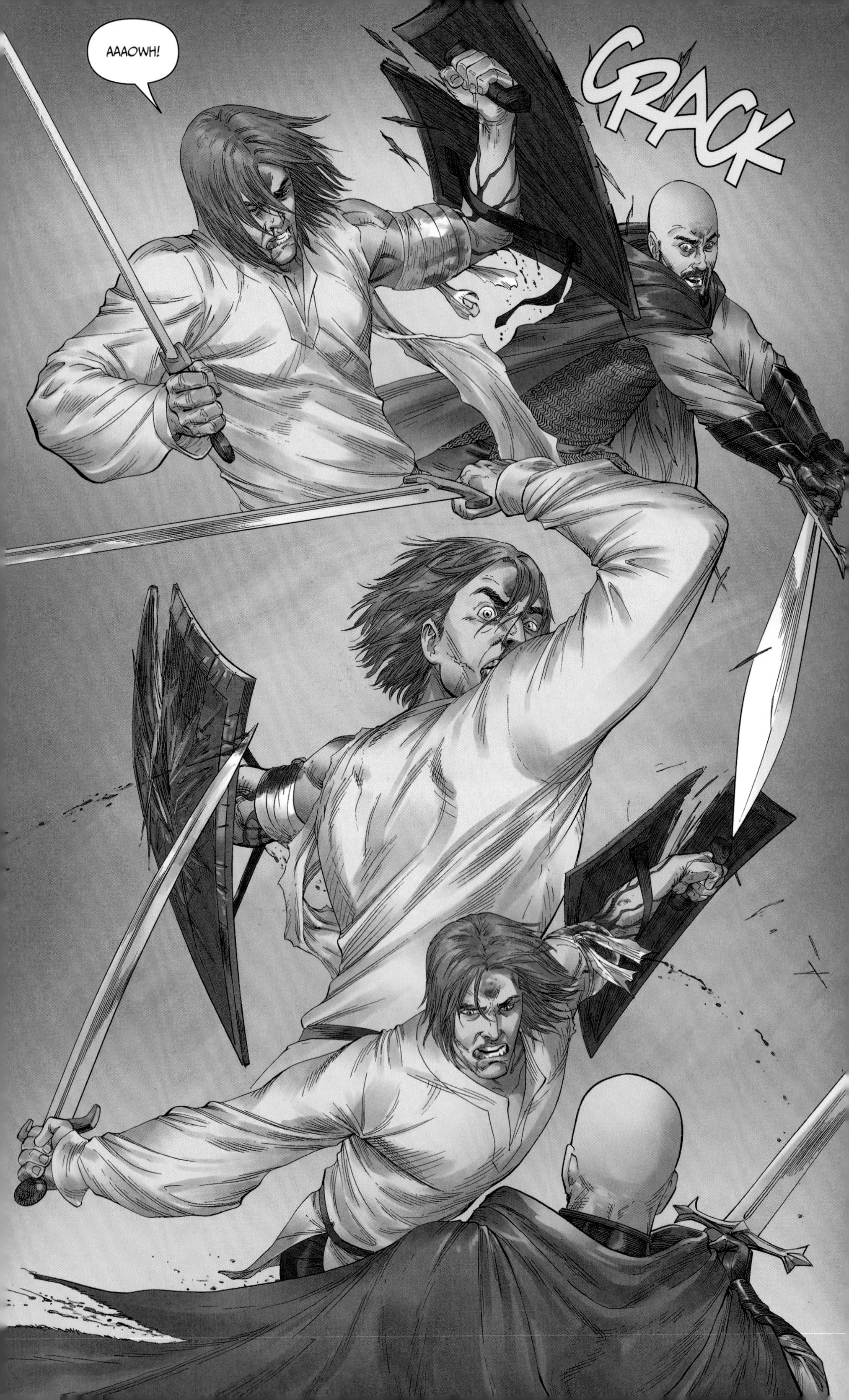
AAAOWH!
CRACK

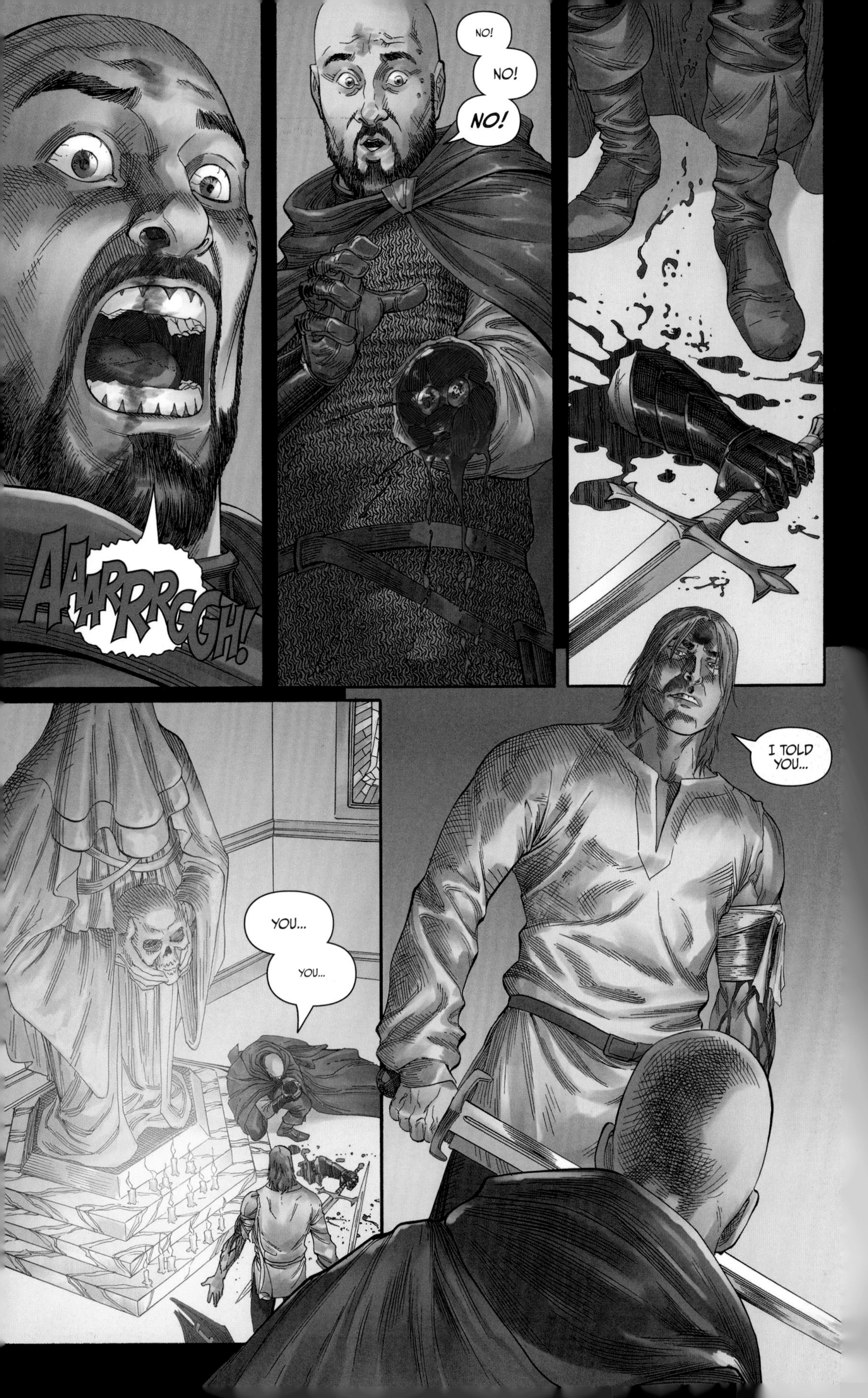
AAARRRGGH!
NO!
NO!
NO!
I TOLD YOU...
YOU...
YOU...

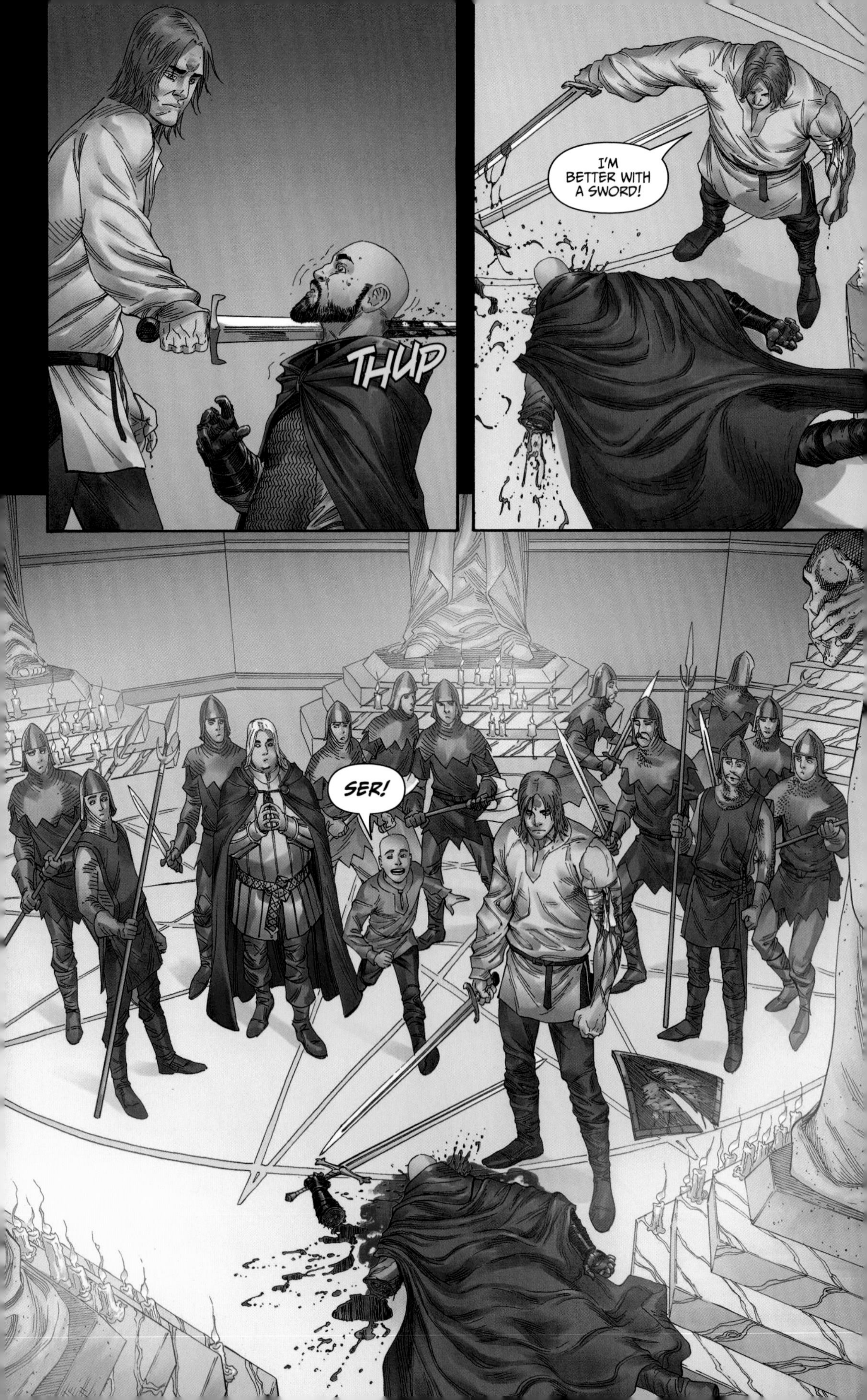
THUP
I'M BETTER WITH A SWORD!
SER!

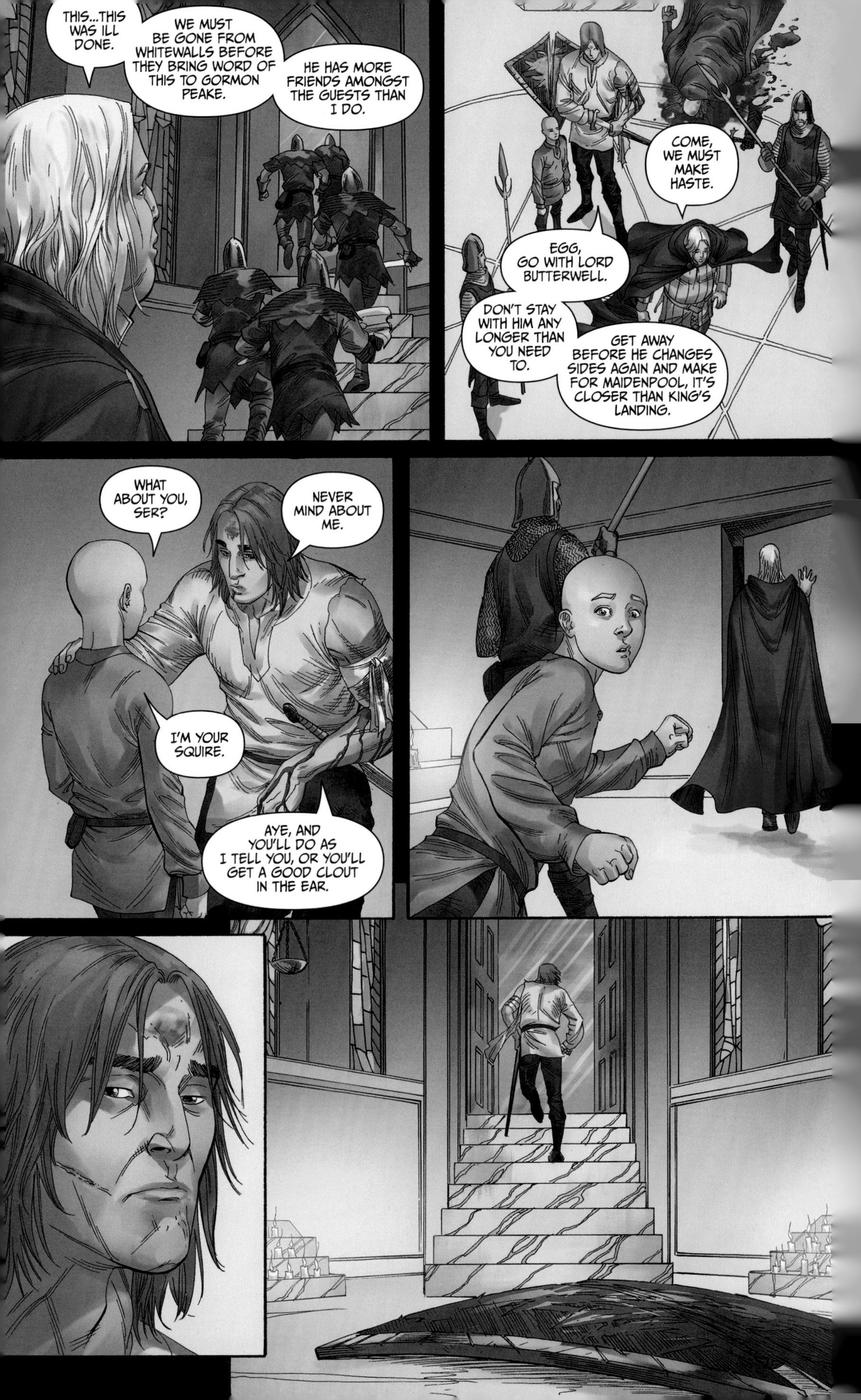
THIS...THIS WAS ILL DONE.
WE MUST BE GONE FROM WHITEWALLS BEFORE THEY BRING WORD OF THIS TO GORMON PEAKE.
HE HAS MORE FRIENDS AMONGST THE GUESTS THAN I DO.
COME, WE MUST MAKE HASTE.
EGG, GO WITH LORD BUTTERWELL.
DON'T STAY WITH HIM ANY LONGER THAN YOU NEED TO.
GET AWAY BEFORE HE CHANGES SIDES AGAIN AND MAKE FOR MAIDENPOOL, IT'S CLOSER THAN KING'S LANDING.
WHAT ABOUT YOU, SER?
NEVER MIND ABOUT ME.
I'M YOUR SQUIRE.
AYE, AND YOU'LL DO AS I TELL YOU, OR YOU'LL GET A GOOD CLOUT IN THE EAR.

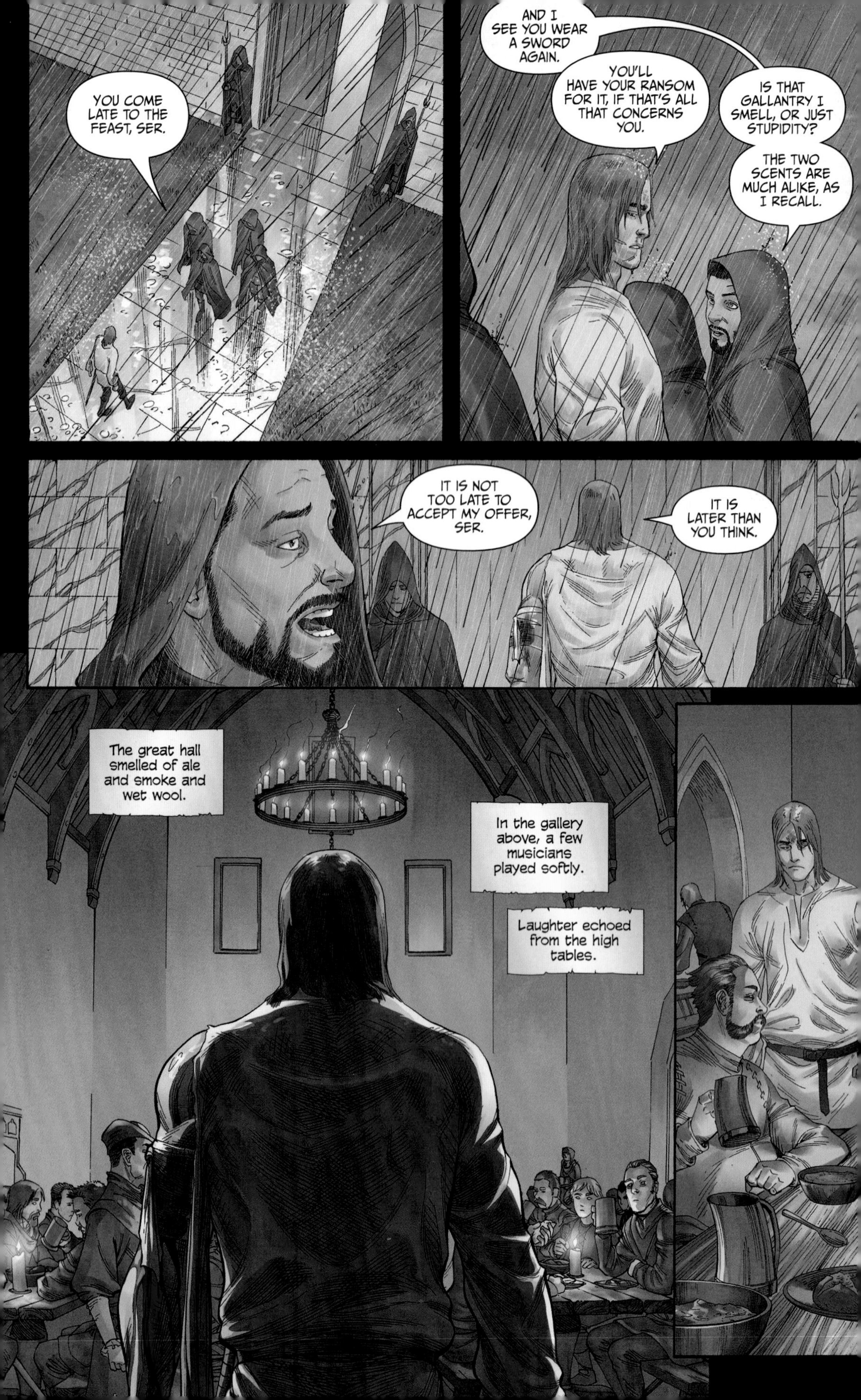
YOU COME LATE TO THE FEAST, SER.
AND I SEE YOU WEAR A SWORD AGAIN.
YOU'LL HAVE YOUR RANSOM FOR IT, IF THAT'S ALL THAT CONCERNS YOU.
IS THAT GALLANTRY I SMELL, OR JUST STUPIDITY?
THE TWO SCENTS ARE MUCH ALIKE, AS I RECALL.
IT IS NOT TOO LATE TO ACCEPT MY OFFER, SER.
IT IS LATER THAN YOU THINK.
The great hall smelled of ale and smoke and wet wool.
In the gallery above, a few musicians played softly.
Laughter echoed from the high tables.

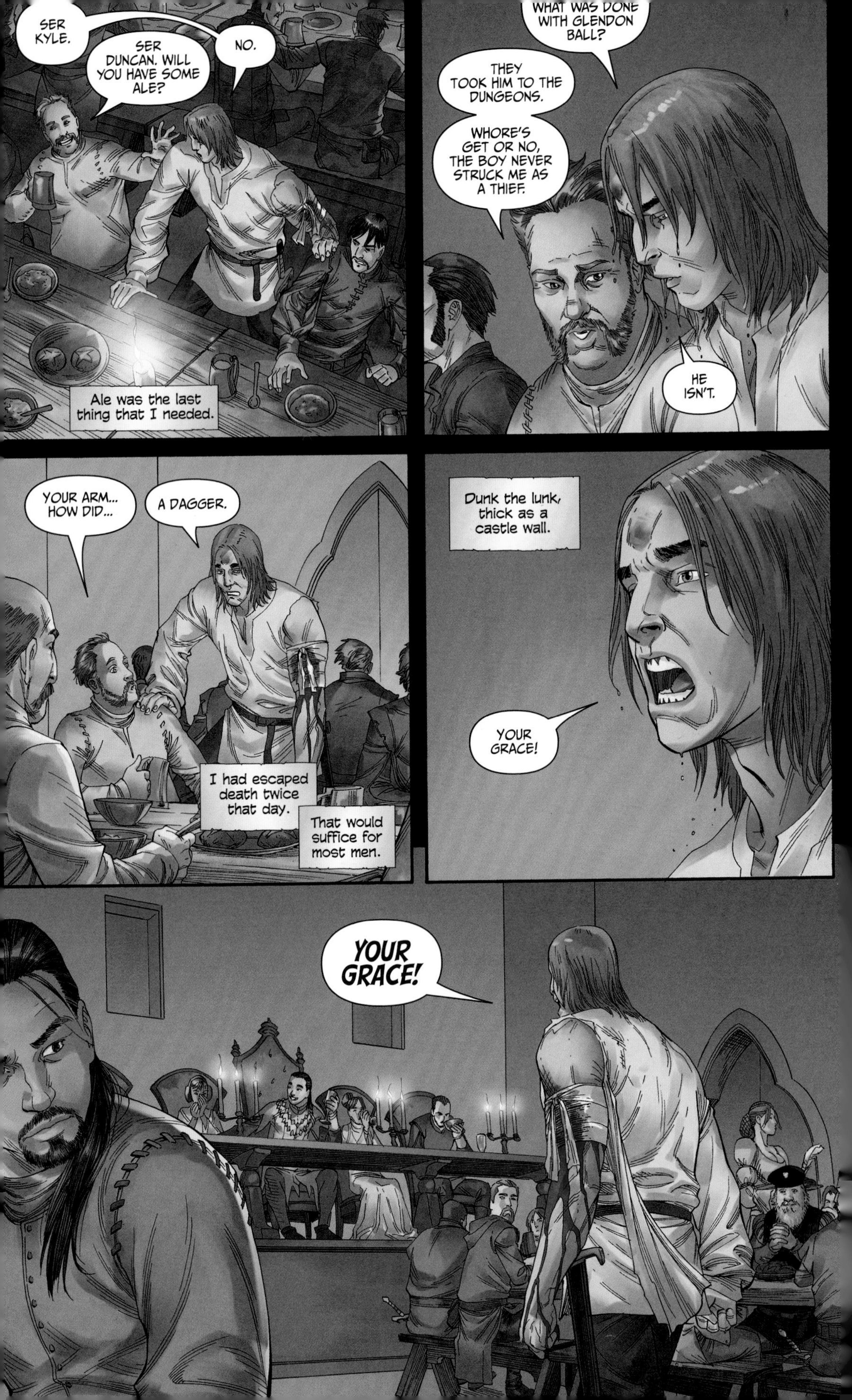
SER KYLE.
SER DUNCAN. WILL YOU HAVE SOME ALE?
NO.
Ale was the last thing that I needed.
WHAT WAS DONE WITH GLENDON BALL?
THEY TOOK HIM TO THE DUNGEONS.
WHORE'S GET OR NO, THE BOY NEVER STRUCK ME AS A THIEF.
HE ISN'T.
YOUR ARM... HOW DID...
A DAGGER.
I had escaped death twice that day.
That would suffice for most men.
Dunk the lunk, thick as a castle wall.
YOUR GRACE!
YOUR GRACE!

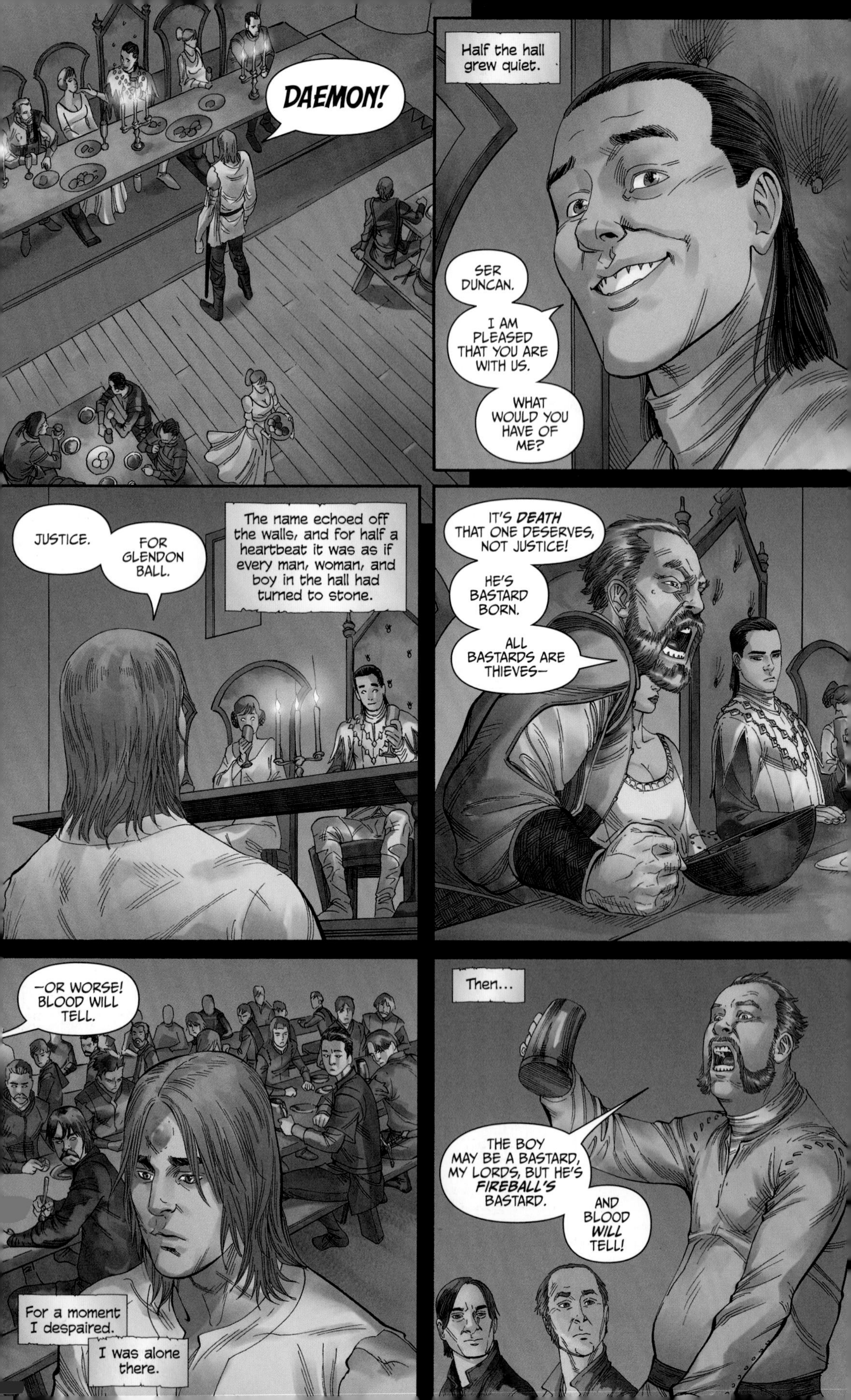
DAEMON!
Half the hall grew quiet.
SER DUNCAN.
I AM PLEASED THAT YOU ARE WITH US.
WHAT WOULD YOU HAVE OF ME?
JUSTICE.
FOR GLENDON BALL.
The name echoed off the walls, and for half a heartbeat it was as if every man, woman, and boy in the hall had turned to stone.
IT'S DEATH THAT ONE DESERVES, NOT JUSTICE!
HE'S BASTARD BORN.
ALL BASTARDS ARE THIEVES—
—OR WORSE! BLOOD WILL TELL.
For a moment I despaired.
I was alone there.
Then...
THE BOY MAY BE A BASTARD, MY LORDS, BUT HE'S FIREBALL'S BASTARD.
AND BLOOD WILL TELL!

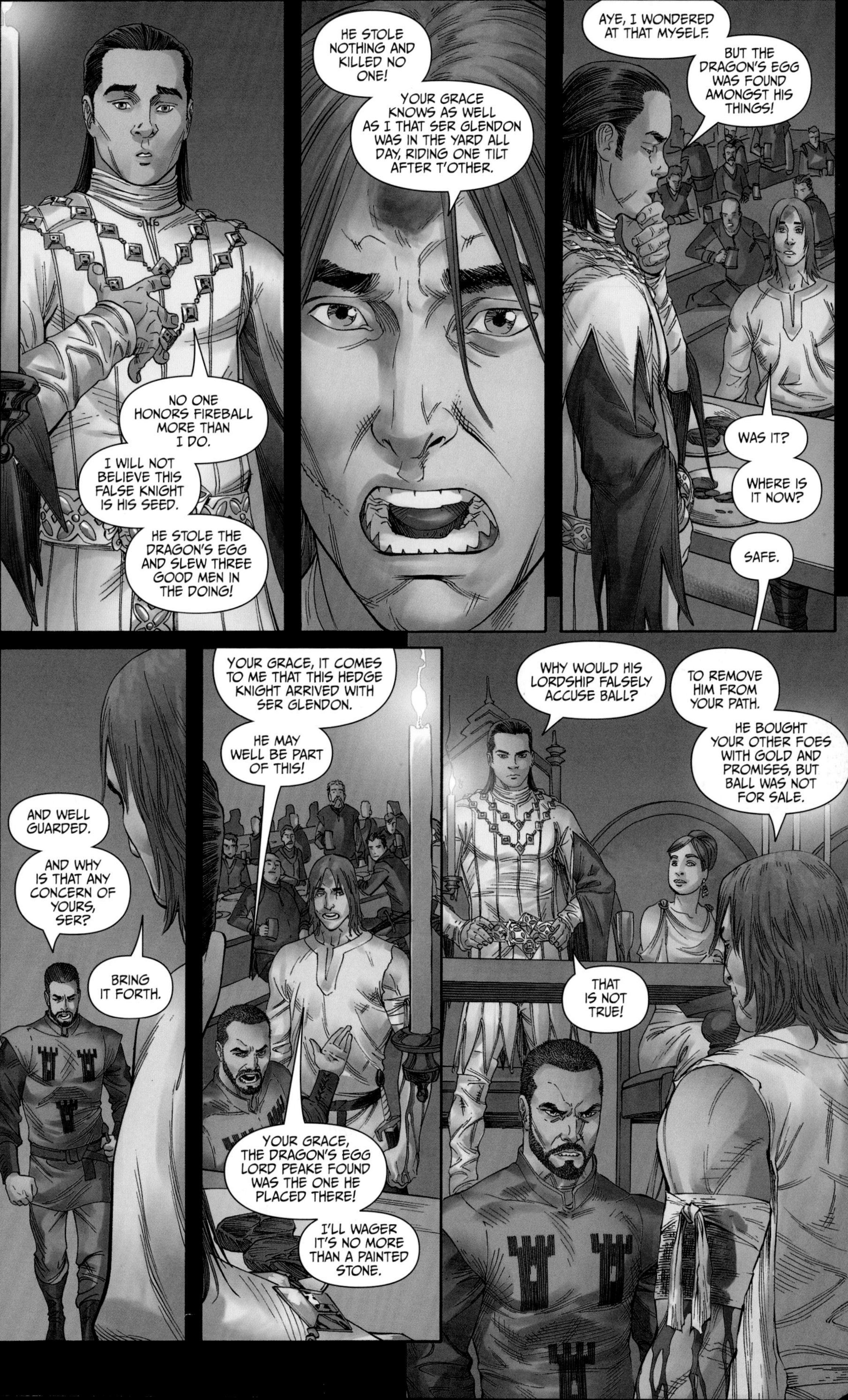
NO ONE HONORS FIREBALL MORE THAN I DO.
I WILL NOT BELIEVE THIS FALSE KNIGHT IS HIS SEED.
HE STOLE THE DRAGON'S EGG AND SLEW THREE GOOD MEN IN THE DOING!
HE STOLE NOTHING AND KILLED NO ONE!
YOUR GRACE KNOWS AS WELL AS I THAT SER GLENDON WAS IN THE YARD ALL DAY, RIDING ONE TILT AFTER T'OTHER.
AYE, I WONDERED AT THAT MYSELF.
BUT THE DRAGON'S EGG WAS FOUND AMONGST HIS THINGS!
WAS IT?
WHERE IS IT NOW?
SAFE.
AND WELL GUARDED.
AND WHY IS THAT ANY CONCERN OF YOURS, SER?
BRING IT FORTH.
YOUR GRACE, IT COMES TO ME THAT THIS HEDGE KNIGHT ARRIVED WITH SER GLENDON.
HE MAY WELL BE PART OF THIS!
YOUR GRACE, THE DRAGON'S EGG LORD PEAKE FOUND WAS THE ONE HE PLACED THERE!
I'LL WAGER IT'S NO MORE THAN A PAINTED STONE.
WHY WOULD HIS LORDSHIP FALSELY ACCUSE BALL?
TO REMOVE HIM FROM YOUR PATH.
HE BOUGHT YOUR OTHER FOES WITH GOLD AND PROMISES, BUT BALL WAS NOT FOR SALE.
THAT IS NOT TRUE!

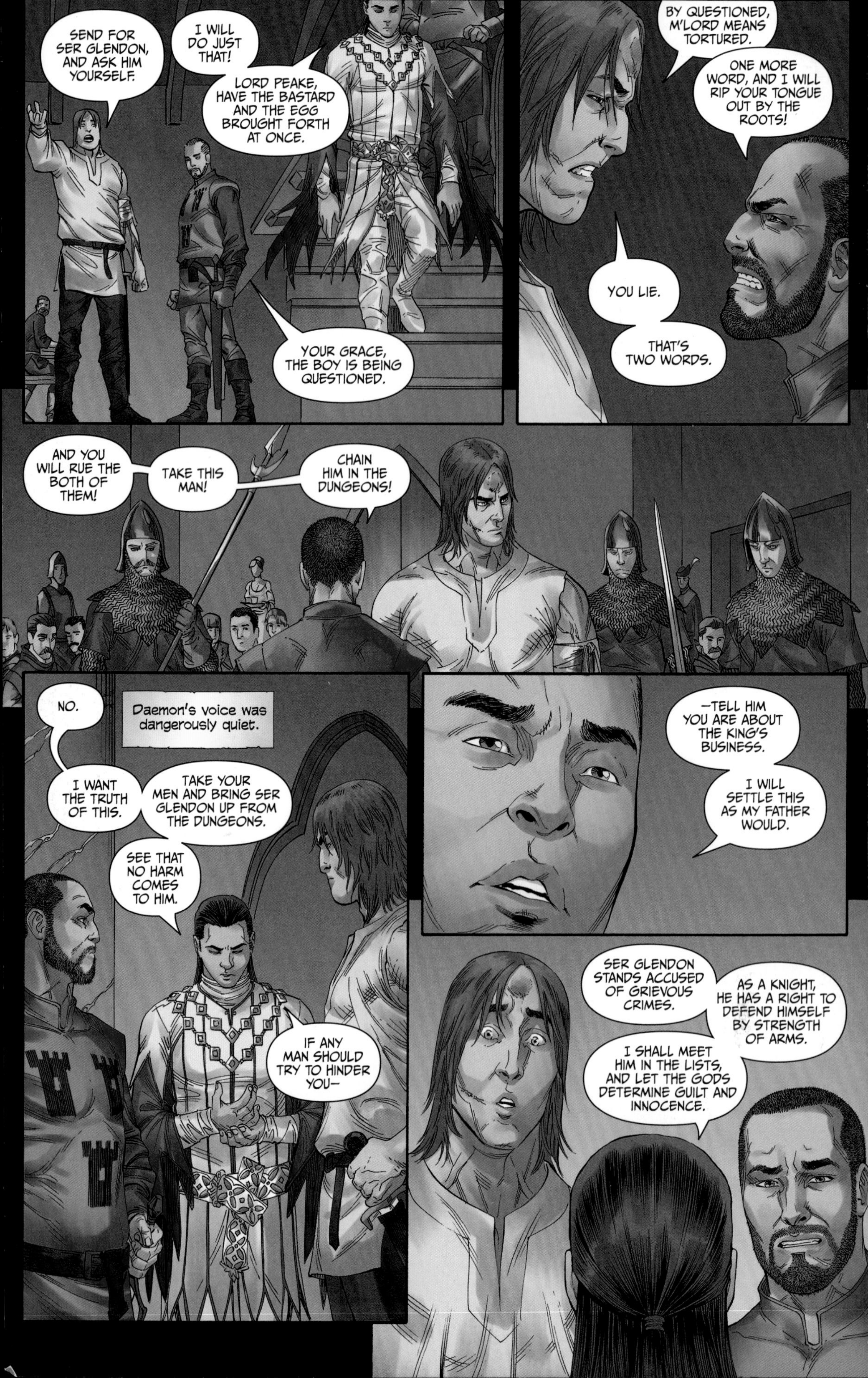
SEND FOR SER GLENDON, AND ASK HIM YOURSELF.
I WILL DO JUST THAT!
LORD PEAKE, HAVE THE BASTARD AND THE EGG BROUGHT FORTH AT ONCE.
YOUR GRACE, THE BOY IS BEING QUESTIONED.
BY QUESTIONED, M'LORD MEANS TORTURED.
ONE MORE WORD, AND I WILL RIP YOUR TONGUE OUT BY THE ROOTS!
YOU LIE.
THAT'S TWO WORDS.
AND YOU WILL RUE THE BOTH OF THEM!
TAKE THIS MAN!
CHAIN HIM IN THE DUNGEONS!
NO.
Daemon's voice was dangerously quiet.
I WANT THE TRUTH OF THIS.
TAKE YOUR MEN AND BRING SER GLENDON UP FROM THE DUNGEONS.
SEE THAT NO HARM COMES TO HIM.
IF ANY MAN SHOULD TRY TO HINDER YOU—
—TELL HIM YOU ARE ABOUT THE KING'S BUSINESS.
I WILL SETTLE THIS AS MY FATHER WOULD.
SER GLENDON STANDS ACCUSED OF GRIEVOUS CRIMES.
AS A KNIGHT, HE HAS A RIGHT TO DEFEND HIMSELF BY STRENGTH OF ARMS.
I SHALL MEET HIM IN THE LISTS, AND LET THE GODS DETERMINE GUILT AND INNOCENCE.

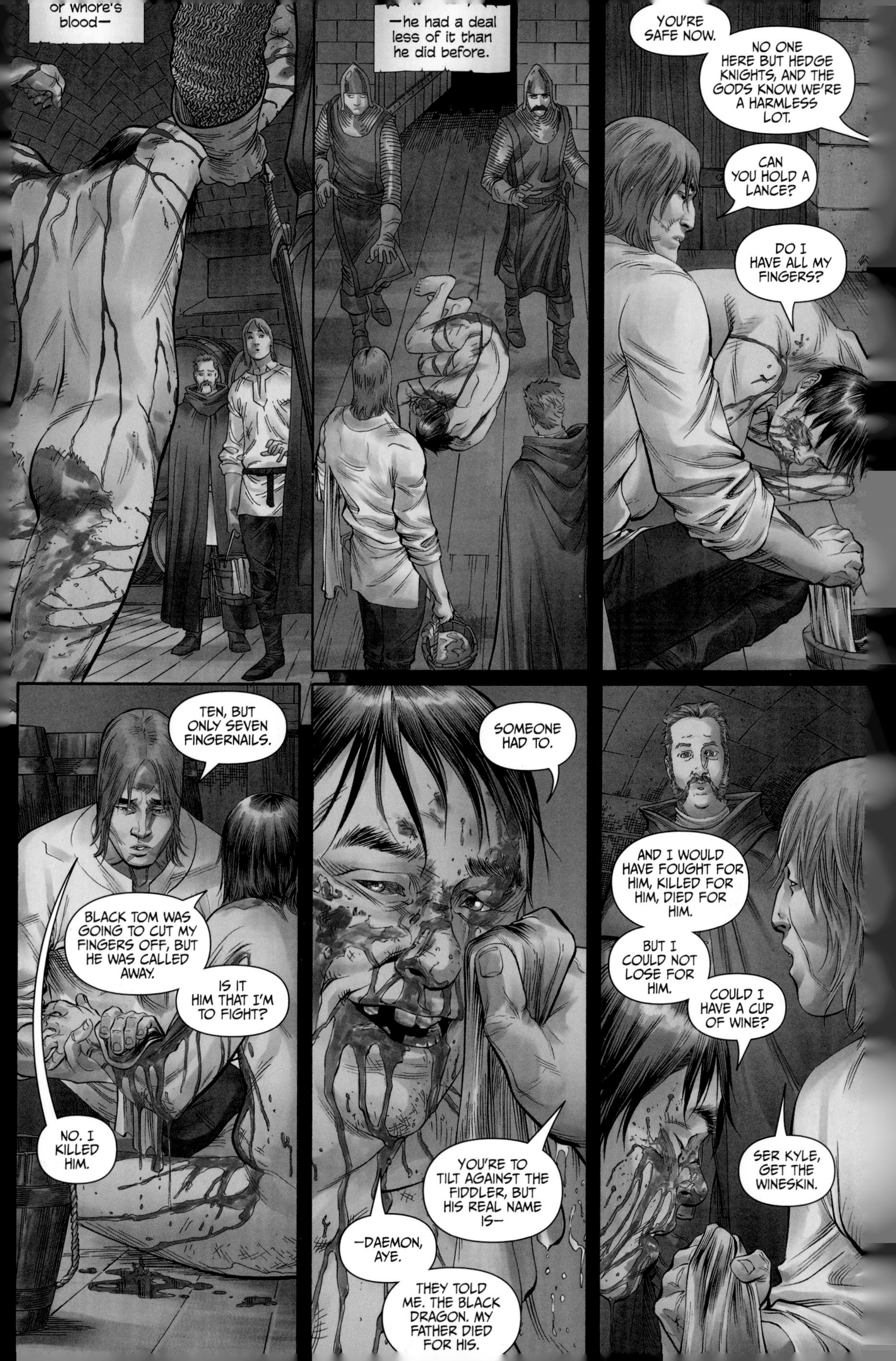
or whore's blood—
—he had a deal less of it than he did before.
YOU'RE SAFE NOW.
NO ONE HERE BUT HEDGE KNIGHTS, AND THE GODS KNOW WE'RE A HARMLESS LOT.
CAN YOU HOLD A LANCE?
DO I HAVE ALL MY FINGERS?
TEN, BUT ONLY SEVEN FINGERNAILS.
BLACK TOM WAS GOING TO CUT MY FINGERS OFF, BUT HE WAS CALLED AWAY.
IS IT HIM THAT I'M TO FIGHT?
NO. I KILLED HIM.
SOMEONE HAD TO.
YOU'RE TO TILT AGAINST THE FIDDLER, BUT HIS REAL NAME IS—
—DAEMON, AYE.
THEY TOLD ME. THE BLACK DRAGON. MY FATHER DIED FOR HIS.
AND I WOULD HAVE FOUGHT FOR HIM, KILLED FOR HIM, DIED FOR HIM.
BUT I COULD NOT LOSE FOR HIM.
COULD I HAVE A CUP OF WINE?
SER KYLE, GET THE WINESKIN.

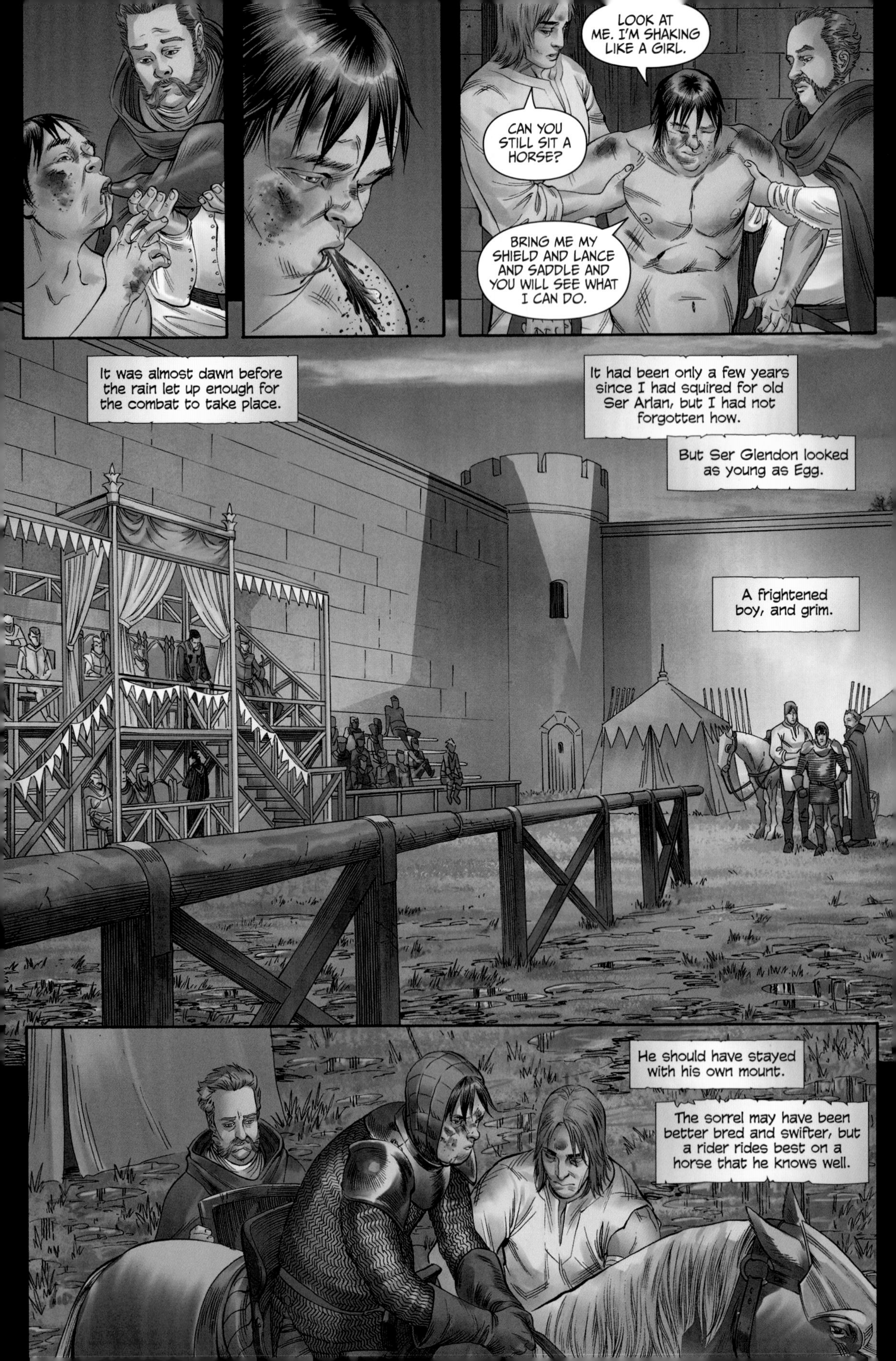

LOOK AT ME. I'M SHAKING LIKE A GIRL.
CAN YOU STILL SIT A HORSE?
BRING ME MY SHIELD AND LANCE AND SADDLE AND YOU WILL SEE WHAT I CAN DO.
It was almost dawn before the rain let up enough for the combat to take place.
It had been only a few years since I had squired for old Ser Arlan, but I had not forgotten how.
But Ser Glendon looked as young as Egg.
A frightened boy, and grim.
He should have stayed with his own mount.
The sorrel may have been better bred and swifter, but a rider rides best on a horse that he knows well.

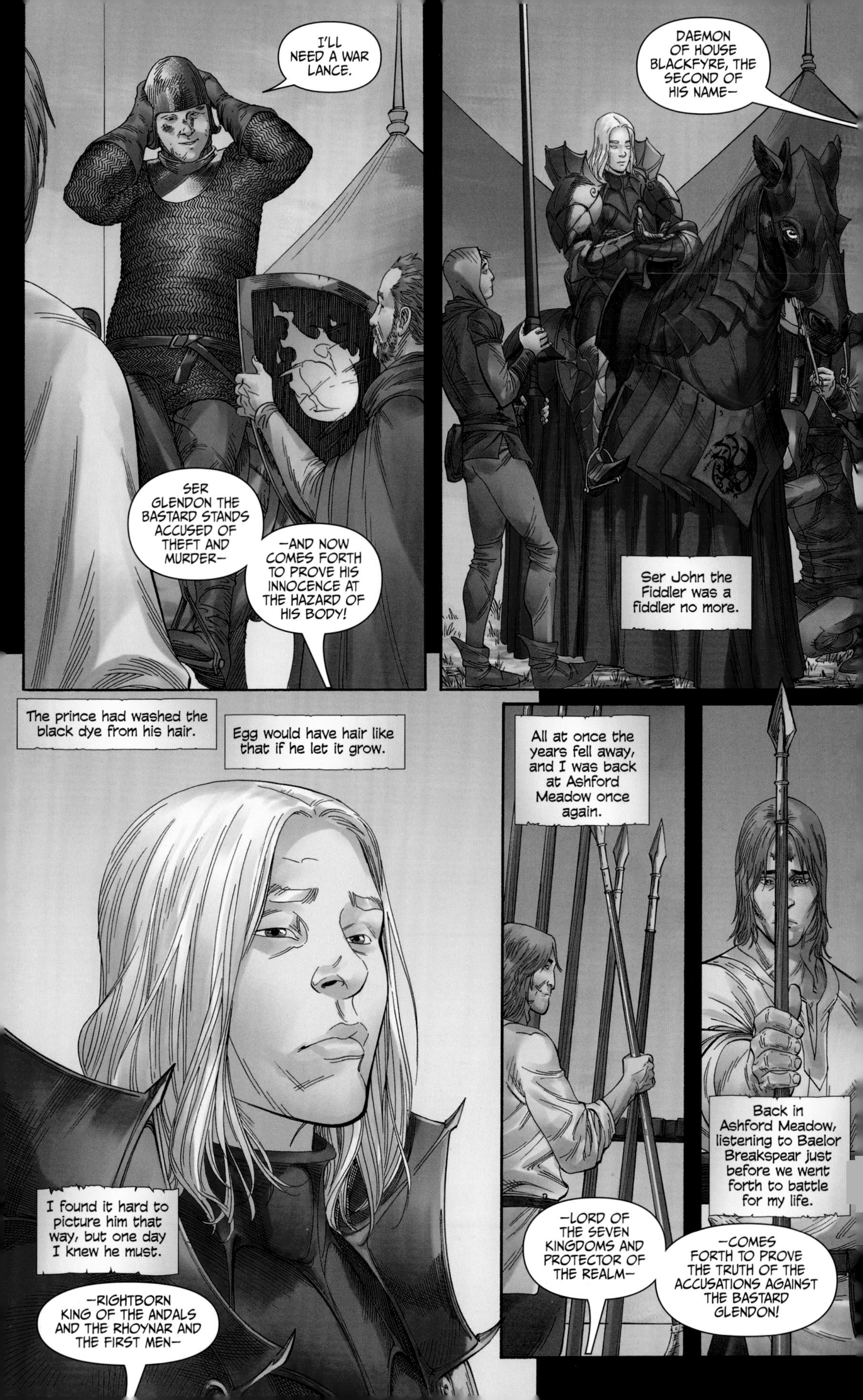
I'LL NEED A WAR LANCE.
SER GLENDON THE BASTARD STANDS ACCUSED OF THEFT AND MURDER—
—AND NOW COMES FORTH TO PROVE HIS INNOCENCE AT THE HAZARD OF HIS BODY!
DAEMON OF HOUSE BLACKFYRE, THE SECOND OF HIS NAME—
Ser John the Fiddler was a fiddler no more.
The prince had washed the black dye from his hair.
Egg would have hair like that if he let it grow.
I found it hard to picture him that way, but one day I knew he must.
—RIGHTBORN KING OF THE ANDALS AND THE RHOYNAR AND THE FIRST MEN—
All at once the years fell away, and I was back at Ashford Meadow once again.
Back in Ashford Meadow, listening to Baelor Breakspear just before we went forth to battle for my life.
—LORD OF THE SEVEN KINGDOMS AND PROTECTOR OF THE REALM—
—COMES FORTH TO PROVE THE TRUTH OF THE ACCUSATIONS AGAINST THE BASTARD GLENDON!

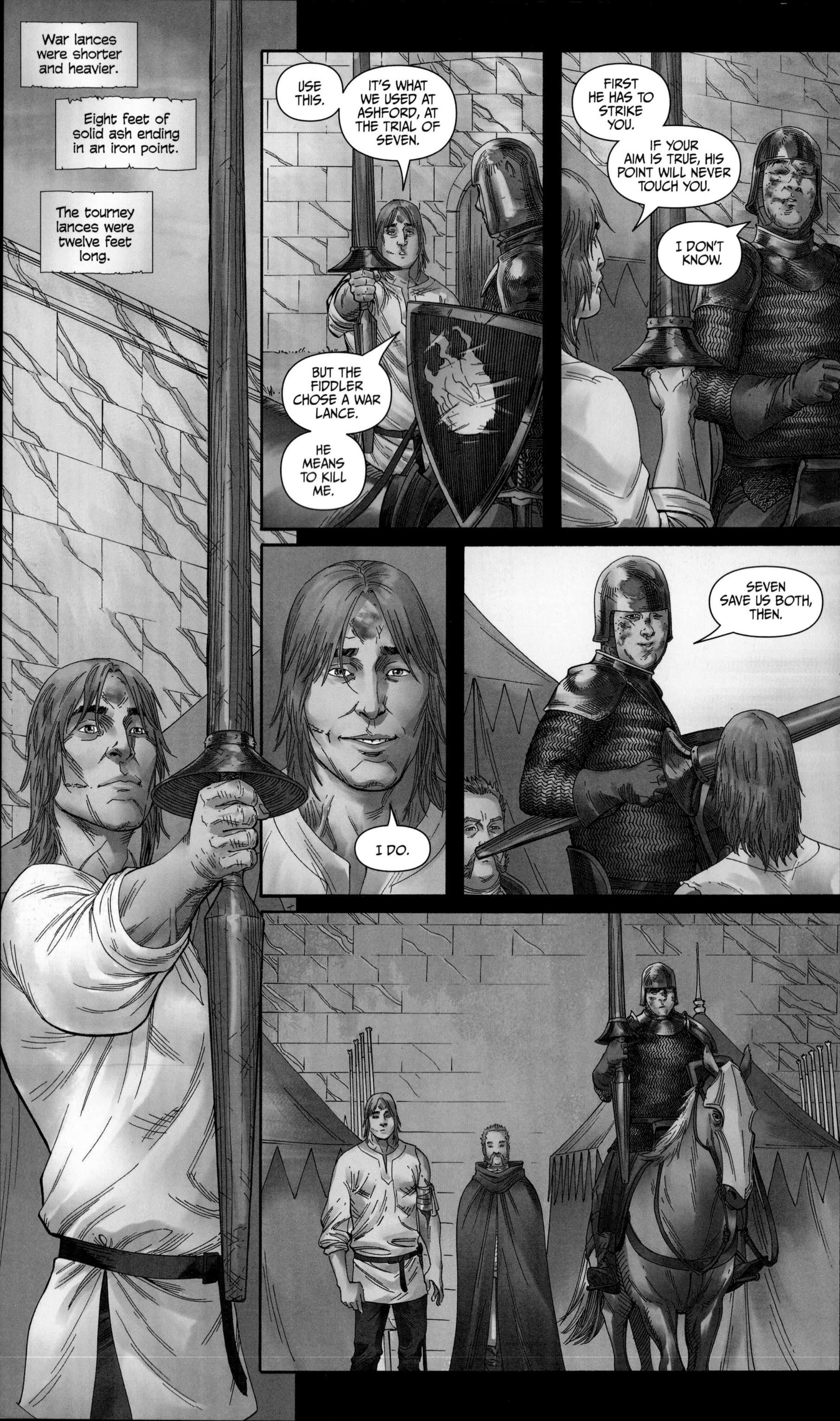
War lances were shorter and heavier.
Eight feet of solid ash ending in an iron point.
The tourney lances were twelve feet long.
USE THIS.
IT'S WHAT WE USED AT ASHFORD, AT THE TRIAL OF SEVEN.
BUT THE FIDDLER CHOSE A WAR LANCE.
HE MEANS TO KILL ME.
FIRST HE HAS TO STRIKE YOU.
IF YOUR AIM IS TRUE, HIS POINT WILL NEVER TOUCH YOU.
I DON'T KNOW.
I DO.
SEVEN SAVE US BOTH, THEN.

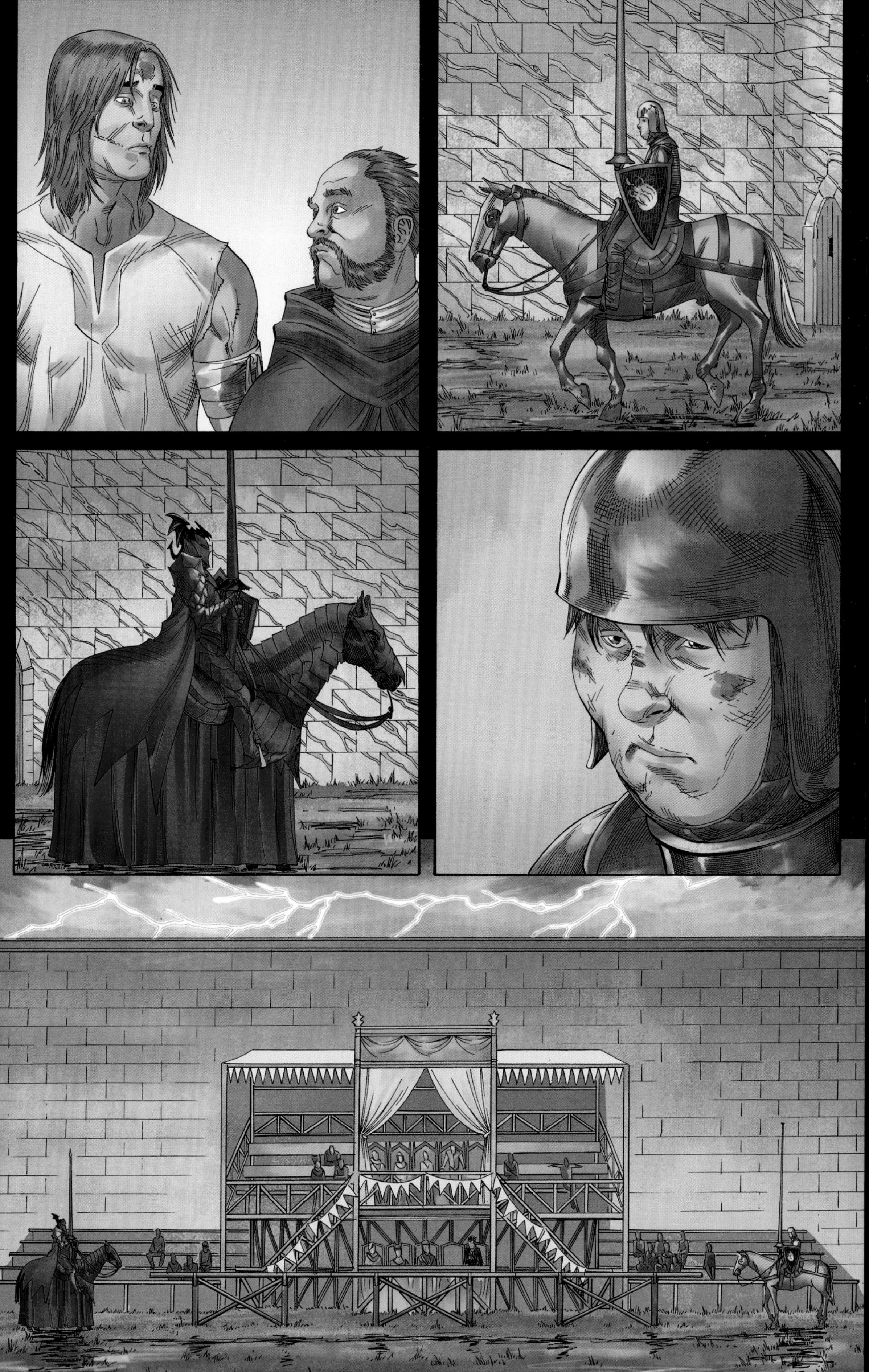

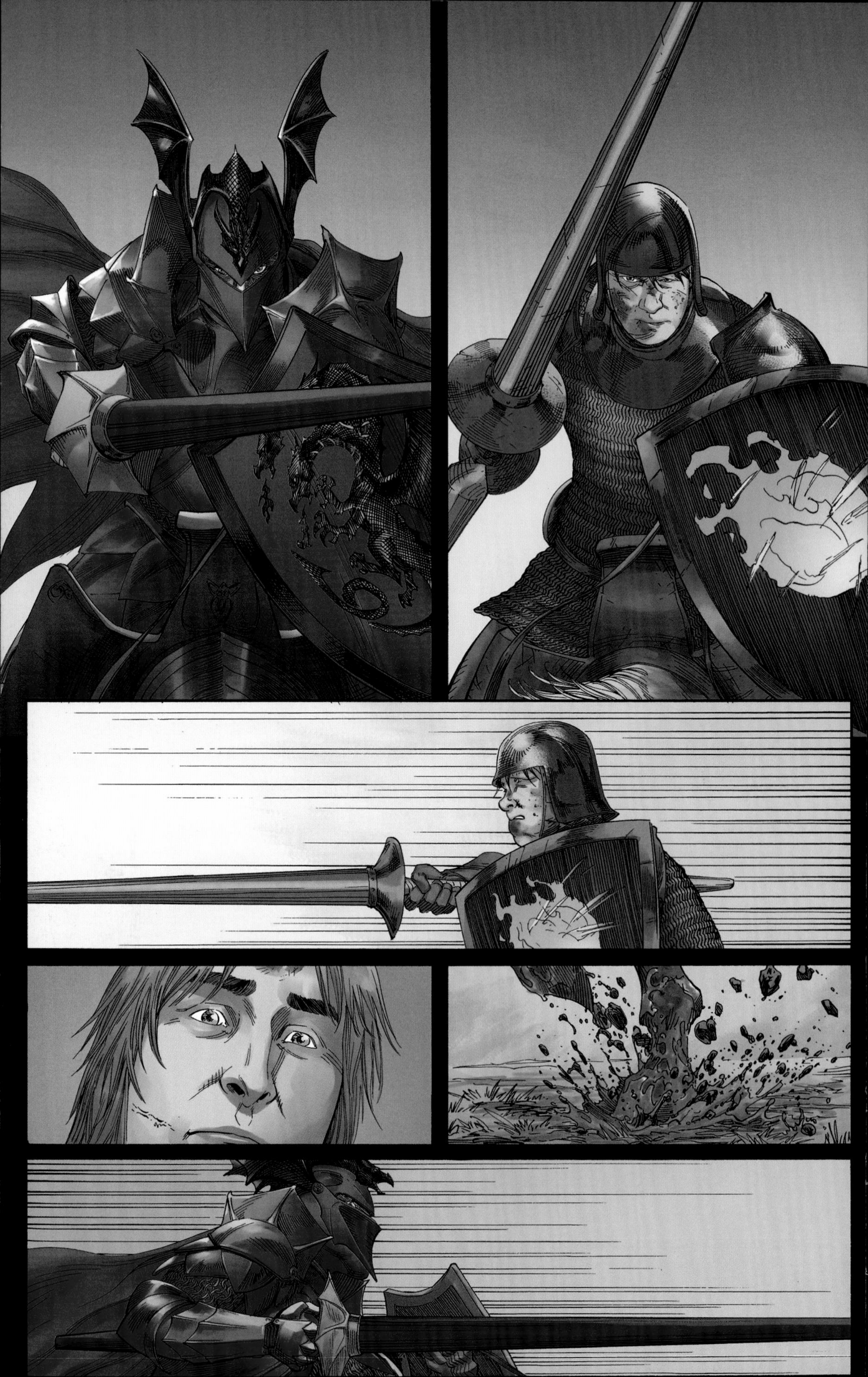

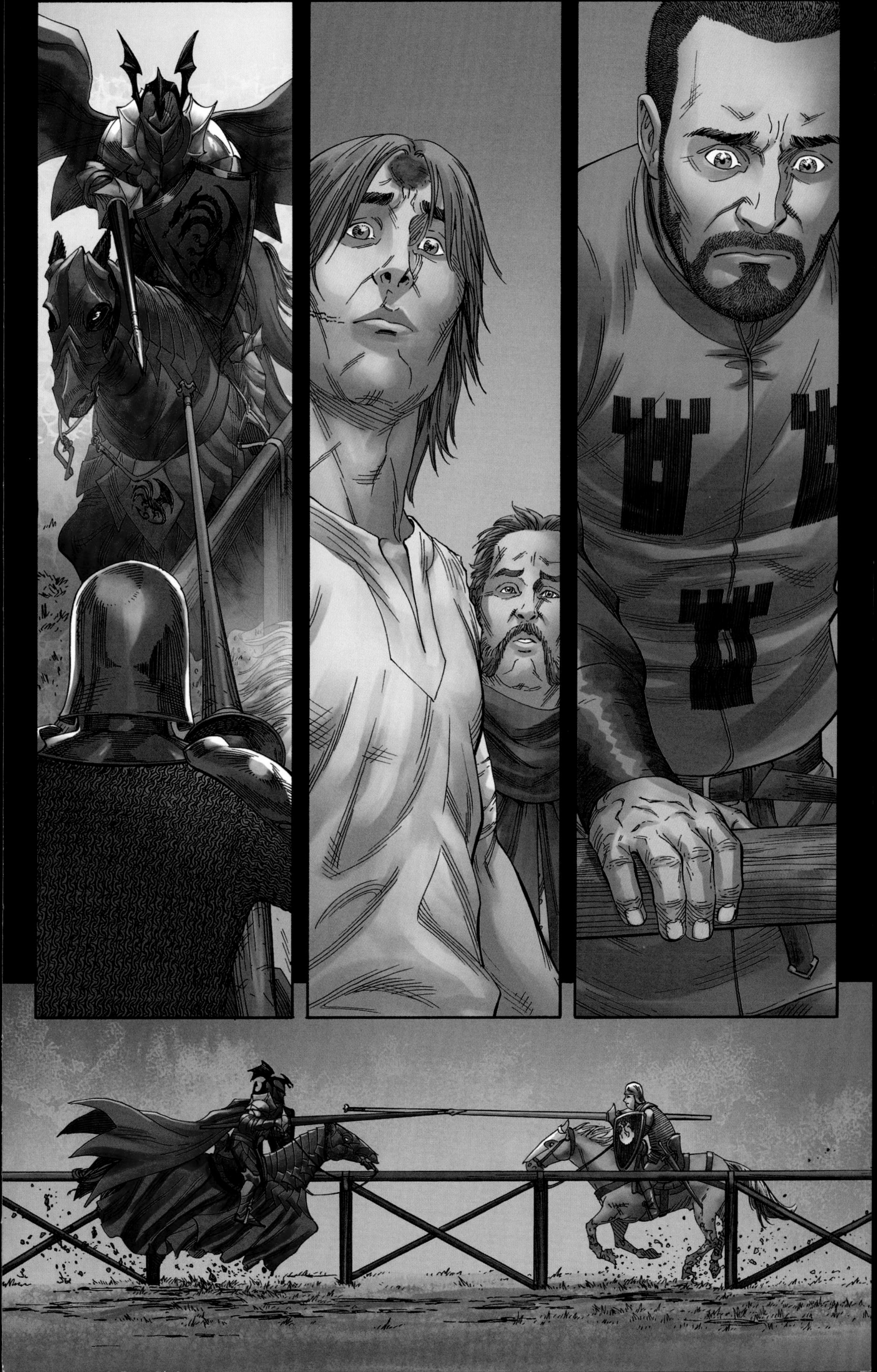

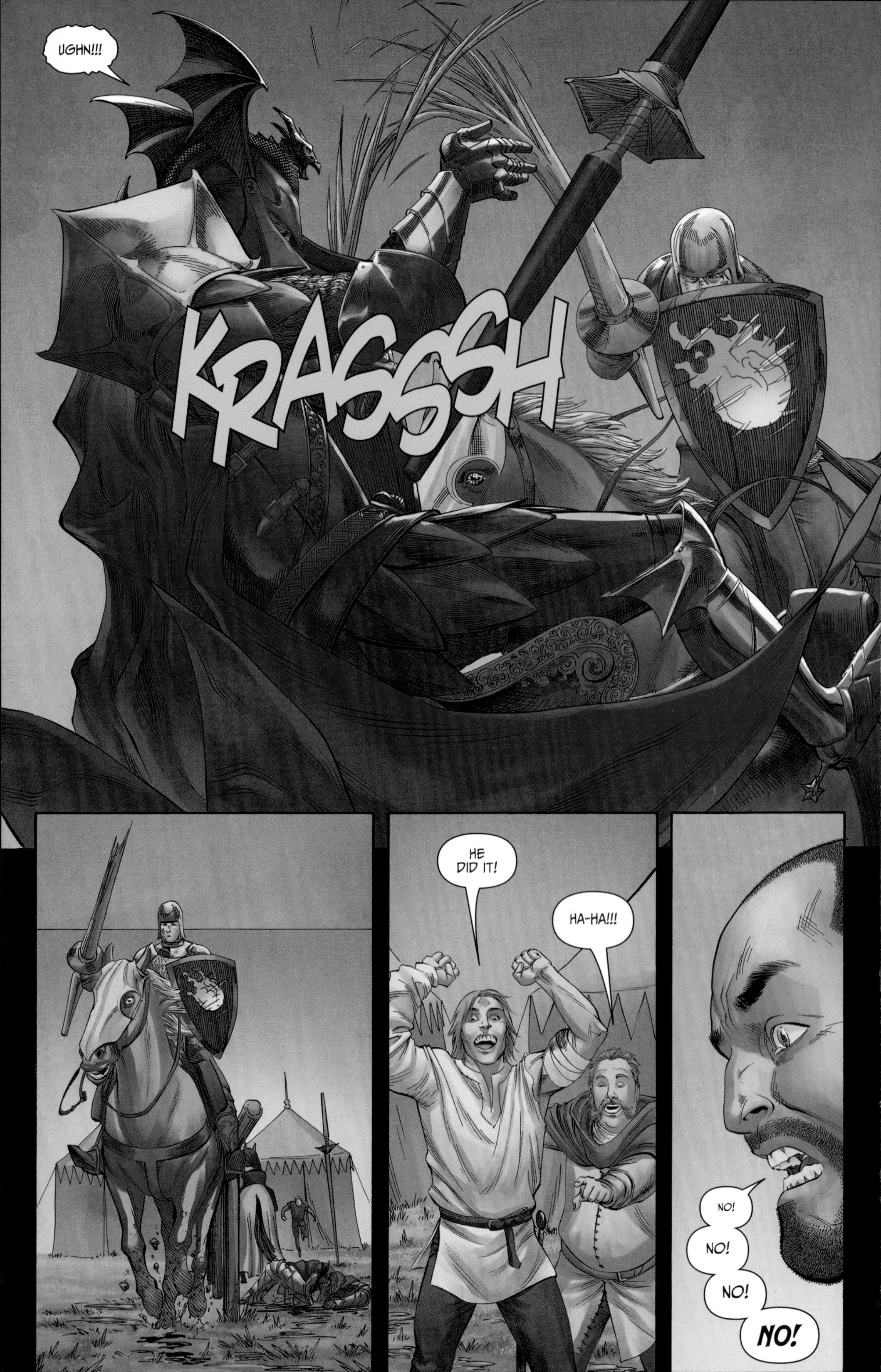
UGHN!!!
KRASSSH
HE DID IT!
HA-HA!!!
NO!
NO!
NO!
NO!

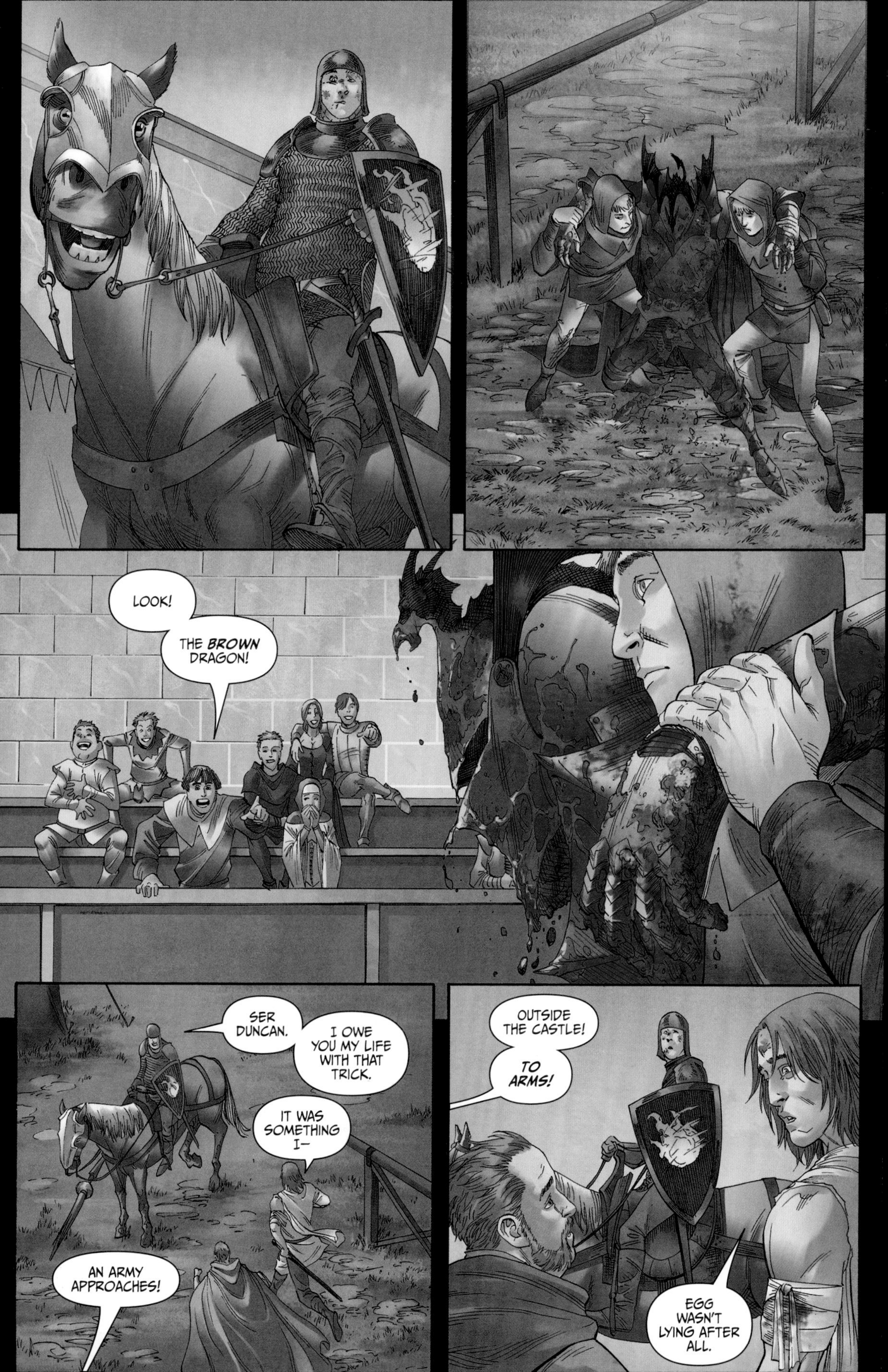
LOOK!
THE BROWN DRAGON!
SER DUNCAN.
I OWE YOU MY LIFE WITH THAT TRICK.
IT WAS SOMETHING I—
AN ARMY APPROACHES!
OUTSIDE THE CASTLE!
TO ARMS!
EGG WASN'T LYING AFTER ALL.

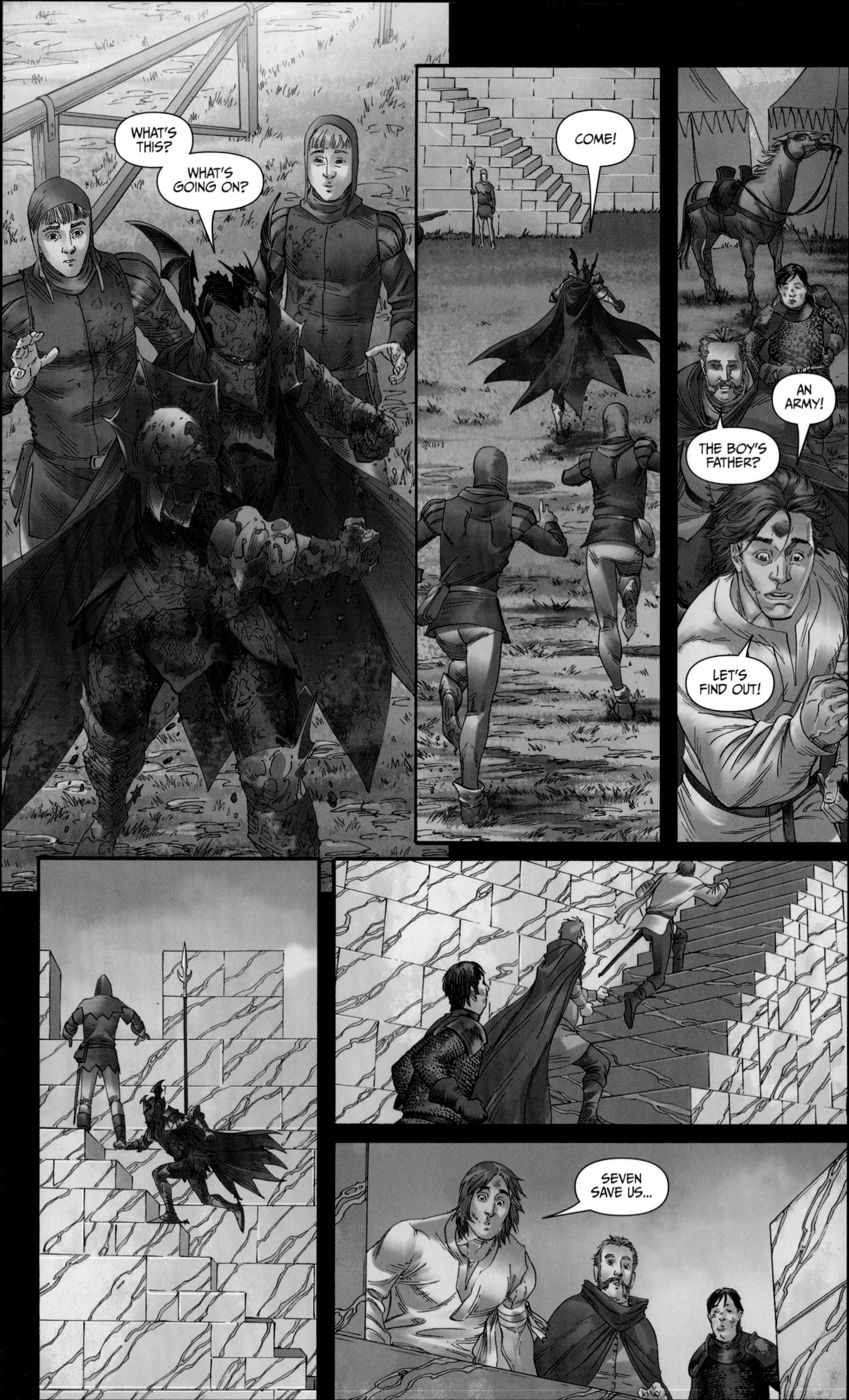
WHAT'S THIS?
WHAT'S GOING ON?
COME!
THE BOY'S FATHER?
AN ARMY!
LET'S FIND OUT!
SEVEN SAVE US...

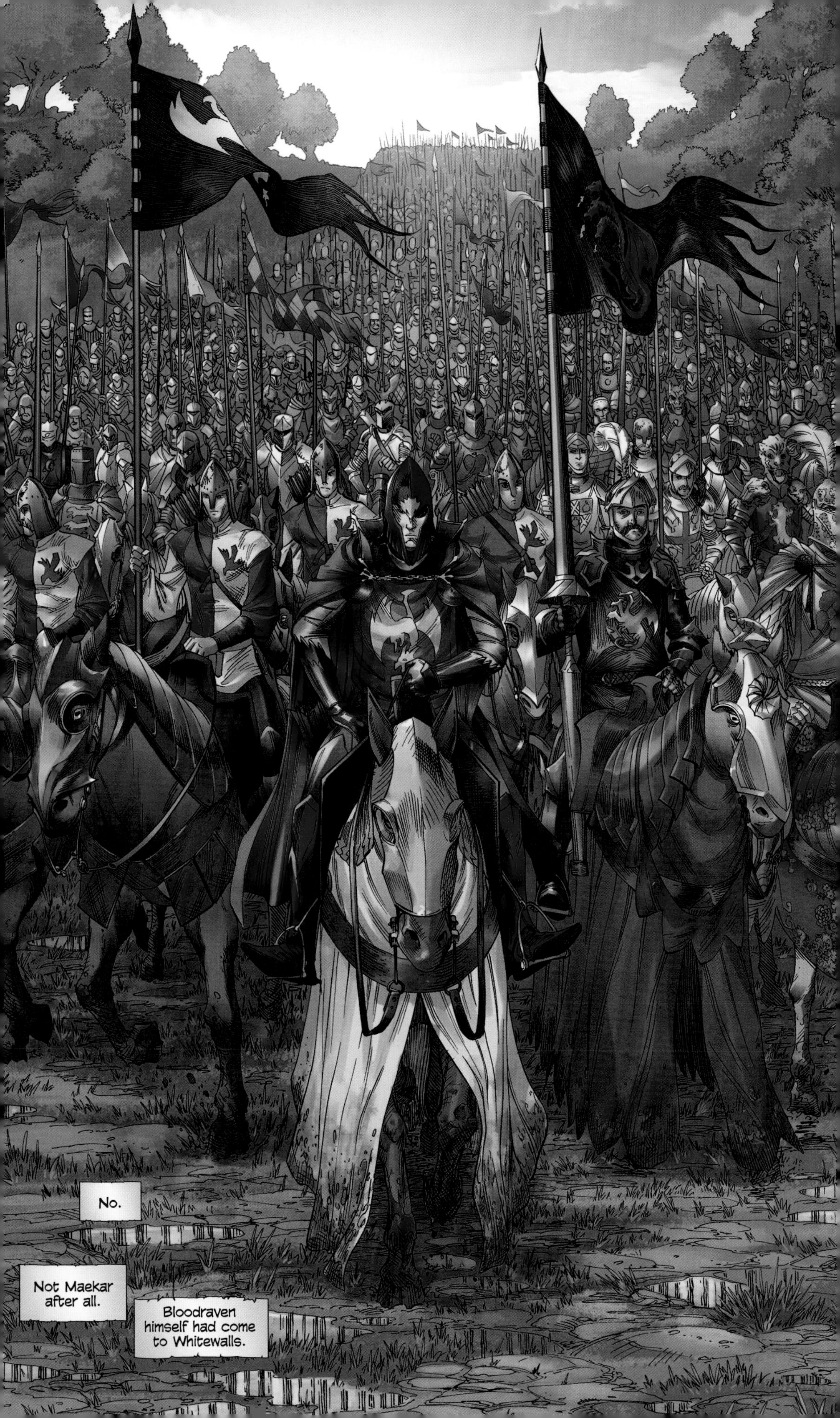
No.
Not Maekar after all.
Bloodraven himself had come to Whitewalls.

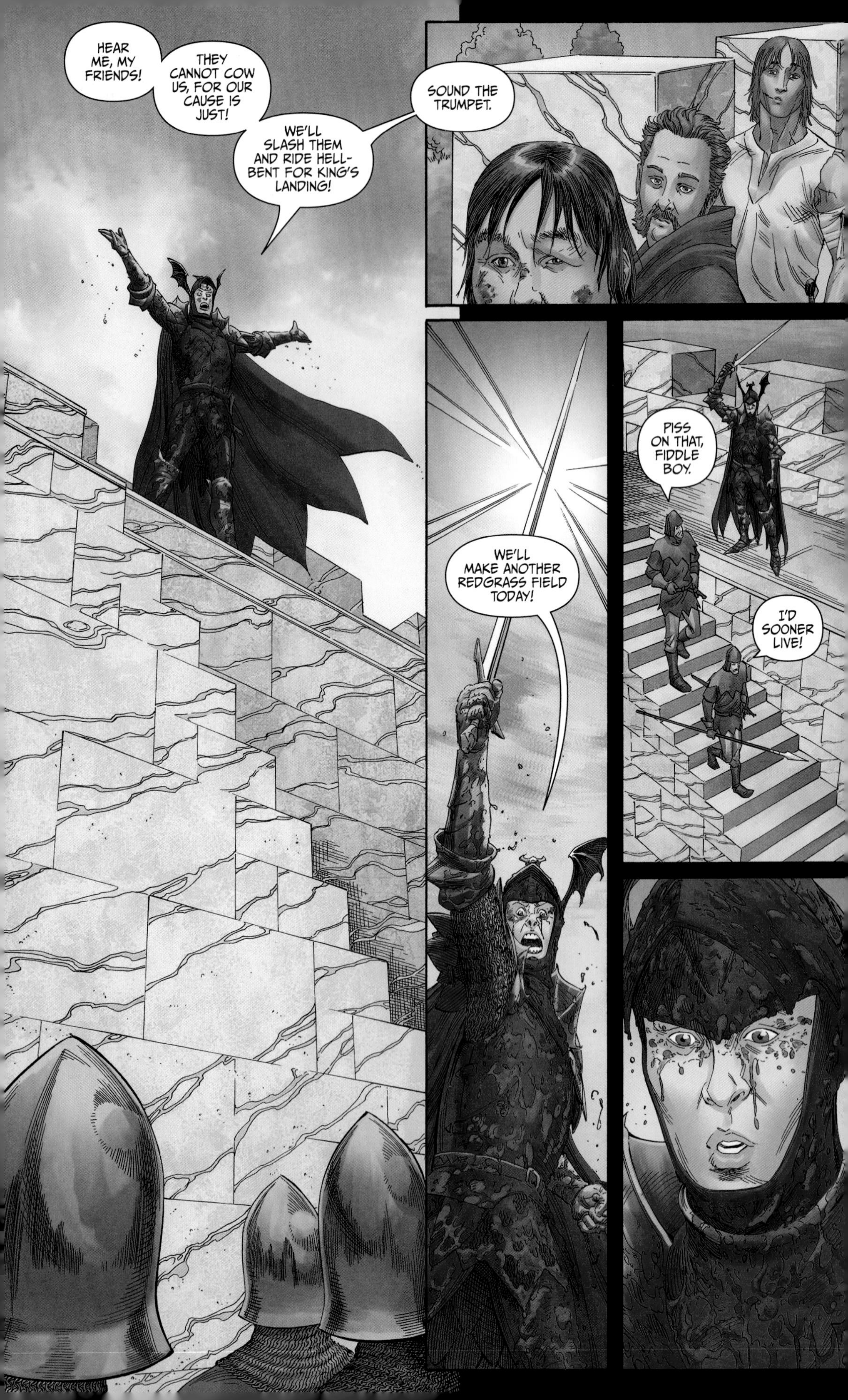
HEAR ME, MY FRIENDS!
THEY CANNOT COW US, FOR OUR CAUSE IS JUST!
WE'LL SLASH THEM AND RIDE HELL-BENT FOR KING'S LANDING!
SOUND THE TRUMPET.
WE'LL MAKE ANOTHER REDGRASS FIELD TODAY!
PISS ON THAT, FIDDLE BOY.
I'D SOONER LIVE!

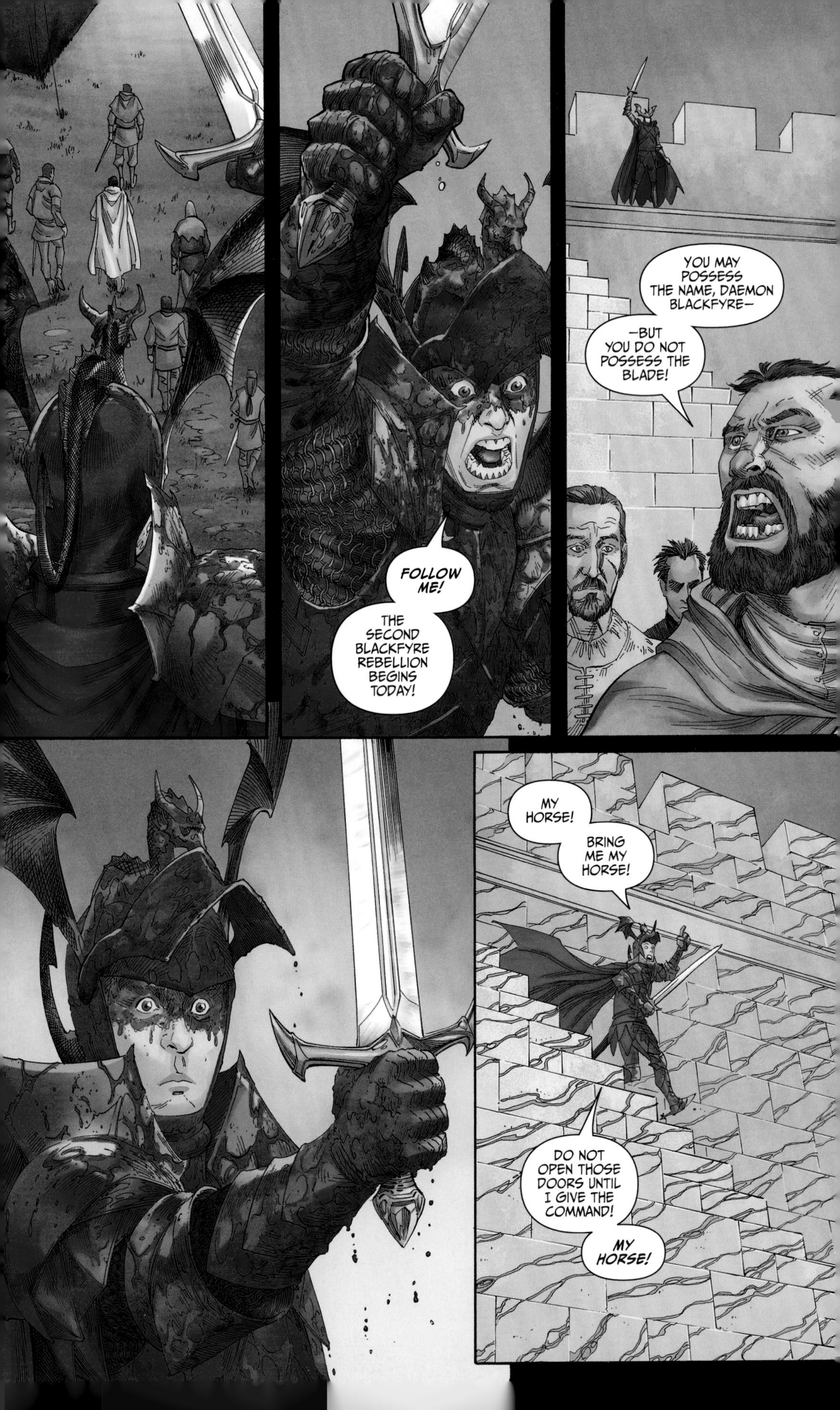
FOLLOW ME!
THE SECOND BLACKFYRE REBELLION BEGINS TODAY!
YOU MAY POSSESS THE NAME, DAEMON BLACKFYRE—
—BUT YOU DO NOT POSSESS THE BLADE!
MY HORSE!
BRING ME MY HORSE!
DO NOT OPEN THOSE DOORS UNTIL I GIVE THE COMMAND!
MY HORSE!

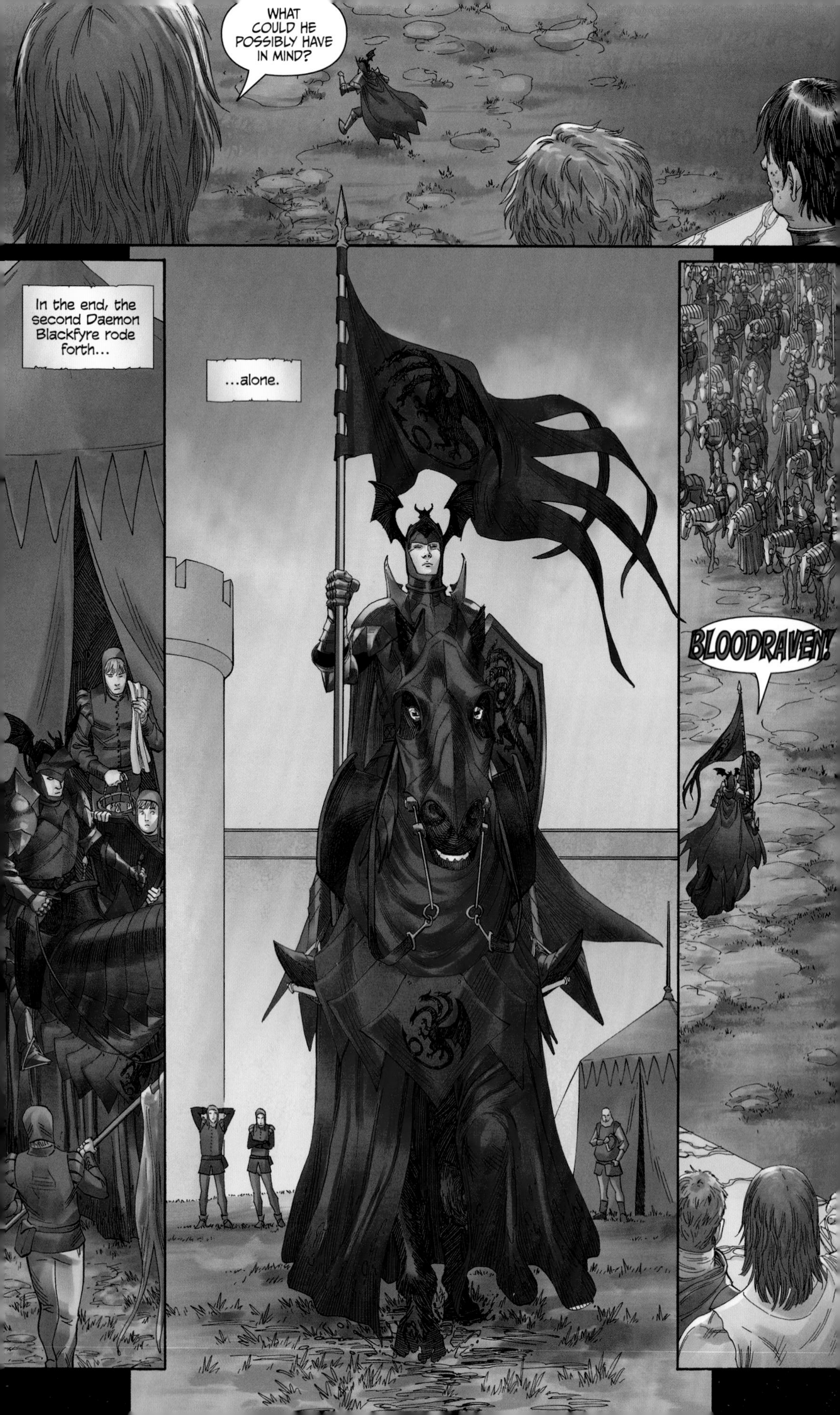
WHAT COULD HE POSSIBLY HAVE IN MIND?
In the end, the second Daemon Blackfyre rode forth...
...alone.
BLOODRAVEN!

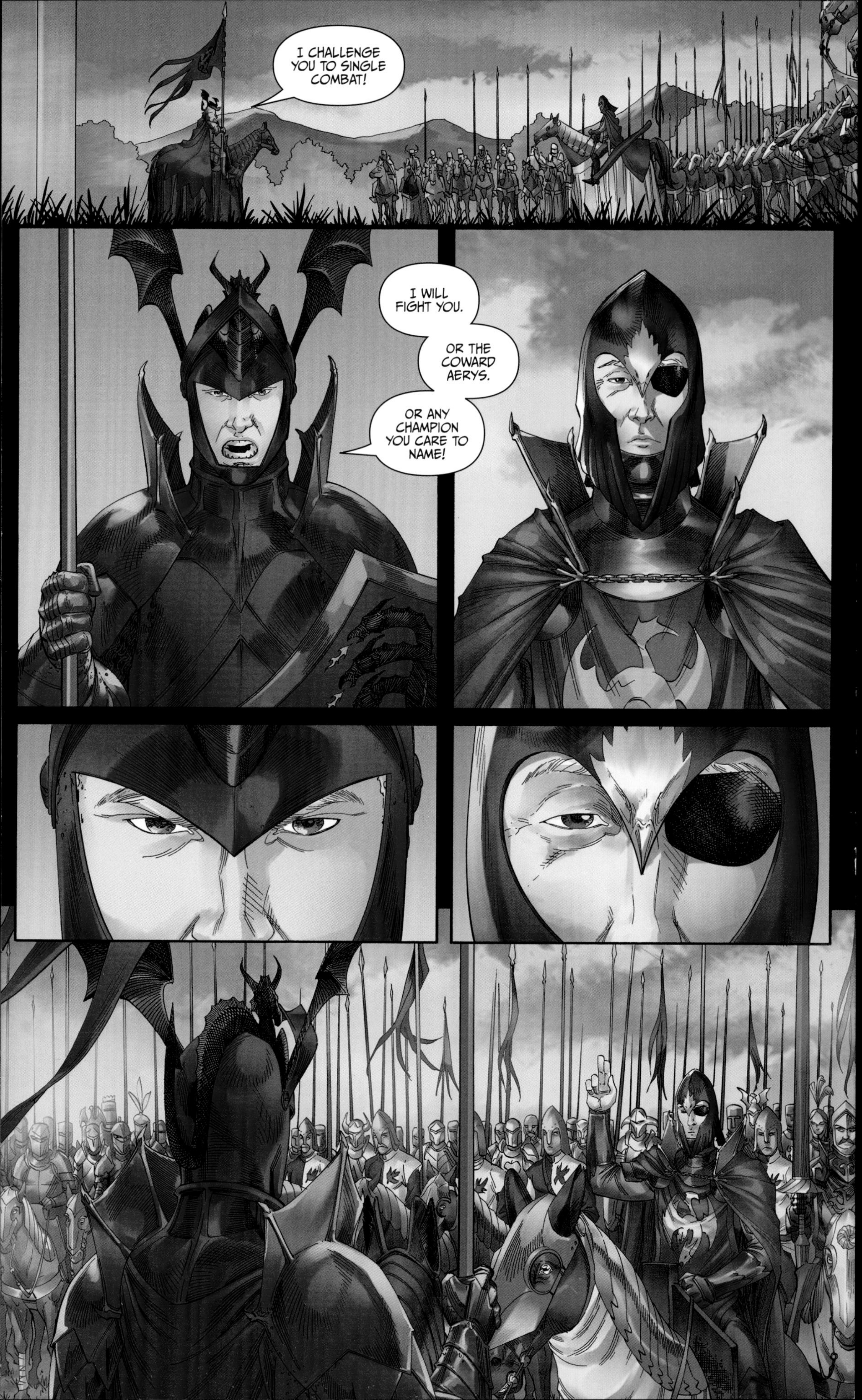
I CHALLENGE YOU TO SINGLE COMBAT!
I WILL FIGHT YOU.
OR THE COWARD AERYS.
OR ANY CHAMPION YOU CARE TO NAME!

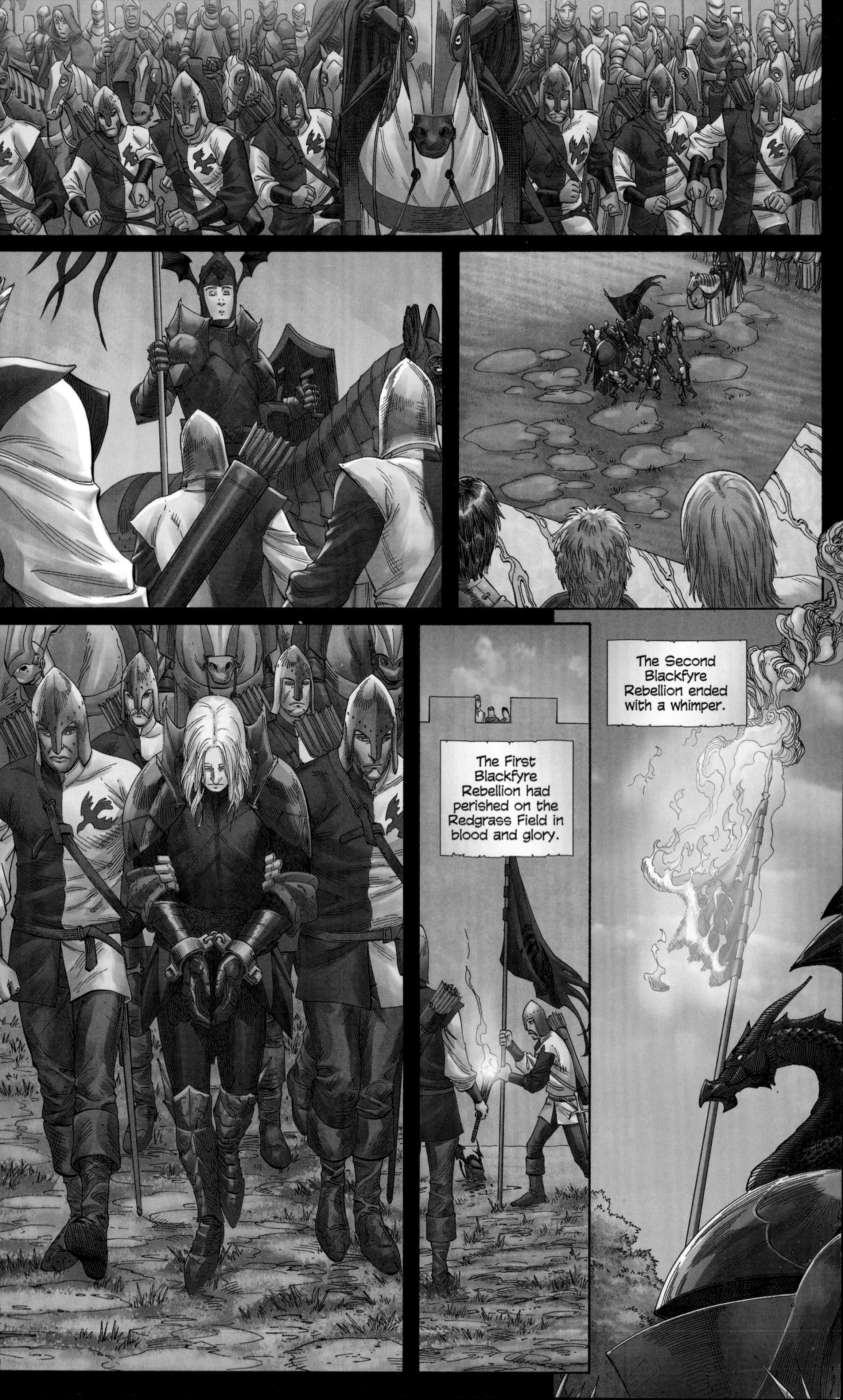
The First Blackfyre Rebellion had perished on the Redgrass Field in blood and glory.
The Second Blackfyre Rebellion ended with a whimper.

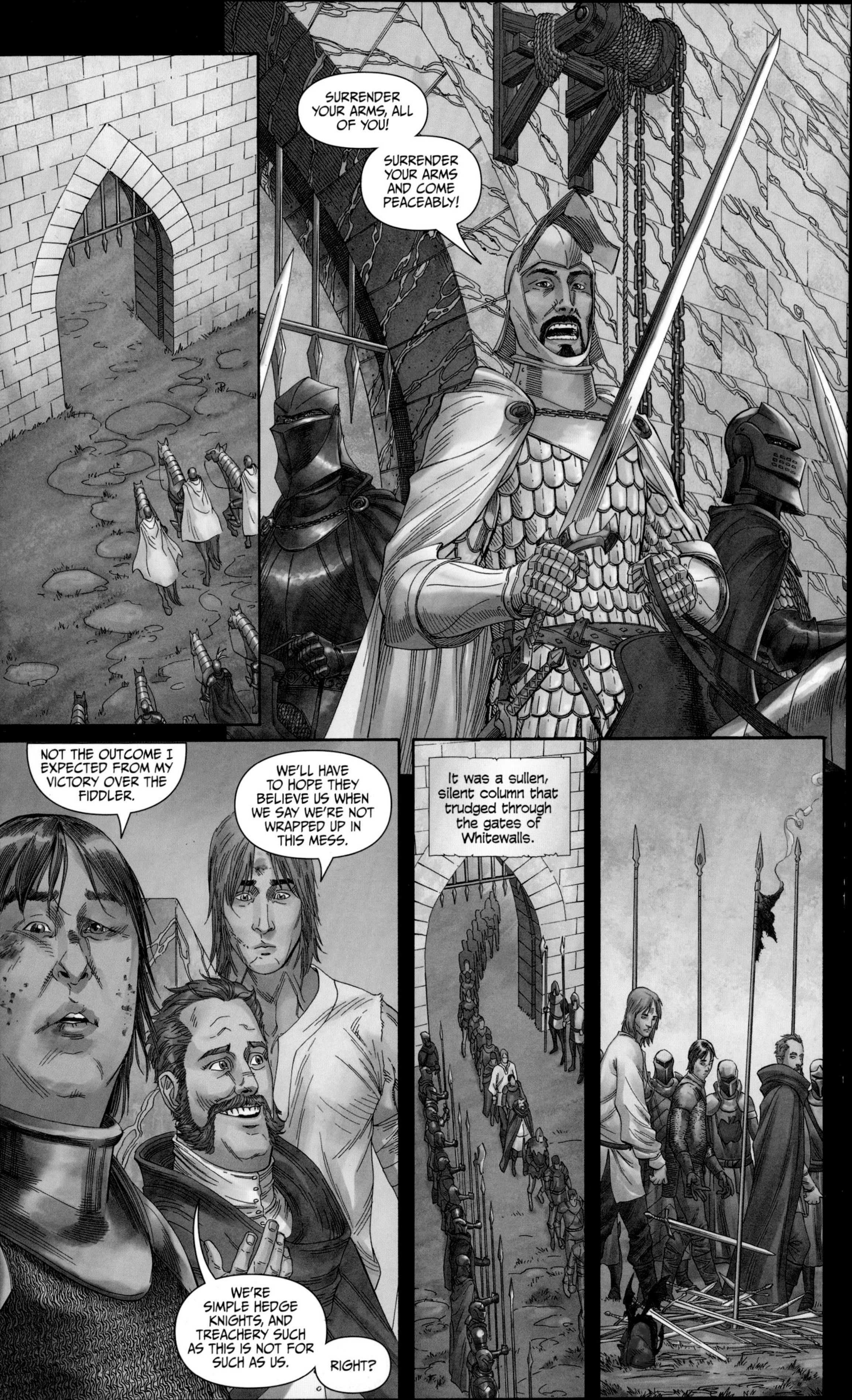
SURRENDER YOUR ARMS, ALL OF YOU!
SURRENDER YOUR ARMS AND COME PEACEABLY!
NOT THE OUTCOME I EXPECTED FROM MY VICTORY OVER THE FIDDLER.
WE'LL HAVE TO HOPE THEY BELIEVE US WHEN WE SAY WE'RE NOT WRAPPED UP IN THIS MESS.
WE'RE SIMPLE HEDGE KNIGHTS, AND TREACHERY SUCH AS THIS IS NOT FOR SUCH AS US.
RIGHT?
It was a sullen, silent column that trudged through the gates of Whitewalls.

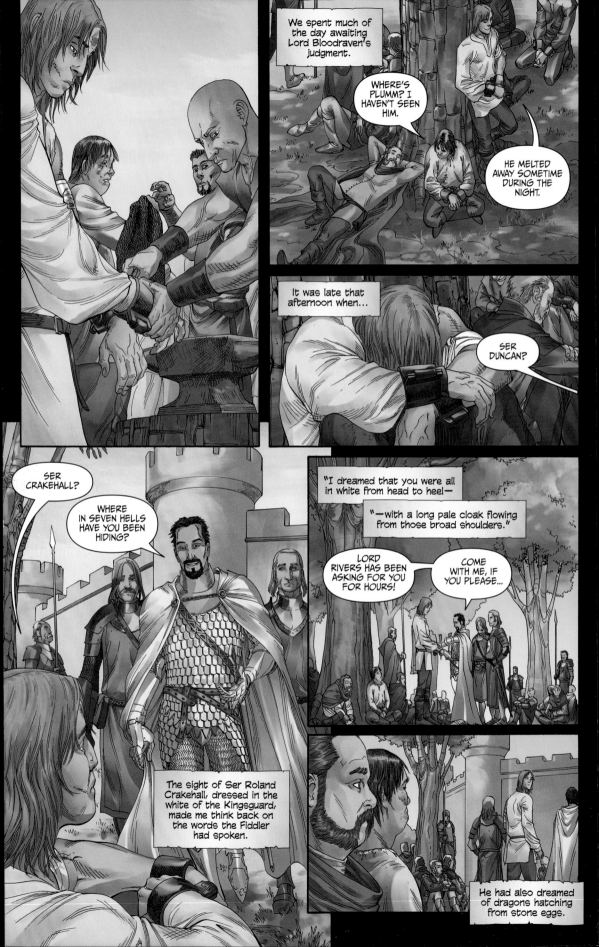

We spent much of the day awaiting Lord Bloodraven's judgment.

WHERE'S PLUMM? I HAVEN'T SEEN HIM.

HE MELTED AWAY SOMETIME DURING THE NIGHT.

It was late that afternoon when...

SER DUNCAN?

SER CRAKEHALL?

WHERE IN SEVEN HELLS HAVE YOU BEEN HIDING?

The sight of Ser Roland Crakehall, dressed in the white of the Kingsguard, made me think back on the words the Fiddler had spoken.

"I dreamed that you were all in white from head to heel—

"—with a long pale cloak flowing from those broad shoulders."

LORD RIVERS HAS BEEN ASKING FOR YOU FOR HOURS!

COME WITH ME, IF YOU PLEASE...

He had also dreamed of dragons hatching from stone eggs.

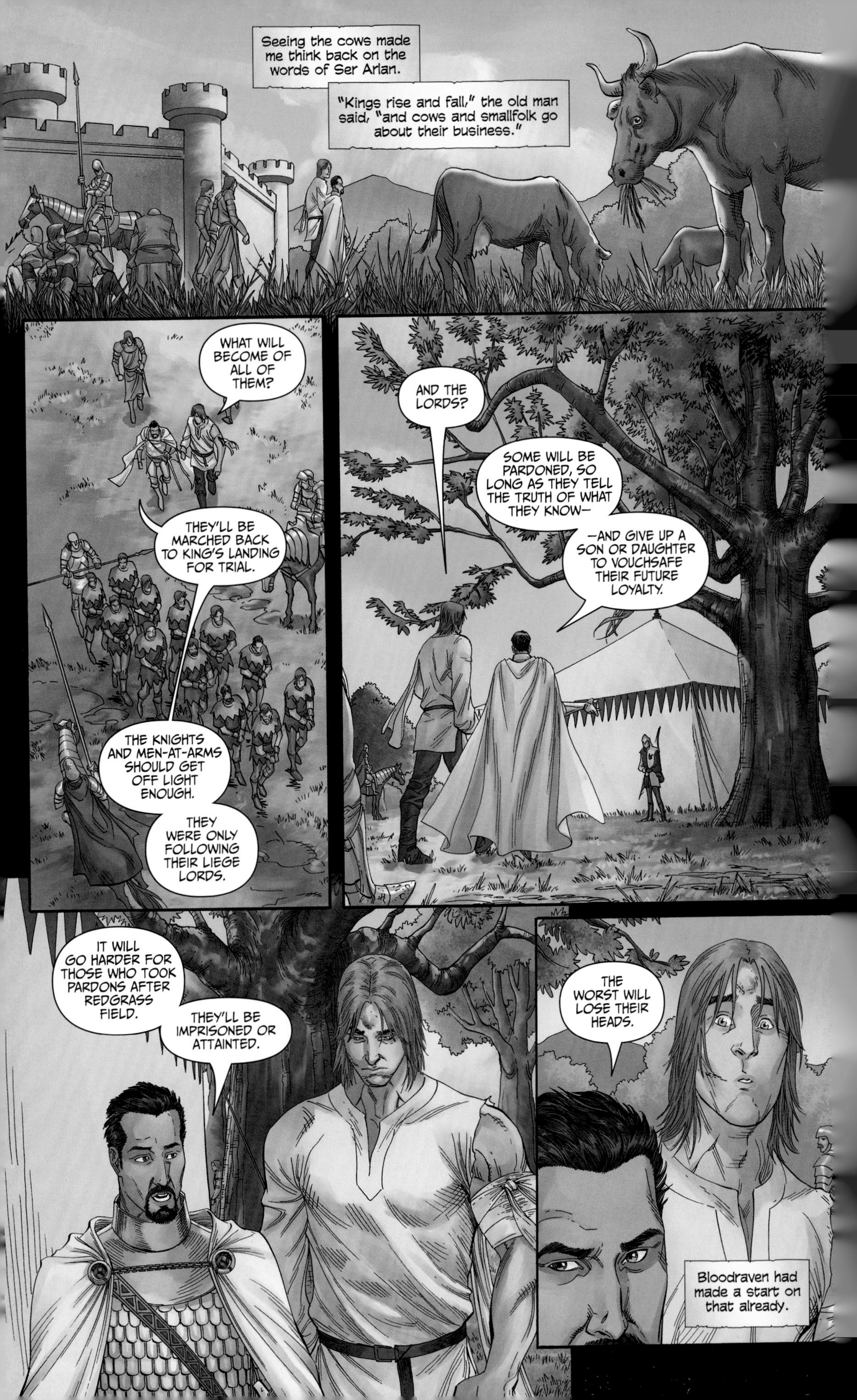
Seeing the cows made me think back on the words of Ser Arlan.
"Kings rise and fall," the old man said, "and cows and smallfolk go about their business."
WHAT WILL BECOME OF ALL OF THEM?
THEY'LL BE MARCHED BACK TO KING'S LANDING FOR TRIAL.
THE KNIGHTS AND MEN-AT-ARMS SHOULD GET OFF LIGHT ENOUGH.
THEY WERE ONLY FOLLOWING THEIR LIEGE LORDS.
AND THE LORDS?
SOME WILL BE PARDONED, SO LONG AS THEY TELL THE TRUTH OF WHAT THEY KNOW—
—AND GIVE UP A SON OR DAUGHTER TO VOUCHSAFE THEIR FUTURE LOYALTY.
IT WILL GO HARDER FOR THOSE WHO TOOK PARDONS AFTER REDGRASS FIELD.
THEY'LL BE IMPRISONED OR ATTAINTED.
THE WORST WILL LOSE THEIR HEADS.
Bloodraven had made a start on that already.

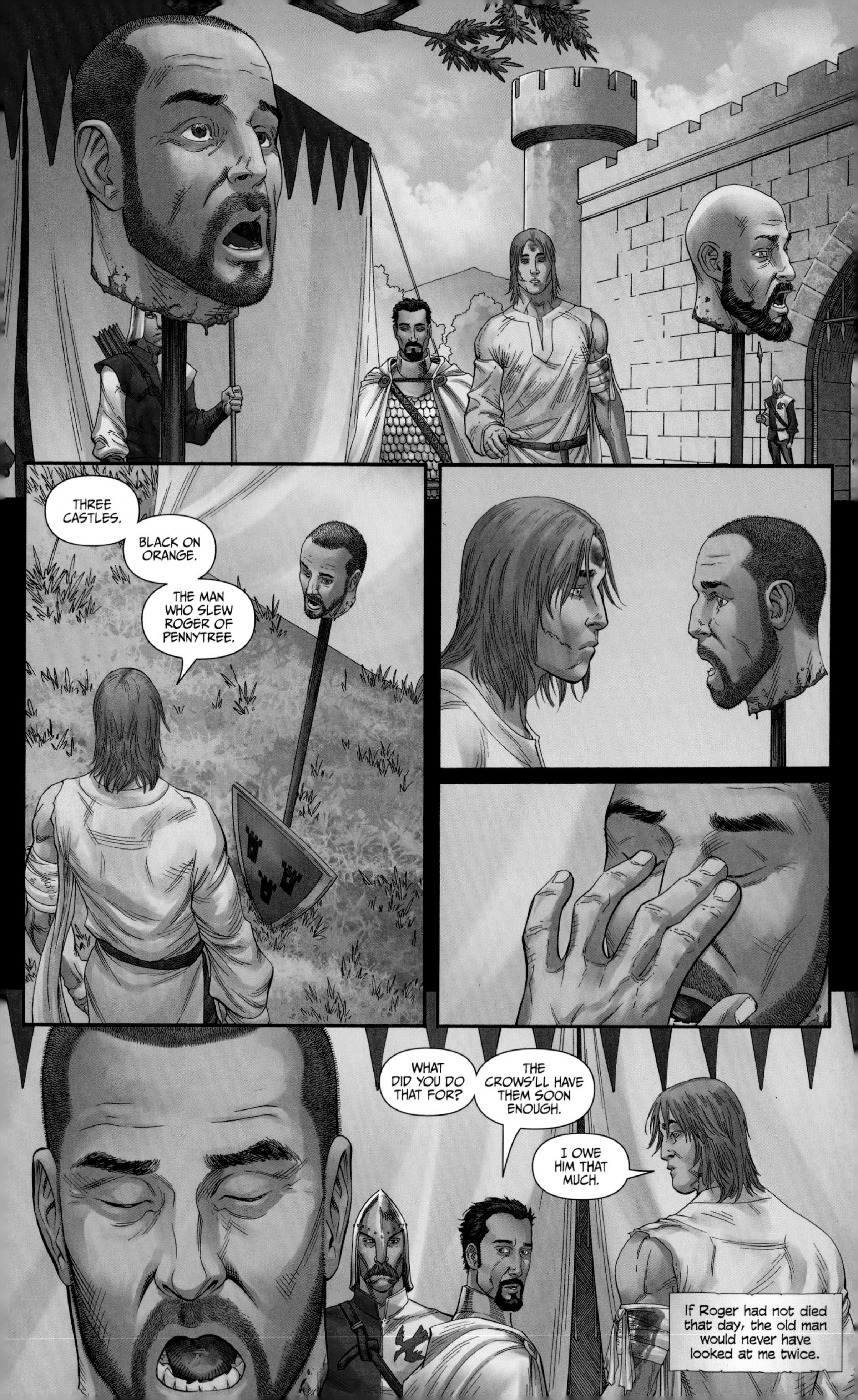
THREE CASTLES.
BLACK ON ORANGE.
THE MAN WHO SLEW ROGER OF PENNYTREE.
WHAT DID YOU DO THAT FOR?
THE CROWS'LL HAVE THEM SOON ENOUGH.
I OWE HIM THAT MUCH.
If Roger had not died that day, the old man would never have looked at me twice.

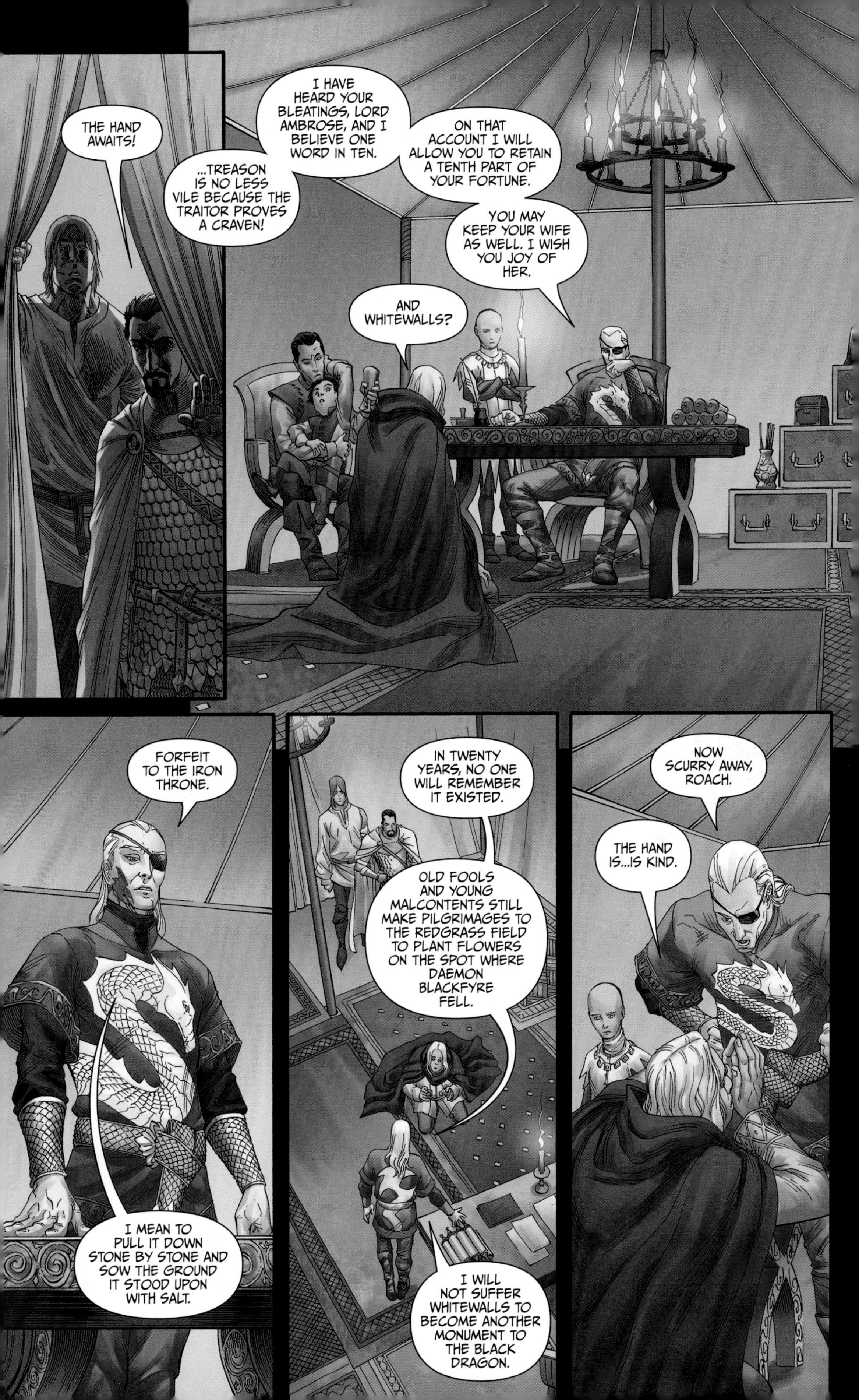
THE HAND AWAITS!
...TREASON IS NO LESS VILE BECAUSE THE TRAITOR PROVES A CRAVEN!
I HAVE HEARD YOUR BLEATINGS, LORD AMBROSE, AND I BELIEVE ONE WORD IN TEN.
ON THAT ACCOUNT I WILL ALLOW YOU TO RETAIN A TENTH PART OF YOUR FORTUNE.
YOU MAY KEEP YOUR WIFE AS WELL. I WISH YOU JOY OF HER.
AND WHITEWALLS?
FORFEIT TO THE IRON THRONE.
I MEAN TO PULL IT DOWN STONE BY STONE AND SOW THE GROUND IT STOOD UPON WITH SALT.
IN TWENTY YEARS, NO ONE WILL REMEMBER IT EXISTED.
OLD FOOLS AND YOUNG MALCONTENTS STILL MAKE PILGRIMAGES TO THE REDGRASS FIELD TO PLANT FLOWERS ON THE SPOT WHERE DAEMON BLACKFYRE FELL.
I WILL NOT SUFFER WHITEWALLS TO BECOME ANOTHER MONUMENT TO THE BLACK DRAGON.
NOW SCURRY AWAY, ROACH.
THE HAND IS...IS KIND.

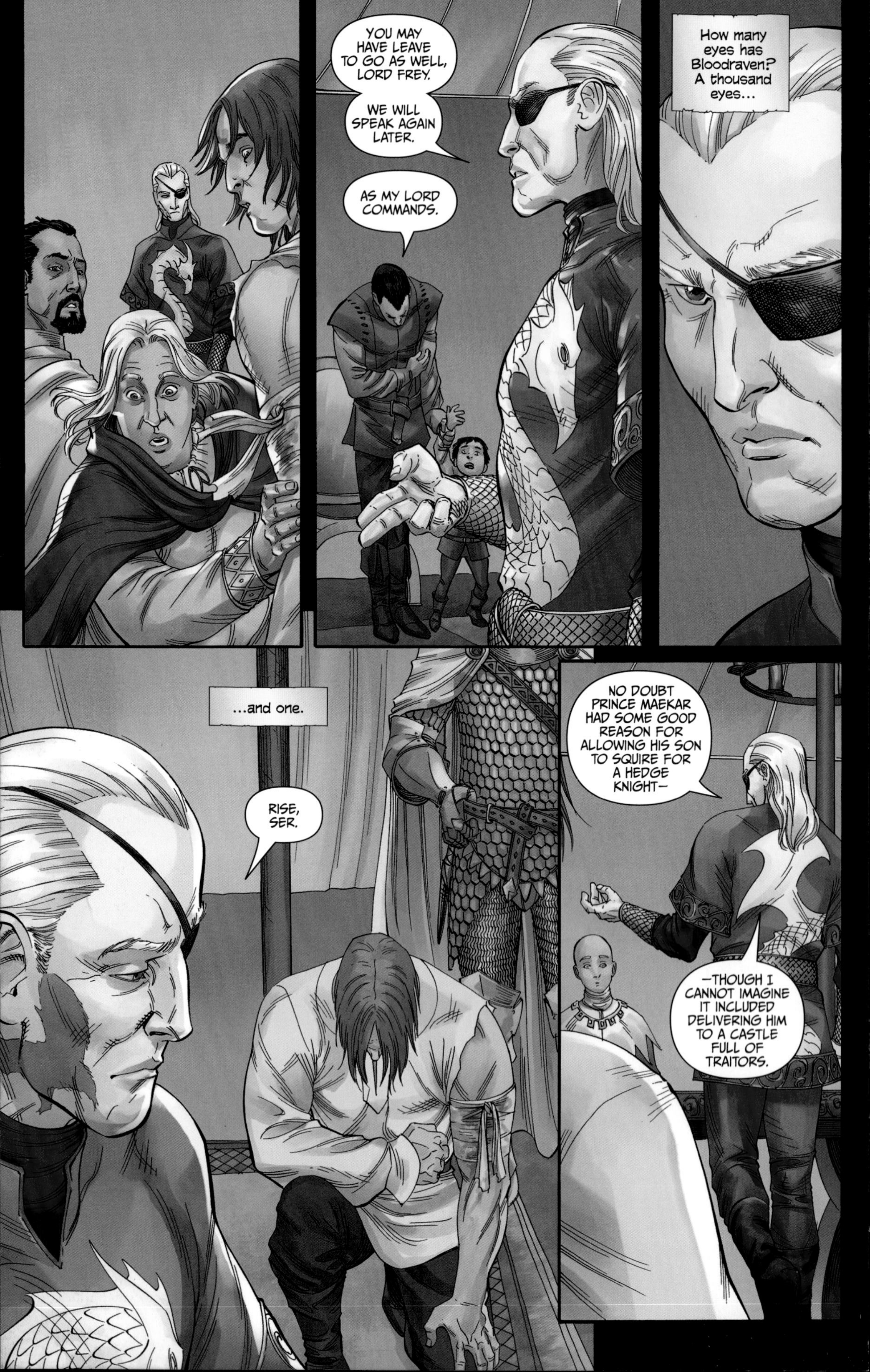
YOU MAY HAVE LEAVE TO GO AS WELL, LORD FREY.
WE WILL SPEAK AGAIN LATER.
AS MY LORD COMMANDS.
How many eyes has Bloodraven? A thousand eyes...
...and one.
RISE, SER.
NO DOUBT PRINCE MAEKAR HAD SOME GOOD REASON FOR ALLOWING HIS SON TO SQUIRE FOR A HEDGE KNIGHT—
—THOUGH I CANNOT IMAGINE IT INCLUDED DELIVERING HIM TO A CASTLE FULL OF TRAITORS.

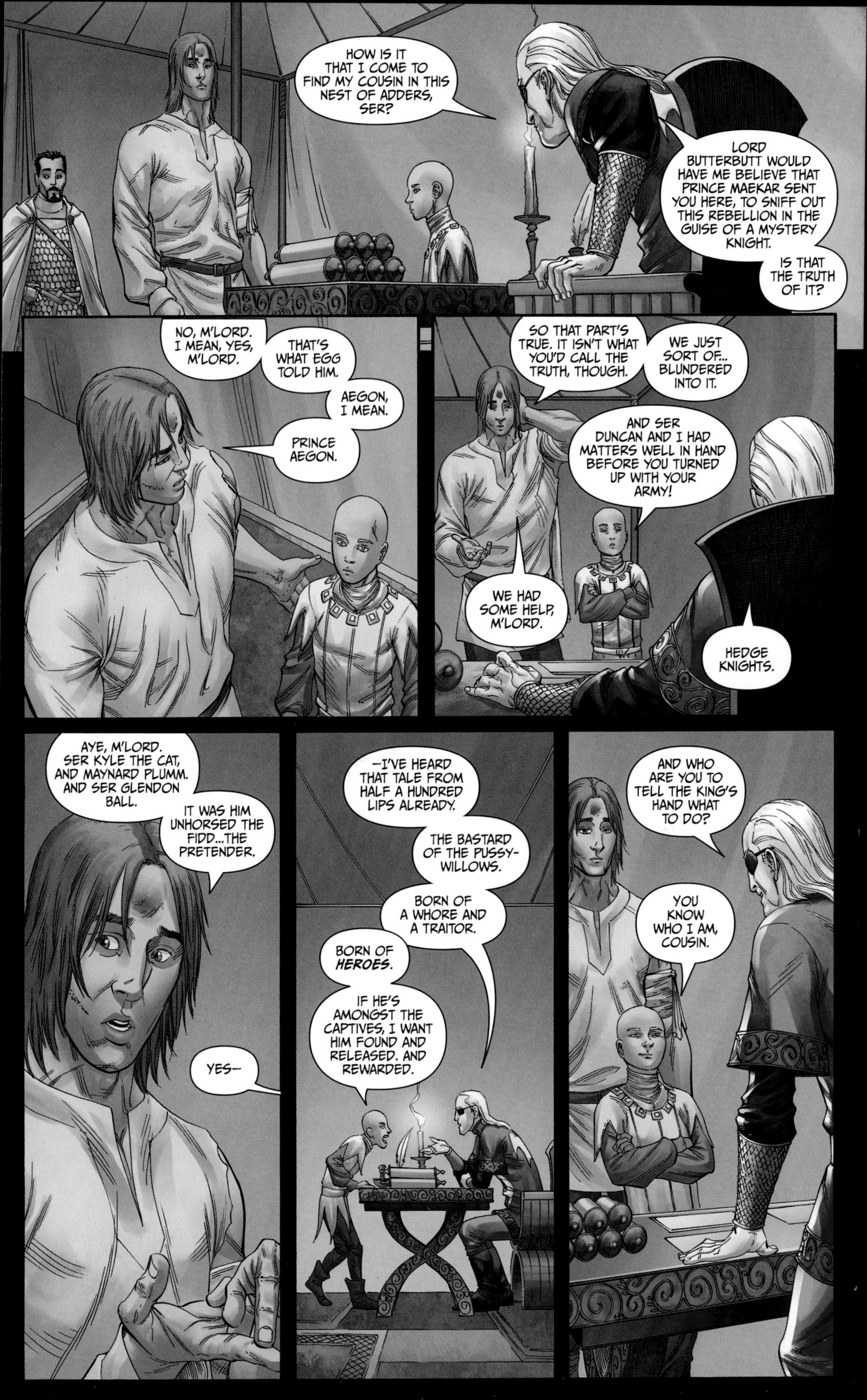
HOW IS IT THAT I COME TO FIND MY COUSIN IN THIS NEST OF ADDERS, SER?
LORD BUTTERBUTT WOULD HAVE ME BELIEVE THAT PRINCE MAEKAR SENT YOU HERE, TO SNIFF OUT THIS REBELLION IN THE GUISE OF A MYSTERY KNIGHT.
IS THAT THE TRUTH OF IT?
NO, M'LORD. I MEAN, YES, M'LORD.
THAT'S WHAT EGG TOLD HIM.
AEGON, I MEAN.
PRINCE AEGON.
SO THAT PART'S TRUE. IT ISN'T WHAT YOU'D CALL THE TRUTH, THOUGH.
WE JUST SORT OF... BLUNDERED INTO IT.
AND SER DUNCAN AND I HAD MATTERS WELL IN HAND BEFORE YOU TURNED UP WITH YOUR ARMY!
WE HAD SOME HELP, M'LORD.
HEDGE KNIGHTS.
AYE, M'LORD. SER KYLE THE CAT, AND MAYNARD PLUMM. AND SER GLENDON BALL.
IT WAS HIM UNHORSED THE FIDD...THE PRETENDER.
YES—
—I'VE HEARD THAT TALE FROM HALF A HUNDRED LIPS ALREADY.
THE BASTARD OF THE PUSSY-WILLOWS.
BORN OF A WHORE AND A TRAITOR.
BORN OF **HEROES**.
IF HE'S AMONGST THE CAPTIVES, I WANT HIM FOUND AND RELEASED. AND REWARDED.
AND WHO ARE YOU TO TELL THE KING'S HAND WHAT TO DO?
YOU KNOW WHO I AM, COUSIN.

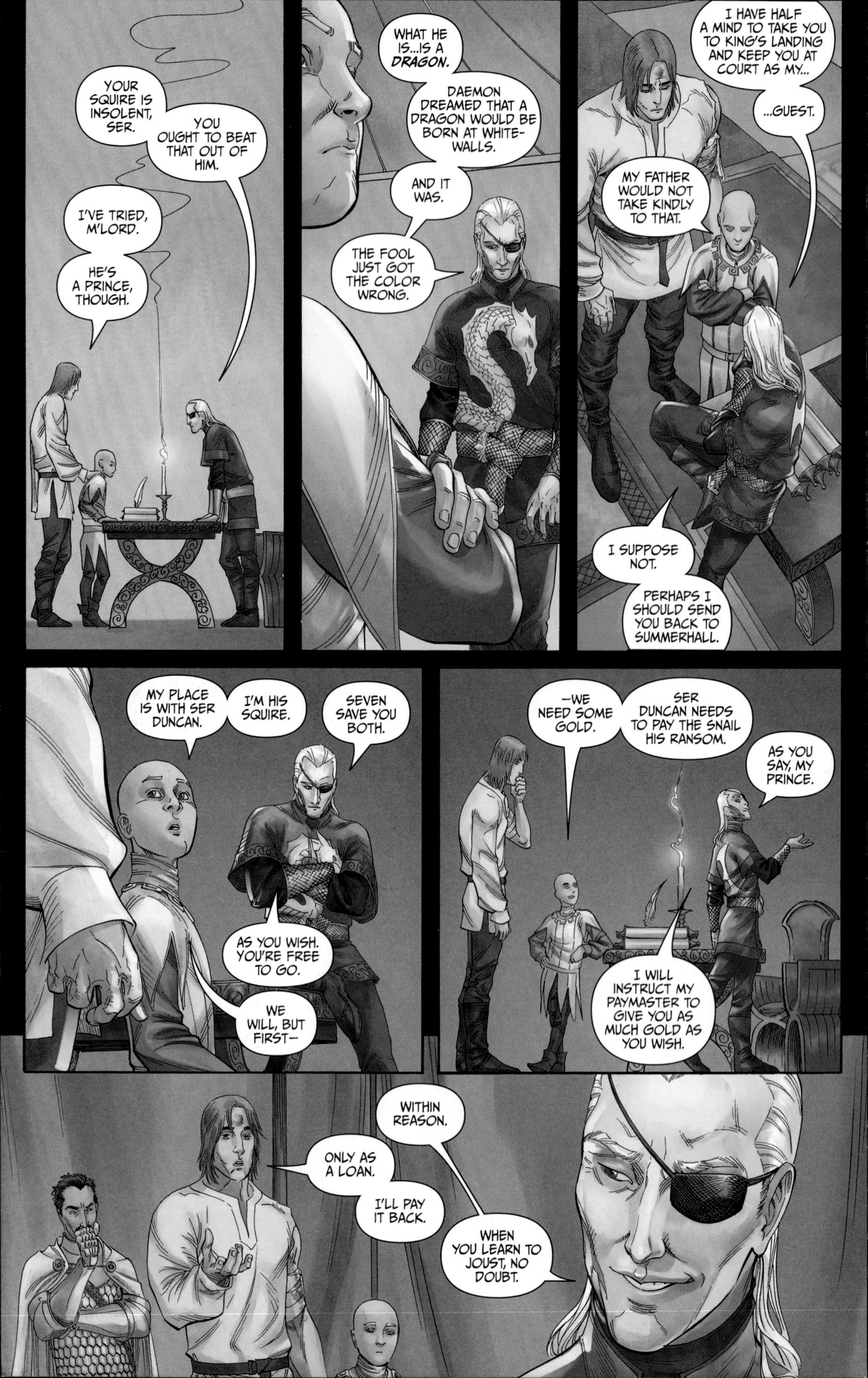
YOUR SQUIRE IS INSOLENT, SER.
YOU OUGHT TO BEAT THAT OUT OF HIM.
I'VE TRIED, M'LORD.
HE'S A PRINCE, THOUGH.
WHAT HE IS...IS A *DRAGON.*
DAEMON DREAMED THAT A DRAGON WOULD BE BORN AT WHITE-WALLS.
AND IT WAS.
THE FOOL JUST GOT THE COLOR WRONG.
I HAVE HALF A MIND TO TAKE YOU TO KING'S LANDING AND KEEP YOU AT COURT AS MY...
...GUEST.
MY FATHER WOULD NOT TAKE KINDLY TO THAT.
I SUPPOSE NOT.
PERHAPS I SHOULD SEND YOU BACK TO SUMMERHALL.
MY PLACE IS WITH SER DUNCAN.
I'M HIS SQUIRE.
SEVEN SAVE YOU BOTH.
AS YOU WISH. YOU'RE FREE TO GO.
WE WILL, BUT FIRST—
—WE NEED SOME GOLD.
SER DUNCAN NEEDS TO PAY THE SNAIL HIS RANSOM.
AS YOU SAY, MY PRINCE.
I WILL INSTRUCT MY PAYMASTER TO GIVE YOU AS MUCH GOLD AS YOU WISH.
WITHIN REASON.
ONLY AS A LOAN.
I'LL PAY IT BACK.
WHEN YOU LEARN TO JOUST, NO DOUBT.

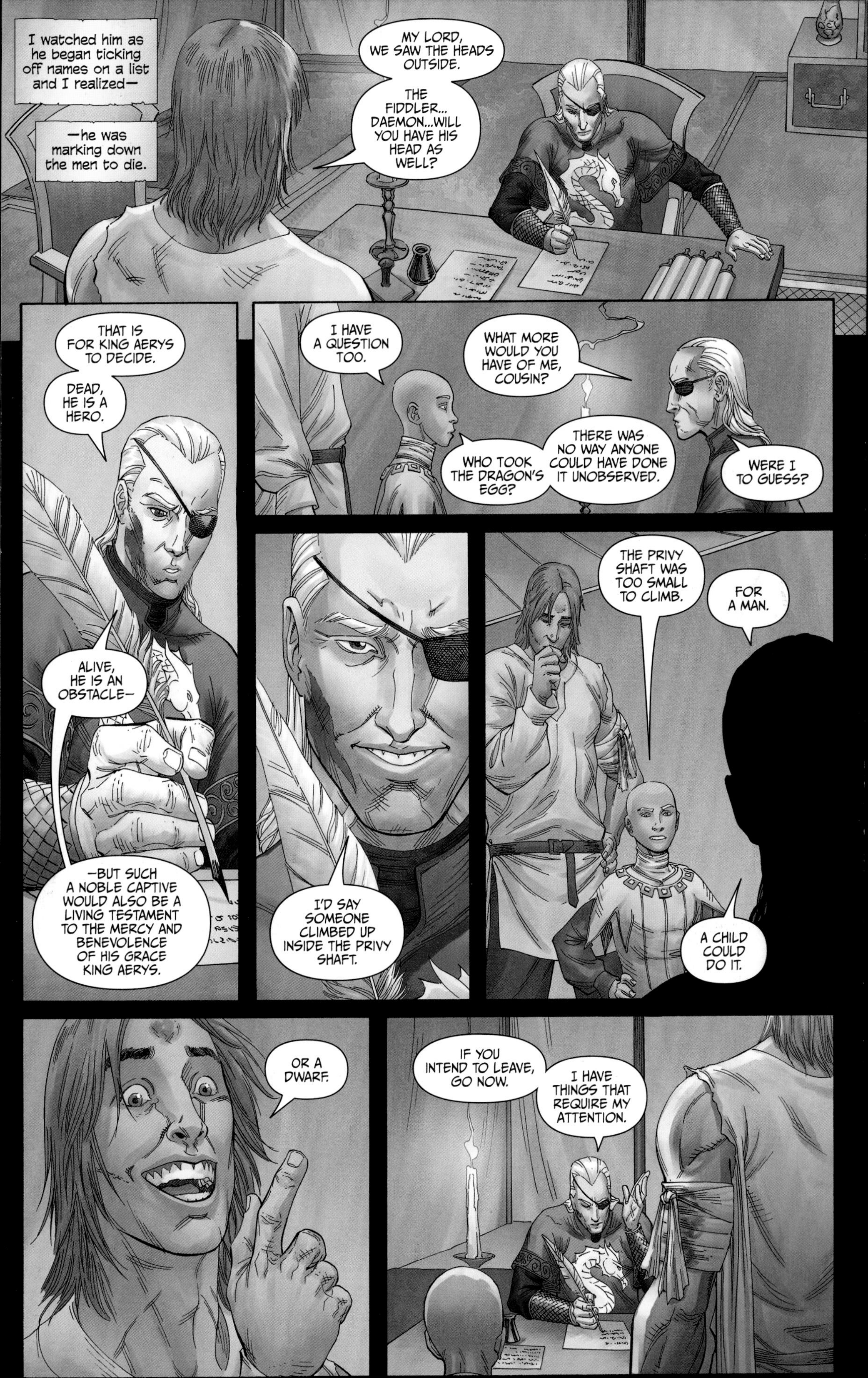
I watched him as he began ticking off names on a list and I realized—
—he was marking down the men to die.
MY LORD, WE SAW THE HEADS OUTSIDE.
THE FIDDLER... DAEMON...WILL YOU HAVE HIS HEAD AS WELL?
THAT IS FOR KING AERYS TO DECIDE.
DEAD, HE IS A HERO.
ALIVE, HE IS AN OBSTACLE—
—BUT SUCH A NOBLE CAPTIVE WOULD ALSO BE A LIVING TESTAMENT TO THE MERCY AND BENEVOLENCE OF HIS GRACE KING AERYS.
I HAVE A QUESTION TOO.
WHAT MORE WOULD YOU HAVE OF ME, COUSIN?
WHO TOOK THE DRAGON'S EGG?
THERE WAS NO WAY ANYONE COULD HAVE DONE IT UNOBSERVED.
WERE I TO GUESS?
I'D SAY SOMEONE CLIMBED UP INSIDE THE PRIVY SHAFT.
THE PRIVY SHAFT WAS TOO SMALL TO CLIMB.
FOR A MAN.
A CHILD COULD DO IT.
OR A DWARF.
IF YOU INTEND TO LEAVE, GO NOW.
I HAVE THINGS THAT REQUIRE MY ATTENTION.

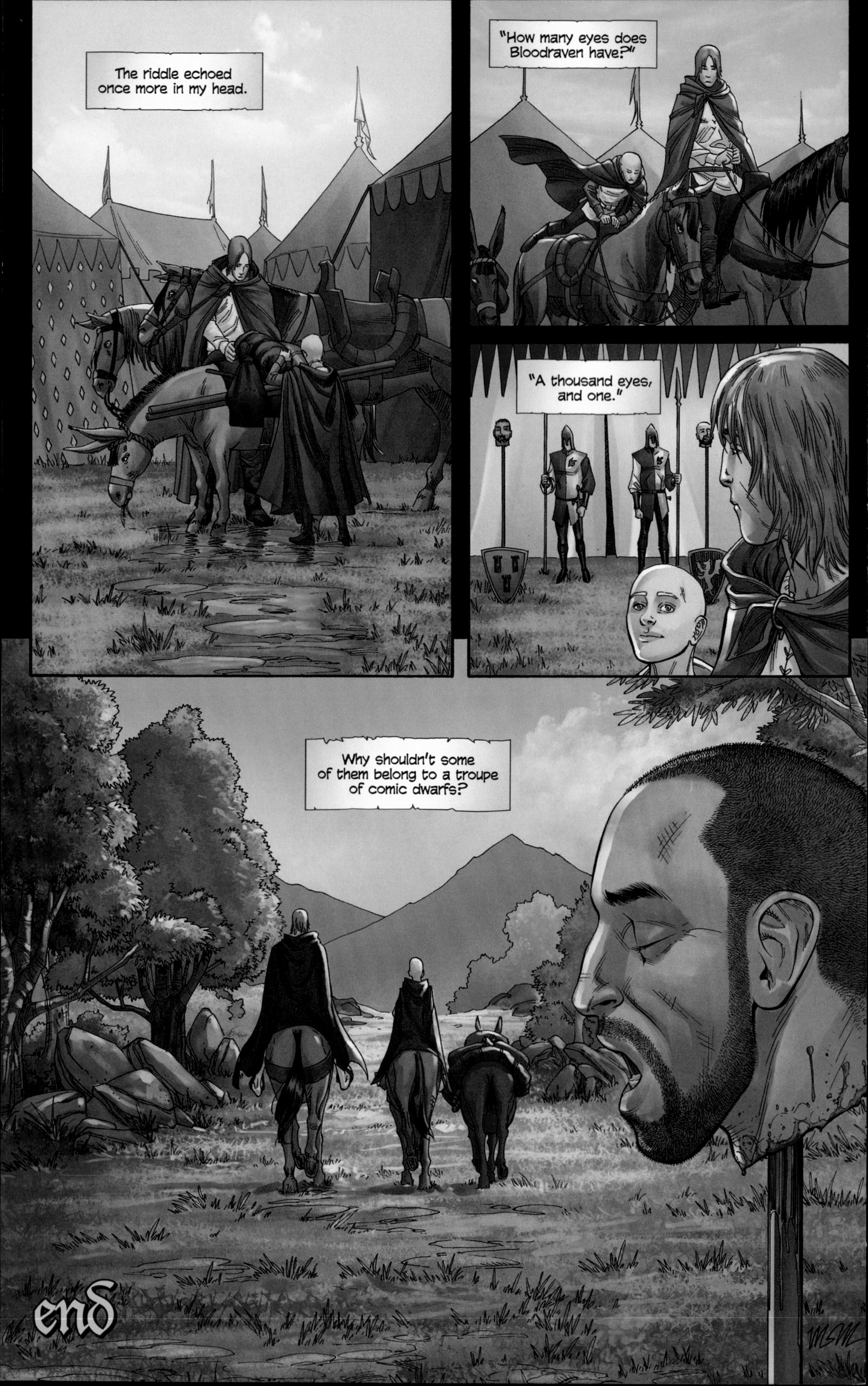
The riddle echoed once more in my head.
"How many eyes does Bloodraven have?"
"A thousand eyes, and one."
Why shouldn't some of them belong to a troupe of comic dwarfs?
end

Bill Tortolini was born and raised in the shadow of Boston. He graduated from Salem State University, and has been working as an creative director for over two decades. Working on large brands and advertisements for Fortune 500 companies, Tortolini also became involved in the comics industry in 1996. Since then, he has lettered comics for companies including Marvel, Dynamite Entertainment, Random House, Disney, and Image Comics, among many others. Notable works include Marvel's Anita Blake comics, the various adaptations of Robert Jordan's Wheel of Time series, Stephen King's *The Talisman*, Jim Butcher's *The Dresden Files*, and George R.R. Martin's *The Hedge Knight*. Tortolini is an avid Boston sports fan, skier, golfer, and pop-culture aficionado. He lives in Billerica, Massachusetts, with his wife, Kristen, their three children Abigail, Katherine, and Cameron, and his sometimes-loyal dog, Oliver.

TORTOLINI.COM | @BILLTORTOLINI

J. Nanjan is the head of NS Studios in Chennai, India, which he started with Sivakami Mohan in 2014. He has a BFA degree from the College of Fine Arts in Chennai, and has worked as a comic colorist for Gotham Comics, Virgin Comics (where he worked on the popular Devi series), and for Digikore Studios (for Soliel Comics) in India. Recently, he has done work for Mike S. Miller, DC Comics, Zenescope, and Dynamite Entertainment. Nanjan has colored Injustice: Gods Among Us, and is now working on its sequel series, Injustice 2 and the Bombshells series. He lives in Chennai, India, with his family.

Sivakami Mohan is the head of operations as well as the senior colorist at NS Studios in Chennai, India, which she started with J. Nanjan in 2014. She has a BFA degree, as well as her MBA degree. She previously worked at Virgin Comics, India, and is currently working with Mike S. Miller, DC Comics, Zenescope, and Dynamite Entertainment through NS Studios.